Sept '04

Darling

D0335233

Continue the obsession......

All love
No2 xxx

WINNER TAKES ALL

WINNER TAKES ALL

a life of sorts

MICHAEL WINNER

ROBSON BOOKS

First published in Great Britain in 2004 by Robson Books, The Chrysalis Building, Bramley Road, London W10 6SP

An imprint of Chrysalis Books Group plc

British Library Cataloguing in Publication Data
A catalogue record for this title is available from the British Library.

ISBN 1 86105 734 2

Typeset by SX Composing DTP, Rayleigh, Essex
Printed by Creative Print & Design (Wales), Ebbw Vale

For Orson, Marlon, Burt, Charlie, Jill, Michael, Shakira, Sophia, Faye, Anthony, Oliver, Mickey and Minnie Mouse, Laurence Olivier, Lassie, Carol Reed, Trigger the Wonder Horse, Judy Garland, Bambi, Walt Disney, Paul Hamlyn, Miss K. M. Hobbs, Marilyn Monroe, Monica, Christina, Caroline, Sparkle, Jill, Georgina, Steffanie, Lorraine, Jenny, Vanessa, Helen and George . . . and Geraldine, who I hope will still be with me when this book is published.

Thanks to

Margaret for starting the typing. Pat for carrying it on. Dinah, more than a receptionist, for keeping order, calm and beauty in the situation. John Fraser for bravely putting up with me for so many decades. Zoe for keeping the cuttings books. Jim for driving the Rolls Phantom. Donata for feeding me. The goldfish for being so lazy. The foxes for occasionally not digging up the flowerbeds. All the people at Robson Books, who were never less than pleasant. And you for having bought this account of my life. If you've got any money left send it all to me (well, leave a bit for yourself) as a donation toward the National Police Memorial to pay tribute to officers slain on duty and to honour their familes who suffer so much. I thank the families of the slain officers, people I would never otherwise have met, for being so warm and for their comradeship over the many years.

I wish all of you great happiness.

Michael Winner
219 Kensington High Street, London W8 6BD

Contents

Prologue: Lights in the Dark

The lamp-lighter started at the far end of the road. I'd peer from my window as dusk deepened on the tiny mansions of Alexander Avenue in the North London suburb of Willesden. He'd stop and reach up from his bicycle with a long pole to ignite the gas-jet on the lamp-post. The first light would flicker in the gloom.

It was my earliest memory. I suppose I was three years old. He went slowly up the hill, turning the little street into a pin-point beauty of wavering flame. When he got to one end he crossed the road and went down the other side. By the time he'd finished the bijou mansions were illuminated by the lights in the dark.

We moved south to an apartment in Lancaster Gate, a road of Victorian houses interspersed with 1930s flats. Now the street lights were electric. But there was a war. So they weren't turned on. The traffic lights went from red to red and yellow, and then to green. Then in reverse order. I'd lean out of the window at night and watch for hours. There were no other lights, because windows were blacked out. When the enemy came, new lights were an incredible display. First the sound of the siren, rising and falling. Then the piercing beams of the searchlights in nearby Hyde Park as they reached into the sky. Barrage balloons, like fat pigs, floated on their long wires to ensnare low-flying invaders. Then the drone of unseen enemy aircraft followed by an enormous roar as the anti-aircraft guns opened up. Marvellous explosions rocked our street! Great flashes in the air! Sometimes I saw a plane caught in the spotlight. The sound of falling shrapnel. Then the bombs! A piercing whistle that descended, darkening in tone. What a bang as they landed! The red glow of fires added to the display. I stayed at the window until I was dragged inside.

Then the most magical light of all. It came from a small hole in the wall casting images on a white screen. I sat bewitched in the smelly stalls. We'd moved to Letchworth in Hertfordshire.

When I wasn't in the old Palace cinema I was in the art deco majesty of the Broadway. Or in the Regal or any of the other picture palaces. These lights revealed an incredible world of action and sophistication. Of laughter and tragedy. Then there were the yellow street lights of Cambridge. Illuminated reflections on the rain-soaked pavements that led between ancient college walls and crowded cafés. I walked under them to cinemas where fellow undergraduates stood in line for the latest European masterpiece or the Technicolor delights of Hollywood.

Then the lights were mine. First I carried them on the bus with a single cameraman as we made our short films. I pushed their thin cables with exposed wires into the round wall sockets and fixed them with matchsticks. Even the electric shocks when it went wrong couldn't take away the pleasure of the work. The lights got bigger. Brawny men carried them on their backs or pushed them into place on wheeled tripods. I controlled them! They lit up the slums of New York, the peasant villages of Mexico, the stately homes of England. They illuminated the greatest talents of the twentieth century. There was Marlon Brando rising from his canvas chair, there Sophia Loren, Charles Bronson, Anthony Hopkins . . . they were lights used to create the magic of cinema.

One day the lights will go out. No lamp-lighter will be there to turn them on. The searchlights will have dimmed. Movie lights will shine on. But not for me. The lights gripped me from the beginning and they will until the end. I've spent my life among them. They've lightened the dark.

1

Winner the Kid

My grandfather's naturalisation papers were personally signed by Winston Churchill, then a Secretary of State. Grandpa was born in Russia in 1874 at Gorod Dovinsk. His name was Davis Winner. The neat handwriting of a civil servant described him as 'a trimming and hosiery merchant' living in Portobello Road in the County of London. On 28th May 1910 Churchill signed his 'Memorial praying for a Certificate of Naturalization'.

Davis Winner had a menswear shop in Notting Hill Gate. Until a few years ago, across the pavement fronting two houses, a mosaic spelled 'Winner's' in Edwardian script. I sat on the cracked tiles one Sunday and a girlfriend took my photograph. I returned when we were filming nearby, intending to buy the tiny squares and lay them on my garden path. But the Council had concreted them over.

Davis Winner had a family of eight. One of the boys was my father George. He, like each of the children, ran a branch of the Winner's clothing chain. One was in Lime Grove where film technicians worked with Alfred Hitchcock at the old Gainsborough Film Studios. Film-crew members used to tell me they bought shirts there. Family legend has it grandfather was known as the King of Notting Hill. He travelled Europe regularly. It was said he had a mistress in every capital city. He died in 1933, two years before I was born.

My mother, Helen, was born in Praszka in Poland in 1906. She came to England with her parents and a brother when she was sixteen. She'd seen terrible persecution of the Jews and the trauma of it affected her forever, causing a highly strung nature that resulted in her losing eight million pounds at the Cannes Casino in the 1970s. She was a congenital gambler who was to take the furniture and paintings left to me and sell them from the back of taxis all over the South of France to pay her gaming debts. In an attempt to acquire more money to lose she instructed ten firms of solicitors to sue me for cash over a period of six years. As I'd done nothing wrong, they refused. She was a character, was Mumsy. My father was an angel. They married in 1934 and acquired an Irish setter called Roger. I arrived a year later.

After the death of my grandfather, George (as I called him) went into property. He wasn't rich. The house at 12 Alexander Avenue was modest. The two little girls next door, Jill and Valerie, were my age so they probably didn't have the large bosoms they were later to acquire. But I always think of them as well formed. I remember setting fire to the waste-paper basket. The fire brigade was called and I was sent next door to be with Jill and Valerie. Our family photo album shows me, beautifully dressed, sitting in the garden on a large tartan rug with a teddy bear and a toy rabbit dressed in long spotted trousers, with Roger. Other photos show me in a toy car, posing with a rubber ball and sitting on my mother, who was very beautiful and spoke like a duchess.

When the Second World War arrived it was assumed London would be devastated by German bombs. In spring 1940 I was at a school at Middleton-on-Sea where the Form Mistress, Miss Murchland, reported it was a pleasure to teach anyone so keen on learning! We re-located to Cheltenham. My parents put me down for Cheltenham College. They were told the Jewish quota was full. 'I thought that was what we were fighting a war about,' Mumsy said. She always had a good turn of phrase. It made no impression on Cheltenham College. We left for Hitchin, a Hertfordshire market town. There I was to attend, for eleven years, a co-educational

Quaker boarding school in nearby Letchworth. St Christopher School had outrageously modern ideas for 1941. It adopted the principles of the educational pioneer Madame Montessori who spoke about 'not working a youngster too hard'. In theory it was governed by the students. It was vegetarian, Quaker and ludicrous. During the war they fed us on grass from the cricket pitch to help the war effort! We all became ill. But we produced the best milk in Hertfordshire.

Letchworth was a Bernard Shaw-type idealistic, socialist town. No pubs were allowed. I was sent to St Christopher because my parents thought the children looked happy. Since co-educational boarding schools were unheard of in the early forties, well they might. A Women's Congress decided at the time 'It would be better if only girls went to co-educational schools.' Aged five, I entered a pleasant house smelling of floor polish where kids were painting. I went up to one of them. 'Why have your cows got no legs?' I asked. 'Because there's a mist,' was the reply. The boy's name was William. He played Macbeth to my Macduff in a horrific school presentation. He was with me at Cambridge University. He later committed suicide.

I started as a day pupil and my parents moved to a small house in Letchworth. They re-located to London when I was six and I became a boarder. On my letters I drew birds and boats. 'Dear Mummy and Daddy,' I wrote, 'I don't like being a boarder very much. Are you still allowed to go fishing in London now? Will you bring chocolates and sweets for all of us please. Love from Michael.' We're told childhood is the happiest time of our lives. It's difficult to grade as one thing or another. Just keeping going was a full-time job. Survival and remaining amused was everything. I remember neither joy nor sadness, but practicality. Being certain you got the best food or a good seat. Keeping warm. Curiosity. It was wartime so sweets and chocolates were rationed. We were fed on salads and hard brown-bread rusks. We sat on the branch of a tree and peed on people below. We looked with interest at each other's genitalia.

Bombs were falling. A favourite game in the dormitory was to tell a child his mother had been killed in an explosion. 'She was in that blue dress she wore when she came to see you last weekend. It was all covered in blood. Her head was lying a few feet away. Her arms were blown off.' The child victim would protest: 'You're making it up!' 'It really is true this time,' we'd say. 'Miss Homfray was told on the phone. We listened in.' When they tried it on me I'd sob uncontrollably. Then gleefully join in the following night to torture someone else.

It was then I decided to be a film director. Was it *Snow White* or *Bambi*? Probably one of those, with the genius of Disney showing good and evil so vividly. I was hooked. At seven I'd make elaborate drawings of a city, cut out the windows of the buildings and paste coloured sweet paper behind them. I'd hold a torch behind, so the colours glowed with the light coming through. I told a story to go with my 'slides'. I was on the toilet after one show. A little girl was on a potty next to me. 'Did you like my film?' I asked. 'I hated it,' she replied. 'Why?' I asked. 'I hate films,' she answered. 'They frighten me.' My first critic, aged six!

I also wrote plays. There was a large window ledge by a bay window on the first floor. There I directed my drama. A boy, Robert, was behind the window curtain waiting to act. I pushed at the curtain. 'Come on, Robert,' I said. But I'd pushed him out of the window! He fell to the gravel drive below. For some time after, he walked around with his left arm in a sling. That was my first memory of directing.

St Christopher School being vegetarian, most of what we ate wasn't affected by rationing. Powdered eggs, milk and cheese were rationed, but we seemed to have enough. Most of the egg dishes were a lumpy concoction made from the powder. Sweet rationing hurt! Sweets were currency, like tobacco or drugs in prison. We weren't allowed meat, so we'd buy meat or fish paste in little glass jars, scoop it out and eat it from our fingers.

My school reports varied. Aged six: 'Michael has suddenly become very noisy and rather fancies himself as a humorist.' The next term I was writing 'excellent and original stories' but was still 'disturbing in class'. I was seven when the nicest thing ever was written about me: 'Michael has a great sense of fairness, and not only where he himself is concerned. He spontaneously interferes on behalf of any child whom he thinks is unable to stand up for itself. He is much respected and listened to by the other children in consequence.'

I remember the lemonade and orangeade at special do's. The sandwiches at the dances. The thrill of a first erection. The occasional bullying. The academic standard at St Christopher's was poor. There was a rag-bag group of teachers, some pleasant, some not. The pretence of the children running the place through School Councils was a sham. Whenever we passed a motion allowing us to go to the cinema more than twice a term, the Headmaster over-ruled it. We did a great deal of cleaning because 'It teaches you community spirit.' It was to save the school money. The Geography teacher took boys on holiday, photographed them stark naked by rocks and pools, then displayed the pictures in his room. The Latin teacher walked hand in hand with pubescent girls along the lanes of Hertfordshire, and sat for hours with them in classrooms at night. We'd peep through the keyhole as he kissed them. Whenever you went into the Maths teacher's bed-sitting room in the evening, there'd be a young girl sitting with him on the carpet. We found it entertaining.

Nice Miss Hobbs who taught French rather well had a close friend, Miss Mouncey. They'd spend hours locked in the bathroom. They were nicknamed Hobbsy-wobbsy and her wobbsy-knobsies and Mouncey-wouncey and her bouncey-wouncies. They went to live in Wales. The English teacher, an attractive lady, gave special diction lessons to a lad from North London. He'd describe in detail how he screwed her. His parents paid for the lessons! I felt disconnected. My fellow pupils were dull. The surroundings were pretty but we slept in rusty, leaky caravans. There were rats galore.

The limited vegetarian diet wasn't healthy. Any disease going, we got. Infantile paralysis struck more than once.

I spent most of my time visiting the cinema, ignoring the twice-a-term rule. In the Broadway I saw *The Third Man* eleven times and Olivier's *Henry V* nine. The Palace was older. It smelt of dirt and food. I was watching Cecil B. De Mille's epic *Unconquered* in the Regal at Hitchin. Gary Cooper and Paulette Goddard were battling all odds, when I felt a hand on my thigh. I was twelve and so innocent I'd no idea what this could mean. The hand moved further up towards my groin. 'Poor chap,' I thought, 'he must be excited by the movie.' I removed his hand. 'Have you got a big one?' asked the man. This was too much! In the middle of Paramount's best! I moved.

In London our block of flats was hit by incendiary bombs. The main damage was from gallons of water poured on by the firemen, which cascaded three floors below. It drenched Mrs Louvain's furniture in the flat above. We got off without blemish. My father kept volunteering for the Army but he had some medical failing. So he ran a building firm that was called in to prop up bomb-damaged buildings. Mumsy invited soldiers round to dinner. British people were asked to entertain soldiers coming to London from abroad. So there'd be Americans, Poles, French – a whole bevy of different, uniformed men sitting at the dinner table. My mother enjoyed this. Her smile sparkled and her eyes twinkled.

Then came the German rockets. There was a droning overhead, followed by silence as the missile stopped in mid-air. We'd throw ourselves on the ground. A pause as the rocket started its fall to earth. Its speed increased, a whistle, high-pitched and fading. Finally an enormous explosion! We got up and carried on. Suddenly it was Victory in Europe, VE Day! May 1945. I was nine. George drove us to Trafalgar Square. People danced, sung, shouted, waved Union Jacks. Soldiers climbed on to the running board and pushed money through the open window to me at the back. I gazed out at this great explosion of excitement. I've never seen such a mass of joy. We'd survived. We'd fought a common cause. We started out a country alone, fearful citizens facing a monster enemy. We won against a terrible evil. We'd been party to the last unifying crusade the nation will ever know. A grand new world would emerge from the killing and the chaos. That's what we thought.

2

A Writer and a Thief

I started writing for the public on a lavatory wall. I was ten. There were two toilets outside the school's back door. Each day I'd summarise the news. Children stood in line to read my version of events. Then I started a film notice board, reviewing films, few of which I'd seen. I'd put up photos to accompany the text. It got me free tickets for the local cinemas. Later I ran a second wall notice board on general events. In 1947 when I was twelve my school report said, 'He has the reputation of being Movie Mad and should try to take up some more creative hobby.' H. Lyn Harris, our Headmaster, continually spoke of the terrible influence of cinema. How the now-classic Warner Brothers gangster films would turn me into a criminal. They glorified slaughter and violence, like that dreadful John Wayne shooting Indians and Japanese. We shot at each other with imaginary guns, falling down fake-dead all over. It didn't mean we grew up killers, any more than it does now. Although people say today's films go further and are more realistic, the ones we saw were very realistic to us.

I felt out of place among the smartly dressed Jewish crowd I met on holiday in London. The girls were so over-made-up and confident that they frightened me. I retired to the movies and collecting autographs. I'd look up the stars' addresses (many of them were in the phone book) and go there. Or I'd leave my autograph book at the stage door. I still have it. A grand affair with cut-out photographs stuck around a space for the stars to sign. Some of them, like Orson Welles and Terry-Thomas, I'd later employ

At school I paid a boy from the class above to do my washing-up and clean my room. When they called 'P to Z' to stand at the cold, exterior, wooden basins and wash the plates, studious John Fraser would be my stand-in for sixpence. He got two shillings a week to clean my room and make my bed. 'It's wrong,' the Headmaster said, facing Fraser, 'it's the power of the purse.' 'What do you want to do, John?' I asked. 'I'd like the money,' he said. He's worked for me ever since.

My school reports continued; 'If there is anything to be done, Michael is usually missing' – this when I was ten. Two years later: 'Michael seems to lack a community feeling.' In contrast other reports describe me as 'considerate', 'reasonable' and 'prone to using bad language'. The Headmaster was a tall, scoutmaster-like figure with a desperately fat wife called Elinore. She proudly told us she took all her clothes off and stood in front of her open window for an air bath every morning.

A serious, red-haired boy, Jim, ran the Young Farmers' Club. This was three rabbits and six chickens in huts. I hated games and the alternative, which was a 'run' round the countryside. A member of staff checked you at the furthest point. Once I hired a taxi, drove past the other 'runners', rolled up to the master, smiled, and drove off. This was so outrageous for a twelve-year-old that they let it go. If you joined the Young Farmers' Club you were excused games and the run. I got a triangular lapel badge with YFC on it. Jim and I were the only members. 'We clean out the rabbit hutches, feed the rabbits and chickens, and collect the eggs,' explained Jim. 'What happens to the eggs?' I asked. 'I give them to the school kitchen,' said Jim. 'How many eggs are there?' 'About twenty a week,' he replied. 'Jim,' I said, 'we'll give the school kitchen five, and sell the rest.' 'Good idea,' said Jim.

The staff bought our eggs. The people who were meant to be leading us upwards in the cause of Shavian socialism. A serious boy called Tony, who was forever in the lab, took my eggs, cooked them on a Bunsen burner and walked through assembled children eating a breakfast of powdered-egg rubbish. He'd place my eggs with a flourish in front of me on the communal table. He and his family were devout Communists.

I got most of the money to pay for all this by stealing. It was very wrong. Today I'm so finickity that I fired one of my staff for nicking twenty-pence worth of curtain hangers from Barkers because he couldn't be bothered to wait at the till queue. I sent someone else back with the twenty pence. My staff member had been my teacher at St Christopher School! As a kid I went shoplifting at Woolworths. I was furious when a packet of foreign stamps had two slightly torn. I got a cash refund. Years later I sent the Chairman of Woolworths five hundred pounds.

At games time, boys left money in their pockets in the changing room. It was disappointing when someone got there before me. With their money I'd buy the kids' sweet-ration cards. A boy called Clotworthy had received ten shillings from his parents. A lot of money in 1948. Fifty pence now. 'I should put this in the Headmaster's office,' he said. 'You must, Patrick,' I admonished. But the lure of the football field was too much for Clotworthy. He trooped out with the others. I nicked his ten shillings.

Thirty-five years later I was sitting in my office with Mr Fraser, the man who'd made my bed at school. 'I feel terrible I stole things,' I said. 'I'd like to give the money back.' I hadn't seen or spoken to Clotworthy for thirty years, but I could see his handwriting in bright blue ink on his envelopes addressed to 75 Knoll Drive, Styvechale, Coventry. I rang directory enquiries. I phoned. Patrick answered. 'Hello,' I said, 'it's Michael Winner.' Clotworthy went into paroxysms of delight. 'I've seen you on television . . . It's *him*,' he told his wife. I revealed my crime. 'What's Charles Bronson like?' Patrick asked. I promised to give him the money plus compound interest and a bonus. I sent an apology and a cheque for a hundred pounds. I invited him to my next film premiere, all expenses paid, hotel, travel, meals, the lot. Later I wrote an article inviting any Christophians to contact me for money back, no questions asked. A few did.

I was devoted to Enid Blyton. 'I'll never read anything else,' I told my parents. I always referred to my parents by their first names, George and Helen. That's what they wanted me to do. It bemused their adult friends.

I adored sausages and chips. Not only did I eat them continually; when I grew up, I'd live in a small semi-detached, save money, and work as a pavement artist on Sundays.

Dad's business was doing well. We started to go abroad. Unusual in 1946. We chose Switzerland, the only country in Europe not ravaged by war. At the Palace Hotel Lucerne I walked on to the balcony overlooking the great lake with the towering mountains beyond. I stopped and drew back, gasping at the beauty of it. The next year we went to Alassio on the Italian Riviera where ragged kids with no shoes begged and ran along the cobbled streets like a scene from a post-war Italian film.

I was thirteen when I was summoned to the Headmaster's office. There was H. Lyn Harris, the benign, grey-haired Headmaster, running a Quaker school renowned for its racial tolerance and religious freedom, and two boys of my age. One of them a Jewish boy called Kissin, the other a Christian called Carr. According to the Headmaster I'd threatened to have Carr run out of the school. That was nonsense. 'You're so popular,' said the Headmaster (news to me!), 'your gang could make his life so awful that Carr here would have to leave.' This was ridiculous! I had no gang! I had no desire to dispose of Carr!

'I remember,' said the Headmaster, 'when the Jews came to Letchworth.' It was getting dark outside and I wondered why he didn't turn the lights on. 'We didn't have any here until the outbreak of war,' he went on. Carr and Kissin sat silent. 'The Jews came down with their money and bought up all the good houses.' This didn't concern me. I just wanted to get out of his dimly lit study and back to normality. 'They used their money, you see,' said Mr Harris, warming to his theme. 'Of course,' he added, 'not all Jews are bad. There are some very talented ones. There's Danny Kaye and Yehudi Menuhin. I don't think you understand the principles of St Christopher's,' Mr Harris said. He was right. I didn't! 'I don't like the way you spend your money getting boys to do things that you should be doing. It's the power of the purse.' I knew that was coming. Though what it had to do with getting poor old Carr thrown out, or Danny Kaye, I couldn't make out. Mr Harris droned on. It was getting even darker. Then we got up and left. It was never referred to again. In my eleven years at school that was the oddest moment. A few months later I went to the St James's Theatre to see Laurence Olivier and Vivien Leigh in their double bill of *Caesar and Cleopatra* and *Antony and Cleopatra*. In the interval Dad and I went to the bar. There was Mr Harris, our Headmaster, with a gin and tonic in one hand and a blonde lady who was not his wife by the other. And he was so proud of the fact he didn't drink!

I struggled through my Barmitzvah Ceremony. My party was in a flat in the grand mansion we'd moved to near Holland Park. My mother spent her life playing poker, gin rummy and bridge with great skill and devotion. Most nights she could be found at Crockford's, an upper-crust gaming club in St James's. When she wasn't there she'd organise games at home. I changed into my dark blue suit. The dinner went smoothly. There were the usual speeches. Then a bevy of staff appeared carrying green-baize card tables. Everyone divided into groups and played poker. I retired to my bedroom, which was being used as a cloakroom. I sat on my bed, made some two feet higher by layer upon layer of mink coats. Occasionally I peeped through the door into the lounge and saw cakes and tea being wheeled round on trolleys. Where did I fit in? I didn't relate to the slick young men and women, the offspring of my parents' card-playing Jewish friends. I wasn't a blond cricket and football player or a well-meaning do-gooder like others at St Christopher's. My happiest times there were walking with a girlfriend, platonic as I was too shy to try anything. I carried my childhood soft blue blanket trimmed with silk on to the school playing field so we could lie in the sun. An eccentric Hungarian boy called Erdeyli would leap from his room bowing like an unctuous head waiter and cry in his thick accent, 'Is everything all right, sir? Can we have lunch served for you in the garden? Will you be in to dinner, tonight, sir?' Then he would double over in peals of laughter. As I lay in my bedroom, the minks having swayed off on the backs of their proud owners, I didn't know salvation was coming.

A thin young man with a blonde girl walked around at the St Christopher School old students' reunion. I was now fourteen. The man had been a student named Hamburger. He changed it to Hamlyn because the kids called him 'Sausage'. He later became Lord Hamlyn and gave three million pounds to the Labour Party and many millions more to charity. Then he worked for a publisher, World Film Publications. He'd once sold books from a barrow outside the London Palladium. He became a legend in the world of publishing. 'Excuse me,' I said to him, 'could I have all your books free?' Paul Hamlyn looked down at me, 'Er, yes,' he said. He now knew coming to Old Scholars' day was a mistake. A few days later I rang Hamlyn, reversing the charges. 'I never got the books,' I said. A large, brown parcel arrived! I now knew a man actively engaged in something to do with films. I had my father ask him to dinner.

I was a loner. I preferred cinema to social activities. I had a girl-friend at school, but I was too scared to suggest sex. Another pretty girl who insisted on wearing make-up, which put me off, chased me up the concrete walkway to the boys' changing room – 'If you'll meet me in the room tonight, I'll do everything,' she said. I muttered an excuse and fled. When I did take a girl to a small unoccupied bedroom which you could lock, on the first floor, we just kissed and held hands. But I was capable of hyping myself up, to be a braver, less shy person. I phoned a small studio at Welwyn Garden City, Hertfordshire. I asked for the publicity department. I said, 'My name's Michael Winner. I'm writing a book for Paul Hamlyn's World Film Publications on film-making from the children's angle. I'd like to come down.' In 1952, children of fourteen didn't behave like this. Now every child of fourteen has a band, has written music, has sex, is on dope, is glue sniffing, has been in rehab, has a life of their own, is pregnant or about to be pregnant, drinks, dresses up, is a real mess. In 1952, children of fourteen were an adjunct of adults. They were an ancillary. They didn't phone film studios and pretend to be writing a book. But a great many films were being made. People were employed to encourage people to write about them. It was a case of supply and demand. They needed visiting journalists. I could provide one.

The film was a part of a British series called *The Huggetts*. It starred Jack Warner, Kathleen Harrison, Petula Clark, Jimmy Hanley and Joan Dowling. A thick sound-proof door opened and I was inside my first studio. The smell of scenery and of must and dust; the darkness, the back of the sets – and beyond them, arc lights. A murmur of voices. I was paralysed with fear and excitement. I inched forward until I could see the camera, the set and the actors. A tea trolley appeared with big, sticky cakes! Heaven! I took a large eclair and a cup of tea. Joan Dowling, a well-known gamine cockney actress, came over. I was standing close to an actress! I stared, unable to speak. A movie star was about to talk to me. 'You've got cream all over your mouth,' she said. My hand shot up to wipe it away. I was shaking. I've since met many of the most famous actresses in the world. Some of them I've made love to. I've lived my life among actresses at work and during the times in between. When I meet a legendary star I still sometimes see the face of Joan Dowling standing in the darkness by the tea trolley in Welwyn Studios. Not many years after our meeting she married an actor, was unhappy and committed suicide.

There are in our business great highs and great lows. If you can't learn to deal with them, and many can't, there enter disillusion, drink, drugs, loneliness and death. They go hand in hand for nearly all of us. They lurk in the shadows, just beyond the lights. They devour some of us every year. The lights shine on most people for a comparatively short time. Then they splutter and dim. Suddenly the offers don't come in. The sycophants are gone. The famous and almost famous are re-graded, re-aligned, reduced. It happens to directors, producers and writers as well as to actors and actresses. I've seen them arrive and bathe in the brilliance of the lights. I've seen the lights swing away to a new attraction. I've seen the desperation as the light moves on. It happened to the young cockney sparrow with her smile and her sweet haircut who was the first to greet me when I entered the world of movies. Few people remember her now. But for a short time the lights shone on Joan Dowling. She was photographed in the magazines, interviewed, talked about. Her parents were proud. She was a rising talent. What rises, falls. In her case rather early. That, as the saying goes, is show business. You shouldn't join it if you can't take a joke.

3

There's No Business Like . . .

In September 1950 I went to Denham village where the movie *Tom Brown's Schooldays* was shooting. It starred John Howard Davies, who was eleven. He'd come to fame as Oliver Twist in David Lean's film of the Dickens classic. I was three years older. He lived near me. I asked how he was getting to work the next day. 'In the studio limousine,' he said. I responded, 'Could you give me a lift?' The next morning John and I got into his Daimler. When I alighted at Denham, the publicity man was apoplectic. 'It took me two hours to get here,' he spluttered. 'I had to take a tube to King's Cross, then a train, then a taxi from Denham station to the set. You walk out of the star's limousine!' 'We did it in forty minutes,' I explained.

John Howard Davies became a top TV director, then Head of Comedy for the BBC and later Thames TV. His father would write my first feature film in 1962. It was thirty years before I saw John again. A group of diners entered a local restaurant in morning suits. One came over. 'I'm John Howard Davies,' he said. 'You're responsible for my being a director; I thought, "If he can do it, so can I."' He sent me a bottle of Dom Perignon as a thank you for introducing his career. A couple of days after my journey to Denham the phone rang. It was Paul Hamlyn. 'Michael,' he said, 'I'm getting complaints about you going to studios saying you're writing a book for us. Give it a rest, will you.' My door to the world of movies had closed! 'You've just met a star who lives in Kensington,' my father said. 'Why not write an article for the local paper about John Howard Davies?' I took the bus to Exhibition Road where a thin office housed the *Kensington Post*. A weary, moustached man with red hair took my article. Three days later, on 8th September 1950, the article appeared complete with a photo of John Howard Davies I'd got from the publicity man. At the bottom was my name! I was fourteen years old. I'd gone from schoolboy to genuine journalist. I wrote for the paper every week for four years. They never paid me. When I mentioned money they gave me a cup of tea. But I had my own column, 'Michael Winner's Show Gossip'. The paper was part of a group. It appeared in seventeen local papers all over London.

I wrote under many different names. My TV reviews were hindered by the fact I never saw TV. Mother didn't want a distraction to her gambling. Occasionally I wrote for the rival Kensington paper, the *News*. Their show-business writer was the young Barry Norman! The first money I got was five shillings (twenty-five pence) from the *Hornsey Journal* for an article about Max Bygraves. I took tea with the sculptor Sir Jacob Epstein. There was his wife, a strange woman with long, lank hair, and his son, a rather loutish young man who read comics. We had a marzipan cake with four coloured sponge squares inside. Later I was in the office of the *Kensington Post*. The phone rang. It was Epstein. 'Can I speak to the Editor?' he asked in his thick German accent. I sensed trouble. 'You're speaking to him,' I said, hoping he wouldn't recognise my voice. 'The young boy you sent to interview me,' said Epstein, 'was he a trainee?' 'Oh no,' I said, 'a very experienced member of staff.' 'Well,' said Epstein, 'he knew nothing about my work, nothing at all.' 'He was one of our best men . . .' I started. Epstein slammed the phone down. The next day the photographer had an appointment at his studio. Epstein threw a chisel at him through the window.

I met nice new people. Sir Malcolm Sargent to Sir Ralph Richardson, James Stewart to Marlene Dietrich. I interviewed all the American stars who came to the London Palladium. I got a letter from Douglas Fairbanks Jnr, KBE, saying he wasn't really entitled to be called 'Sir' as he was American, even though he'd been knighted. But would I call him 'Sir' anyway. Another from Joyce Grenfell when I wrote to her as 'Joyce Grenfell' in the King's Road. She objected to my not putting 'Miss'. 'I'm not a shop,' she wrote.

The London Palladium public relations chief, John Carlsen, had an enormous moustache. The Palladium was home to top American stars coming to Europe for two-week variety stints. It was a time of glamour after the privation of combat. 'You're terrific,' Mr Carlsen said as he walked me to yet another legend. 'You come on Monday, and on Thursday the press cuttings service sends me your column in seventeen different papers. The star doesn't know they're little London locals. He thinks it's like America and you're a syndicated columnist!' I met Sophie Tucker, Bob Hope, Chico and Harpo Marx, Debbie Reynolds and Eddie Fisher, Guy Mitchell, Les Paul and Mary Ford, Nat King Cole and more. One act particularly took London by storm. The American singer Johnnie Ray, a handsome, gangling, blond with immense vitality. Almost into rock and roll before rock and roll had arrived. In his dressing room, I wondered who those men in mackintoshes were. 'Would you like to come out the front with us?' said Johnnie. We walked through the vast empty-seated Palladium to the front lobby to avoid the girl fans at the back. 'Can we give you a ride?' asked Johnnie. 'No thanks,' I said, not realising what he meant. I watched confused as Johnnie, the blond beauty, got into a modest grey car with three dowdy men and drove off. Johnnie was later engulfed by homosexual scandals. I saw him in 1969 in Australia. Still a terrific performer. He died quite young, by then working in tacky clubs in America.

Eddie Fisher played the Palladium before he married Debbie Reynolds. She sang a duet with him. My photo with them shows Debbie wearing a crucifix necklace, Eddie Star of David cufflinks. Years later I employed their daughter, Carrie Fisher. I told her I'd met her parents before they were wed. 'You should have stopped the marriage,' she said. Another great hero was Nat King Cole. In my many visits to the Palladium dressing room there was only one when nobody else was there but me and the star. That was with Nat King Cole. The normal group of hangers-on and fans were absent. This was the 1950s. Anti-black prejudice was rampant. The only two of my heroes I never met were Dean Martin and Jerry Lewis. With typical English snottiness the press murdered their terrific act. They refused to see anyone.

I kept visiting film studios. A big star then was a handsome Irish actor, Maxwell Reed. He became Joan Collins's first husband and one of the first men to sue his wife for alimony. Maxwell had black silk sheets and his white Jaguar convertible was 'it'. He was making a movie called *The Dark Man*. It starred two girls, so pretty I was transfixed: Natasha Parry and Barbara Murray. Maxwell Reed had all the self-assurance and glamour I lacked. 'You know,' he said, 'I get a lot of begging letters. I don't open them.' 'If you don't open them,' I said nervously, 'how do you know they're begging letters?' Maxwell thought about that. 'I can smell them,' he said. He then declined to give me a lift back to town.

My father was impressed with my press cuttings and the people I met. The kids at school weren't interested. My mother remained besotted with her gambling. My junior triumphs were dismissed. The only other thing my mother was devoted to, other than gambling, was Tweetie Pie. Tweetie Pie was a canary who resided in a large cage hanging in front of the French windows. Unfortunately, on one memorable morning, I came downstairs to find Tweetie Pie lying on his or her back (I never knew its gender) with its legs in the air. The bird was assuredly dead. This caused my mother great consternation. Tweetie Pie was never replaced.

A few of the stars I met became friends. Terry-Thomas visited our house from time to time. Dad and I used to go down to Alexandra Palace where Terry did his live BBC show in black and white. The fifties were marvellously different. You'd go to a restaurant for lunch and there'd be a twenty-piece string orchestra playing in full evening dress. At the Empire cinema in Leicester Square there was a revue with twenty dancing girls and an enormous orchestra before the movie. Hardly anyone had cars so you could park anywhere. There were no yellow lines or parking meters. It was unheard of to go to a theatrical first night without being in evening dress. At the 400 Club in Leicester Square you had to wear evening dress just to get in. After every big event stars would gather in The Caprice. I'd sit on the red plush banquettes in black tie with Noël Coward on one side and Ivor Novello or Laurence Olivier on the other. In the mid-fifties you could get a top-class meal with wine for two for £1.50 in today's money.

The Croisette that ran along the front in Cannes was a narrow two-lane road and many of the buildings were still villas with red wavy-tiled roofs and large gardens. At the Carlton Hotel the largely Jewish clientele sat on wicker chairs by the front wall facing the entrance driveway. It was called the Wailing Wall because they were always complaining. We spent New Year's Eve at the Cannes Casino. A vast 1900s ballroom with a thirty-piece orchestra. Uniformed attendants took your car and parked it under the palm trees in grounds that led to the sea. As midnight chimed all the picture windows were alive with the showering sparks from Catherine wheels positioned above. In the high-ceilinged, chandeliered and marble gaming rooms people sat in evening dress around the roulette and *chemin de fer* tables. Darryl Zanuck and King Farouk of Egypt played for hundreds of thousands. There would be Yul Brynner, Noël Coward, Grace Kelly and Cary Grant.

We stayed up late at school to listen to Donald Peers singing 'By a Babbling Brook . . .' in evening dress in a BBC radio studio. For excitement there was radio's *Dick Barton, Special Agent*. In those days very daring. Irate parents wrote to say a thriller in the early evening was demeaning the morals of the nation. Melbury Road, the street where we now lived, was lined with vast mansions built for the famous artists of the Victorian era. Holman Hunt, Lord Leighton and, in our house, Sir Luke Fildes, whose studio was described by Edward VII 'as one of the finest rooms in London'. It's now my bedroom. Holland Park wasn't open to the public. It had a bombed-out Jacobean mansion in the middle. We'd climb into woodland so vast you'd think you were in the middle of the country. David Lean lived behind me and Michael Powell, another legendary film director, opposite. Two doors down I stood and watched as Moira Shearer, the beautiful red-haired ballerina star of *The Red Shoes*, set off to marry Ludovic Kennedy. It was an enchanted world where you needed no bars on the windows to stop burglars. No alarms. No terrorists. No tower blocks stood ugly against the sky. There were fields and ponds where now are housing estates. The solar system was a mysterious landscape where strange beings surely lived. You could look at a tree and not worry if acid rain was affecting it. A river was a wild and natural thing: not smothered by pollution. We believed it would be like that forever.

In the summer holiday we went to the Palace Hotel, Torquay. Once a week the guests did cabaret. I befriended two brothers from Liverpool. Brian and Clive Epstein. Brian and I were rehearsing our impersonation of a group called The Ink Spots. Brian said, 'You can't sing at all, can you?' Brian later discovered and managed the Beatles. I discovered that the Fleet Street papers hired extra reporters on Saturday to prepare for the Sunday editions. I was taken on by the *Sunday Express*. On my first outing I was sent off with Dudley Smith, who was later knighted and became a Tory MP. I transferred to the *Sunday Pictorial* (now the *Sunday Mirror*). The News Editor, Fred Redman, sent me to a hospital in Hammersmith where Captain Carlsen had been helicoptered from his ship to attend the bedside of his sick daughter. Carlsen had become famous a year earlier for staying on board his ship *The Flying Enterprise*, refusing to leave until seconds before it sunk. Journalists waited for a statement. I got bored with hanging about so I walked into the hospital and asked for his daughter's room. I knocked. 'Come in,' said a voice. I opened the door. There, sitting forlorn and grieving, stooped on a chair by the bed of his dying daughter, sat Captain Carlsen. I was appalled at what I'd done. Captain Carlsen looked up; there were tears rolling down his cheeks. I mumbled and left. Not realising I was meant to wait for the hospital report, I phoned the News Editor and told him I'd seen Captain Carlsen and no one else had. He instructed me to return to the office and write my story. In the excitement I forgot I didn't have one!

At school I was fed up with chasing rats round the rotting caravans where they had us sleep. I wanted education. I knew I wasn't getting it. It was the year of the General Certificate of Education exam. GCE, it was called. A girl in the class above me had left to go to a tutorial establishment in London. Miss K. M. Hobbs MA (Oxon) of Guildford and Buckingham Gate. A stone's throw from Buckingham Palace. I phoned Miss Hobbs and asked if she'd take me. She was surprised. Parents usually called. But yes, if I passed her interview. I wrote a letter to my father on why I thought St Christopher's stank. I said I was going to leave.

Miss Hobbs was an imposing lady of the old school. She looked at my schoolwork. 'You're illiterate,' she announced. 'You cannot write, you cannot punctuate. Academically you are non-existent.' This woman I liked. In my final report at St Christopher School the Headmaster wrote, 'Michael has an influential personality, what he undertakes he does well. He has very great possibilities, but at his present stage of development he has experienced a difficult clash with some of his own standards and some of the school's. This has created some conflict in his mind and it may be as well that he should work it out somewhere else.' I used a wire recorder for exam passing. Early recording devices used wire. They were the size of three briefcases piled on top of one another. Later they recorded on grey paper tape which broke easily. The wire ran from one spool to another. I'd record essential information and play it under my bed at night until the whoosh of the tape running loose woke me up. When the exam results came I'd passed three O levels and one higher level, OA in Economics. I'd failed Latin, which I needed to get to Oxford or Cambridge. I wasn't going to university anyway. The film industry was waiting! Following on from my childhood triumphs in journalism, I'd become a director at once! I told my parents as we drove along the South Carriageway of Hyde Park. They stopped the car and leaned over from the Rover's front seats to scream at me in the back. 'You will get in to Cambridge! If you do not you will be cut off, abandoned to fate, thrown out into the streets.' I've never seen two people so determined to influence another. Perhaps I knew they were right. Perhaps I was scared. I decided to go to Cambridge.

On 30th September 1952, Miss Hobbs wrote to my father saying, 'After seeing something of Michael's work and receiving tutors' considered reports it is only fair to tell you that if you imagined he was almost up to entrance standard for university, this is far from being the case.'

Less than a year later I'd passed the entrance exams and at seventeen was up at Cambridge. At Miss Hobbs's establishment there were only three pupils to a class. The teachers were brilliant. The few students were interesting and cheerful. I could live at home, go to the movies and the theatre and carry on my show-business column. After my second term my report said, 'Few students have tried so hard as Michael to re-adjust. He is lively, vigorous and ambitious.' At the end of the summer term, I was to take my Advanced Level exams which, if I passed, would get me to Cambridge. I took an interview at Downing College, Cambridge. I learned that the colleges themselves set exams. If you passed you got into that particular college. You couldn't use the exam, like the General Certificate of Education Advanced exam, to get anywhere else. So why bother with A level? The Downing College exam was three weeks earlier. They gave you the results in a few days.

Cambridge was a beautiful place and Downing was its only Georgian college. I sat in the exam room looking on to the large central court. Policemen were everywhere! A column of limousines was driving to the Master's Lodge. It was President Tito of Yugoslavia visiting the Master of Downing, Sir Lionel Whitby, who was Vice-Chancellor of the University. Then I looked round the room at the other boys. I said to myself, 'Someone in this room has to pass. If these dull-looking people can do it, so can I!' A few days later I learned I'd passed. I'd also passed my second attempt at O level Latin.

My joy at academic triumphs was somewhat abated by the fact that Great Britain still had National Service and I was due to enter the Army for two years before going to Cambridge. I considered this a complete waste of time. We were carrying an enormous standing army of National Servicemen and regulars which MPs said was draining the resources of the country. It was bound soon to be abolished. In those days there were some medical examining boards in London where you could buy your way out of the Army for five hundred pounds. I put this to my father as a reasonable proposition! I suggested he lend me the money. He said, 'Of course you've got to go in the Army!' So I went to Shepherd's Bush, took my medical, and passed. Now I stared in disbelief at the card telling me to report to Catterick Camp. I was to become a soldier!

I had an idea. National Service was bound to be abolished in the next three years. If I went to Cambridge immediately I'd stand a chance of avoiding it. It was July. I telephoned the Bursar of

Downing College and said, 'Could I come up in October this year?'
The Bursar replied, 'We've had a cancellation from an African
student. We do have a place available.' I said, 'I'd like a room
overlooking the main courtyard, because I thought it very attractive
when I came . . .' The Bursar interrupted, 'This is not a hotel, Mr
Winner, you can't select your room. The college will allocate you
one.'

That left three months with nothing to do before going to
Cambridge. I don't know why I was in the National Union of
Students building, but on their notice board I saw that a pastor was
organising cheap trips to show students the American Way of life.
America was not a place people went to in 1953. Very few people
travelled in Europe, let alone across the Atlantic. Here was an
opportunity to visit the place I'd only seen in the movies.

4

America, Here I Come

The flight to New York by propeller plane took sixteen and a half hours! The jet hadn't been invented. We stopped in Iceland to refuel. I was met in New York by a bespectacled, pudgy young man, Irving Slomowitz. We were to stay with assorted people all over America. Irving and his friend Jack drove me past the amazing New York skyline at sunset, and on to Ossining, a dormitory town famous for housing Sing Sing prison. There, in the Fuller Gardens apartment block, Irving showed me his one-room pad and lowered his bed from the wall. It had been a long time since I'd shared a room. I'd never shared a bed! But in his infinite wisdom God had decided my first night in America was to be the first night I slept with another human being and that was to be Irving Slomowitz. Sometime during the night, Irving's hand, not deliberately, landed on my thigh. With as much grace as I could muster, because he was asleep, snoring and my host, I removed it. Then I found somewhere else to stay.

Thirty years later I spotted Peter Falk, of *Columbo* fame, at a restaurant in London. We'd met briefly in Los Angeles. I asked him out to dinner the next night. Like many stars Peter is extremely shy. I drove through Hyde Park with him and his wife Shera, searching for something to say. 'Where were you brought up, Peter?' I asked.

'In Ossining,' he replied. 'Oh,' I said, immediately regretting the silliness of it, 'did you know Irving Slomowitz?' 'I lived in the same apartment block!' said Peter. 'Not the Fuller Gardens?' I said. 'How did you know?' said Peter. 'I spent my first night in America there,' I answered. 'I shared a bed with Irving Slomowitz. He turned over while asleep and his hand ended up on my thigh.' 'I stayed with Irving Slomowitz in New York,' said Peter, 'in the same bed!' Peter and I became blood brothers! We'd both slept with Irving Slomowitz!

The train from Ossining into New York had straw seats. Near the local railway station there was a soda fountain with a creaking outer door covered with mesh to keep flies out and a counter with high stools. Just like in the movies. In New York I worked the phone. 'I'm Michael Winner from the British press,' I said. Tickets to theatres, movies and TV shows showered upon me. I went to Eddie Fisher's TV show and met his guest, Duke Ellington. I attended the Ticker Tape parade for golfer Ben Hogan and stood with the press photographers as Mayor Impelliteri of New York handed Hogan a scroll of honour. I saw Cinerama, the new film experience, where three screens joined together to produce an enormous image featuring a roller-coaster ride which had the audience screaming at its reality. The other cinema gimmick was 3-D. You wore red and green spectacles. In *The Charge at Feather River* the Indians flew off their horses into your lap. Accompanying the movie were Dean Martin and Jerry Lewis in their stage act. 'They won't see English people,' their PR man said. 'The press there gave them a terrible time.'

But Howard Johnson's had endless flavours of ice-cream and at Gallaghers, New York's famous steak house, I saw Marilyn Monroe dining with Joe Di Maggio. Then I set off with nine other students from assorted countries on our trip round America. Various do-gooders, local church groups, Rotary Clubs and others put us up. In Philadelphia, an Isaac Stern concert was rained out after half an hour. In Baltimore, we walked down narrow alleys between rotting wooden fences in the black slum area, with howling dogs and ramshackle shacks made of wood. At the Johns Hopkins Hospital, the President of the Philippines was wheeled past us from the operating theatre. In Washington, we visited the Senate and the

House of Representatives, and more slums, again housing African Americans. We went on to Pittsburgh where, in order to get into the YMCA, I signed a form saying I wished to propagate Christ and all his teachings. Outside Columbus, Ohio, I stayed with a poor farmer who gave me a dollar when I left to buy myself a present. We did a lot of broadcasts taking questions such as 'In England do they still have oxen pulling the plough?' It was before travel and TV had informed different countries of the world how we all lived.

The Illinois State Fair had an exhibit labelled 'Korean War Atrocities – See The Commie War Crimes'. If you looked closely you could see that 'North Korean tortures' with American soldiers being clubbed were touched-up pictures of German war crimes. All the 'Communists' wore German uniforms. The next exhibit was 'The Lobster Family', a display of human freaks. In the evening there was a concert by Guy Lombardo and his Orchestra. One of our travelling students was a marvellous black man from Zanzibar, Omar Abdullah. I nicknamed him Reggie. At the Rotary Club, our hosts in Lexington Kentucky, a speaker boasted of the message of tolerance the Rotary Clubs offered the world. He pointed out with pride that Reggie was the first Negro ever to be allowed to dine there! In Georgia, we had picnics. No restaurant would allow Reggie in. So Reggie and I decided to de-segregate a restaurant. It was in mid-town Atlanta, called the SF Cafeteria. Junior executives and women shoppers went there for lunch. We didn't understand the risk, but we knew what was going on was wrong. Reggie was a classical African with completely Negroid features. Together we entered the whites-only restaurant and stood in line for the self-service counter. Heads turned, but no one tried to stop us. This was 1953. For a black man to eat in a white restaurant was unheard of! It was so unheard of that diners didn't believe it was happening! We sat down and ate. People turned and looked. They talked. But they were so amazed that they did nothing. As we left we passed two women. One turned to the other. 'He must be Spanish,' she said.

At Nashville, where my host's son spoke of the inferiority of black people, adding the poor were no better, I visited The Grand Ole' Opry, a legendary Country and Western venue televised on the network each week. At nearby Evansville I went to my first drive-in movie. Later, on our way to Monmouth, Illinois, my diary entry read, 'We were turned out of a pokey restaurant because the owner wouldn't serve Reggie. I was stung by a bee.' In the afternoon I went to my first ball game where the visiting team, from Philadephia, were booed on every possible occasion while the home team were cheered to the rafters. Then on to Detroit and Niagara Falls where I thought the long promenade of balconied hotels facing them made it look like the Falls had been put in a museum.

Back in New York, America was in the grip of anti-Communist fervour. 'In the event of enemy attack please remain in your seats and await further instructions' was printed in heavy black type at the top of my theatre programme. Every skyscraper had a sign on it: 'Air Raid Shelter This Way'. On roads leading into the city huge hoardings read 'In the event of an enemy attack this highway will be closed to public transport.' My white-haired Quaker host in Philadelphia, a sweet lady, had told me, 'I think we should kill all the Communists, it would be so much simpler.' The pleasure-boat going round Manhattan Island glided past a thin, rectangular skyscraper. 'On your left, the United Nations building,' bawled the guide, 'built by America to protect the rest of the world from Communism.' 'That's where we meet the foreigners,' explained a hot-dog-eating parent to his offspring. 'Don't they owe us a lot of money?' replied his son.

I was not to return to America for fourteen years. Then, instead of a student charter plane with earnest young men playing guitars, it would be first class paid for by Universal Pictures. Instead of being met by Irving Slomowitz, my Hollywood agent would escort me to a studio limousine. Instead of sharing a bed in a small apartment, I'd be in a suite at the Beverly Hills Hotel. Instead of travelling in old cars and greyhound buses organised by earnest do-gooders, it was a first-class flight to Los Angeles because Steve McQueen wanted to do a movie with me. The journeys of youth, through countries and a life which seem so permanent, fade into photos in an album. Events hung together by the fragile thread of memory. When you're young you want to pass through it quickly and join the grown-ups. You don't realise adulthood creeps up on you and stays for an eternity. The thin and fresh-faced adventurer turns into a figure only loosely connected to what you were. Was it really you? Or did some other person play the role in Act One, to be pushed off-stage after the intermission? And was there an intermission at all between childhood and after-life? There was. It was called Cambridge.

5

Superstudent

I went up to Cambridge, aged seventeen, in October 1953. I had a bedroom and a sitting room in Downing College overlooking the gardens, the wrought-iron entrance gates and the Porter's Lodge. There was a butler who brought hot water in an earthenware jug in the morning and poured it into a bowl so I could wash. On my first evening an undergraduate came towards me with an apple impaled on the end of his umbrella. 'Why have you got an apple on the end of your umbrella?' I asked. 'I'm walking up and down to see how many people ask that,' was the reply. Everyone was wearing thick, tweed, herringbone jackets. We ate in the vast, cold College Hall. At my first dinner I met a lot of earnest young men who talked endlessly about poetry and novels. After coffee in my rooms they sang dirty songs into my tape recorder for five hours.

Although undergraduates were aged up to thirty and many of them had been in the Army fighting in Malaya, no one was allowed to leave their college after ten o'clock at night. We had to be in by midnight. If you came in after ten you were fined a penny and if you came in between eleven and midnight you were fined two pennies! Undergraduates would climb out of their colleges after hours. They often fell, breaking legs or arms. The front-page leader of the

University newspaper, *Varsity*, read 'Curfew Remains'. College landladies (we all spent our last two years in lodgings) had voted by a large majority in favour of maintaining the curfew, because they feared if students were allowed to bring friends in till 11 p.m., 'they would have to stay up more often until midnight to make coffee for them'. To enforce this rule a Proctor, a member of the University staff in full formal dress with wing collar, would walk the Cambridge streets with two 'Bulldogs' – college porters in black suits and bowler hats. Undergraduates had to wear their gown after dark. This was a black, academic cloak.

The Bulldogs would run up and ask, 'Excuse me sir, are you a member of the University?' If you weren't wearing a gown there was a fine of one pound. If you were out after hours you could be heavily fined or 'rusticated' – which meant being sent away from the University for a week or more.

There were only two girls' colleges. Girls weren't allowed to join men's colleges. Men outnumbered girls ten to one. Since I'd not yet dared do much with girls, this didn't bother me! I was reading Economics, but this was not a full-time occupation. I sought out the small, cluttered offices of the student newspaper, *Varsity*. My columns from the *Kensington Post* impressed the Editor and I was accepted. The paper was a well-produced twelve-page tabloid, crammed with advertising. It made a healthy profit selling seven thousand copies a week. My first job was to go to a theatre to interview escapologist Alan Alan. He told me hanging upside-down helped him do crossword puzzles. In the same issue of *Varsity* I was pictured surrounded by knives which had been thrown at me by Denver, another act on the bill. I became a life member of the Union (the debating society). I joined both the Labour Club and the Conservative Club! Fellow-student Cecil (now Lord) Parkinson was a leading light of the Labour Club. He later became Chairman of the Tory Party. Tam Dalyell, the venerable left-wing MP, was active in the Conservative Party! Cambridge was great fun. I was glad my parents forced me to go. Each day I'd cycle to the *Varsity* office where I was soon promoted to edit one of the sections. I acquired fancy waistcoats, cowboy-type bow-ties with long hanging strands and a black sword-stick with an ivory dog's-head handle. I learned to hypnotise people and became Director of Hypnotism for the Cambridge Psychic Research Society.

After my first year at Cambridge I decided attending academic functions was a waste of time. I'd passed Part One in Economics and switched to Law. There were long, tedious textbooks, but you could buy a precis of them in short-form books. Cambridge education consisted of lectures, often by the people who had written the textbooks. The lectures were basically spoken versions of the books. Then there were tutorials where Professors would take small groups in their rooms. All needed information was available in the short-version books. My Tutor at Downing was a dull, earnest man who was supposedly guiding me through University life. He spent his time telling me I shouldn't be writing for the University newspaper. I replied that I didn't intend to go to any academic functions at all. Nor did I wish to pay for them. He telephoned T.S. Ellis Lewis, a world expert on the Law of Tort, whose tutorials I attended at Gonville and Caius College. The Professor said he didn't mind at all if I didn't come.

For two weeks before the exams I worked like mad. We filed into the Senate House, a gracious Georgian building where desks were laid out for the Cambridge degree tests. We were allowed to go in up to half an hour late and to leave up to half an hour early. I took the crammer book with me and sat, after the exam had started, in the deserted corridor outside reading up one section of the work which I'd not studied. Then I rushed in and, before even looking at the exam paper, wrote what I'd just read on my blank paper. Then I looked at the exam questions and answered them as best I could. So as not to confuse myself, I left half an hour early. I passed.

I also carried on with my London show columns and wrote for many magazines including a wonderful sepia movie publication called *Picturegoer*. I was the film critic and feature-writer on the *New Musical Express*, a frequent contributor to the *Spectator* and did film reviews for *Films and Filming*. In Cambridge, I wrote about a group of rugger rowdies who'd invaded the swimming pool of a girls' college. When I entered my digs four men in black balaclavas with slits for eyes greeted me. They threw me into a van and drove to the freezing waters of the River Cam. They bundled me out. 'You embarrassed us,' they said in the clipped tones of the British public-school bully, 'now we're going to chuck you in the river.' 'I hope you can swim,' I said. 'Because I can't. So one of you is going to have to get me out, or face a murder inquiry.' They thought about that. Their eyes flickered from one to the other through slits in their balaclavas. Then they ran to their van and drove off. 'Hey!' I yelled as they sped away, 'how about a lift home!'

I was a celebrity within the confines of Cambridge University. I interviewed visiting big-wigs from Hugh Gaitskell and Clement Attlee to Chris Chataway. I led campaigns against the Union debating society, inviting the Fascist leader Sir Oswald Mosley. I was *Varsity*'s film critic. In a poll, the most famous person at the University was Jonathan Miller, known by 87 per cent of the students; I was second, known by 76 per cent. Other contenders were Giles Shaw (who became a Tory Minister) at 69 per cent, Tam Dalyell at 57 per cent, and James Ferman, who became the Film Censor, at 42 per cent! The *Varsity* article concluded, 'If you can't be Michael Winner (and believe us nobody could actually be Michael Winner), then be yourself!'

At the *Varsity* newspaper it was custom that if you were Features Editor, which I'd become, you automatically went on to be Assistant Editor and then Editor. These appointments were made at the end of each term. At the end of my fourth term at Cambridge a new Editor was to take over. I would normally be made his Assistant and the following term become Editor. In the undergraduate world this was important. The Assistant Editor, Ted Taylor, hated me! If as Editor he failed to choose me as his number two, I'd be out! The new Editor could be elected by the fourteen-man editorial team. But never was. The number two simply became, unopposed, the new Editor. I decided to contest the election! I had only two good friends among the fourteen-man executive. To win I needed eight supporters, because if it was a draw, seven-all, the existing Editor had a casting vote. He would favour his friend Ted whom he'd chosen as his Assistant. Three against eleven didn't look like victory!

My *Varsity* supporters were Bill Hopper, a cloth-capped man from Durham, the newspaper's Business Manager. And Graham Cleverley, a thin, soft-spoken lad from Southampton, an Assistant

Features Editor. We'd not been able to find anyone who remembered an election for the Editorship, so long had it been carried out in the gentlemanly way of letting the next chap in automatically.

We agreed I'd be particularly nice to everybody who had a vote. I'd ask them to my room for a drink and a chat. We put in my nomination at the last minute, so as to give the other side less time to organise. It didn't seem to worry Mr Taylor. He thought I was an unpopular, over-publicised upstart for whom the *Varsity* board would never vote. We started work. Photo Editors were promised new darkrooms, everyone who was liable to remain on the paper was blatantly offered opportunities galore. On the day before the vote we reckoned my supporters had increased from two to three! The new certainty was a pleasant, dark-haired chap called Cass Robertson, the paper's Sports Editor. Bill Hopper, our blunt Northerner, was particularly cross about the Photo Editor and the Photo Manager, Redmayne and Hargreaves. He tried to get them on my side. 'I should've said, "Listen Redders old chap, if you don't vote for Winner I'll close your bloody darkroom down," ' he said gruffly and then gave out a short, nervous laugh. The Features Editor, Marshall Gorridge, had vanished altogether. Gorridge had been at school with my rival Ted Taylor so we reckoned he'd vote against me. 'All right,' I said to my group of three, 'you stand on either side of the photographic chaps Redmayne and Hargreaves. It's a small room and they have to vote knowing whoever's next to them may see them writing their choice. It might swing them if you're close by.' 'I reckon we may have Fitch, the Advertisement Manager,' said Cleverley. 'If we do, that makes, with Redmayne and Hargreaves . . . and us four . . . seven votes.' 'Not enough,' I said, 'and only four of them are certain!'

On election day Gorridge was still missing. My loyal three came in early to the tiny *Varsity* office. Left on the notice board was a single, hand-delivered envelope addressed to the Editor. 'I think it's Gorridge's writing,' said Cleverley. 'Steam it open,' I said. 'What if it's a vote for Taylor?' said Hopper. 'We put it back,' I said. The envelope was from Gorridge. He voted for me! We re-sealed it.

A clatter outside announced Ted Taylor and his people, including the Chairman, Harrison, trooping in. Crammed into the tiny front office, along with two large desks and filing cabinets, were fourteen young people, shoulder to shoulder. Hanging in the balance, one of the key positions at Cambridge University. Unimportant in the real world, but supremely meaningful at the time. Hopper handed over Gorridge's envelope. 'Here,' he said, thrusting it forward to Harrison, 'Marshall Gorridge gave me this. Could be his vote.'

Harrison handed out voting papers. Everybody scribbled a name. Harrison collected the papers and counted them into two piles, his back to us. His body hiding the votes. He fished in his pocket and opened Gorridge's. 'Michael Winner's next term's Editor,' he announced.

My voters applauded. The Taylor group left disgusted. The next day I held my first meeting in the office. Gavin Lyall, now a famous author, had been campaigning heavily for Taylor. He turned up with a big lapel badge reading 'I like Mike' based on the US Presidential 'I like Ike' badges. He smiled and congratulated me. 'Arsehole!' I thought. But I was magnanimous. I appointed him to the board as Art Editor.

The defeated opposition had one more edition of *Varsity* in which to spit revenge. They printed, 'During the last few weeks Winner has been working hard on a cartoon transcription for Walt Disney of *Whisky Galore* and *How to Make Friends and Influence People*.' What did I care? I'd won.

In 1954 I got Christmas vacation work as a Call Boy at the BBC Television studios. The name came from the theatrical title for the lad who went round the dressing rooms calling artistes on to the stage. Lime Grove was Britain's only TV studio. There was just one black-and-white TV channel. All programmes were 'live'. If a play was repeated the sets were left standing. The actors came back a few days later and did it again. The studios had been the Gainsborough Film Studios where Hitchcock made *The Lady Vanishes*. Where Margaret Lockwood and James Mason starred in *The Wicked Lady*. My grandfather had a menswear store on the corner. I arrived particularly disadvantaged to work for BBC Television. We didn't have TV. My mother was dedicated to playing cards.

I was working on an afternoon children's play. An old actress turned round. 'Go to my dressing room and get my handbag, would you?' she said. I looked behind me. 'Some idiot's got to get her handbag,' I thought. But she was talking to me! This didn't fit my view of myself as Cambridge undergraduate wit, writer and general genius. The trouble with university, and I see little difference today, is that it induces in the students the belief that they're special. That they are somehow, at Oxford and Cambridge particularly, above other people. Clever. Destined for great things. In fact they are, on the whole, a load of lazy, over-opinionated twits. That's what I was as I walked along the corridors looking for the old actress's dressing room to fetch her handbag.

In my second week I was on a quiz show called *Find the Link*, produced by a man later Chairman of London Weekend Television, Brian Tesler. The compère, Peter Martin asked a panel to find some link between guests. My job was to position the contestants ready to go on. I'd wave them forward to make their move from back-stage. People came and went. Then came the celebrity guest, the film star James Mason. Mr Mason appeared, did something, I forget what, and then started towards the steps for his interview.

I was standing at the back with the next two people due on. One was Eric Williams, who'd written a famous book called *The Wooden Horse* about how he and some fellow prisoners of war escaped from a German prison camp by making a tunnel, with the prisoner digging it hidden under a wooden vaulting horse. Mr Williams was with one of his fellow ex-prisoners. They had ropes round them with grappling irons and little shovels. Since the war they'd got fat. James Mason and the compère were at the bottom of the steps when I pushed my two Wooden Horse contestants forward. I didn't know the compère interviewed the celebrity guest. Just as Peter said, 'Now Mr Mason, what film are you making?' my two heavily clad escapees clomped down, knocking into James Mason and the compère at the bottom! There was confusion! The compère looked appalled! James Mason had been physically pushed from the TV screen! Eric Williams and his mate stood bemused. I watched this on the TV at the back as viewers saw it at home. The compère said 'Sorry' to the off-screen James Mason, took Eric Williams, his grappling irons, his ropes and his friend to their place at the desk and then returned to James Mason. I'd fucked up on live TV! After the show the Producer, Brian Tesler, came to congratulate everyone. For one fleeting moment, which I will never forget, Brian Tesler's eyes looked into mine. There was within them all the contempt and hatred I so truly deserved.

Years went by and I became well known. I found myself seated opposite Brian Tesler at a dinner organised by the British Academy of Film and Television Arts. 'Brian,' I called, 'I've waited thirty-eight years to apologise to you.' He looked surprised. 'When I last saw you, you gave me a look of great hatred,' I said. Brian's wife looked nervous. I told the story. Tesler didn't remember any of it. My remaining time at the BBC was memorable for the extraordinary furore that developed over a production of George Orwell's *1984*. The play, about Big Brother in a futuristic society, shocked the British Establishment and press beyond belief. They thought it politically subversive. There were threats to blow up the studio to prevent the play being repeated a couple of days later! The corridors and sets were patrolled by the Metropolitan police! To the confusion was added my presence as Call Boy. But this time I did nothing wrong. Another furore was blowing! A second television station was to be allowed, called ITV. The BBC's monopoly would be broken! This delighted employees, who saw a chance of getting higher wages. The BBC regulars were full of disdain. There wouldn't be enough talent to go round. There'd be no audience for it. It would lower standards. All the claptrap that came up when it was proposed the BBC have a second channel returned yet again when ITV got its second channel. And again when Sky and the satellite and cable channels came in. Every time something increases choice for the public and threatens the status quo, the cry is the same. It didn't matter. I wasn't planning to work in television. I'd go back to Cambridge and then into movies.

6

The Editor

My first edition of the *Varsity* newspaper appeared on 15th January 1955. The headline was 'UNDERGRADUATE MINDS!' The piece continued, 'Students are neurotic, says a Psychiatrist. Students go through many difficult phases. They grow beards, become Communist, contemplate suicide, study obtuse philosophies, turn against their parents and friends, become seclusive or seek gaiety and dabble in the arts.' Thus spoke Dr Russell Davis. His remarks seem okay for today! I used my acquaintance with celebrities to have a guest writer in the paper each week. The first was the famous radio comedian Kenneth Horne. His radio show *Much Binding in the Marsh* was a cult hit in the fifties. Other celebrity guests were Eric Williams, the famous escaper I'd pushed through at the wrong time on BBC television; Ronald Waldman, Head of Television Light Entertainment at the BBC and who was later to reject me for a job in Television; Bernard Braden, probably the first alternative comedian on the BBC; and Spike Milligan. His article started, 'Hercules Bleriot snuggled down in his favourite chair, he was a tall man (as you dear reader will observe when he stands up).'

My most controversial move with *Varsity* was to bring it out in Oxford. I said, 'The price of the Oxford edition will be threepence instead of fourpence for the Cambridge edition. It's the cheapest piece of education Oxford ever had.' We had Oxford students to run the edition but they were frightened off by the fury of the Oxford newspapers, *Isis* and *Cherwell*. When I went to rally the troops I was told Oxford's student journalists would throw me in the river. So I took the Cambridge University Water-Ski Team. *Varsity*'s finances were in a healthy state when I arrived. It was broke when I left! I'd go to the Market Square in Cambridge, take taxis from the rank, and say 'Oxford!' My Cambridge staff were in two taxis and the Cambridge Water-Ski bodyguards were in two behind! The *Manchester Guardian* wrote, 'Oxford had better look out or the press lords of Cambridge will be imposing all the horror of the Cambridge way of life upon the impressionable minds of its freshmen. Policies of *Varsity* are those often associated rightly or wrongly with Cambridge. It is brisk, efficient and professional.'

This was true. Our circulation of 6,000 was three times bigger than any Oxford publication. *The Times* on 28th January 1955 wrote, 'Mr Michael Winner of Downing College, like any other editor worth his salt, is not to be turned from his set purpose by the opposition even when, as he might say, it copies the worst excesses of the French revolution. Do they threaten in Oxford to plunge him in a convenient river? Do Oxford undergraduates rip down posters pasted up for their own good? It will make no difference.' John Gale in the *Observer* noted that I was wearing an impeccable but faintly checked yellow waistcoat and wrote, 'Michael Winner had not made a courtesy call upon the Oxford student paper *Cherwell* when they invited him last Sunday. "Because (a) I'd left, and (b) I understood they wanted to throw me in the river."' The *Sunday Times* wrote, 'Suppose the *Sunday Times* were to suddenly publish a Moscow edition. It would hardly start more argument and publicity than has attended the incursion of the Cambridge undergraduate newspaper *Varsity* to Oxford. At least we may reflect in this country there is still room for enterprise and competition.' As a sop to the Oxford undergraduates, my guest writer that week was Enid Blyton.

The owner of a local Cambridge cinema, the Rex, was a marvellous cockney, George Webb. His cinema manager, Leslie Halliwell, became a famous film historian and writer. When a woman complained to George that the spring in one of his seats had protruded into her bottom he said, 'Madam, you were in the one and nines. Them seats are reserved for the yobbos!' The 1/9d seat was the equivalent of 7p. That's what it cost to go to movies in the fifties. One night after dinner at an Indian restaurant we went to George's cinema. Ingmar Bergman's *Smiles of a Summer Night* was on. There were queues all round the block. This was because of a scene lasting four seconds where a nude woman ran into the sea. Nudity was completely unknown in movies. The sight of it, even in long shot and out-of-focus black and white, had the students turning up in their hundreds.

Marlon Brando's classic film *The Wild One* was banned by the British Film Censor because he considered it a bad influence. I'd found out a cinema could get a licence to show a film (as they can today) if the local council permits it. I suggested George ask the Cambridge Council to pass *The Wild One* for his cinema. They did. This caused an outcry in the press. Many celebrities came down, including Jackie Collins who I knew from London. She visited my modest rooms with her boyfriend, before going on to the movie.

I spent even more time on my national writing career, driving up two or three mornings a week to London to see movie press shows in Leicester Square. Undergraduates were not allowed to have a car in Cambridge until their third year. But if you joined the Yacht Club, you could have a car to travel to the nearest suitable lake, six miles away near St Ives. I went to the Yacht Club premises in Cambridge and found, early on, how valuable it is to be well known. They welcomed me with open arms. I paid a tiny fee and became a member. I said to my tutor, 'I need permission for a car to go and sail at St Ives.' I never went to St Ives. My car was a modest black Austin A35 with bright red leather. It could do the journey from Cambridge to London in an hour and a half going at sixty-five miles an hour. Anything faster and you felt it would fall to pieces. The journey from London to the centre of Cambridge now is considerably more. It shows what extraordinary non-progress we've made.

I carried on writing for the *Spectator* and the film magazine. I also wrote for *Showgirl Glamour Revue*. This was a precursor of *Playboy* and *Penthouse*, except they didn't dare show a nipple, let alone any other part of a woman's anatomy. It just had cleavage and pretty girls and what would be the equivalent of intelligent men's magazine articles. A magazine I particularly liked was *The Cheshire Cat*, billed as 'An intimate journal and review of London coffee house circles'. Coffee had become a great thing in the fifties. The first espresso machine arrived in London in 1955 in Park Lane. There was a coffee bar in Northumberland Avenue, where young people met. They produced *The Cheshire Cat,* where I had a column. An article appeared saying the coffee in Forte restaurants, called Black and White Cafés, was so dreadful old dray horses wouldn't drink it. Forte sued. We thought of filling a trough with coffee from the Forte cafeterias and bringing some old dray horses to court to see if they'd drink it. No one could afford the legal fees, so the magazine collapsed.

It was in my *Varsity* that playwright Michael Frayn got his first chance to see his name in print. Shortly before I finished Cambridge, Michael wrote an article headed 'WINNER AND ALSO RANS'. He said:

> There are only two men left in Cambridge whose names everyone has heard of, Jonathan Miller and Michael Winner. The only survivors of the group, Bricusse, Boxer, Raphael, and Woodthorpe which made Cambridge a colourful place to live in and something more, for the rest of the country, than a town which produces television sets. People have often doubted whether Winner was a good thing. While he was editor of *Varsity* he inspired a widespread personal dislike among a lot of people who had never even met him, and the brash vulgarity of his ideals caused a lot of sensitive noses to turn up including this column's. Can Winner be a good thing in spite of all this? Yes he can. Ambition whatever the saints think is one of the things, like love, which makes the world go round. Cambridge is growing grey and anaemic because far too many people here have drowned their ambitions in listlessness or politely suppressed them to suit a code of pseudo modesty. People without ambition are so much dead weight and people who are ambitious and pretend they aren't are phonies. In a world of

mock humble minds and self-effacing jeers, Winner is certainly a very good thing. After all this is Cambridge University and not as you would sometimes think a school for backward children.

Years later Frayn came to Shepperton Studios to watch me direct a strange movie, *The Cool Mikado*. He was writing for the *Observer*. The stage was dark except for the area where we were filming. Michael didn't notice a large swimming pool and fell in!

While I was at Cambridge I interviewed Benny Hill for *Showgirl Glamour Revue* and we became friends, in as much as anyone could be a friend of Benny Hill. Benny lived near me in a flat in Queen's Gate. He was extremely tight. I said to him once, 'What did you have for breakfast, Benny?' He said, 'Soup'. I said, 'Why did you have soup?' He replied, 'Because in the supermarket are cans from which the labels have come off and nobody knows what's in them. They're much cheaper than the other cans.' This was when he was earning a fortune. Benny was so mean he couldn't even leave money to anybody. He died worth millions without a will. So a lot of strange distant relatives whom he didn't know or care about got lucky. Years after I met him, I was dating one of the girl dancers in *Hot Gossip* who was a regular in his show, a beautiful redhead called Lorraine. We went to Barbados together. The following year we were going to Barbados for Christmas and New Year. Lorraine said, 'Benny's called a rehearsal on 27th December.' I said, 'Nobody rehearses on 27th December! They wait for the New Year.' So Lorraine had to leave Barbados early. She flew back, ending up at 10 a.m., having flown overnight, at a rehearsal room in Fulham. The cast of Benny's TV show were sitting there. When Lorraine entered Benny said, 'I've changed my mind. We're not going to rehearse until 2nd January.' I've no doubt Benny called this one day of pretend rehearsal to show Lorraine who was boss, because she was going out with me. I said to her, 'If you didn't need him for your career I'd give him a blast he'd remember for the rest of his life.' But I stayed friendly with Benny, seeing him occasionally and talking to him on the phone. He was very distressed when his lease came up on the flat in Queen's Gate which he'd had for over thirty years.

Benny said, 'I've got to get a new place, it's dreadful.' I said, 'You don't have to move, just buy a new lease.' He said, 'They're asking me much too much. Because it's me they're taking me for a ride.' I said, 'Don't be silly, they can only sell the lease for what it's worth. They're not going to ask you for more than anybody else.' Benny said, 'No, no, they're going to cheat me.' I said, 'Why don't you go to other estate agents, see the price of flats and buy one.' He said, 'Because the minute I come they put the price up.' I said, 'You mean estate agents selling highly expensive flats in Kensington rush to the window and change the prices just for you!' I couldn't convince him. So Benny bought a little house in Teddington near the Thames TV Studios where he did his programme. A short time afterwards John Howard Davies, the same person who'd given me a lift to Denham village and who was now Head of Comedy at Thames, called Benny in and said, 'We're cancelling your programme.' This was terrible, bowing to so-called political correctness. It caused Benny's death.

Another thing I did while at Cambridge was take a holiday job on a column called 'In London Last Night' on the *Evening Standard*. It was a witty social diary of evening events much loved by Lord Beaverbrook who owned Express Newspapers. Six of us would go out every night to parties, film premieres, politicians' cocktail parties, debutante dances and so on. There was also a photographer and someone in the office to manage things. We were highly paid. The minute Lord Beaverbrook died, the column was killed off. It was too expensive. But it was a wonderful experience for a young person to get out and about round London, going to all the night clubs that were very popular at the time.

'In London Last Night' was edited by Jeremy Campbell, who became the US correspondent for the *Evening Standard*. Together we invented a debutante called Venetia Crust. In those days people spent £5,000–£10,000 on a dance for five or six hundred people. That's the equivalent of over £100,000 today. The same girls would dance every night and the same weary debutante escorts wore evening dress and filled up space. The dances were preceded by a cocktail party and then a series of dinner parties. The girls were nice, normally around seventeen years old. But not very bright. So we invented Venetia who said things worth putting in the column. Venetia glued five-pound notes to the pavement outside the Dorchester Hotel and then poured champagne from a window on to the heads of men who tried to pick them up. She put all the money she'd been given for her debutante dance on a horse in the Derby. This was palpable nonsense because the girls were never given the money. It was a world which no one else knew or understood. We'd leave this stuff at three o'clock in the morning in the smelly ink-filled room of the *Evening Standard* and it would appear at 11 a.m. the same morning. Today they're lucky if they get theatre reviews in the next day! Venetia became so famous I invented a father for her called Arnold. He appeared in a restaurant owned by Tommy Yeardye, boyfriend of the actress Diana Dors, where people were given easels and oils and naked girls were strewn around for them to paint! I reported in the *Evening Standard* that Venetia's father Arnold created a picture called *Trauma* with a stirrup pump. He and Venetia became famous. Other journalists would say, 'Where's Venetia?' I'd say, 'She's just left, you just missed her.'

There was a man on the 'In London Last Night' column called David Stone, who later co-wrote the movie *Repulsion* with Roman Polanski. Stone lived with a man called Richard Berens at 15 Ilchester Place, which was behind my parents' house in Melbury Road. As a gag, they put an announcement in *The Times* – all debutante dances were announced in *The Times* – 'On June 15th 1957, Mr and Mrs Arnold Crust for Venetia at 15 Ilchester Place.' A lot of journalists turned up to meet Venetia. They were greeted by Richard Berens in his pyjamas. I was sitting in the *Evening Standard* office that night typing out my story. The phone rang. A voice said, 'Get the *Daily Mirror*, Venetia's exposed.' I went and got the *Daily Mirror* from their offices. James Pettigrew's diary headline was 'MEET MISS UPPERCRUST THE DEBUTANTE WHO ISN'T'. Jeremy Campbell was at the press table at a Savoy Hotel Derby Day dinner. I whispered in his ear, 'The *Mirror*'s exposed Venetia.' Jeremy shot up like a rocket. He was very tall and thin. At that moment he was also very white! We went to the Savoy lobby where other journalists hid behind the pillars thinking I'd arrived with a scoop. I've never had a scoop in my life. The next day the Editor, Charles Wintour, asked to see Jeremy. He had in front of him two envelopes of press cuttings from the *Standard* library. One was headed 'Crust, Venetia,

Debutante'. The other 'Crust, Arnold, Painter'. The final *Daily Mirror* cutting announced they were fakes. Jeremy was demoted to the News Desk. By chance my first film script was then purchased, a thriller called *Man with a Gun*. I left the column. Arnold Crust lives on. I edit my own films. Arnold is credited as Editor. He's had some wonderful reviews. He gets a full screen credit. It's nice to think he's still working.

My Cambridge days were ending. The government had not yet terminated National Service. I'd have to go into the Army. This seemed a waste of time and of no benefit to the nation. The only fighting was in Malaysia where we were attempting to keep the local population slaves to the British Empire. This didn't strike me as a noble cause. There were tens of thousands of National Servicemen with nothing to do. At Catterick Camp they were painting coal white in order to give the soldiers activity. My father still refused to lend me money to buy myself out! I then did something, which in retrospect I deeply regret. But we all make mistakes from time to time. I devised a way to get out of the Army. It was rumoured that if you were homosexual, in those days, they wouldn't have you in the army. I went to the London Yellow Pages directory in the Cambridge post office and looked under P for Psychiatrists. I counted the degrees after each name. The man with the most degrees operated out of a flat in Harley House. This was where Joan and Jackie Collins lived. I occasionally took Jackie out, although we did not have an affair. I phoned the psychiatrist, I'll call him Dr Grant, and made an appointment. I said, 'I bite my fingernails [True]. I set fire to paper in ashtrays [True]. I think I'm homosexual [Untrue].' Dr Grant said, 'Have you had a homosexual experience?' I said, 'No. But I want to.'

The sessions cost three guineas each. That's just over £3. I could see Dr Grant's eyes lighting up. A hefty 1950s income was sitting opposite him. He said, 'We won't put you on the couch until you come down from Cambridge. Then we'll do a serious examination. For now, I'll just talk to you.' On my fourth visit Dr Grant opened his diary and said, 'We'll have to book you in three times a week as you're leaving Cambridge soon.' I said, 'I'd love to, but I'm afraid I have to go in the Army.' Dr Grant said, 'You don't want to go in the Army do you?' I said, 'No.' Dr Grant stood up and said, 'Wait there.'

He went into a room at the back where his secretary was, and I heard him talking. I heard the secretary typing. Dr Grant returned and handed me a letter. He said, 'Show them that.' A few days later I arrived for the Cambridge University Army Medical. I had a pee here. They felt my testicles there. I did the eye chart. It was the same routine I'd gone through at Shepherd's Bush. I was holding my letter, wondering 'What do I do with it?' At the end of the examination, there was an old Colonel type sitting at a table. He looked up. 'Well, Winner,' he said, 'which of the services do you want to go into?' I held out my letter without saying anything. The 'Colonel' read it. His eyes flickered to me with utter contempt. He said, 'How long have you been feeling like this?' I said, 'About three months.' That was it. I was medically unfit for the Army. I'm really quite ashamed of myself. I don't think it would have done any good my being in the Army. The chances of my having been sent to fight in Malaya were as near nil as possible and I didn't want to kill Malaysians anyway. It was an improper thing to do. But in those days I was far less socially responsible than I am now. I can only apologise to the nation for being denied the opportunity of having me paint coal white in Catterick. I might have done an incredibly artistic job. Shortly thereafter National Service was abolished!

I went three more times to Dr Grant. He kept asking me to go to cricket with him at Lord's. I guess he was gay himself. It was highly improper of him to ask a patient to go on a social event. Eight years later I was becoming well known as a motion-picture director. I received a phone call. Dr Grant said, 'Could I please see you?' I said, 'What about?' He said, 'I'll tell you privately when we meet.' I thought, 'Oh my God! He's going to reveal I cheated to get out of the Army!' Dr Grant came to my apartment with an enormous envelope. I thought, 'That's my file! He's going to blackmail me!' He offered me the envelope. 'I've written a play,' he said, 'I wonder if you'd consider putting it on.' That was the final moment of an episode for which I have great regret. Not because I think the Army would have done me any good. Or that I would have done the Army or the nation any good. I think it's something I should have joined in regardless. I again apologise for not doing so.

7

A Start in Movies

It was 1956. I was twenty and out of Cambridge with an Honours Degree in Law and Economics. I was ready to enter the film industry. I wrote endless job application letters, but got very few answers. Those I received said I wasn't required. I persuaded my father to lend me two thousand pounds. With that I made a short film called *The Square* and put up half the money with an existing company making shorts for the cinema circuits for a film called *This Is Belgium*. It rained a lot in Belgium, so this was largely shot in East Grinstead. It figured in the *Guinness Book of Records* as the only film about Belgium shot in East Grinstead. In those days short films played in the cinemas together with the second feature, deliberately made to support the main film, and a newsreel. Shorts and second features led many young directors to bigger movies. *The Square* was a twenty-minute film script I wrote about an old man living in a rundown area of King's Cross. He'd arrived when it was very grand and was alienated from the rest of the modern community. His terrace of houses was to be knocked down. He was all alone. The last night he was there he answered the door and all the local residents had gathered together to give him a party. For the leading actor I employed a wonderful character called A. E. Matthews who was famous on the London stage and in movies. He was very old. When he did plays he invariably forgot the lines and invented something new, which delighted the audience. He was also a very distinguished-looking man and a very heavy drinker. We got him a dressing room in a terraced house in King's Cross and I advised the old cockney lady living there to hide her drink away. When the film finished she said, 'Mr Matthews drank all my lighter fluid.' Sadly the film never made it to the screens. The two people I employed, as the entire crew, cameraman and sound man, had a deal with the Rank Organisation and when I rather messed up the final editing, they offered to buy the film from me. They said they'd get it shown on the circuit but I couldn't have a credit as Producer, Director or Writer. They would take those credits themselves and I would only be called Associate Producer – which is a kind of general dogsbody. I was so outraged that I didn't sell the film. Which I probably should have done because at least it would have got shown!

In the case of *This Is Belgium* I learned early on the shenanigans that happen in the movie business. I put up £700 and they gave me an account of how they'd spent the first £350. When they sent me a letter about the second £350 I noticed £40 was in it for a reconnaissance to Belgium. I knew they'd never taken this, so I declined to sign. Later a friend of mine from Cambridge said, 'Tell 'em you're going to send in the lawyers and the accountants – the film was already playing the Odeon circuit and would have been making a lot of money – and they'll cave in immediately.' So at least I got my money back plus bank interest. And was able to give that back to my father.

Another event occurred in those films which was to greatly affect my life. I was casting for *The Square* in my father's real estate office opposite Olympia. The next day I was back at home when his secretary rang me and said, 'A girl's turned up for the audition.' I said, 'The audition was yesterday.' The secretary said in a rather meaningful way, 'I think you'd like to meet her!' Her voice told me this was something special. I went to my father's office, where there was the most beautiful eighteen-year-old girl called Geraldine Lynton-Edwards. She was an actress and dancer and later was very successful both in the West End and in France. She was in the film and we had a relationship. From time to time we'd do an encore over the intervening years. As with nearly all my girlfriends we stayed very friendly. A few years ago we met up yet again and she has lived with me ever since. And added years to my life by forcing me to do Pilates for forty-five minutes every morning and walk for an hour every night. In the early days Geraldine was tested for the lead in the famous Cliff Richard film *Summer Holiday* and got the part. At the time she was in the chorus of Lionel Bart's *Blitz* at the Adelphi Theatre in the Strand. The Producer of that show, Donald Albery, said to her, 'If you leave the chorus we'll sue you.' This was a shatteringly horrible thing to do because she would have been an immense success in her film role. But she was so frightened she stayed in the chorus and then went to live in Paris, where she was very successful as an actress in many major French films and also as a dancer. So it's funny how incidents in your early life can come back to give you considerable pleasure. After making *The Square* and *This Is Belgium*, to my extreme surprise the world wasn't knocking at my door. There was a wonderfully abrasive American, Al Parker, who in silent movies directed stars such as Douglas Fairbanks Snr, Gloria Swanson, Norma Talmadge and John Barrymore. In 1936 he moved to England where he directed routine thrillers and then became a talent agent. I'd interviewed him for my local paper column. He'd become a good friend. Al was one of London's top agents, representing James Mason, Jack Hawkins and Richard Attenborough. I asked his advice about how to become a director. 'You can't become a director until you're forty,' said Al. This was the general thinking at the time. The British film industry was run by men in three-piece grey suits who drank a lot of gin and tonic. Directors were old. So was the audience.

Al said, 'Work for me as an agent.' I had no other offers so I joined him. It taught me a great deal about behind-the-scenes activities of movies. It taught me about professionalism. Al had a luxurious office in a Mayfair house. I was in a very small room next to the toilet on an upper floor. Although we met and spoke all the time, Al would send me letters. They were typed in red and blue ink. 'Office hours start at 9.30 you came in today at 9.34. This is not acceptable,' he wrote. In another letter he said, 'I can hear laughter coming from your office. May I remind you this is not a pub or a club.' The words 'pub' and 'club' were in red ink. The rest was in blue.

Aged eighteen, I became a late entry to the world of sex. I took girls out from time to time. A girl I'd been friends with at school was in my bedroom at home. She had all her clothes off and was lying in bed with me. She said, 'Aren't you going to take your clothes off?' This terrified me beyond belief! So I didn't do anything. Later I was dating Monica, daughter of a rabbi at the Golders Green Synagogue. We were sitting in a cinema in the Edgware Road watching an English film where soldiers were running around with white bands across them and muskets. I put my hand on Monica's knee. Before I could plan where it might go next, she grabbed my hand and stuck it under her jumper, on her naked breasts! I thought, 'My God! I'll have to go the whole way!' Thus I was introduced to sex. Monica later became well known in movies. She re-voiced foreign actresses whose English wasn't clear enough. Monica was top in her field. She re-voiced many of the female stars in the early Bond movies. She'd carry reviews of these actresses referring to their voices and proudly say, 'That was me.' She thought she'd be given a part as a Bond girl. But Monica wasn't up to that standard. Later, when I became a director, I used Monica on two films to re-voice foreign artists. She was brilliant at acquiring a voice similar to theirs but more comprehensible. Monica eventually became a barrister.

Once I'd got my toe in the water I found that, although I was very shy, when I plucked up courage to ask girls out, they came! Later, when I became a famous film director, I had to put up with journalists writing that the only reason girls ever went out with me was because I was a film director. That's absolute nonsense! My greatest success was when I was not a film director and poncing around London as a total failure. No girls will go out with anybody, in my opinion, just for money or for a chance of fame. They may have an occasional one-night stand for that reason or that may enter into it as part of the attraction. But for any sort of relationship girls wish to have fun. They wish to be entertained. They wish to feel comfortable and at ease with the person they are with. They want to be amused. The idea that all girls are prostitutes and will only go out with someone for money is ridiculous and deeply insulting to womanhood in general.

I have very few qualities, but the one thing all my girlfriends have said is that they enjoyed being with me because it was entertaining and fun. To some of them I may have appeared handsome, to some of them I may not. Beauty is in the eye of the beholder! A lot of girls resent you as a film director. They're suspicious of success. They think, 'He's a film director – he can have anybody! I'm not going to be one of those.' A lot of girls are more attracted to lame ducks. Men who they feel want them for themselves and who they can help. When I started out on my devoted quest to have as many girls as possible in the space of a short time, rather like how many students can you pile into a Mini, I did, to my surprise, remarkably well. In those days, when I ventured into the world of sex, there were no discotheques. I frequented the Betavon Swedish Club in a terraced house in Notting Hill where Scandinavian au pair girls went at the weekend. Also the Linguists' Club, a lovely old house in Campden Hill where the hideous Kensington Town Hall now stands. They had dances three times a week. I also met girls through my journalism.

It was not until 1956 that I first experienced real love. The girl was a young actress named Jill Ireland, who later married Charles Bronson, the man so much in my movie career. I saw Jill on the cover of *Picturegoer*, a sepia fan magazine. She stood in shorts and a striped football shirt. A football bounced in mid-air, by a fake goal post. It was the edition of 7th May 1955. She was quite simply the most beautiful girl I'd ever seen. I rang her agent and said I wanted to meet her. Jill was nineteen, I was nineteen. She was under contract to the Rank Organisation and had just started a film called *Oh Rosalinda* as a ballet dancer. She'd trained for ballet but, while driving with her boyfriend, she stubbed a cigarette out on his hand! This, not unnaturally, caused him to swerve the car. The resulting accident damaged Jill's legs and prevented her continuing in classical ballet. We met at Lancaster Gate underground station. Whenever I pass the station I still see her standing there as she did that day in July 1955. Slender, with close-cropped blonde hair, a light blue jacket, a white pleated skirt, no stockings, no make-up. Jill Ireland was an exceptional character, even in her teens. Her public face in the fifties was of the pretty starlet available for premieres, medium parts in Rank comedies like *Three Men in a Boat*, or to add glamour to tough films like *Hell Drivers*. Above all, Jill loved life. I have never known anyone before or since who had so much charm, or so much fun just getting through the day. It was a characteristic to be severely tested by later tragedy.

We met regularly and became good friends. By the end of 1956 I had my first tiny flat in Thurloe Place, South Kensington, above an Indian restaurant. A living room and bedroom were reached by a staircase with peeling linoleum. The decoration was 1950s kitsch, which I threw away. Today it would be worth a great deal of money! The living room featured a hideous oil painting of a woman with bare feet, which I'd bought from the artist. One girlfriend looked around this absolute mess of a room, with a green-and-purple three-piece suite which a manufacturer had tried out and rejected for mass production. There were trailing plants on white ironwork shelves and various other monstrosities. This girl eventually settled on a piece of grey wall that had nothing on it. 'I like that area,' she said. 'It's simple.' That summed the place up.

It was here that I brought Jill Ireland for my seduction. We'd become very friendly. We used to go riding in Edgware with a wonderful man called Colonel Jimmy Younghusband. Jill later became a champion rider and horse breeder. I introduced her to the sport. Believe it or not, I jumped over five-bar gates! Well, the horse did it. I sat on its back and managed to stay on. On a particular evening I got all Jill's clothes off. But she declined to go the whole way. I was upset. I put my clothes on and stormed out of my own flat. Jill grabbed at me crying, 'I'll do it! I'll do it! Please come back!' But I was having a major tantrum. There followed a scene I can see to this day. Jill often referred to it, later, giggling, on the film set, dangerously close to Bronson. I got in my open Sunbeam Alpine sports tourer and pulled into Thurloe Place. Suddenly I saw Jill naked at the windows of my first-floor apartment. In troughs immediately outside were flowerpots full of earth. Jill picked them up one by one and hurled them down at me. It was like a war movie. The pots hit the ground – thank God they didn't hit the car or they would have ruined it! If they'd hit me, I'd have been dead! As they hit the road the pots exploded with a bang. Earth showered about the place. I accelerated away with pots still falling in the road behind me.

By the time I calmed down and went back to my flat, Jill had left. But the next night we became lovers. Her previous boyfriend, Richard Lyon, was insanely jealous. He followed us around and often parked outside her place all night. She shared a luxurious flat with two other girls on the corner of Sloane Street and Hans Place. It was a more glamorous location than where she'd lived with her parents in Isleworth. Her father ran a local newspaper shop. She was considered one of the great beauties of the day. But like all men who are chauvinistic and piggish, the minute she came to me I took her for granted. It was not until she left that I realised how much I loved her. By the beginning of 1957 I'd been fired from the theatrical agency. I had no work. My father said that unless I came into his property business he'd cut me off and stop giving me any money. He'd given me some from time to time to keep me going. Particularly as my salary at the agency had been only £10 a week. My secretary got £11 and ten shillings.

Knowing I could sign on the family accounts at both Harrods and Fortnum and Mason, I went round to stock up for winter. I ordered an enormous amount of pressed duck, tinned peaches and other delicacies, only to be called in to meet the credit managers! They explained my name had been taken off the account! All I was left with was my luxurious blue touring open car, the petrol account, which Dad didn't close, and £5 a week pocket money, which he'd given me when I was at school and which he forgot to stop. I was sitting with Jill in El Cubano, a wonderful restaurant in Brompton Road which featured parakeets, macaws and other rare birds in cages and served the most wonderful chilli con carne. Jill said, 'I don't mind paying for myself, Michael, but I really don't think I should pay for you.' This was a humiliating moment! Shortly thereafter I went on to the *Daily Sketch* newspaper on the Diary which was edited by Barry Norman, who I'd met when he was on the *Kensington News* and I on the *Kensington Post* some years earlier. I also went back to the *Evening Standard*, while writing film scripts and occasionally making documentaries during the day. After two weeks on the *Daily Sketch* I was asked to meet the Features Editor, who later became the legendary *Daily Mail* Editor, David English. 'He's going to congratulate me,' I thought. He said two words:

'You're fired!' We later became great friends. David often asked me to tell the story at parties.

I continued to see Jill. I wish we'd both been older because she'd have made a wonderful wife. She was desperate to get married. I don't say this to flatter myself. She was quite simply desperate to get married. Why, I never knew. She was living in a flat in Knightsbridge. She had a career. She was under contract to the Rank Organisation and she was making a film called *Robbery Under Arms*. She said, 'The minute I'm twenty-one I'm going to be married. I'd like to marry you, Michael. Let's get married!' I said, 'I'm far too young to marry, Jill. I have no money. I have no prospects. I can't take that on right now.' Jill said, 'If I don't marry you I'll marry somebody else.' I said, 'You don't know anybody else. I'm the only person you're going out with.' Jill's twenty-first birthday, on 24th April 1957, coincided with Easter. She was giving a party in her apartment for her film friends, actors, actresses, producers. I was unbelievably shy. I simply didn't have the courage to go to her party. I know this sounds ridiculous, but it's true. So over Easter I went with my family to the South of France. On my return I immediately went round to Jill's flat. She opened the door.

Her attitude had changed. She didn't welcome me. There was a long corridor leading from the front door. It had bedrooms to the left and right. At the end was a large living room with three windows overlooking Sloane Street. There were no lights on. But a man stood silhouetted at one of the windows. I knew I was in trouble. He was David McCallum, a young Welsh actor with whom Jill was working on *Robbery Under Arms*. I realised the girl I loved was slipping away. We were all rather embarrassed. In a desperate attempt to make friends I asked if I could give David a lift home to his bedsit in Highgate. He must have known I was Jill's previous lover. We spoke in a polite but frigid way and I dropped him off. Then I went back to Jill's flat and she didn't let me in. I'd phone, but she wouldn't speak to me. Two weeks later I got up early and bought the Sunday papers. There was a story that Jill Ireland had married David McCallum at a register office in South London. I went back to my tiny flat in South Kensington. The telephone rang. It was Jill. She said, 'Have you seen the newspapers?' I said, 'Yes.' She said, 'What do you think?' I said,

'You wanted to marry me three weeks ago, I think it's ridiculous.'
Jill said, 'I know it is. I don't love him. I still love you. But I told you
I was going to get married.' I thought, 'This is strange!' 'Where's
David McCallum?' I asked. 'He's hurt his toe. He's in the hospital,'
said Jill. After that Jill phoned a lot and asked to meet me. But I felt
very strict about such things. I met her once only. We lay together on
Hampstead Heath and I fondled her bosoms. That was the last time I
saw her for many years.

Some months later I was getting petrol at a garage in Queensway
when a man got out of the car behind and started to come over. I
thought, 'Oh Lord! I must have cut him up. He's going to hit me.' It
was David McCallum. He said, 'Michael, I want to thank you. Jill
was very flighty when we first got married. I know how many times
she telephoned you. Thank you for not seeing her.' Then he got back
into his car.

It was thirty-five years before I saw David McCallum again.
Then he played a part in my movie *Dirty Weekend*. I said, 'David,
do you remember when I last met you? It was in a garage in
Queensway and you thanked me for not seeing Jill when she was
asking me out all the time.' David said, 'I remember it well. She was
very unfaithful during our marriage.' She left him in 1963 shortly
after he and Charles Bronson finished the movie *The Great Escape*.
I said to David, 'You know, it's extraordinary. Jill was determined
to get married at twenty-one. She wanted to marry me and I said, "I
can't marry you, Jill, I'm too young and you don't know anybody
else."' David McCallum said, 'Yes she did. She knew me. I was the
poor schmuck from the Welsh Hills she decided to marry!' David
was the only person I met who wasn't crazy about Jill. She'd led
him a merry dance during the marriage and then walked out on him
for Charlie Bronson. But she did have two wonderful children with
him. She and Charlie brought them up very well and David loved
them and kept in touch.

I didn't see Jill again until 1968 when Bronson was in England
making a film called *Twinkie*. He was dining with Jill and her two
children by David McCallum in the Aretusa in the King's Road. It
was 'the' dining place for show-business people. I didn't go over. I
felt it would have embarrassed Jill. Later she said to me, 'Why didn't

you come and talk to us? I told Charlie that was you, and that I knew you. And you ignored us.'

It was fourteen years since I'd spoken to Jill when United Artists said to me, 'If you get Charles Bronson for *Chato's Land* we'll make the movie.' Charles and Jill were in Paris where Charlie was making a film. On 14th November 1970, I rang the bell of their suite at the George V hotel. Jill opened the door. She was youthful and beautiful as ever. 'Michael,' she said, 'how wonderful to see you! I've told Charlie all about us! Do come in.' 'This is puzzling,' I thought. 'Charles Bronson doesn't seem to me a man who'd welcome his wife's ex-lover to direct his movie.' Jill introduced me to Charlie. She was extremely helpful in keeping the atmosphere cheerful and positive. We had lunch in the hotel and Charlie's Rolls took me back to the airport. He agreed to do the film.

In April 1971 I arrived in Almeria for the shooting of the movie, a Western, *Chato's Land*. Charlie was already there finishing off another film. 'It's so nice to see you here, Michael,' Jill said. 'I'll need my old friends when Charlie goes.' 'Where's he going?' I asked, 'We're starting the movie in a couple of days.' 'He's very old you know,' said Jill. 'He's only fifty-two,' I replied. That was Charlie's age in the publicity material. 'You don't believe that, do you?' said Jill. Later Jill told me Charlie had taken eight years off his real age. He was born in a mining camp and I doubt if they kept proper records. The three of us dined together every night at our hotel in Aguadulce. I was in their suite one night, standing on the balcony with Jill. The wind ruffled the palm trees. Charlie was still in the shower getting ready for dinner. Jill spoke very quietly as we looked at the sea. 'I've told Charlie we were friends,' she said. 'I didn't tell him about the rest of it. Whatever you do, don't tell him.' 'Jill,' I said, 'my lips are sealed. This is the safest secret in the world.' I was not about to tell Charlie I'd screwed his wife. He'd probably have killed her. He'd definitely have killed me.

During all my time with Charlie, both when we made the movies and seeing him in between, Jill was a wonderful friend. She was also very much in love with Charlie and was a marvellous and faithful wife. When she met him Jill was starring in an American TV series called *Shane*. Charlie was a small-part player. By the early seventies

Charlie had become a big star in Europe. Jill remained full of fun, giggling, gossiping and running a home and family with great success. Charlie often spoke to me of how much he loved Jill. Also of his own youth in a Pennsylvania mining camp and how he'd witnessed the lingering death of his father from cancer, where they lived in a two-room hut. 'I hope I never have to see anything like that again,' he said. How ironic those words were. He would have to go through the same awful experience with Jill. When we did *Death Wish* in 1974 Jill, who thought she couldn't have more children, had a baby daughter, Zuleika. Later, in 1983, when the publicity lady on one of her films died suddenly, Jill adopted her daughter, Katrina. She already looked after her two boys from McCallum and another they'd adopted. By the time we were making *Death Wish Two* in 1981, in which Jill had a leading role, she was becoming increasingly incautious. She'd reminisce about old times with me on the set. 'Do you remember when I threw all the flowerpots?!' she said. 'Sshh, Jill,' I said, 'Charlie's just over there.'

In March 1984 Jill and Charlie were in London on a private visit. They came to my house for tea. 'I've been a bit off lately,' Jill said. A few weeks later she went in for a check-up. They discovered cancer. Her breast was removed. She spent a year in treatment. In April 1985 we made *Death Wish Three* with Charlie. On Jill's forty-ninth birthday we went to New York's Tavern on the Green and toasted her restored health. Jill was desperate to help others who had cancer. I was with her and Charlie in a London restaurant. Jill said, 'Charlie, I'd like to give a party at the Dorchester for children who have cancer. I'd like to tell them they can beat it and let them see how I've beaten it. I think it would be wonderful for them.' Charlie said, 'That's the most stupid idea I've ever heard, Jill. One of them may fall over and sue us.' 'I think the party just took a dive, Jill!' I said. That was typical Charlie. He was very, very cautious. He never wanted to put his neck out. Jill wrote a book about her experiences called *Life Wish*. It was published in 1987. She sent me a copy. She wrote on it, 'To Michael with love and fond memories Jill'. But life was not to be that kind. Cancer struck anew. 'It's like a fire,' Jill said to me, 'you put it out in one place and it starts in another.' All the terrible treatment re-started. Jill told me, 'I'm very happy with my life. I'm starting a new book, a novel, and I've got a new doctor who says he can give me a year and a half to live. That'll be enough to finish the book and have a great time.' There was no self-pity, no moaning. As always, Jill was positive. But the new treatment, involving massive doses of radiation, chemotherapy and radioactive implants, burned away at her increasingly frail body. She was dying. Painfully. She lived to face the tragedy of her bright and lovely adopted son, Jason, dying of a drug overdose. She was getting thinner and thinner. She was down to six stone. 'I'll never see England again,' she said to me, in a rare moment of sadness. I visited Charlie and Jill at their new house in Malibu about six months before she died. It was full of enormous crystal which they believed might cure the cancer.

Jill gave a small dinner party for me. She was painfully thin. But she was a wonderful and cheerful hostess, with the spirit I'd known when I was with her in London. She even insisted on getting up and carrying the dirty plates away, even though Charlie cautioned her not to. When I hugged her goodbye there was nothing there. It was as though my arms would go through her and I'd be hugging myself. My last sight of her was Jill standing with Charlie at the door, silhouetted by the hall light. Behind them, sparkles came from the great crystal pillars she hoped would protect her. She waved as I got into the car.

In London the *Daily Mail* asked if I'd write a tribute to Jill. Everybody knew she was desperately ill. I couldn't write while she was alive. It felt as if I was writing an obituary for someone who might make it. I kept in touch with Charlie's house by phone. Sometimes Jill could speak, sometimes she couldn't. Finally her manager told me she was going in and out of consciousness and couldn't live much longer. I wrote my piece for the *Daily Mail*. They came and collected it from my house. Two hours later, at seven o'clock on the evening of 18th May 1990, an editor from the paper rang. 'We've just had it on the wire service. Jill Ireland died a few minutes ago. I'm afraid your tribute missed the first edition.' I sat there stunned. The most beautiful person that ever lit up my life was gone. I didn't know what to do. In her final years Jill flew. She showed that human spirit in adversity can be a wondrous thing. Her thoughts were not of herself but of others who suffered. Of her friends, of her family. The world suddenly saw in the little girl from Isleworth a grandeur and humanity that placed her in a space all her own. 'I'd better comfort Charlie,' I thought. I rang the house. Charlie answered the phone. 'Charlie,' I said, 'I want to say how sorry I am.' 'About what?' said Charlie. 'Well, you know I just want to say, Charlie, it's a terrible thing, and my thoughts are with you.' 'I don't know what you're talking about,' Bronson said. My mind was racing. Had I been given incorrect information? Was I phoning to console him about a death that hadn't occurred? 'Charlie,' I said, 'a newspaper here just rang and told me Jill died.' There was a pause. 'Jeeze!' said Charlie with an intake of breath. 'It only happened ten minutes ago.' I thought back on the girl I'd met at Lancaster Gate tube station. Our incredible love-making. The joy of her spirit. I remembered how I'd cried when she left. I leaned against the door of my tiny flat, weeping. She'd been a very long-time friend. Part of a strange threesome. Me, Charlie Bronson and Jill Ireland. Jill and I had been together on film sets and in private life for thirty-three years. I remembered once when we were in London on *Death Wish Three* we were having dinner at an Indian restaurant. I told Charlie the story of how Jill always said she was determined to get married at twenty-one. Almost regardless of who she married. 'Were you one of the people Jill might have married?' said Charlie. I was sure he knew there'd been something between us. 'Jill had more sense, even in those days, Charlie,' I said.

I thought back to a time in Naples when we were making *The Mechanic*. Charlie, like all Scorpios, including me, was very fond of his food. Jill decided to play a joke on us. She had the hotel make spaghetti with chocolate sauce. She told Charlie she'd prepared it specially for him. It was dreadful. Because it was from Jill, Charlie said how much he liked it. Until Jill revealed it was a joke. We were neither of us terribly happy about that. But it was typical of Jill. Her sense of fun, which never left her, made her the most outstanding girl I'd ever met. If I'd been a few years older, I'd have married her. When people ask me why I never married, I say, 'The timing was never right' or 'I screwed up.' I have many letters in bright blue ink that Jill sent me. They're all over the house. I used to read them, and put them in the nearest drawer. That's where they remain. A lot of girls followed. Many of them I loved and respected. Perhaps I deluded myself that the only person I could have married was Jill Ireland. It was getting dark one night when I opened the drawer of an eighteenth-century commode. In it was an old letter from Jill asking me to send her parents a Christmas hamper. It rested on the *Picturegoer* magazine where I'd first seen her. I'd bought it at a film fair. There was Jill, left hand on left hip, in shorts, right hand out bouncing the football, photographically frozen in mid-air. She looked up at me in the vast emptiness of my living room. Above her was a caption: 'Cup Final Girl'. But the game was over.

8

Shorts and Nudes

My first job in movies came in 1956 after I'd been fired by Al Parker. To work in a highly unionised industry I had to join the Association of Cinematograph and Television Technicians. At their offices in Soho Square was a lovely, plump union official called Bessie Bond. She often advised young people who wanted to get in. It was helpful if you gave her lunch at a nearby Italian restaurant. She said, 'Michael, we're trying to unionise Autocue. Anyone who's an employee of Autocue can get in the union at once. Then you can change your grade to whatever you want.' By good fortune the owner of Autocue was John Whitney, a man I'd met and befriended years earlier when he was producing radio programmes. Autocue is a system used on television to this day where presenters look at a screen above the camera from which they read the words they're meant to say. Look at TV without sound and you'll see their eyeballs rolling from left to right! John Whitney put me on the Autocue payroll even though I didn't take money. I thought I'd better discover what Autocue did in case anyone at the union asked me. So I turned up at the BBC studios in Lime Grove as an Assistant Autocue Operator for a day. The Senior Autocue Operator, on a sports programme about wrestling, said, 'Here's some tape – tape our cable to the television camera cable.' I saw this enormous cable running across the studio from the Autocue machinery at the side. 'Get on your hands and knees and do it,' said my new boss. I struggled along the floor of the studio with some white sticky tape. Throughout the rest of the afternoon and evening I worked hard as an Assistant Autocue Operator. At dinner I sat in the canteen with my Autocue boss and sports commentator, Kent Walton, who later became famous for marrying Michael Grade's mother. Kent said, 'If you work hard, Michael, you could become a Senior Autocue Operator like Gerry.' He indicated my boss. I didn't tell him I was really bound for Hollywood, because it would have been impertinent.

While I worked with Al Parker as an agent I'd dealt with the two Danziger Brothers. They made television series and second feature movies at their studio in Elstree. I'd negotiate with them over whether the artists I represented would be paid £10 or £12 per day. They were impressed by my fight for the extra £2. I asked for work. Eddie Danziger said, 'You can be First Assistant Director on the second unit of the *Mark Sabre* TV series.' I was paid £27 a week. Unfortunately I'd no idea what a First Assistant Director did! On the two documentary films I'd made we only had a unit of three people, myself, the cameraman and an assistant. On my first day at the Danziger studios the second unit was shooting the detective hero (played by Donald Gray, a one-armed actor who'd been a TV news-reader) introducing the series, leaning on a parapet in front of a blank screen on to which was projected the Houses of Parliament with boats going by on the Thames. It was all in black and white. Mr Gray spouted his bit about being Mark Sabre. I had no idea what to do. The Second Assistant Director, Tony Hearne, who was extremely peeved at not having been made First Assistant, came over and said, 'Would you like me to run the set?' I said, 'Yes.' So he did a bit of shouting and yelling. After one day I realised what a First Assistant Director did. Thereafter I did it with reasonable competence.

The second unit spent most of its time on London's streets with a double for Donald Gray. We'd film the double arriving in a car, getting out, and going into various locations. Or coming out, getting into the car, and going away from various locations. We shot in all weather. If it rained they'd add commentary, 'As we got to Covent

Garden it started to rain!' If the sun came out they'd say, 'As we reached Knightsbridge the sun came out.' I thought this very tacky. Twenty years later the great screen actor Robert Ryan was working for me on *Lawman*. I referred to his part in *The Professionals*, a mammoth hit movie in 1966. 'I never quite understood what your character was about, Bob,' I said. Robert Ryan replied, 'I had the most important line in the film. We were shooting in New Mexico and the weather kept changing. So to explain it Richard Brooks [the Director] wrote a line in the script where I say, "This goddam desert. Freezes you one minute and burns the hell out of you the next!" That,' he said, 'dealt with all the weather changes!'

My job was to lead the Danziger second unit, some twenty people, around London. Our Camera Operator was Nicolas Roeg who later became a famous cameraman and director. At meal times I'd choose a restaurant and pay for the company. My film unit didn't look at the food on offer. They only looked at the price. If the price was high, they ordered it. This I found very useful later when ordering wine. If you look at a wine list and don't understand it, there has to be a reason why the higher-priced wine is better than the lower priced. I've since learned a tiny bit about wine and can just about make a choice based on minimum expertise.

I left the Danzigers when I was offered a job as Director by Sheldon Reynolds, an American making a TV series called *Dick and the Duchess*. It starred Hazel Court as a Duchess with the American actor Patrick O'Neal and a superb English character actor, Richard Wattis. In those days British trade unions were rampant and obstructive. Shelley had directed three of the series, then the technicians' union told him not to direct any more. They wanted an Englishman. So I sat on a chair with my name painted on it. When Sheldon Reynolds nodded, I shouted 'Action!' When he nodded again I shouted 'Cut!' My name appeared on the call sheet as the Director. But Shelley directed. Shelley's Co-Producer was a French lady, Nicole Milinaire, with whom he was having a stormy affair. They were always arguing. Sometimes the grips would pick up the fake wall of a room, and carry it away. It would reveal Shelley and Nicole having a screaming row. The Duke of Bedford was brought down for a publicity stunt to be photographed with Hazel Court who played the Duchess. The real Duke met Nicole Milinaire. He married her. She is still the Duchess of Bedford.

I was very happy going to the MGM studios at Elstree every day to shout 'Action!' and 'Cut!' But the technicians' union said to Sheldon Reynolds, 'We won't accept Winner on the set unless he directs. And you can't be there when he's doing it!' I was to direct. After all, I'd already directed my documentaries. The actors helped. I thought we got through the day rather well. I was shattered when Reynolds brought in a more experienced director to take over!

I contacted one of the directors I'd worked for at the Danzigers, Ernie Morris, a lovely man who used to be an electrician. He made me First Assistant Director on a TV series, *The White Hunter*. It starred an actor called Rhodes Reason. There were lots of African huts and painted backgrounds of the African veldt. The Africans, with rings through their noses, grass skirts and spears, were largely played by law students from London University. I'm extremely proud of being fired from the job of First Assistant Director on *The White Hunter*. The English extras, always a motley crew, said to the American producers, 'We refuse to change in the same room as blacks because they smell.' The producers said to me, 'You're to order a separate dressing-room caravan for the blacks!' I was appalled! Like most Englishmen I'd been brought up to believe black people had inferior brains but could sing and tap dance. It was only when I went round America with a black student and then to Cambridge and had black friends, who did better than me at the exams, that I realised what nonsense this was. I said, 'I refuse to order a second dressing room. It's a disgrace that you take note of these ridiculous English extras, most of whom are louts anyway. If anyone smells, they do!' This historic speech in the cause of racial equality made no impression on my American producers. They fired me. I went to the set and told the Jewish Camera Operator, who was the union representative. He said, 'They can't fire you! The union will come out in support!' The technicians' union spoke to the American producers who still insisted on separate changing facilities for the blacks. They demoted me to a non-job in an office with no function. This was so boring I did what they wanted, and left. I was unemployed again. This is quite common in the motion-picture business. I continued to write scripts, some of which I sold as second features. I continued writing to people seeking work. In order to boost my rather meagre career as a director I invented a series of documentaries I'd made in Africa but which unfortunately were unavailable to be seen!

I can trace my career as a director to a letter I wrote in 1958. *The Enemy Below*, a submarine epic starring Robert Mitchum, was on at the Carlton Cinema in the Haymarket. I arrived in the middle of a short film about Ireland which preceded it. Words came on the screen. 'The End – A Harold Baim Production'. This was a new name! I wrote to Mr Baim and got no answer. A few weeks later the phone rang in my tiny flat in Thurloe Place. Harold Baim said, 'Are you busy, Michael? I'm going to direct a film on an aircraft carrier. I need an Associate Producer.' I could truthfully answer that I was not busy. I was looking out of the window at a line of double-decker buses going by. Baim had cornered the market in making short films to go with all United Artists pictures. This was highly lucrative because a fund existed called the Eady into which cinemas paid a small percentage of the seat money. It was then redistributed only to British films. Short films got triple Eady and second features got double Eady. This petered out a few years later when British cinemas were doing badly and the owners said, 'Why should we support British films which nobody wants to see?' Americans ruled the roost then, as they still do. Even though British films had the Eady subsidy, and the National Film Finance Corporation to finance them, and a quota system whereby cinemas were forced to play a large number of British movies, you could not buy people into the cinema. So while some good films got made, the British didn't support their own product. It is, with few exceptions, the same today.

What Harold Baim meant by 'Associate Producer' was an assistant on a crew of three: the cameraman who kept a flask of Scotch in his back pocket, Mr Baim who came from Leeds and was very pleasant. And me. I was flown to Malta where I carried equipment and vaguely assisted in the directing. Then we boarded the aircraft carrier HMS *Victorious* with two thousand British sailors. The carrier was to traipse around the Mediterranean stopping off at Malta, then on to Marseilles and Plymouth. I was given a bunk bed with a tiny space beside it and one of the sailors was delegated to chaperone me. We ate in the officers' mess where I complained about the ship rolling from side to side. Since they'd just spent millions of pounds putting in stabilisers, the officers found my discomfort ridiculous. One Sunday I went on deck with the Petty Officer who was looking after me. Two thousand sailors were sunbathing. As I appeared all two thousand men started to hiss. They hissed continuously. There was this unbelievable sound of two thousand sailors hissing. I turned to my Petty Officer and asked, 'Why are they doing that?' 'Because they fancy you,' he said, 'and if they don't have you, I will!'

When we returned to London Harold Baim asked if I had any ideas for short films. I suggested *Danger Women at Work*. It was a black-and-white twenty-minute film about women doing various things, including learning how to model and being at a dance school. Years later I was sitting on my balcony with Marlon Brando and he said to me, 'I hate acting. The only film I ever enjoyed was the one I made with you. I always hated acting.' I said, 'Marlon, if you hated acting why did you go to drama school?' Marlon replied, 'To get laid.' I won't say the sole motivation of these early twenty-minute shorts was for me to meet girls. But it figured! The film took only a couple of weeks to shoot. Then Harold Baim said to me, 'Can you edit?' While writing commentaries for a firm making 16mm documentaries in North London I'd worked close to an editor so I had some idea of what they did. 'Why?' I asked. 'Because if you can edit the film you get another two weeks' work,' said Harold Baim. 'I'm a very experienced editor,' I said. So now I'm in a basement cutting room in Wardour Street with four cans of film that had to be sliced up into little pieces and joined together as a movie. There was a machine called a Moviola through which you ran the film, and a very complex and irritating little machine which joined the film together with cement. I had not the slightest idea how to operate these! There was an editor working next door. He, together with the owner of the complex, Frank Green, gave me an hour's instruction in editing and off I went. It was very enjoyable. My mother used to call people in to watch me doing jigsaw puzzles when I was a child. Editing is just dealing with a mammoth jigsaw puzzle. You slice up bits of film, join them at the appropriate sprocket and they give the impression of movement and continuity. Unfortunately nobody had told me you had to cut the film along what is called the rack line, the line between the frames of picture. Anyone who has a 35mm camera knows that there are frames of picture and there's a line between them before the next frame comes along. I cut the film, brilliantly in my opinion. Baim was coming to see it.

I took my two ten-minute reels to Frank Green who was also the projectionist. I said, 'Let's look at it before Harold comes.' I sat in the cinema to see my first ever editing job. It was horrific! Every few seconds the picture jumped and half of it would suddenly be off the screen and half would be on! I rushed back to the projection room and screamed 'You're a fucking idiot, Frank! You can't even project film! How dare you rent out a preview theatre when you don't know how to run the projector!' Frank came into the cinema, looked at the film and said, 'Did you make the joins on the rack line?' I said, 'What rack line?' Frank turned and ran back into the projection room. He took the reels off the projector and rushed into my cutting room. There he redid every join himself so it was on the rack line. This involved cutting the film, scraping each side of the celluloid so half of the very thin celluloid was cut off and then joining it with a cement glue. Shortly thereafter the Italians created a joiner that did all this with Sellotape, which took a tenth of the time and you didn't lose a frame each side when you made a join. The Americans kept the cement joiner for years because they were old-fashioned!

Back in the cinema, Harold Baim saw the film and loved it. *Danger Women at Work* cost three hundred pounds. It opened at the London Pavilion in Piccadilly Circus, supporting *Some Like It Hot*. Following that I did many short films for Harold and went on to use well-known actors and actresses in many of them. One was about behaviour called *Behave Yourself*. It garnered excellent reviews. It still plays on cable today. As for Frank Green, the man I had so unfairly screamed at, we remained great friends. Frank was a wonderful Wardour Street character of the fifties, sixties and seventies. He would shuffle around in carpet slippers going between the three buildings he owned, all of which had private cinemas, offices, and rented cutting rooms in them. It's rumoured he made a second fortune producing pornographic movies! Either way he was a total delight. When Frank finally retired I was asked to give the speech, paying tribute to him, in one of his packed private cinemas. It is somewhat a mystery as to what happened thereafter. But somehow or other Frank, who was a multi-millionaire by the time he retired, lost all his money in a silly sale of his properties, had a stroke and died a broken man. I remember him with great affection.

A cameraman employed by Harold Baim recommended me to a wonderful cockney character, E. J. Fancey. E. J. had a company making second feature and low-budget feature films. He made Peter Sellers' first movie when he signed up The Goons. He also released pirated copies of Charlie Chaplin's films. When Charlie Chaplin came to England for the first time after many years in the early sixties, he got off the plane and reporters said to him, 'Why are you coming back, Mr Chaplin?' Chaplin said, 'To sue that bastard E. J. Fancey who's been making money by pirating my films.' 'I'll sue the git for libel!' E. J. said to me!

In 1959, E. J. had a deal to make a travel film for the Swiss Tourist Office called *Swiss Holiday*. The Thomas Cook representative on it was Francesca Annis' father. E. J. intended to stay on in hotels provided by the Swiss government, using the opportunity to make a second feature film. I sat in his enormous offices overlooking Leicester Square, E. J. handed me a single sheet of paper, supposedly a story, for an hour-long movie that was to start shooting three weeks later. I said, 'It's a bit short!' E. J. said, 'It's about this man. He goes into a restaurant and this woman's there. Then he goes into a church and the same woman is there. Then he goes to Egypt (I have some Arab tent material) and the same woman is there.' 'Who is she?' I asked. 'I don't know, boy,' said E. J., 'you'll have to figure it out.' The film was called *Shoot to Kill*. It starred an actor called Dermot Walsh who was going through a period of anonymity at the time and this picture sealed it. The third day of shooting in Geneva involved Dermot jumping over a wall. A big action scene, one man and a wall! As he landed on the other side of the wall Dermot appeared to have broken his ankle. He was carried off on a stretcher! It's very upsetting when your first feature movie is terminated because the actor's broken his ankle. We went back to London where we discovered Dermot hadn't broken his ankle, just sprained it. He was now better. I said, 'E. J., the world must not be deprived of an opportunity to see this film. We may be in London. But nobody will know. We'll shoot in London as if it were Geneva.' E. J. thought this a cracking idea. We didn't have, in those days, an art department as I've had since. Hundreds of people to transform a place from one country to another. All we had were three thousand fake, cardboard Swiss car registration plates. So we'd go to Regent's Park and Sellotape these Swiss plates on to all the cars. In our enfeebled minds we believed this made it look like Geneva! People came out of their houses and drove their cars away. London was full of British cars with cardboard Swiss registration plates. I remember thinking at the time, 'This is not normal. One day I'll be in an industry where it's organised and proper and things are done meticulously.' I'm still waiting!

The trade paper, *The Daily Cinema*, review of *Shoot to Kill* said, 'Pleasant shots of Geneva and other Swiss scenery create further interest.' In fact hardly any of it was in Switzerland. It was shot in and around London locations. The *Kinematograph Weekly*, another trade paper, said, 'Its Geneva backgrounds are the real thing and lend a touch of validity to the extraordinary hanky panky.' Ninety-five per cent of the Geneva locations were London! But in those days very few people travelled. E. J. Fancey once said to me, 'You know what's ruining the industry, boy? Travel is ruining the industry! In the old days we'd make a documentary about Spain and put it out. Then we'd re-cut the same shots of Spain, put a different commentary on it and call it *This Is Italy*. Then we'd re-cut the same material, put another commentary on, and call it *This Is France*. You can't do it today, boy. They're travelling!' Another wonderful E. J. Fancey wheeze came to fruition in *Shoot to Kill*. E. J. had the re-release rights, for a limited number of years, for the 1940 Alfred Hitchcock movie *Foreign Correspondent*, starring Joel McCrea and Laraine Day. It contained a famous sequence, which I later heard Hitchcock describing on television as his greatest technical achievement ever. An old-fashioned airplane was flying across the Atlantic and crashed. The camera was behind the two pilots who had a large cockpit window in front of them. You saw the plane suddenly dipping toward the sea. Without any cut in the sequence, you saw the plane, from behind the pilots, going right down and into the sea. When it crashed water poured in breaking the glass of the cockpit, deluging and drowning the two pilots. This was achieved years before computer effects! Hitchcock built a back projection screen of rice paper. It was very thin and would easily break. A film of the sky and then the dip into the sea was projected so you could see it from the cockpit. At the exact moment the back projection reached the plane dipping into the sea thousands of gallons of water were poured through the rice-paper screen. Water deluged the cockpit of the plane. E. J. Fancey said to me, 'We'll use the air crash from *Foreign Correspondent* in your film, Michael.'

So in *Shoot to Kill* you have Dermot Walsh sitting in a mock-up plane on his way to Geneva. Then London Airport traffic control (filmed in a coffee bar in South Kensington) hears an SOS call from the plane, 'One of the engines is going, we're in terrible trouble!' This was supposedly over Lake Geneva! Dermot Walsh looks round and sees Joel McCrea sitting behind him looking worried. In the London Airport control room a man says, 'Report your position.' Dermot Walsh looks round in another direction and Laraine Day faints into the aisle of the plane. Then we go to Hitchcock's shot behind the pilots and the plane crashes into the sea. This was difficult to follow! But I managed! We cut to the beach at Worthing where various members of the Worthing repertory company, including Lynn Redgrave in her first ever movie, were thrashing about in the water as if they'd swum to the shore of Lake Geneva after this terrible plane crash! Dermot was still clutching his suitcase in which were top-secret documents. Lynn always reminds me of this episode, adding, 'You had Aleta Morrison in the film. She had the longest legs in show business.' This was some showgirl-cum-actress who I'd had in one of my short films. Years later I was working with the American actor Bruce Dern who was also starring in Hitchcock's *Family Plot*. I met Hitch and told him the story of his sequence being used in *Shoot to Kill*. He laughed. I continued in the late fifties making short films and second features for both E. J. Fancey and Harold Baim. Then something happened that was to change the whole ethos of cinema as well as my own fortunes.

In 1960 a British distributor had a twenty-minute short called *Nudes in the Snow*. It showed three girls clad only in ski boots and socks on a mountain. They were skiing, falling over and throwing snowballs at each other. The distributor decided to ask the British Board of Film Censors to give this a certificate. No nudity was then permitted on the screen at all other than an occasional long shot of somebody's bosom such as in Bergman's *Smiles of a Summer Night*. If nudes appeared on stage they had to stand absolutely still. There was no chance of this film being passed. Amazingly the Censor, John Trevelyan, passed it with a U Certificate for general audiences. It played in the West End to absolute uproar. There were queues all round the cinema. It broke barriers that led to the freedom of the sixties. Small distributors decided to make nudist documentaries. At first these pictures had to show people completely naked. Later they were allowed to wear pants or knickers. E. J. Fancey had a daughter, Adrienne, who worked with him. She rang me up and said, 'I want you to make a nudist film. Immediately!' I was delighted to do almost anything. These films had no sex in them. Mine simply showed naked bodies in a ridiculous story about nudists under threat from local citizens who didn't like them. The nudists played a lot of volleyball! It was difficult to get girls to appear nude. Page Three didn't exist at the time. There were no nude magazines for men. They bought a magazine called *Health and Efficiency* which had genuine nudists on the cover.

We shot this movie, *Some Like It Cool*, in three weeks around England from Walton-on-Thames to Devon. I'd phone up mothers and say, 'I do assure you, it's perfectly respectable for your daughter to appear naked. It may well do her career considerable good.' We got a rag-bag of girls. Not the prettiest! The best one was a real nudist we saw at a camp. She immediately got the lead! The Censor's rule was that everyone had to be completely naked, thus genitalia were showing. But they couldn't be shown too close to camera. As the cast approached the camera the men would have a copy of *The Times* that was conveniently held over 'it'. The women would have either a deckchair or a ping-pong bat or something else to cover them. One of our locations was the Marquis of Bath's estate at Longleat. His house and grounds were open to the public. I arrived with sixty nude people. They frolicked amid the formal gardens. Lord Bath came out to watch. I suddenly saw two coachloads of tourists coming down the long winding drive towards the house. I turned to his lordship and said, 'I thought you'd closed the place. You can't let sightseers in, they'll see my nudes! We'll be up before the local magistrate.' 'Don't worry about that,' said Lord Bath, 'I *am* the local magistrate.' Sightseers were being shown round the house. The guide was pointing out a marvellous painting on a wall. But the public were looking out of the windows gobsmacked at my nudists. Lord Bath even provided us with his own daughter, Lady Sylvie Thynne, to join our group stark naked. She was only eighteen months old at the time!

The film opened at a cinema in Oxford Street in May 1961. It was a phenomenal financial success. Outside the cinema was a photograph taken at a real nudist camp with our actors in the front and ordinary nudists at the back. One of these was a bank manager from Hastings who became the subject of ridicule and abuse among his friends. He didn't sue the company so I guess it was all sorted out. The movie cost nine thousand pounds to make and got its money back in four weeks. Queues spread way down Oxford Street for this nonsense. The financial success of it did me good. Lord Brabourne, one of our most distinguished film producers, and Lewis Gilbert, a top director, who had befriended me and liked many of my documentaries, personally financed me to make a short film, *Haunted England*, for Columbia Pictures. This was to go out with Lewis's feature film *HMS Defiant*. So now I had both a red-hot box-office success, however silly it was, and the public sponsorship of two of Britain's most illustrious film-makers. Lewis became a great friend and introduced me around the industry as his protégé. I will always be deeply grateful for that.

I was also becoming upwardly mobile. My father had invested money I'd got for my Bar Mitzvah in property for me. This permitted me to leave the curling linoleum of Thurloe Place and get a nice balcony flat in nearby Cornwall Gardens. It started my lifelong interest in antiques and paintings. A friend of mine, David, whose father owned an antiques shop, helped me furnish the flat. We were both at the auction room Sotheby's one day to get a piece of furniture. David was bidding for me. But I got so over-excited I started bidding myself. Eventually the auctioneer took pity on us. 'Are you two together?' he asked. We then realised we'd been bidding against each other, my decorator and me! So the item went for much more than it should have done.

At the beginning of December 1961 I was in a cutting room re-editing Nazi film material for a feature documentary for E. J. Fancey. David Deutsch, the Head of Production at Anglo-Amalgamated, an important small distributor, phoned and offered me the job of directing a feature film at Pinewood Studios. It was called *Play It Cool*, Britain's first Twist film starring three famous pop singers of the day, Billy Fury, Helen Shapiro and the American Bobby Vee. He offered me two thousand pounds for twelve weeks' work from 11th December 1961, which included the pre-production and four weeks shooting at Pinewood Studios. I was under contract to E. J. Fancey. He was known as being very tough. But when I told him I had a chance to make a feature film he tore my contract up in front of me. 'Good luck to you, boy!' he said. With E. J.'s good wishes ringing in my ears, I entered a new world.

9

Musical Me

To a British population reeling from the introduction of on-screen nudity there came, in the 1960s, a further upheaval. Rock and Roll. Until the sixties grown-ups had money. They gave some to their children as pocket money. The children earned little, and basically copied the lifestyle of their parents. By the beginning of the sixties enough money was filtering down to young people for them to be able to afford their own choices. They didn't want Donald Peers singing 'By a Babbling Brook' in evening-dress suit on BBC radio as I had when at school. Youngsters – adults called them 'messenger boys' – were forming bands and playing in the cinemas. The owners of cinema circuits noticed that on the pop-concert days the take quadrupled from movie days. The gin and tonic three-piece grey-suit brigade realised that if they wanted profit they had to succumb to this ghastly trend. They started to put these young singers – 'upstarts who wouldn't last' – into movies. Cliff Richard was okay, he looked clean. But when it came to people such as Billy Fury, a Liverpool version of Elvis Presley, the parents objected. And with the Rolling Stones a couple of years later parents went berserk.

The French New Wave employed directors in their early twenties. This was unheard of outside France. But the need to have directors who were able to communicate with the young pop singers, plus the fact that the French had done it so it might just work, allowed younger people to direct. The script of *Play It Cool* was written by Jack Davies, by coincidence the father of John Howard Davies, the Oliver Twist youngster who'd introduced me to professional writing. Jack wrote *Those Magnificent Men in Their Flying Machines*. He viewed the job of writing for Billy Fury as well beneath him. So on the credits he called himself Jack Henry. My first feature-film assignment took me into the hallowed halls of Pinewood Studios. I'd been making documentaries in real places. In clubs, in pubs and in houses. I saw no reason for an art director to knock up a second-rate pre-fabrication of these things just to keep everyone working at Pinewood because it had a lot of permanent staff. But I had no power. I was twenty-six years old. I was instructed to film in the studio and only go on location for street scenes.

In those days pop concerts were not a single band or person performing for two hours. There were often ten performers on the same bill. Whoever was doing well in the charts got top spot that week. I'd see Billy Fury on tour and on the same bill would be John Leyton, Eden Kane and other people who've since gone into musical oblivion. Billy would start with a spotlight on his genital area which was much padded! The spotlight enlarged and Billy then did Elvis Presley movements with a voice not unlike Presley. But he was a very good singer. My other British star, Helen Shapiro, was having great success at the time. She dressed like a Jewish princess and behaved like a Jewish princess. It didn't take long for fans to spot this. Later on we managed to get Bobby Vee, the American rock and roll singer. It was exciting to be welcomed into the edge of the mainstream of British cinema. I was written about as the youngest director in the English-speaking language and, strangely enough, I remained that for some years. 'Do you want a dolly or a crane?' I was asked. I had no idea what they were. We didn't have them on documentaries. There we carried the lights round ourselves on the bus and put the wires into the round electric sockets, fixing them with matchsticks. We spent the day getting electrocuted. Directing is a business much clouded by mystique. Basically you should just get on with it. Later you acquire a deeper thought process.

I couldn't bring much of what I'd learned from studying Luis
Buñuel, my favourite director of all time, or Hitchcock, or Carol
Reed, to *Play It Cool*. Although I tried to bring a bit of Billy Wilder!
The cast included many famous names of the day. Richard Wattis,
who I'd pretended to direct on *Dick and the Duchess*, Peter
Barkworth, Bernie Winters, Lionel Blair, Jeremy Lloyd, who went
on to become one of television's top writers, and singers such as
Danny Williams and Shane Fenton who later reinvented himself as
Alvin Stardust. And Dennis Price, as nice an actor as I ever met, who
I'd had in my short films. My Producer, David Deutsch, was the
most marvellous man I encountered in the film industry. He was
kind, considerate, witty and knew exactly how to handle people. We
remained friends until he died tragically young. The Executive
Producer, Julian Wintle, typified the gin and tonic three-piece-suit
brigade. He was horrible. He viewed the film he'd been asked to
oversee by Nat Cohen of Anglo-Amalgamated as infinitely beneath
him. Everybody who was anything to do with it was beneath him.
But he promised me a box of cigars if I finished on schedule. I'd
started smoking very expensive Havana cigars. I did so for thirty-
five years until they so damaged my health I had to have a heart
operation!

Billy Fury's gang, his band, were Michael Anderson Jnr, the son
of a famous director, Keith Hamshere, who'd been the original
Oliver in *Oliver Twist* on the stage and who went on to become a
film-stills photographer, Jeremy Bullock and Ray Brooks. There was
a problem making Britain's first Twist film in January 1962. The
Twist hadn't reached England! None of the extras knew how to do
it. So we had Twist instructors from America! Just when the extras
thought they'd got it and I screamed through the loudhailer, 'Action!
Everybody! *Twist!*' the veteran Soundman, Dudley Messenger,
would play Bach or Beethoven through the loudspeakers as a joke.
On another occasion, since I used the loudhailer a great deal because
of the crowds, when I screamed 'Action!' ten loud-hailers on ropes
came down from the top of the sound stage. On the first day of
shooting Billy Fury was lunching in the Pinewood canteen. He sat
awkwardly on the corner of a table while the four boys who played
his gang had all the space and were making all the noise. 'William,'

I said, 'why are you sitting on the corner without enough room to eat your lunch?' Billy was extremely shy. He murmured something about it being 'all right'. 'No,' I said to the other four actors, 'it's not all right. You are only here in Pinewood Studios getting paid because of Billy Fury. I suggest you show him the respect he deserves and give him room to eat.' Billy was a delight. Except one morning. We had a hundred and fifty extras on a big dance-hall scene and he didn't turn up! My Producer David Deutsch was still in London. I rang him. 'David,' I said, 'our star isn't answering his phone and he's not with us!' Billy was managed by a man called Larry Parnes, a gay entrepreneur who, reasonably for him, lived opposite the Baden-Powell Scout headquarters in Cromwell Road, Kensington! He shared his flat with many of his young stars. That does not mean all were homosexual with him. David Deutsch went to the flat. He phoned me from a callbox outside. He said, 'I rang the bell of Larry Parnes's flat and Billy Fury, looking out of it, appeared and slammed the door in my face.' I said, 'Hang around, David and hope for the best.' Somehow or other we scraped through.

At the same time in Pinewood Studios they were making the first James Bond film with Sean Connery. Everybody thought this would be a total disaster. Sean hadn't done any big movies and to spend that much money on what appeared to be a dopey English thriller was considered a great insanity! Sean came on to the set to see me. Everybody in Pinewood came on the set, because my directing was rather robust! The *Kinematograph Weekly*, the bible of the trade in England, wrote:

There are those who think that film-making should be conducted in a cathedral-like calm, those who go along with a little light relief between takes, and Michael Winner. He directs like a frenzied *Sunday Night at the Palladium* compère with a constant stream of gags broadcast to the world at large through his loudhailer. Of course artists and crew occasionally get their own back. The other day Winner started to give a stream of instructions. When he stopped it looked as though he'd started making up for a nigger minstrel show. [See how they wrote in those days!] Someone had smeared his loudhailer mouthpiece with black make-up. His exuberance is of course absolutely right for this film, a pop musical laced with a substantial dose of twist.

In the *Daily Sketch*, a then national newspaper, Fergus Cashin wrote:

Tired publicity men who have seen it all before crowd the floor at Pinewood studios. Actors leave their own films and join the crush. Chippies and scene shifters jostle for position. Tea trolley girls fight to serve the cuppas on the set. What's going on? Well, Billy Fury's out there singing. So is Helen Shapiro. And there's a crowd of shapely dolls twisting to a band with a way out beat. But what's the main attraction? Why is Janet Munro, who a few minutes ago was sobbing glycerine tears in *Life for Ruth*, laughing real salty tears? She says 'These days you don't need a head shrinker, all you need is a few minutes down here on the set of *Play It Cool* to unwind. Look at him. Now isn't he a nut? I adore him.' The nut is a man you will never see. An extraordinary over-confident charmer who is directing this film with the loudest voice ever heard on a film set. His name is Michael Winner.

I've always believed a director should jolly people along as well as being a disciplinarian. If you're doing a musical comedy why not a bit of joviality? We finished the film on schedule. When I went into his office Julian Wintle picked up a box of very cheap cigars and threw them across the room. They landed on the floor and broke. He said, 'There's your cigars, Michael!' He was a real charmer.

Nat Cohen, the greatest movie executive I ever encountered in England, whose company made popular films as well as getting Academy Awards for *Darling*, was very pleased with the movie. In those days there were only three cinema circuits. Two of them owned by Rank, one owned by Associated British. The circuit bookers saw my film and said, 'This is awful! Messenger boys. They won't last! We don't want it!' Nat Cohen insisted they try it out. *Play It Cool* was previewed in three places, one of them being Luton. On

3rd June 1962 we drove down there. It was an amazing sight. The cinema was surrounded by young people, hungry to see something that related to them, rather than Gregory Peck as a lawyer. The theatre was full. When the titles came up they applauded the name of Billy Fury. They applauded Bobby Vee. When Helen Shapiro's name came they booed. Which shows how fleeting is pop fame. When we contracted Helen to do the picture in late 1961 she was a big attraction. But she was a prima donna and the kids sensed it. Her star career was short. We paid her enormous money in those days – £1,500 a day for two days. We were limited on the make-up, hair time and the preparation time we had with her. Before shooting we went to EMI Studios in Abbey Road, later made famous by the Beatles, to hear her pre-record our songs. My Producer, David Deutsch, bought a very expensive box of chocolates. He gave it to Helen who didn't even say thank you. She just plonked it on the shelf. I thought, 'What a cow.'

Years later, for my sixtieth-birthday lunch party, which I gave in the Leighton House Museum near my house, I had the whole museum decked out, and the whole street outside, dressed with Victorian extras. We had carriages and coaches and Victorian gardeners and nannies and children. We had an Arab hall with an Egyptian band and harem girls in the Arab harem area. Guests ranged from Eric Clapton and Bill Wyman through to the Commissioner of Police, Lord Foster and Diana Rigg. Speeches were by Michael Caine, John Cleese, Roger Moore and Bob Hoskins. I wanted Helen Shapiro to sing 'Walking Back to Happiness', her big hit. Her agent said, 'She'd be thrilled.' I said, 'I just want "Walking Back to Happiness". We'll pay the full £6,000, but that's all we want.' The agent said, 'She does a forty-minute act.' I said, 'I don't want a forty-minute act.' The agent re-checked with Helen, called me back and said, 'She's suddenly remembered she's busy that day! ' Helen's 'starry' attitude hadn't changed!

As a result of the enormous success of the *Play It Cool* previews the movie played the full circuit and did immensely well. David Deutsch got profit cheques for the rest of his life. I wasn't allowed a percentage. I just got my meagre salary. After that I sat in an office in Soho. I'd been put under contract as an Associate Producer, although I never performed that role, by veteran Producer Daniel M. Angel. Angel was strong-willed and opinionated. He'd been crippled by infantile paralysis and insisted on being called Major Angel even though the war had finished seventeen years earlier. He'd made *Reach for the Sky* and many important films. With another major film producer, John Woolf, he was the first British producer to sell his films to television. Film distributors and cinema owners in England were so furious that Danny and John were banned from making films. The circuit refused to show them for five years! If any of their films were shown on re-issue their names were cut out of the print! That sort of thing went on in the late fifties! Danny Angel's period of purgatory was graciously ended by these morons who ran the cinemas and the circuits. He took me on because he was going back to making movies. So I sat in this small room in his offices in Dean Street quite certain everyone would know I'd directed *Play It Cool* and the phone would never stop ringing. If I received a wrong number it was a big event. I got one offer from the producer of my short films, Harold Baim. Harold thought the end of copyright on Gilbert and Sullivan music was something the world cared about! He would produce an updated version of *The Mikado*! With his short films he always got the music from a library and then the film was edited to the music. So Harold spent a fortune having a very large orchestra record all the music for *The Cool Mikado* in a somewhat new version. It was still very Radio 4-type stuff! He had no script and wanted to shoot in a hurry. With Lou Schwartz, a top television writer, I wrote a script. I persuaded Harold to bring in John Barry, now a top film-music writer. Then he had a rock band, The John Barry Seven. In *The Cool Mikado* they played the 'Tit Willow Twist' while Lionel Blair and the dancers performed. It was all absolute nonsense, shot in four weeks on the silent stage at Shepperton. But I got some wonderful artists.

The lead actor, playing Coco, was Frankie Howerd. I'd been an immense fan of Frankie from his early days on *Variety Bandbox* on the radio. His career had been going wonderfully until the wife of an electrician who became his boyfriend went to the Sunday papers and revealed Frankie had stolen her husband and was homosexual. In 1960 that was unacceptable. Frankie's name went from the top of the bill to bottom. He was unemployable. Luckily United Artists in America knew nothing of this and Harold Baim was happy to go along with it. So I booked Frankie Howerd for five hundred pounds for four weeks. When employers saw United Artists starring him, they sheepishly went along and forgave what they'd considered sexual deviancy. I also had an old friend in it, Tommy Cooper. I'd met him through my father. Tommy was in my father's Masonic Lodge in Shepherd's Bush. Also Mike and Bernie Winters, Stubby Kaye, who was so brilliant in MGM's *Guys and Dolls*, and Dennis Price because he was a lovely man and a great actor. And a host of British stalwarts including Dermot Walsh who'd jumped over a wall in my first ever semi-feature movie.

I'd decided to have these rather ropey sets (all we could afford) built at Shepperton depicting Japan, and then I'd have a blue screen behind them and on to that blue screen would later be superimposed pictures of real Japanese countryside. I'd go to Japan and shoot this with a small second unit. This appealed to me because it had never been done before, a mixture of real waving cherry trees blossoming backing obviously fake sets. It would also give me a chance to go to Japan paid for by United Artists! Harold Baim had budgeted the film at forty thousand pounds, which was far less than it needed. *Play It Cool* had cost seventy-five thousand pounds but that was in black and white. *The Cool Mikado* was in colour. They were both a four-week shoot. After two weeks we ran out of money. United Artists sent auditors over. All they could report was that the original budget was ridiculous. UA would not pay for the enormous technical post-production costs of superimposing Japanese scenery on to the blue screen surrounding every set. So when the film was finished the blue screen backing stayed behind the sets, but with no pictures on it! Although I did get to Japan for a week to shoot the title backgrounds. I was very impressed when I was there. A major Hollywood film was being made with Richard Widmark. They had a famous Japanese cameraman who not only lit the film but operated the camera as well. That was totally unheard of in England! You had to have one person to light, another person to operate and two more assistants. It took thirty years before English and American cameramen also operated.

The film was not a great success! That's putting it mildly! But it was the only time Tommy Cooper and Frankie Howerd acted together. The Producer, Harold Baim, was so thrilled with the movie. But when I was called to the office of Bud Ornstein, the UK Head of United Artists, he held up his left hand showing six sheets of paper. In his right hand were another six sheets of paper. Bud said, 'Michael, in my left hand are my notes on what's wrong with *The Cool Mikado*. In my right hand are my notes on what's wrong with *Tom Jones*.' I got equal billing with a film that went on to win the Academy Award for Best Picture!

I'd taken the precaution of looking for seriously excellent material and nurturing it and getting it written. I realised if I didn't dig myself out of pop musicals, nobody else would. It's important in movies to be self-motivated. Never accept 'No' for an answer. Whenever I'm asked by people, 'What is the best way to become a director?' I always say, 'Don't wait for work. Get hold of scripts. Write scripts. Do things yourself. If you try hard enough and you've got any talent you'll eventually come through.' I was not to be aware that the little English script I had cooking in the background was to turn me from a British rock-and-roll director into a member of the Hollywood 'in' set. But before that other things happened.

10

Julie and Success

The veteran Producer Danny Angel, who I was under contract to as an Associate Producer, had a movie script based on the book *The Furnished Room* by Laura Del Rivo. She was the girlfriend of the sixties avant-garde writer, Colin Wilson. It was about misfits in early sixties Notting Hill Gate, then full of seedy bed-sitting rooms. An underworld of failed intelligentsia. Danny had given the book to Joseph Losey who wanted Warren Beatty and Claudia Cardinale. What Warren Beatty would have been doing in a bed-sit in Notting Hill Gate I can't imagine! The film didn't get made, so Danny offered it to me. The script was by two distinguished writers of the day, Keith Waterhouse and Willis Hall. It was a sombre story about an aimless loner living in Notting Hill Gate. He's picked up by a self-styled ex-army captain to commit a murder for him. It gave me a chance to direct a 'real' film even though the script and book were downbeat and unlikely to be commercial. For the leading girl we tested three actresses, Julie Christie, Kathleen Breck and Suzanne Farmer (who was in Hammer Horror films and had very large bosoms). We viewed the tests at Associated British Studios in Elstree. Myself, Danny Angel, the Associated British Casting Director and Danny's Assistant Producer, a lovely man called Vivian Cox.

The lights came up and everyone waited for Danny to speak. He said to me, 'What do you think?' 'There's no question,' I said. 'We should have Julie Christie. She's wonderful. She'll be a major star.' I'd seen Julie's work on television. I'd had her round and personally coached her for her test. But her career was going through a bad patch. She'd been under contract to the Rank Organisation where she played the pretty blonde on the back of Leslie Phillips' motor scooter and they terminated her contract. She was tested for *Nothing but the Best* by Clive Donner, who rejected her in favour of Millicent Martin. She was tested for *Billy Liar* by John Schlesinger, who rejected her in favour of an actress called Topsy Jane. There was silence after I suggested her name. It was broken by Danny Angel. 'Julie Christie's a B-picture actress. Everybody knows she'll never get anywhere,' he said. 'I still think she's the best,' I responded. Danny Angel asked, 'Who'd want to fuck Julie Christie?' I said, 'I would!' Danny responded, 'Well, you're homosexual!' This was a typical Danny Angel exchange. He knew I wasn't a homosexual. Once Danny had put me down everyone else concurred sheepishly in choosing Kathleen Breck for the part. She was a reasonable actress but no Julie Christie.

After I'd made *West 11* I produced my own film, *The System*, a few months later. I again wanted Julie in the lead. By now she'd been in *Billy Liar* because Topsy Jane, the original choice, had become ill. I met John Schlesinger in Sackville Street near my Mayfair office. I said, 'John, I thought you were meant to be in the north of England shooting *Billy Liar*.' He said, 'I am. But a terrible thing happened. Topsy Jane became ill and they're making me take Julie Christie.' I said, 'I think that's good. She'll be great in your film.' When I wanted her for my next film *Billy Liar* hadn't come out. Julie said to me, 'They think I'm so dreadful in *Billy Liar,* they insist I go to Birmingham rep to learn how to act.' I got plaintive postcards from her up there telling me how much she hated it! Anyway, back to the casting of *West 11*.

Sean Connery was dying to play the leading man. He'd finished shooting James Bond which everyone thought would be a disaster. I thought he'd be terrific. Danny Angel said, 'Another B-picture actor! No one will ever be interested in Sean Connery.' Another brilliant actor, James Mason, wanted to play the seedy army captain. Danny Angel dismissed him as 'a has-been'. Instead of a film with Julie Christie, Sean Connery and James Mason we ended up with Alfred Lynch, Kathleen Breck and Eric Portman. Lynch was a good actor but not suited for the role. Eric Portman was a superb screen actor who I'd been brought up on as a child, but he didn't have the charisma of Mason. The movie gave me an opportunity to employ many of the actors I'd enjoyed watching as a youth, including Diana Dors, Freda Jackson, Finlay Currie, Marie Nay, Patrick Wymark, Kathleen Harrison and newcomers Francesca Annis and David Hemmings.

The film was lit by a wonderful cameraman, Otto Heller, who spoke in a thick Jewish middle-European accent. Anybody who was with him ended up speaking the same way! Sometimes I spent days on end speaking like Otto Heller in this German-Jewish accent! It was obvious that the place to make a film about Notting Hill Gate (the picture had been re-titled *West 11*) was in Notting Hill Gate. Everything was there. The crumbling buildings, the peeling staircases, the bed-sitting rooms. But Danny Angel said, 'We don't want a lot of wobbly cameras like they have in the French New Wave. In England we make films in studios.' As the film was financed by Associated British which had a studio, I was again forced to make most of it in a studio. I found an ideal bed-sit in Notting Hill Gate. The Art Director said, 'I'll build it much bigger for you, so it's easier to shoot in.' I said, 'I don't want it bigger. I want it exactly the same size as it is. It's the sort of place people here live in.' I was determined everything should be authentic. I was nearly fired after the first day's shooting because Danny Angel didn't understand my style of directing. He was used to the old-fashioned way of making movies where the director plonks the camera down facing the entire set and actors play the whole scene that is to be done that day in what is called a master shot. Then the camera moves in and picks up various closer angles, over the shoulders, close-ups, etc. I shoot in little bits that need to be joined together. They overlap only slightly. This is better for the actors because they don't have to say the same lines endlessly throughout the day. Also, if you want to change anything you're not stuck to the master shot. You can adapt your shooting and dialogue as you go along. When I later made *Lawman* the veteran star, Robert Ryan, said to me, 'The only person I've met who makes films like you is John Ford.'

Danny Angel sat watching the rushes of *West 11*, then phoned me up in hysterics. He said, 'This will never cut together. You haven't done a master shot.' We had another of our endless rows. I was always having rows with Danny! He was an old friend of my family. One day his wife Betty phoned my father George and said, 'Your son's impossible. Danny's so shattered, he came home this evening and had a glass of Scotch.' My father said, 'I have a glass of Scotch every evening.' Betty replied, 'Danny hasn't drunk for thirty years.'

The film was not a commercial success because it was so downbeat. But it did get some good reviews. Alexander Walker in the *Evening Standard* said, 'Director Michael Winner has probably made the definitive work on bed-sitter land. I commend the film.' David Benedictus in the *Daily Express* described it as 'Remarkably and scabrously authentic'. And the Editor of *Films and Filming*, Robin Bean, wrote, 'An excellent example of the atmosphere and feeling that can be evoked by using locations to effect, which could never come from a studio set'. If only he knew!

We were only a few months into 1963 and I'd finished shooting *West 11* when a script I'd been preparing was ready for presentation. It's a dreadful time, when you have to offer your script and hope some company will make it. The original story, by a new writer, Peter Draper, dealt with kids at the seaside. During the short season they worked on the deckchairs and other summer activities. It showed how they tried to screw all the girls and make the most of the summer while they could. It was an intelligently written piece where the leading actor got involved in an affair with a richer girl who treated him as he treated all the other girls and dumped him. I'd met Oliver Reed in 1962 when casting *West 11*. I'd always thought he was a wonderful actor. He was very sensitive and quietly spoken. Unlike the image he was later to acquire as a roustabout drinker. Oliver showed me poetry he'd written. He wanted to make a short film about people on a hill living in a wardrobe! I liked him very much. He, too, was dismissed by Danny Angel as 'another B-picture actor'. Oliver had only done Hammer Horror films, but I thought he had more to offer. So in my new role as Producer I gave Oliver Reed the lead. I also went back to Julie Christie whom I'd not been allowed to employ before. I couldn't get Julie for reasons I've mentioned. So we had a new girl, Jane Merrow, who was fine in the film but never became a star. Few British girls do! It took some thirty years from Julie Christie becoming a major star in 1963 before Catherine Zeta-Jones became a major star. I used David Hemmings who'd had a small part in *West 11*. It was my first outing with a wonderful character actor, Harry Andrews, and there were two excellent girls in the film, Barbara Ferris and Julia Foster, who I later cast in my commercials. I also auditioned a young Ian McKellen. During the interview I asked, 'Are you homosexual?' I was not against homosexuals and it would not have affected anything. I shouldn't have said it. Ian said, 'No.' Twenty-five years later we were guests at a party hosted by Elizabeth Taylor. Ian said to me, 'Do you remember when we met before?' I said, 'Yes. It was 1963 when I interviewed you for *The System*. I did something I've been ashamed of ever since. I asked if you were homosexual.' Ian said, 'And I said "yes".' I said, 'No, you didn't, Ian, you said "no".' He said, 'Well, ask me again and you can come upstairs for a kiss.' Ian's a great character, absolutely charming. He'd remembered this incident as I had for twenty-five years. I was glad to apologise.

The System was made because Sir Michael Balcon, the most important and distinguished executive in British movies, greatly liked the script and what I had done with *West 11*. He was the genius who'd run Ealing Studios, making many of the best films in the history of British cinema. Balcon had moved on to Bryanston Films where he made *Tom Jones*, *Saturday Night and Sunday Morning* and many other great movies. Bryanston financed *The System*. In those days the normal way of financing a film was that an English company put up 70 per cent of the money, the National Film Finance Corporation put up 25 per cent and the director and producer would defer most of their fee, working for more or less nothing, to provide the other 5 per cent. In this case the National Film Finance Corporation didn't put up any money, although they had for *West 11* – a greatly inferior script. My Co-Producer, Kenneth Shipman, put up some money himself. I put up most of my small fee. The film cost a hundred and twenty thousand pounds. As Cameraman I chose the man who'd been with me operating the camera on the Danzigers' Mark Sabre second unit, Nicolas Roeg. Nic gave me some advice which at the time I thought ridiculous.

Nic Roeg said to me, 'You know, Michael, you'll never be successful if you direct as if you're enjoying it. You've got to look very serious. You've got to give it a bit of this.' Nic raised his right hand and pinched the top of his nose with his thumb and forefinger and lowered his head as if in deep and intellectual thought. He said, "Make them think you're intellectual."' Nic took his own advice in respect of his own career. I often wondered what would have happened if I'd taken it! I was at last able to get a film made the way I wanted it. Entirely on location. The story was set in Torquay and Brixham. The film crew and actors echoed the theme of the movie, of boys in the summer at a seaside resort screwing as many girls as they could! I had a large apartment in an old-fashioned house overlooking Torquay. Every Saturday night I'd have parties where we'd dance to the Everley Brothers. The sort of things you dream of happening in movie-world actually happened! The finale of the film was a big beach party where a bride and groom burn in effigy. It became quite vicious, like a Nazi rally. We had three hundred local people as extras. It rained a great deal so for three nights we were on a cold and damp beach shooting this scene, with extras with flaring torches. To this day people come up to me in the street and say, 'What a wonderful party you gave on the beach at Torquay!' It was cold, wet and rough. But the glamour of filming obliterates everything.

I was in Torquay driving with my local eighteen-year-old girlfriend, when I saw people in sleeping bags outside the Palace Theatre. I said, 'Is it the Bolshoi Ballet?' The girl said, 'It's the Beatles.' I bought their one LP that was out, listened to their single 'Love, Love Me Do' and decided they'd be major. I wrote to their manager, Brian Epstein, whose name I'd seen in the newspapers, suggesting he came to Torquay to see me as I was prepared to give the Beatles a chance in movies. Brian replied, 'I don't know why you're writing to me "Dear Mr Epstein" when you know me well.

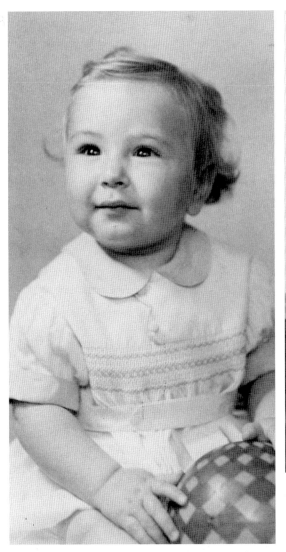

Above left and right: When I was somewhat younger. There is no question that after these photos were taken I was on a downward slope, appearancewise.

Left: My father George and my mother Helen. When I look at this picture I realise how dreadful it was that I didn't pay them more attention and show them more love.

In the London Palladium dressing room with Bob Hope in 1953, when I was eighteen. And better dressed.

In the London Palladium dressing room in 1954 with Nat King Cole, who was showing me an oil painting a fan had done for him. I was still well dressed!

With girlfriend Christina Svensson, attempting to dance.

At a debutante dance circa 1957 when on the 'In London Last Night' column, with Lola Wigan.

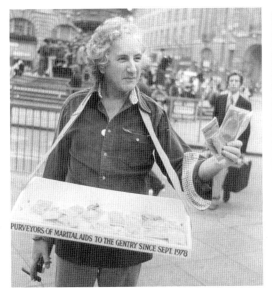

PURVEYORS OF MARITAL AIDS TO THE GENTRY SINCE SEPT. 1978

Above left: At Piccadilly Circus selling 'French ticklers' in September 1978, having lost a bet with Marlon Brando.

Above: With Billy Fury on the set of *Play It Cool* in 1962.

Left: With Terry-Thomas and Wilfrid Hyde-White on location for *You Must Be Joking* in 1965.

Below: With Frankie Howerd, Stubby Kaye, Jacqueline Jones and Jill Mai Meredith in 1962 on the set of *The Cool Mikado*.

Left: Testing Julie Christie in 1961 for the lead role in *West 11*. I chose her. The producer rejected her, saying she was a 'B-picture actress', Sean Connery was 'B-picture' and James Mason was 'a has been'! That's when I decided to be my own producer.

Below: The unit at Hallsands South, Devon, on *The System* in summer 1963, with actors Oliver Reed and Jane Merrow, and cameraman Nicolas Roeg.

With Oliver Reed and
Michael Crawford at
a pre-production
reception for *The Jokers*
in 1966.

Orson Welles and
Oliver Reed on the
set of *I'll Never Forget
What's'isname* in 1967
at a golf club in north
London, which was
standing in for
Orson's mansion.

With Marianne
Faithfull, naked in the
bath, on the set of *I'll
Never Forget
What's'isname*. That
was the nearest we
got to a meaningful
relationship!

Above: With Michael Crawford and Stanley Baker during the shooting of *The Games* in Rome in 1969.

Left: With Oliver Reed in the Austrian Alps during the shooting of *Hannibal Brooks* in 1968. This was when we had to change Oliver's hotel every night because he was rather rumbustious and the hotel objected!

With Charles Aznavour, the least fit marathon runner ever to grace the screen, during the shooting of *The Games* in Rome.

With Burt Lancaster in Durango, Mexico, during the filming of *Lawman* in 1970.
Sadly, I don't have a photo of Burt holding me by the lapels over a 2,000-foot drop and
threatening to kill me.

With Marlon Brando in a field in Cambridgeshire during the filming of *The Nightcomers*
in 1971. This was the smiling and witty Brando I knew. If there was another one I never
met him.

With Marlon Brando at Sawston Hall, Cambridge, the location for *The Nightcomers*.

Left: The cover of *Picturegoer*, showing Jill Ireland in May 1955. I wrote for the magazine in the 1950s. It was the sight of this picture that made me phone up her agent and arrange to meet.

Below: With Jill Ireland and Charles Bronson on the set of *Chato's Land* in 1971.

We were on holiday two years running at the Palace Hotel, Torquay. You and I and my brother Clive were good friends.' I hadn't realised this was the same man who was now managing the Beatles. At our hotel then they used to have nights when guests did the cabaret. Brian and I imitated The Ink Spots. Brian said he couldn't come to Torquay. He was going to be in London on 13th October 1963 as the Beatles would be on *Sunday Night at the London Palladium* that night. We arranged to meet the following evening. My friend Lewis Gilbert guaranteed me £40,000 to offer them. Brian and I dined at the Empress. He said, 'I've got the Beatles on at the Finsbury Park Empire for five weeks over Christmas. We're not selling many tickets. Would you like to invest?' At the time I had no money. I'd received £3,000 for making *The System*, £3,000 for *West 11* and £2,000 for *Play It Cool*. I said, 'Brian, how can you tell me you're not doing well at the theatre? The Beatles were so successful on television last night.' Brian said, 'The box office picked up a bit today, but not much.' I discussed doing a movie with the Beatles. Brian said, 'We're close to a deal with United Artists.' I asked, 'What is it?' Brian replied, 'For the first film they're getting £5,000, for the second £10,000 and for the third film £15,000. United Artists get the right to release the records.' I said, 'That doesn't seem much to me.' Brian answered, 'But Cliff Richard only got £3,000 for his first film.' I said, 'Cliff Richard was one person. You've got four. You're sitting on something much more valuable than Cliff Richard.' I offered Brian my £40,000 and it was rejected. Because the deal he outlined to me was the deal that went through. That's why the Beatles, for their third United Artists film, delivered just a 16mm load of nonsense called *The Magical Mystery Tour*. By then they were earning millions. They really didn't need £15,000 for a movie!

As the Beatles were signed with United Artists I telephoned Bud Ornstein, the man who had held up critical notes of *The Cool Mikado* and *Tom Jones*, and asked if I could direct the film. He'd already taken on Dick Lester. He said to me, 'Why on earth would you want to do that sort of film, Michael? You've gone past pop musicals now. It's only a low-budget quickie. ' The film took a fortune. So did the second Beatles film. This produced a strange event. Bud Ornstein had farmed out the job of producing the Beatles film to an ex-publicity man, Walter Shenson. In those days producers at United Artists got an enormous share of profits, usually 50 per cent. Later Walter Shenson said to Bud Ornstein, 'I did nothing to get these Beatles movies at all. You handed them to me on a plate. I'd like to give you some of my profits!' Bud Ornstein asked his United Artists boss in America, the legendary executive Arthur Krim, if he could take the money from Walter Shenson. Krim said, 'Of course you can't, Bud, you gave out the job as an executive for United Artists. You can't take a cutback from a producer.' Bud Ornstein was so upset that he took the money, quit United Artists, and went to live in Spain. There he died an unhappy man. Walter Shenson went on to make a fortune! Brian Epstein died of drugs. I never got the Beatles. I did use a group called the Searchers to do the title song for *The System*. The *New Musical Express* said at the end of 1963, 'Pity the poor Searchers. If it hadn't been for the Beatles it would have been them.' Which it wouldn't, because the Searchers were nowhere near the Beatles.

The System would be the film that was to change my entire life. I had no idea of this when it came out in England to fairly good reviews, but certainly not what I felt it deserved. The reviewer for *Time and Tide*, an 'in' magazine, Gina Richardson, said, '*The System* is intended to break down some of the clichés that have been built up about layabout youth in the decade or so since they became fashionable amongst us busy adults and it really does so.' Robin Bean in *Films and Filming* was one of the few to give it major attention, calling it, 'One of the best British films of the year. Well constructed, actors are handled with a genuine awareness of character and motivation. The photography is excellent.' Patrick Gibbs in the *Daily Telegraph* said, 'It's a single merit of *The System* that it takes a consistent, undivided view of its subject. A pleasing film handled with skill and tact.'

Before *The System* was released it became a *cause célèbre* in the British film industry. The film was extremely tame. There was a tiny bit of bare-breasts for a second or two, but other than that, nothing. No one expected any problem with the Censor, John Trevelyan, the man who had passed *Nudes in the Snow*. A man of considerable daring. He looked like a cadaverous old headmaster and smoked incessantly. He was good at defending the rights of film-makers and presenting himself on television. I got a long letter from Trevelyan saying *The System* had to be cut to ribbons because it was so offensive. As I was reading the letter he rang me and said, 'You'd better come and see me, Michael. We have problems.' I went to Trevelyan's office. He told me that as Secretary of the British Board of Film Censors, he normally had all the power. They now had a new Chairman, Lord Herbert Morrison, an ex-Labour Cabinet Minister. Normally the Chairman did very little. But on the morning *The System* was shown to the Censors, Lord Morrison asked, 'Can I sit in on this?' The film produced no adverse reaction at all from John Trevelyan or the other censors. But Morrison was apoplectic! He thought the whole attitude of these boys trying to get laid and screw girls on the beach would damage society. He turned to John Trevelyan and said, 'This should not be shown ever, anywhere.' It became a battle to define who had power at the British Board of Film Censors, the Chairman or the Secretary. Trevelyan would have made no cuts at all. I went to see him and Lord Morrison, bringing Sir Michael Balcon. Balcon was appalled at Morrison's attitude regarding a film which he was proud to be associated with. Lord Morrison said it showed a society he didn't think should exist. Sir Michael Balcon said his company had made many of the most distinguished films in the history of British cinema and wouldn't make a film unless it had value. John Trevelyan won the battle and became the real head of the censorship office. We made a few cosmetic cuts, a quarter of a second here and there. That, I thought, was that regarding *The System*. But it wasn't.

11

Crown Jewels

In 1964 my career came to a halt! In the two previous years I'd made four movies, which is practically unheard of. But the movie business, for directors as well as actors and actresses, is a stop/go affair. I was developing a screenplay inspired by an Army initiative test for which soldiers were asked to get as far away as possible from their camp at Catterick. One of them ended up in New Zealand having smuggled his way on to various aeroplanes! I wrote a story and got writer Alan Hackney, who'd done some of the Boulting Brothers classic comedies, to write a screenplay. I showed it to Harry H. Corbett, one of our top comic actors. He loved it. I asked companies if they'd finance it. Then my *Play It Cool* Producer, David Deutsch, said he had an assignment from Anglo-Amalgamated to make a pop-music film with the Dave Clark Five, the 1960s band led by a young drummer from North London and famous for recording its discs at a higher decibel rating than anyone else! David and I went to Blackpool to meet Clark who was playing in a theatre. He presented us with his own storyline where he lived in a cave and was eaten by rats! This didn't strike us as a great idea for a pop musical.

An American producer, Charles H. Schneer, had seen my Army-initiative script, *You Must Be Joking*. He offered to make it under a deal he had with Columbia Pictures. So I left the Dave Clark project. I suggested to David Deutsch a young television director, John Boorman. John took over the Dave Clark film. It was his first movie. I continued with *You Must Be Joking*. Charlie Schneer didn't want Harry H. Corbett. Columbia wanted Michael Callan, who was the juvenile lead in a hit film at the time, *Cat Ballou*. I had to take Michael Callan. A nice fellow who didn't sell the film in America and didn't help it in England either! I assembled a wonderful cast including Terry-Thomas, Lionel Jeffries, Wilfred Hyde-White, James Robertson Justice, Leslie Phillips, Denholm Elliott, Arthur Lowe and many more. Schneer was the only producer I'd met who didn't run scared of the unit. In England the unit usually ran the movie. Most producers just trailed along and put up with whatever nonsense they had to. Overtime bans, people walking out all over the place and general chaos.

We started shooting *You Must Be Joking* in early 1965. It gave me the chance to work with Geoff Unsworth, one of the most important lighting cameramen in the world. He'd been nominated for an Academy Award for *Becket*. The British film industry was at a low ebb. Only three other films were shooting. Schneer had a far less distinguished cameraman start pre-production. He went into a small house location in St John's Wood, came back to Schneer and said, 'Winner's crazy, no one can shoot in these small rooms.' I said to Schneer, 'We've shot in far smaller places before.' So in came Geoff Unsworth, not a likely candidate for a black-and-white British comedy after the major international films he'd done. I'd selected a very modest set of lights for our cameraman. I always believe that the more lights you give the cameraman, the more time he's going to spend lighting and the less time there is for the acting and making the movie! Geoff came to see me and I handed him the short list of the lights available. Geoff looked at it and said in a very quiet voice, 'I normally choose my own lights.' I said, 'Yes, Geoff, but the cameraman who's just left was an idiot. If he could do the film with these lights, I'm sure you can!' Unsworth, who was the most marvellous man, simply nodded and said, 'Yes.' And he did. Brilliantly.

One scene called for a rock band in an old open Rolls-Royce to be chasing Michael Callan and his girlfriend in a sports car. The

Rolls-Royce got into the middle of Piccadilly Circus and blew up. Amazingly we couldn't get permission from the police! I said to Charlie Schneer, 'Who cares! We've got a car full of special effects. It's not really blowing up. It won't hurt anybody. Just do it.' Schneer said, 'I won't be there that day because I'm a visiting American. They may throw me out of the country. We'll leave the Production Manager with you.' The Production Manager was the only person against this. We went into Piccadilly Circus at 11 a.m. The car stopped, there was a loud bang and smoke and water poured from it right in the middle of Piccadilly Circus! The police told us off but did no more. Unfortunately we didn't get enough shots before the police insisted it was driven away. So we had to return two weeks later.

The unit was all around Piccadilly Circus with walkie-talkies when I got a message that the Rolls had collapsed in the Hyde Park underpass. It would be towed into Piccadilly Circus. By now the police had got wind of something and increasing numbers were appearing. The Production Manager told me I should stop but I said, 'We'll carry on. It's a laugh.' Our Rolls was pulled into Piccadilly Circus, the ropes were severed, the Rolls was left, and there was this big bang! Billows of smoke and water poured out of it and bits of lightweight material showered down from it. The police were furious. Ten of them came to push the car out of the way. They weren't too happy, because water was still shooting out of it in all directions. They got drenched. I was not well known at the time. One officer came to me and said, 'Are you in charge?' I said, 'I'm just doing some shopping. I've no idea who these people are.' The police arrested the Production Manager, the only person totally against the scheme. They also arrested the man who'd driven the car into Piccadilly. They were both up in court and were given minor fines. For years after, if anyone called up the police in London and said, 'We're going to shoot a film,' the police said, 'Is it anything to do with Michael Winner? If so don't come anywhere near us.' It was immense fun making *You Must Be Joking*, particularly being with these extraordinary comedy actors who were among the greatest this country has ever produced. There was one scene where Wilfred Hyde-White, getting very old, bless him, was briefing the soldiers on the initiative test. After the take Wilfred said to me, 'I hope you didn't mind my reading from the script, Michael.' I said, 'I don't mind you reading from the script, Wilfred. But it would help if you didn't turn the pages over in the middle of the shot!'

You Must Be Joking has a wonderful line, written by one of our additional writers, Johnny Speight, who wrote *Till Death Us Do Part*. Michael Callan has got to find a set of porcelain ducks, the sort that 'fly' on people's walls. He rings the bell of a cheap apartment. The door is opened by that terrific old character actress Irene Handl. Michael Callan says, 'I'm collecting for starving people.' Irene replies, 'Starving people! Is that a good cause then?' The film was well received. The *Guardian* described it as 'A high-spirited British romp'. Alexander Walker in the *Evening Standard* said, 'Michael Winner's direction is nimble and the jokes come thick and fast.' Ralph Blum in New York *Vogue* called it 'A hilariously funny film done in black and white humour with a refreshingly upper-class bias'. It was not a box-office hit. I was still waiting for my breakthrough.

I'd written a story based on my own experience at Cambridge University. In my time your bicycle was speedily stolen by another student. So we'd just take any bicycle, ride it to a place and leave it. Thousands of bicycles were used as communal bikes. I cycled to the offices of the *Varsity* newspaper every day from Downing College. Once I'd got there I'd meet people and walk back. One day I took the Downing College Porter's bike. He looked out of his lodge in his bowler hat and saw. He called the police! They met me at the *Varsity* office, notebooks rampant, and said, 'You've stolen this bicycle.' I said, 'No, I haven't. I've no intention of keeping it. I simply rode it from Downing College to this office.' The police agreed that if you took something it had to be proved you intended to keep it before you could be done for theft. So they reported me to my college Master. I was called up before the college disciplinary board and sent down for two weeks. Ten years later I wrote *The Jokers*, about two brothers, seeking recognition, who steal the Crown Jewels as a gesture of defiance against society. They leave notes that they're only borrowing the jewels and intend to return them. Except one of them doesn't leave a note and pins it all on his brother, who he hates because he's jealous of him. To put my story into a screenplay I employed two young men who were not yet fully professional writers, Dick Clement and Ian La Frenais. They've since written many famous films and TV series. The three of us worked on the script. Then I started touting it around. Without success. At the suggestion of my friend Lewis Gilbert I joined up with two mediocre producers, Maurice Foster and Ben Arbeid. They couldn't get *The Jokers* going either.

I'd been unemployed for almost a year but I still went into my office in Piccadilly every Saturday. I was there on Saturday 30th April 1966 when I opened a letter from a writer I'd employed, John Gardner. John wrote a series of books about a detective called Boysie Oakes and went on to write the James Bond tales after the death of Ian Fleming. In his letter John congratulated me on my reviews in *Time* and *Newsweek*. I said to myself, 'This man's insane. I can't possibly have reviews in *Time* and *Newsweek*. I've no film out in America.' Furthermore, *Time* and *Newsweek* came out on Wednesday. This was now Saturday. If I had rave reviews, someone would have told me. I bought copies of *Time* and *Newsweek*. To my amazement I was being heralded as the new genius of English-speaking cinema. *The System*, which I'd made three years earlier, was showing in New York titled *The Girl-Getters*. *Newsweek*'s film critic wrote 'Michael Winner is the unheralded director of this consistently intelligent and often brilliant low budget import.' The *Time* magazine critic wrote, 'Director Michael Winner coolly catches the feverish gotta-keep-busy restlessness of youth on the go. Wherever the action is Winner gives a commanding end of summer air to every moment of it.' I drove to the London offices of *The New York Times* where they had a paper with display advertisements for movies in New York. Every New York critic was raving about my film. John Simon, the leading film critic in America at the time, writing in the *New Leader* said, 'Winner has a strong feeling for detail. He has elicited telling performances from a large and motley cast. Michael Winner, whose debut this is, should turn into a noteworthy director.' Howard Thompson in *The New York Times* referred to 'the simple lubrication of the sharp-eyed director Michael Winner'. I got a copy of a large display advertisement in *The New York Times*. In those days photocopying was in its infancy. There were photocopy machines at railway stations where you put in money and got a photocopy where the white came out black and the black came out white. I photocopied the ad of New York reviews for *The System* at Victoria Station.

The only company chief in England who'd not rejected *The Jokers* was Jay Kanter. He'd recently opened an office for Universal Pictures. In the early sixties Britain was considered useless by the Americans. We didn't make commercial pictures. Suddenly we had three movies which took money! The James Bond film *Dr No*, *Tom Jones* and the Beatles' film *A Hard Day's Night*. The Hollywood movie companies decided that as United Artists had an office in London producing these hits, they should too! People arrived to finance British films! This euphoria lasted about four years. A large number of pictures were made, which overall made an enormous loss. Then the Americans called their executives back and closed the UK offices. Jay Kanter had my script of *The Jokers* but hadn't responded to it. I knew his private address. I took my reviews and put them through his letterbox. I rang my partner, Maurice Foster, and told him. Maurice said, 'Nobody cares about reviews the director gets!' and hung up! On Monday morning Jay Kanter rang Maurice Foster, and said, 'If you can get Michael Winner to sign a six-picture deal with Universal, you can start the movie.' On Saturday I'd been unemployable. On Monday I was being offered a six-picture deal by the most important film company in America! All because of the New York critics! Jay Kanter had seen *The System*. He was a great fan of Oliver Reed and wanted him for one of the brothers. They gave him a six-picture contract.

We already had Michael Crawford for the other. Universal said he was essential for the deal. Michael Crawford was a marvellously mercurial character, given to the most enormous and hilarious bursts of humour. And enormous bursts of temper! He didn't want Oliver Reed as his brother. He knew I'd made a picture with him, and that we were friends. He thought Oliver might get special treatment. He said Oliver Reed didn't look like his brother. He wanted Stanley Baker. 'Michael,' I said, 'if Oliver Reed doesn't look like your brother, then Stanley Baker, who's about twenty years older, looks even less like your brother!' Crawford was in a play in the West End.

I persuaded Oliver to go and see it. I said to Crawford, 'I'm bringing Oliver Reed to the theatre to meet you.' On the afternoon of the day we were going to the play Michael Crawford rang. He said, 'Don't bring Oliver Reed. I refuse to have him in the part. If you bring him to my dressing room I'll throw him out.' I said, 'Michael it's three o'clock in the afternoon. We're going to be in your dressing room at ten-thirty tonight. As Oliver Reed is extremely fit and strong I suggest you start training now to throw him out!' The last thing I wanted, having forced Oliver to go and see this rather dreary play, was to have Oliver go round to the dressing room and have Michael Crawford scream at him. The dressing-room door opened and Michael Crawford greeted Oliver Reed like an old friend. Within seconds they were like real brothers. Later Michael asked for Oliver Reed to be with him in another film.

We made *The Jokers* on locations all over London with some difficulty as the police weren't mad about me. But in those days they took bribes galore. I was shooting just off Sloane Street once. We had the unit base in a garage. It was night and I could see all the lights turning on in a block of flats as residents phoned the police to complain about the noise. Policemen came round to the garage where the unit were set up for dinner. The Location Manager gave each one five pounds and they'd sit down and have a cup of tea. This is an ethos that has long gone. But it was prevalent in the mid-sixties! As well as Michael Crawford and Oliver Reed, *The Jokers* starred Harry Andrews and featured more of our great artists, including James Donald, Daniel Massey, Michael Hordern, Frank Finlay, Warren Mitchell and Edward Fox. We were allowed to shoot a bit in the Tower of London but soon outstayed our welcome and were asked to leave. So I sent in cameramen with hand-held cameras disguised as tourists.

Michael Crawford was a great prankster. One day he and Oliver put a massive amount of laxative in my coffee. While I was on the toilet at home the telephone rang. It was Michael Crawford. He said, 'How are you feeling, Michael?' I said, 'Very well.' He said, 'Nothing wrong?' I said, 'No, nothing's wrong.' Crawford said, 'You're sure?' I said, 'Absolutely sure, I'm fine.' The next day Michael said to me, 'Something had to be wrong, Oliver Reed and I filled your coffee with laxative.' I said, 'I was sitting on the toilet when you rang me. But I didn't feel like telling you!'

Michael Crawford is the most wonderful comic actor. But although he got on with Oliver Reed well and was deeply professional, he'd never pay for anything. Oliver was very generous and paid for a lot of meals. I'd pay for a lot of meals. Michael has since become extremely generous in his donations to children's charities. Oliver kept telling him off about his personal meanness. So Michael asked us to dinner at the White Elephant Club, which was the 'in' club of London. We were filming a few houses away. I said to Oliver, 'Michael will never turn up to pay for this dinner.' Oliver said, 'Of course he will.' I said, 'I bet you fifty pounds, Oliver, he doesn't.' Oliver took the bet. At about ten to six (we were going to break at six) I saw Oliver rushing up and down the backstairs of our location in Curzon Street. He said, 'I'm looking for Michael Crawford.' I said, 'Don't worry, Oliver. We'll have dinner without him.' Oliver looked all over the place. He couldn't believe someone would do this. So Oliver, Harry Andrews and I went to dinner at the White Elephant. I happily paid. Later that evening we were shooting in Trafalgar Square. Oliver and Michael were in evening dress. Michael came on the set. Oliver, who normally sits very quietly, got up, rushed over to Michael, picked him up and held him over the pool which the fountains splash into. He said, 'Michael, unless you pay for the dinner we've just had I'm going to drop you in the fountain.' Michael was screaming in fear! I was screaming, too! Because if Oliver dropped Crawford in the fountain Michael's evening suit would be ruined and we'd have to stop filming. Michael paid the bill!

When *The Jokers* opened in London I thought up a publicity stunt. There were two students at Cambridge University who'd been in the papers because they'd got a Morris Minor car on to the roof of King's College Chapel! My idea was that these two boys, on the Saturday after the movie opened on Friday, would climb into the Tower of London with a big banner saying, '*The Jokers* were here!' They'd be arrested. They'd be in court on Monday and say to the magistrate, 'We were doing this as a joke because we saw the film *The Jokers*.' Jay Kanter, the Head of Universal, agreed and gave me some slush money. I got a private detective who found the students. They got scaling irons, they got ropes, they got all the things necessary. The Saturday this jape was planned for was, by coincidence, the Saturday when the Crown Jewels were being moved from an old jewel tower at the Tower of London to a new jewel room that had just been built. There were hundreds of troops, police and security people added to the normal Beefeaters and troops that guard the Tower. The troops and extra police left at 2 a.m. after the jewels had been transferred. Early in the morning my two boys threw their grappling irons up to the Tower, scaled the walls and went in.

At three o'clock in the morning my detective rang me at home. He said, 'We've done it. The boys climbed into the Tower, they walked around the place, they've put the banner up. They're here with me at the phone box.' I said, 'They weren't arrested?' He said, 'Nobody saw them or heard them!' I thought, 'The people at the Tower will see this sign, they'll take it down and if we tell the press about it they'll deny it was ever there. I'll get no publicity!' I said to my detective, 'Phone the papers and tell them you've got the two boys there who put the banner on the Tower. Let them photograph the banner and the boys!' The detective rang round the national press. They didn't have their most alert staff member on at 3 a.m. on Sunday morning. He rang me back, saying, 'I've phoned seven papers. Five of them either told me to "Piss off" or said, "Don't waste our time with jokes," and put the phone down.' I said, 'What about the other two?' He said, 'They sent people round and they've taken a photograph of the boys and the banner.' When the newspapers rang the Tower and asked for comment, an official said, 'It was a very dangerous thing to do – the boys could have been shot.' I thought, 'You can't shoot people if you don't see or hear them!' The story appeared, but didn't get the attention I felt it deserved.

On the other hand, *The Jokers* did. It was an immensely praised picture and for a long time held the box-office record at the Sutton Theater in New York, where it was one of Universal's biggest hits. It was one of the very few British movies in the sixties to make a substantial profit. I still get profit cheques from it. It's shown on TV everywhere. In *The New York Times* Bosley Crowther called it

'Another of those wonderful eccentric British crime comedies. Michael Winner spins a frantic web in what is surely the most frenetic style yet dared in a British film.' Arthur Knight, a very senior American critic, in the *Saturday Review of Literature* called it 'Thoroughly absorbing, constantly amusing'. David Robinson in the *Financial Times* called it 'An extremely well-constructed comedy always keeping its surprises in reverse and timing them effectively'. Dilys Powell in the *Sunday Times* said, 'It made me laugh more often and more unrestrainedly than I have laughed in the cinema for months.'

I now had two enormously praised films in America. I was a very hot director! But my entire life had been in London. I didn't understand how to make the most of this. Shortly before *The Jokers* I'd taken on a legendary Hollywood agent. A tiny Magoo-like figure called Irving Lazar. It was Irving who smashed Otto Preminger in the face with a broken glass in the 21 Club in New York when Preminger insulted his wife. He was a great art collector and party giver. His house was always full of stars. Gene Kelly came over to me and said, 'I'd love you to direct me in something because *The Jokers* is the most wonderful film I've ever seen.' It was like a dream come true. I was much heralded in Hollywood. But I had no idea how to capitalise on it. Orson Welles once said that making a movie is like having the biggest toy-train set in the world. I was a great success. I had the money, the girls, I was my own boss. My childhood dreams had come true. People say to me, 'How did you feel? What were you thinking?' I was thinking it was all bloody marvellous! Who wouldn't? I had another of my own pictures to make for Universal from a script by Peter Draper who'd written *The System*. Irving Lazar took the view that as they had me under a six-picture contract I might as well do it. In fact I'd have been far better taking some of the very big offers I had from Hollywood. But I was happy to be working and happy to be hot within the film community. I set about my next project in London. It was to introduce me to a man who became a great friend. A man who was my absolute hero. Orson Welles.

12

Orson and Oliver

I'll Never Forget What's 'isname is about a young man in advertising who goes to work, smashes up his desk with an axe and decides to return to the simple life. It dealt with themes later to be highly significant, such as pollution, the desire to get out of the rat race and man's inability to come to terms with an increasingly complex and industrialised world. It featured a sarcastic and witty chief of an advertising agency. Peter Draper, who wrote the script, said, 'Wouldn't it be wonderful if we could get Orson Welles.' I said, 'We will!' Universal had given approval to go ahead with Oliver Reed as the lead. Orson Welles was contacted through an elderly Irish lady in Maida Vale called Ann Rogers. We sent her the script. She rang to say Orson loved it and would like to do it. Miss Rogers said Orson would be coming to London and he'd call me. We carried on with the pre-production of the movie, finding locations and casting.

For one of Oliver Reed's girlfriends I chose Marianne Faithfull. Marianne at the time was considered the harlot of the world. She'd been involved in various sexual shenanigans and was widely believed to have had a Mars bar between her legs which had been eaten by all the Rolling Stones, one after the other! Mick Jagger was at the height of his 'bad boy' period. He'd been doing things as dreadful as peeing on the ground in petrol stations! Marianne came to see me in my office early in 1967 looking absolutely beautiful. She was wearing a white trouser suit with a wide-brimmed white hat. We walked four blocks to the Empress restaurant off Berkeley Square. Marianne spent the entire time apologising, saying she hoped she wasn't embarrassing me by being so outrageously dressed. She was dressed in a simple and nice manner. Here was someone who was considered utterly shameless, and yet she was a very polite person, concerned in case she was letting me down! She said Mick Jagger had wanted to come to the lunch but felt embarrassed to do so.

I'd met Mick Jagger with the Rolling Stones shortly before making *You Must Be Joking* in 1964. The wonderful E. J. Fancey, for whom I'd made shorts and a nudist film, rang me and said, 'I've got four boys here. They're so ugly we'll 'ave to make an 'aunted 'ouse film with 'em! That's all you could do with 'em, 'aunt an 'ouse! They're called the Rolling Stones.' He sent them round to my office. They sat nervously on a long sofa facing me. We briefly discussed a musical film we might make. As they left, Brian Jones said to me, 'Our first LP is out next week, be sure to buy a copy.' When Marianne and I got to the Empress Mick Jagger appeared at a nearby table with Chris Stamp, the manager of The Who. I said to Marianne, 'Why not ask Mick to join us for coffee?' She said, 'He's very shy. Would you mind if we joined him?' The two most 'outrageous' people in the country were carefully observing social niceties.

Weeks passed and I'd not heard from Orson. I rang Miss Rogers. I said, 'We're all thrilled that Orson's going to do the picture. Do you think he'll do it at the same time we do? Because we start in two weeks' time!' A day later came a magical moment. My phone rang and the wonderful deep Orson Welles' voice spoke. 'Michael,' he said, 'this is Orson Welles.' I'd sat through *Citizen Kane* and his other films, mesmerised like any other film-obsessed human being. Now Orson Welles was calling me. Orson said he was coming to London. He wanted me to book him into the Mayfair Hotel incognito. No one was to know he was there. I now had a mission in life: to book Orson incognito into the Mayfair Hotel. A few days later Miss Rogers rang and said, 'Mr Welles is in the Mayfair Hotel.

Would you call him?' I rang the Mayfair Hotel and said, 'Orson Welles, please.' The girl on the switchboard said, 'He's not staying here.' I said, 'No, no, I understand that. It's very good of you, I told you to say it. I'm Michael Winner, I'm paying for the room. Please put me through to Orson Welles.' She said, 'We don't have anyone called Orson Welles here,' and rang off. I rang Miss Rogers and said, 'I can't get through.' 'He's expecting you,' she said. 'Just walk round. He's in room 633.' Thus I had my first meeting with Orson, the most wonderful human, witty and considerate person. Everyone told me he'd be difficult. He wasn't difficult at all. He was deeply sensitive and concerned about everybody around him. At the first meeting we did a deal for his services, I scribbled it on the back of an envelope and he signed it.

Then we talked about the billing. Orson said, 'I want to tell you a story. There was a time when Ellen Terry was acting with Sir Herbert Beerbohm Tree and she said to Herbert Beerbohm Tree, "You know, I think the billing should read Ellen Terry and Sir Herbert Beerbohm Tree. My name should be first because I'm more popular than you are." Sir Herbert Beerbohm Tree said to Ellen Terry, "Miss Terry, unless you stop this nonsense the billing will read Sir Herbert Beerbohm Tree but Ellen Terry."' Orson roared that deep throaty laugh. I said, 'Orson, that's brilliant. That's how we'll do your billing. It'll be the first film ever to get good reviews for the billing. We'll say Oliver Reed, Carol White, Harry Andrews but Orson Welles."' I scribbled that down and Orson signed it. The next time I rang the Mayfair Hotel and said, 'Room 633, please,' the operator said, 'Who do you want to speak to?' I said, 'The man in room 633.' She said, 'Who is it?' I said, 'Orson Welles.' The operator said, 'He's not staying here,' and put the phone down. A few days later Orson had gone back to Paris. I still have the telegram he sent: 'Dear Michael, Afraid second thoughts particularly from my own production company make first billing necessity. All best, Orson.' Orson did not have a production company insisting on anything. He'd just changed his mind and wanted to be billed first. So what? I did it.

Before we started shooting, Orson said, 'Would you mind if I re-wrote a few words of the script?' I said, 'Not at all, Orson.' Orson told me he'd personally written the famous Ferris-wheel scene in *The Third Man*. Every day on the set Miss Rogers would take Orson's script pages, type them out and hand them back to him. The following day Orson said our dialogue. Eventually I said, 'Orson you told me you were going to re-write the script. Yet every day you say the lines we gave you.' Orson said, 'Miss Rogers just takes out the stage directions for me. The script's so good I don't need to change it.' We were shooting at the Bluebell Line, a private railway line near Brighton. Early in the morning my assistant said, 'Mr Welles wants to see you in his caravan.' Orson said to me, 'Michael, you're not being fair to me.' I said, 'Goodness me, sir! What am I doing wrong?' Orson said, 'You're always photographing me from below. If you photograph me from below it makes me look fat. I want all my shots to be eye-level shots.' I said, 'I promise, Orson, they'll be eye-level shots from now on.' Orson said, 'Not your eye-level, my eye-level.' Then he roared with laughter. To this day if ever I'm being filmed for television in my garden for a soundbite or photographed I always insist that the lens of the camera is above my eye-level. It takes pounds off! Orson was unbelievably fat in those days. Wherever you put the camera wouldn't make much difference. If we needed to put the camera low, we'd ask him and he'd agree.

Orson had done a number of films wearing a false rubber nose. He had a box of them. He showed them to me. I wanted the Orson Welles I knew and loved, not some tarted-up thing. We'd been shooting a week; Orson couldn't suddenly put a nose on because we'd have had to re-shoot everything. The scene was in a cutting room in Wardour Street. It was very hot and Orson was sweating. I said, 'It's just as well, sir, you haven't got a rubber nose! That would be falling off all over the place. Why didn't you wear one?' Orson said, 'I only put them on for a serious film. This is a comedy.' I wasn't sure at the time whether that was a compliment or not. Because it was a serious film even though it was also very sardonic and funny. On another occasion I came into the caravan and Orson, who was very careful about his weight, and always had hot water and lemon in the morning, was eating frankfurter sausages from a tin. Orson said, 'I don't know why you're looking surprised. The whole unit spend their entire time eating. Whenever I eat anything they all roar with laughter.'

It was a very jolly film. Orson fitted in wonderfully and everybody loved him. One day, when I was doing a close-up, Orson said, 'You know, Michael, I only had three close-ups in *Citizen Kane* and none of them worked.' Later on when we were looping and I'd used a long shot of him, Orson said, 'You should have used my close-up there.' I saw *Citizen Kane* in a re-release in London. There were four people in the audience. I gave up after I counted fifteen close-ups. But there weren't that many.

We had an arrangement whereby Orson was going to buy his own clothes for the movie and we'd pay him back later. We never got the bill. Weeks after the film, when we were doing the re-recording of his voice, Orson suddenly said, 'Michael, I need three thousand pounds and I'd like to keep the cashmere coat I bought.' I said, 'Do you have receipts I can show Universal Pictures?' Orson produced a receipt for three bow-ties. I said, 'This comes to seven pounds and you're asking for three thousand. Do you have receipts for anything else?' Orson roared with laughter and said to Miss Rogers, 'Go and print up some receipts for Mr Winner, will you?' The man was so utterly charming you couldn't deny him anything. Orson was also a very wounded man. We remained friends for a long time. I kept many of the letters he sent me. I would get cables saying, 'Dear Michael, Urgent. I have immediately need for young bright lighting cameraman to replace French cameraman called away on another job. No lamps, no reflectors, only natural sun. We have been photographing with apertures hitherto unheard of and need adventurous youth to continue.' Orson was always in trouble with films he was personally financing. He'd written a script set on a yacht. He wanted Sean Connery. He said, 'Michael how can I send this script to Sean Connery?' I said, 'Why don't you just write him a letter? You're very famous. You've directed some of the greatest films in the history of cinema.' Orson said, 'How do I do that? What should I say? Will you come to the hotel and write it with me?' So I went and co-authored a letter to Sean Connery, which Orson wrote by hand. Sean didn't do the movie. Some time after the shooting of *I'll Never Forget What's'isname*, *The Jokers* came out in America. I have the telegram Orson sent to the Leicester Square Theatre on the day of the opening. 'Dear Michael I know it's a great hit because I've seen it. So will millions more. Fondest, Orson.' That was Orson. So warm and considerate of other people.

There was a particularly strange incident on the shooting of *What's 'isname*. Directors always get insanely carried away. We were in a London cemetery shooting a scene where we were supposedly filming the burning of a body in a crematorium to go into a bizarre commercial that Oliver Reed makes at the end of the movie in the hope of losing his employer, Jonathan Lute, all respect in the industry. Instead it wins the most important advertising prize. In the crematorium I saw lots of urns on the shelves. I said to the man who burned the bodies, 'Do you ever get the wrong ashes in the wrong urns?' The man said, 'I don't bother with the ashes! I just burn everybody during the day. Then I put the ash in the pots.' I said, 'You mean everybody gets an ash cocktail?' The attendant said, 'Yes.' This man came out of a Pinter play. He said to me, 'Have you got a body to burn?' I said, 'Just a coffin.' The attendant said, 'Why don't you burn a body? You can use one of mine!' I said, 'All right.' The attendant said, 'I want ten pounds!' My Location Manager gave him ten pounds and we put this body into the furnace in the coffin. We prepared to film it from both ends of the oven.

There's a small door at one end and a bigger door at the other end. My Cameraman was the wonderful old Jewish man, Otto Heller, who'd done *West 11*. He said, 'Michael, I have a space reserved in the Golders Green Cemetery. I can't watch this body being burned. Please forgive me?' Within seconds the Camera Operator, who was the number two, said, 'I can do it, Michael, I've got my own meter!' The attendant asked me, 'Do you want it done on 300 gas or 700 gas?' I said, 'I don't burn bodies very often. I'll have to take your advice!' The attendant said, 'Do it on 700. We've got a religious ceremony in the chapel in an hour and a half. It'll be quicker.' So we burned the body and filmed it from here and there, although you couldn't see anything because of the flames. The second half of the day was in a supermarket in King Street, Hammersmith. When the film finished, I got phone calls in my office from the press. They left a message with my secretary saying they understood I'd burned a body and that I was eating a ham sandwich and poking the body with a poker. The man from the cemetery rang and said, 'Michael, we've had a call from the press saying you burned a body.' I said, 'They can't possibly use this if you don't say anything. Don't say anything at all. They'll have to get back-up!' The cemetery owner said, 'We've been going since 1760. If this gets out we'll be finished.' I continued to get calls from newspapers. Somebody was going round every paper selling the story. I refused to comment. The man from the cemetery didn't comment.

About four weeks after the calls had finished a man came through saying he was 'Mr Jones' and I took the call. He read the whole rigmarole to me: 'I understand you burned a body, and you had a poker and you were all eating ham sandwiches and drinking tea.' Thus he went on. He was from the *People* newspaper. I said to him, 'Are you so steeped in filth that you can say these words? Do they not have meaning to you? Do you not understand the awfulness of what you're saying? How can you possibly even say this to me and believe there might be any truth in it?' The man said, 'We have to check up . . .' I interrupted, 'No, you don't have to check up. There are certain stories that are so palpably ridiculous that you don't have to check.' The reporter apologised and rang off. He wouldn't today but that's what he did in 1967. A few days later Orson came back to do his post-production voice-looping. He said, in his booming voice, 'Michael, I had the most extraordinary call in Spain. A British reporter rang me and said you'd burned a body.' I said, 'Well, Orson, you know how it is on a Wednesday.' Orson said, 'Oh my God, you didn't, Michael!' and roared with laughter.

I continued to see Orson for years after the movie. He asked me to Los Angeles when the American Film Institute gave him their Life Achievement Award. They staged a wonderful tribute. Orson stood up and said, 'I am honoured to see here every studio chief and every producer in Los Angeles. You've all come to pay me tribute. But not one of you will employ me.' That was a deeply touching moment. Everyone listened and was very moved. And none of them ever employed him! That sums up the film industry. Although Orson was being feted by many of the very rich directors and producers, none of them would put in a penny to finish the little films he was making. I once said to Orson, 'You've made the most famous and acclaimed film in the history of cinema, *Citizen Kane*. You've made other movies like *The Magnificent Ambersons* and pictures that have placed you in the highest regard of all directors. Is there anything left you'd like to do?' Orson said, 'Yes. Before I die I'd like to make one film that makes a profit.' I said, 'Surely *Citizen Kane* made a profit, Orson?' He said, 'Not at all. It was a complete disaster at the box office.' Orson died a great man and a marvellous human being. But he never made a profit.

The leading girl in *I'll Never Forget What's'isname* was a wonderful actress, Carol White, who later became very successful. She then killed herself with drink and drugs. Carol had been acclaimed in Ken Loach's TV movie about the homeless, *Cathy Come Home*. She was married to Mike King, part of an act, the King Brothers, with his two brothers. She lived in Hammersmith and had a sister who was agoraphobic. *I'll Never Forget What's'isname* was the first movie where Carol White had the lead. Ken Loach was going to star her in his movie *Poor Cow*. He insisted there wasn't time for her to do my film. So we'd given up on Carol White. The first time we had lunch I said, 'What are you going to do this afternoon?' and her husband, Mike King, said, 'We've got to go back home because Carol has to cut my hair and cook the dinner.' I thought, 'This marriage won't last once Carol stars in movies.' Anyway, we'd written Carol off because it was a clash with the Ken Loach film. One afternoon my secretary said, 'Carol White's here and insists on seeing you.' In came Carol. She said ferociously, 'I've told that cunt Loach exactly what he can do with himself. I told the fucking arsehole I'm going to do your film and if he didn't like it he could get stuffed and I wouldn't do his.' This seemed a fairly straightforward statement. I said, 'Carol, that's marvellous. I'd love you to do the movie.' She said, 'Ken Loach isn't starting for eight weeks, so as long as you guarantee to finish with me by then, he'll have to put up with it. It means I'll finish your film on Saturday and go to his on Monday.' Thus Carol White did the movie and was absolutely wonderful in it. I still have a stopwatch on my desk which says, 'To Michael my favourite director with love from Carol'.

During the course of the filming Carol started an affair with Oliver Reed. Her husband, Mike, rang me and said, 'Is Carol screwing Oliver Reed?' I said, 'I've never been in the room when intercourse was taking place. As far as I'm concerned, she's not.' One evening Carol came to my flat at 8.30 p.m. and said, 'Phone Oliver and get him over here.' I said, 'Carol, please, it's eight-thirty and I'm going to bed at ten. We're filming tomorrow morning.' She said, 'I don't care about that. Just get Oliver Reed here.' I said, 'Carol, dear, please, go home.' She said, 'I'm not going home. I'm going to sit here until you get Oliver Reed!' I knew the steel that was within this girl. I thought, 'If I'm going to get any sleep I'd better get Oliver Reed here.' I rang Oliver at home in Wimbledon where he was with his wife and child. Oliver responded in that wonderful quiet voice, 'Don't worry, Michael, I'll come over.' Around ten o'clock Oliver got to my flat. He'd been there thirty seconds when Carol White turned to me and said, 'All right, Michael. You can go now!' I said, 'What do you mean "go", Carol? This is my flat! I live here!' Oliver took Carol off and I went to bed marvelling at the magic of the movie business. Next day I said, 'Oliver, what happened?' He said, 'I took her to a hotel. Then I went home to my wife.' As was fairly predictable, Carol left her husband, went to America and had an affair with a very rich studio chief. She became additionally famous when he gave her three mink coats which she brought back to London. Carol was grabbed by Customs. She was put on trial for smuggling mink coats. Her defence was, 'I wanted to see them in the English light before I chose which one to keep.' This made no impression on the judge. But Carol was a great girl. I was deeply saddened to see her get into drink and drugs in America. She died at the age of forty-eight.

I'll Never Forget What's'isname had a wonderful cast, including Harry Andrews, Michael Hordern, Wendy Craig, Frank Finlay, Edward Fox and Norman Rodway. It was an enormous critical success, thus cementing my reputation in America as one of the most praised British directors. A. H. Weiler in *The New York Times* said, 'In a computerised age of speeding youth and instant success, *I'll Never Forget What's'isname* stands a chance of being memorable. It's illustrated in swift, funny, violent, candidly sexy and sometimes poignant strokes that give the picture the towering virtues of honesty and force.' Charles Champlin in the *Los Angeles Times* said, 'Michael Winner proves again he is a vigorous showman of a movie-maker. He has a gift for creating vivid characters swiftly and for propelling them into memorable scenes and compelling sequences.' In England, Margaret Hinxman in the *Sunday Telegraph* wrote, '*I'll Never Forget What's'isname* confirms the promise of Michael Winner as an important director. It's very pointed and very telling.' The movie had one bizarre distinction. There was a scene where Oliver Reed and Carol White are on a houseboat. After a row, Carol goes on the floor and Oliver disappears off screen between her legs and later she knocks over a pot of white paint in a fairly obvious piece of symbolism. The Catholic Legion of Decency in America, which at the time held some sway, decided this was the first time cunnilingus had ever been seen on the screen and banned the film. This didn't make a great deal of difference because the Legion of Decency had very little pulling power.

The film still plays on television and is released, as many of my films are now, on special Director's Edition DVDs where the director talks through the film telling stories of what happened during the shooting. As a result of these two Universal films, *The Jokers* and *I'll Never Forget What's'isname*, and the enormous critical success of *The System*, released in America titled *The Girl-Getters*, the leading studio owner in Los Angeles, Lew Wasserman of Universal, decided to give me the studio's major project for 1968. Intending to echo the success of *Spartacus* where they took a young director, Stanley Kubrick, who led them to glory, Universal had an excellent script for *William the Conqueror*. It was an incredible story of the love-hate relationship between Harold, King of England, and the bastard, William of Normandy. Oliver Reed would play William and we were testing newcomers for Harold. Because of that picture I turned down *The Prime of Miss Jean Brodie*, which I now regret. Particularly as *William the Conqueror* never got made! The budget kept spiralling and the picture was cancelled. Even though they paid me for two years every week as if I was making it!

I'd already got into the Rolls-Royce league with a marvellous grey-green Silver Cloud III. I later sold it to Oliver Reed who was promptly sick all over it. It didn't last long as a thing of beauty! We were driving back from Hastings on a reconnaissance for the never-made *William the Conqueror*. My chauffeur and my Associate

Producer were in the front. I was in the back with the film's Producer. As we sped home along the motorway there was an enormous crashing sound. The car veered and, mercifully, came to a stop. I looked around. There were feathers floating all over the place. The front window was completely smashed. On the ledge behind the back seats was a very large and very dead pheasant! It had come through the windscreen, miraculously missing both the two people sitting in the front and me and my Producer at the back! The glass had shaved off a lot of feathers, which wafted gently to the pile carpets and the leather seats. An incredible escape, but not for the pheasant.

In 1968 the American companies, who'd opened up offices in London, were counting their losses and pulling the executives back to California. Jay Kanter, who'd supported me at Universal Pictures, was one of those to leave. I think, other than *The Jokers*, he'd not made a money-making picture during his four years in charge. If I'd learned one thing in the movie business, it was not to wait for people to employ you. Have your own scripts available to put forward. I had ready a very different type of film for me. A film that was to lead me into a completely new career as an action director.

13

Alpine Elephant

I'd been sent a story by Tom Wright, a house painter from Norwich. He'd been a prisoner of war in Munich during the Second World War working in the zoo with elephants. He constructed a tale about a man who escaped over the Alps to Switzerland with an elephant. I wrote it into a full-length treatment and gave it to Dick Clement and Ian La Frenais who'd written *The Jokers*. We went to Austria to look at locations. Two years earlier when I'd worked with Clement and La Frenais, they wore tweed sports jackets. They looked like they'd just come from the provinces. Now they were dressed in full late sixties gear: velvet jackets, ruffs, frilly shirts. At a small hotel in Bludenz the wine was poured. Ian La Frenais wafted the scent of the wine towards him and said to Dick Clement, 'Smell the aroma, Dick.' I thought, 'I'm in trouble!' And I was. The script had none of the panache of their work on *The Jokers*. Even their agent agreed they should do additional re-writing, which, mercifully, they did. It took only a few seconds for my agent Irving Lazar to transfer me from the sponsorship of Universal Pictures to United Artists, another important American movie company. I went to see their Head of Production, David Picker, in the Dorchester Hotel. He agreed to make *Hannibal*

Brooks as long as we had Oliver Reed. We discussed the budget. Picker said to me, 'Why have we got this 10 per cent contingency in for the elephant?' I said, 'Because nobody since Hannibal has taken an elephant over the Alps. Things will come up I can't reasonably budget for.' Picker said, 'If you take the 10 per cent contingency out of the budget we'll approve it and do the movie.' I said, 'Fine, David. The elephant contingency is out. But don't you think somebody should tell the elephant?!'

Hannibal Brooks was a big action film. I'd no idea how action films were made. The scenes included a train coming off the rails and crashing down a ravine into a river. German convoys were blown up. People were set on fire. People were shooting to and fro. In one scene the elephant pushed an enormous pile of logs down a hill, killing SS troops advancing up it. They in turn rolled down the mountainside under the logs. A watchtower with troops on it collapsed into a ravine when the elephant pulled a rope attached to one of its struts. I now know it would have been normal to take a Stunt Co-ordinator, together with a team of at least twenty stunt men. But I didn't know that then. I'd only had one stunt in a movie, on *You Must Be Joking*, where one of the actors had to fall off the Lutine Bell stand at Lloyds. For that we had used a pleasant, but dopey, cockney stuntman who when you said, 'Jump!' jumped without much thought or preparation for where he'd land. He was my only nod towards the army of people I should have had on the movie. For the role of the fearsome American guerrilla fighter I cast, out of type, the dwarf-like, fey American actor Michael J. Pollard who'd been nominated for an Academy Award for *Bonnie and Clyde*. Most of the other parts were for Germans. Pollard was a very 'in' name. He and Oliver Reed satisfied United Artists. I set up an office in Munich and another office in the Vorarlberg area of Austria. We scouted locations in the snow for scenes we'd film in spring and summer. I learned elephants are herd animals. You can't travel with one, you have to take two. The elephants weighed two and a half tons each. We took five tons of elephant plus an enormous amount of feed, plus great tents for them, often along tiny little roads with narrow and insecure bridges. The bridges were either too weak to go over or too low to go underneath. It was a major exercise.

I was by now producing my own movies. So I was in charge of all the physical side of it as well as the directing. This was a good thing because there's nearly always conflict between director and producer. Nowadays it's quite common for the director to produce as well. It was my fourth film with Oliver Reed.

Oliver was nothing like the caricature that has been presented in the press and which he often presented to the public. Oliver was not against drinking. But he was very professional on the set. In all six pictures I did with him he never missed a second of work through being drunk. He'd become one of my dearest friends. I didn't see him much in the evening because he drank in the evening and I found that boring. But when sober, Olly was the quietest, most gentle, well-spoken and gentlemanly person you could meet. Once Oliver Reed came back from the Albert Hall where he'd met the wonderful Welsh actor Stanley Baker, who was also not frightened of a tipple. Oliver said in a very quiet voice, 'You know, Michael, I met Stanley Baker. He was terribly noisy. It was embarrassing.' In view of the reputation Oliver rightly acquired for being noisy and drunk that was an odd remark! It showed Oliver's Jekyll and Hyde character. Oliver and I sat together on film sets all over the world. We'd discuss girls, we'd take heavy cash bets on the dates of when books were published, we spent hours together. You could only respect and admire Olly the more you got to know him.

It was many years later, when Oliver was more or less unemploy-able because everyone thought he was an alcoholic and he'd pranced around rather a lot, that I employed him on *Parting Shots*. It was that employment which alerted people in the industry to the fact that he was still around and that he must be all right to work with because, if Michael Winner would take him, then Oliver Reed was 'safe'. One day Oliver said to me, 'Ridley Scott wants me to go and read for him for a part in *Gladiator*. I can't audition, I'm a star.' I said, 'Oliver, read for Ridley Scott. You need a last act of your life. You need the money. You need the prestige.' So Oliver went and read for Ridley Scott and got the part. Sadly, he died on that film. It reminded me of a time on *Hannibal Brooks* when we were shooting in the mountains above Innsbruck. It was very misty and the crew could do nothing because cloud enveloped the mountain. There was this enormous convoy of trucks and caravans with nobody working. I walked around keeping everybody cheerful. As I walked from truck to truck I heard on the radios about the assassination of Bobby Kennedy. Oliver had again asked my advice during that film, too, 'There's a man called Ken Russell coming. He wants me to do television. I don't want to do television, Michael. You've turned me into a movie star. I'm going to tell him I can't do it.' I said, 'I've seen some of Ken Russell's work. He's immensely talented. I don't think it would hurt to do television with him. I recommend you do it.' I've no doubt it was those words that turned Oliver from rejecting his association with Ken Russell to accepting it.

Oliver had a marvellous quiet and supportive side. He was immensely loyal. One day on *The Jokers* Michael Crawford had been particularly difficult. He's a wonderful actor, Michael, and I'm very fond of him. But he has flashes of dreadful temper. On this day he'd been chastising me! At nine-thirty that night the doorbell rang and it was Oliver Reed. He said, 'I've just come round, Michael, to tell you that I support you completely. That you behaved very well today when Michael Crawford was abusing you. I'm completely on your side and I love you.' And then he went away.

Many years later two Granada executives producing *This Is Your Life* came to me. They said, '*This Is Your Life* is normally recorded in advance but we've decided to do a live one with Oliver Reed.' I said, 'Obviously you wish to leave Granada. You have another job to go to.' They said, 'We're told by Oliver's family that the person he most respects in the world is you. If we tell him he's going to be on your *This Is Your Life*, Oliver will keep sober. So if you'll meet him in the lobby of the Adelphi Theatre, we'll then reveal that it's his *This Is Your Life* and we'll all be all right.' I said, 'It's very generous of Olly's family to have this great faith in me. You've got at best a 50/50 chance.' They got Michael J. Pollard over from America and had him on an elephant ready to ride in. They had friends and family assembled in the Adelphi Theatre. I'd read in the newspapers that TV electricians were causing lightning strikes on Granada Television. I rang the producer and said, 'Look, if any programme's going to be struck, it's you. Don't ask me to come in until forty-five minutes before you need me.' Sadly, I was right. An hour before the programme was due to start, they rang me and said, 'The electricians are on strike!' They did Oliver Reed's *This Is Your Life* later. They took the wise precaution of recording it. I did my tribute from a beach in Barbados. Oliver in the studio gave me a wave and said in a funny voice, 'Hello, my dear!' He did it with great affection. I could see he was very moved by what I said.

When he died I was the only person from show business at Oliver Reed's funeral. All the friends, who supposedly loved him, some of whom had just worked with him on *Gladiator*, failed to turn up. I sat in the church in Mallow, near Cork. I looked down the aisle and there was the coffin. Lying in that wooden box was my friend. I didn't cry at my mother's funeral or my father's funeral. But I walked down the aisle and stood in front of Oliver's coffin. I touched the coffin to say farewell and when I turned to walk back, tears were streaming down my face. It was a wonderful funeral because Oliver had all his friends there, including his first wife Kate, a lady called Jacqui Darrell with whom he had a daughter, and his last wife, Josephine, who he'd met when she was sixteen and he took her from school to Barbados. Josephine turned out to be the most wonderful influence for him. She looked after him marvellously. The last time I saw Oliver Reed was when he came to the funeral of his agent Denis Selinger and I said, 'Oliver, as you're in London, would you come and re-record a couple of lines for me in my house? They're slightly unclear in *Parting Shots* because of an air-conditioning unit nearby.' The next morning I rang the hotel where he was staying in Hampstead. The hotel manager said, 'Oliver was arrested in Hampstead High Street at midnight.' I rang the police station and said, 'I believe you have my friend Oliver Reed there. I'd appreciate it if you'd let him go because I need him to do some sound recording.' The policeman said, 'He's just left, Mr Winner. We locked him up for the night for his own good.' A very chastened Oliver Reed came to see me. His voice was now far too rough so the recording was useless. He said with a sigh, 'I mustn't travel without Josephine, Michael. I need her so much to look after me.'

I had a Western script based on the Johnson County War. Later another version was made by Michael Cimino and called *Heaven's Gate*. But in 1973 my script was the hottest script and I was the hotter director. Steve McQueen had my script and was very keen on it. I met Steve in the offices of Jay Kanter, now President of First Artists, a company jointly owned by McQueen, Barbra Streisand and other stars. Steve McQueen looked at me coldly and said, 'You're a friend of Oliver Reed, aren't you?' I said, 'That's right.' He said, 'I was asked to come to London to meet Oliver Reed by my agents. They wanted him to co-star in one of my movies. We went to Tramp discotheque. Oliver Reed got drunk. He was sick all over me.' I said, 'I'm sorry about that, Steve. But it really wasn't my fault.' McQueen went on as if I hadn't spoken. He fixed me with those piercing blue eyes. 'They got me some new jeans to wear but they couldn't find shoes. So I had to go round for the rest of the evening smelling of Oliver Reed's sick.' Needless to say, Oliver didn't get the part with Steve. Just as he didn't get other parts because of his drinking. He also turned down many parts in America because he was terribly shy and wouldn't go anywhere he felt insecure.

When we were shooting *Hannibal Brooks*, Michael J. Pollard was massively into drugs and pills. He later went to both Alcoholics Anonymous and Drugs Anonymous. Drugs were being brought in from suppliers all over the place. In one scene we panned along a German convoy on the road below which had gone over landmines. The convoy is blowing up and people are running burning from the vehicles. Michael J. Pollard's guerrillas are shooting them with machine guns. We go along this line of guerrillas on top of the hill; the last one is Michael J. Pollard. He has to wave them forward and say, 'Come on fellows, let's go.' And they run off down the hill. The first time we shot this, we panned along everybody and everything was blowing up perfectly. When we got to Michael J. Pollard, who was stoned, he waved his hands in the wrong direction, and told everyone, 'Back up, fellows!' That shot took three hours to re-stage! I said, 'Michael, you're meant to lead them down the hill.' Then I said, 'Michael, you know I'm very fond of you and you're a wonderful actor but you have to straighten yourself out. You have a great future ahead. You've been nominated for an Academy Award in one of the most important pictures of last year. Why is it you have to keep taking drugs and keep taking pills? There's no reason for that.' Michael J. Pollard looked at me and said, 'You don't share a hotel with Oliver Reed.' I said, 'Michael, you just won the argument.'

Oliver at night was absolutely nuts, bless him. Nearly every day we'd have to move his hotel because he'd pissed on the Austrian flag, or thrown flour over the guests, or run amok through the dining room. I made sure my hotel was at least ten miles from Oliver's. That didn't mean he was not a marvellous person. Oliver had a terrific life, he enjoyed himself. He finally went to rest in Ireland. As Oliver's coffin was driven from the church to a field at the back of a pub in his local village where he was to be buried, Irish people were lining the roadside. It was like a mini version of Princess Diana's coffin going through London. As we passed through the villages all the people crossed themselves. It was very, very moving to see the affection in which Oliver Reed was held. We got to the field at the back of the pub. A lovely, quiet spot where he was to be buried. His first wife, Kate, still looked absolutely beautiful. She was Irish with red hair. As everyone was admiring the peace and beauty of this little field and the fields beyond it and the tall trees, Kate said, 'What a place to be buried. Look at this rubbish! It's full of shit, it's full of flies. I can't wait to get out of this bloody field.' Oliver would have enjoyed that. I can see him now sitting with me and saying in his very quiet gentlemanly voice, 'Did she really say that, Michael? She always had a wonderful sense of humour, Kate. God bless her.'

Before we started *Hannibal Brooks* Oliver said, 'I want to sleep with the elephant for three nights. I've got to get to know the elephant.' One thing you learn on movies is: leave animals to the trainer. The trainer has been with the animal for years. He knows how to handle it. The animal cannot have two masters. I said, 'Oliver, the elephant won't give a fuck that you're sleeping with him.' Oliver slept with the elephant anyway. Elephants are not sweet animals. This elephant spent the entire film trying to kill Oliver. If they were walking along a narrow mountain path with a two thousand-feet drop one side and a hard rock face on the other, the elephant would try to squash Oliver against the rock. Or flip him with his heavy tail. We shot in the Munich Zoo. One week after we left, one of the zoo elephants we'd had in our movie curled his trunk around a child's arm as he was holding out a bun, carried it in the air over the moat that protected the public from the elephants, stamped on the child and killed it. For our two elephants the trainer had what looked like a bamboo pole with a hook which he looped on to the elephant's ear. In fact it was a metal pole with a hook and that guided the elephant where to go. If the elephant misbehaved he slapped it in its face with the metal pole, which may or may not have been cruel, but it was necessary in order to keep the rest of us alive. In the scene where the convoy was blown up Oliver Reed appears with the elephant. With about sixty Austrians playing German soldiers lying down as corpses, the elephant suddenly went berserk! It threw its trunk in the air and started galloping down the road. This sight I shall never forget. I watched in terror! A large Indian elephant rushing down a road with the trainer running after it trying to hit it on the head with an iron bar to stop it. And with sixty Austrians lying there! How they were not trampled to death I'll never know!

Another incident was even more frightening. Michael J. Pollard was at the top of a thousand-foot drop. Oliver's character had fallen down a mountainside. He was at the bottom and Michael J. Pollard throws him down a grappling iron on the end of a rope and shouts, 'Coming down!' We had two cameras, which were supported by ropes in the rock underneath him, looking up at Pollard. Michael was stoned. When I shouted 'Action!', he said, 'Coming down!' and threw the heavy grappling iron! But he forgot to let go! So Michael went over the cliff with the grappling iron. In split seconds, I was writing out the insurance report and preparing the press release about how Michael J. Pollard had died. By an absolute miracle the rope holding up the two cameramen went between Michael's legs! So we now had Michael J. Pollard half against the rock with the rope between his legs. The two cameramen were on the same rope. I could see the struts put into the mountainside holding the rope were beginning to come loose. We were going to lose our star and two cameramen. It was like some movie where the heroine is about to be run over by the train or the building is about to collapse. We were saved by our local Austrian mountaineers. They leaped down the mountain on the end of ropes held by their friends up above and got everybody to safety. Michael J. Pollard dusted himself down, looked around and said, 'Hey, man, that was some trip.' I don't think he knew where he'd been.

What saved me from my lack of knowledge about stunt organisation was the extraordinarily competitive spirit and bravery of the Austrian people who lived in the mountain villages where we were filming. This was 1968 and there wasn't much tourist development. We'd get the villagers of Schrocken determined to do better than the villagers of Igel and the villages of this place determined to do better than the villagers of another place. They'd dress up in the SS uniforms or German soldier uniforms, and I'd say, 'Now you six people are going to roll down this hill and these very large balsa wood logs are going to roll on top of you.' They'd love it. They didn't have any padding on as stuntmen would have done. They didn't prepare themselves as movie stuntmen would have done. They just did it. They were prepared to let you set them on fire, to jump off trees – they'd do anything! Although I found it a bit unsettling seeing the look of awe on their faces when our actors playing German generals and SS officers came up in their staff cars with the Nazi swastika flag flying. The Austrians would look at them as if demi-gods had arrived. At the end of the day's shooting the Austrian villagers would hold up our Nazi flags so they could be photographed in front of the swastika.

There was a bad-taste remark I made on this film which became legendary. I'd fly on Saturday afternoon to England to see the rushes and fly back to Austria on Sunday which was a day off. When I came back after one of these trips, my English Production Manager said, 'A terrible thing happened. While you were away our English stuntman was practising driving the German vehicle he has to drive into a tree on Tuesday. He went through a crowd of Germans and hit a nineteen-year-old boy. He's in the hospital with a broken collar-bone and a broken leg.' I said, 'That's one back for the six million.' This remark was reported in the London *Evening News*. I thought I'd be banned from right-thinking society. I got letters of congratulation.

Another funny remark on *Hannibal Brooks* was a unit story. Two of the German actors, Hans and Willi, were in the bar after shooting. Hans said to Willi, 'You know, Willi, I've been on this movie four weeks and Michael Winner spoke to me for the first time today.' Willi said, 'Really, Hans, Michael Winner spoke to you! What did he say?' Hans replied, 'He said, "Come here you fucking arsehole!"'

It was an incredible experience going with this enormous crew around Austria and Germany making *Hannibal Brooks*. There was the most beautiful scenery, the most wonderful people, the most lovely old Austrian villages with churches with onion-shaped domes and housewives giving me freshly baked apple strudel. There were fifteen action sequences that today would have cost hundreds of thousands of pounds each. All were done, unintentionally, on a shoestring.

The film, when released, went to Number One on the Variety Box Office chart. The film received a U Certificate in 1968. It was passed by the British Film Censor as suitable for a family audience, for children of any age to see. For twenty years *Hannibal Brooks* played on British television during family-viewing hours uncut. About fifteen years ago I was watching the film on television one afternoon and I saw about ten cuts in it. It's absolutely amazing that censorship had increased so much that a family film had been cut when it was harmless! It just shows how very censorious the British authorities have become since 1968. 'The film has a disarming desire to please. To me there's always been something basically self-serving in such stories about the interdependence of man and beast. Everyone plays it well and honestly,' said Vincent Canby in *The New York Times*. In the London *Sunday Telegraph* Margaret Hinxman wrote, 'A sly whimsical send up of the cherished conventions of the action war movie, *Hannibal Brooks* is an engaging entertainment, surely the best, most confident film Michael Winner has ever made, which isn't an idle compliment.' In the London *Daily Mail*, Cecil Wilson wrote, 'You should enjoy every minute of it. The film begins as whimsical comedy of man's humanity to animal but changes swiftly and violently to a grim drama of man's inhumanity to man.'

Just after *Hannibal Brooks* the legendary James Bond movie producer, Harry Saltzman, told me he was selling his Rolls-Royce Phantom V, one of those enormous black things the Queen drives around in. Harry was selling it because the Phantom VI had come out; it looked exactly the same but he wanted the latest car. He sold the V to me for £8,300! When they stopped making it a few years ago it was worth £350,000! I still have this car and it's in wonderful condition. There was a problem, though, buying it from Harry. On each of the four doors he had his initials HS embossed in gold. I either had to change my name or have the car re-sprayed. At this time I had a wonderful cockney chauffeur called Dave. Dave assured me he knew the perfect place to bring the car to and he would personally put a pencil mark each time they re-sprayed it to make sure they covered the pencil mark. 'They re-spray Rollses eight times,' he explained. When the car returned I called Dave over. 'What can you see if you stand here?' I asked. Dave said, 'I can see HS, sir, embossed under the black.' The garage hadn't even bothered to scrape off the HS! Although I'm sure they gave Dave a good commission. It all had to be done again.

Dave was a considerable character. He drove this enormous stately car telling me proudly, 'I have my hands on the ten-to-three position, sir, do you notice?' At his initial interview he said, 'I drive with dignity.' This meant that any time anyone pulled out even fifty yards ahead he would scream, 'You fucking arsehole, prick, cunt!' at the top of his voice. Eventually I said, 'Dave, you know it's very distracting to the passengers in the back to hear this terrible language you're screaming out all the time.' He said, 'You mean to say you can hear it through the glass division of the Rolls-Royce, sir? Those divisions are not what they ought to be.' Dave had another interesting habit. He'd sell goods from the back of my Rolls which I think, to use the vernacular, had fallen off the back of a lorry. Thus he said to me one day when I had the car radio stolen, 'Never mind that, sir, I'd four televisions taken from the boot.' My friend the film director, Lewis Gilbert, came up to me one day and said, 'My watch isn't waterproof.' I said, 'So what, Lewis? Nothing to do with me.' Lewis said, 'I bought it from your chauffeur.' We once had an accountant on a movie with a very high-pitched voice who wanted some carpet. Dave got him some. The accountant said, 'That wasn't the colour I wanted. I wanted light green and you've given me blue.' Dave said, 'You can't choose the colour, sir. They nick what's nearest the door.'

On another occasion I received a letter from the solicitor of a titled lady saying that my Rolls had pursued her down Mount Street and crashed into her on the corner of South Audley Street in Mayfair because the chauffeur didn't like her and was screaming abuse at her.

Dave said, 'Don't worry, sir, I'll deal with it.' I said, 'Dave, you'll be in prison.' He said, 'Never mind sir. I could do with a rest.' He was later in court and I asked him what happened. Apparently the corner of South Audley Street and Mount Street had been full of cockney people with similar voices to Dave, all of whom swore blind the woman ran into the back of him. Dave would keep my Rolls in his garage in Mayfair where he had a council flat and a garage with it. He kept telling me how much the garage was costing him, which couldn't have been much as it was a council flat, so I said, 'Dave, let's put the car in a proper garage. Don't worry yourself, please.' Dave found a garage in the Marriott Hotel off Grosvenor Square and said, 'I'm placing it in the Marriott Hotel garage, sir.' And I duly paid the Marriott Hotel each month for parking this large Rolls.

One weekend I desperately needed cigars. I knew I had a box of Havanas in the back of the Rolls. I telephoned the Marriott Hotel garage and said, 'Excuse me, you have my Rolls-Royce NAN 509D in the garage. I'm coming to it to get some cigars.' The garage attendant said, 'We've never seen a car like that, sir. We don't have a Phantom V Rolls and we don't know your car at all.' I said indignantly, 'I've been paying rent for six months for this car. It must be in your garage.' The garage attendant said, 'Well, it isn't.' When Dave came in on Monday morning I said, 'Dave, where do we keep the Rolls-Royce?' He said, 'In the Marriott Hotel garage, sir.' I said, 'Are you sure?' He said, 'Yes, sir, before I put it in the garage I went down, examined the garage myself and it's a perfect place for it.' I said, 'Well, Dave, I phoned them at the weekend and they've never seen the car and I've been paying for the garage space for six months. So how could the car possibly be there?' Dave said, 'It's not there, sir. It's in my garage where it's always been.' I said, 'Then, why am I paying the Marriott Hotel garage?' Dave said, 'I tried to get the car down there but when I went down the ramp the car was too big to turn the bend, so I just put it in my garage again.' Dave eventually left my employ and went on to work for a judge.

14

Games Directors Play

Michael Crawford got a multi-picture contract with Twentieth Century-Fox as a result of his success in *The Jokers*. He starred in *Hello Dolly* for them. In their movie, *The Games*, he would be an English milkman who becomes a marathon runner and competes at the Olympics. The script was from a best-selling book by Australian writer Hugh Atkinson, scripted by Erich Segal, who later wrote the book and script of *Love Story*. Michael sent it to me and hoped I'd direct it. The scene headings read 'Exterior London', 'Exterior Prague', 'Exterior Tokyo', 'Exterior the United States of America', 'Exterior Sydney Australia', 'Exterior Rome' and so on. That was nice! I also looked forward to working with Michael again. The script was exciting. The Producer was Lester Linsk. His main claim to fame was that he played tennis with Richard Zanuck, the head of Twentieth Century-Fox. He knew nothing about film production. So although I was billed as the Director it was left to me to organise the movie. The film followed the fortunes of four people from different countries who end up in the Olympic marathon in Rome. It was typical of a strain of Twentieth Century-Fox pictures that had been made over the years, following a group of people. Like *Three Coins in the Fountain*, where three American girls go to Rome, chuck coins in the Trevi Fountain, and we find out what happened to them.

The Games was a monster of a movie. It called for enormous crowd scenes. The Rome Olympic stadium and others had to be filled with people. Today this can be done digitally, using very few people. In 1969 what you saw was what you got. I decided to fill the Rome stadium with seventy-five thousand plastic people! It was a daring move to manufacture seventy-five thousand plastic dummies cast in groups of twelve with people in slightly different positions. I'd place real people among them to give movement. And put different bits of clothing on dummies that were in shot! As many as five thousand at a time. It was an enormous enterprise. To say nothing of closing streets all over the world for the marathon to run through. Twentieth Century-Fox were in panic about my plastic people. Lester Linsk phoned me continually saying, 'I can't sleep at night, Michael, worrying about it. Will it work?' I replied, 'It's never been done before, Lester. But I don't see why it shouldn't!'

The marathon had been set in Rome because Twentieth Century-Fox believed there would be masses of library footage of the Olympic Games held there a few years previously. We'd use that as the basis for much of our film. The shots would have been quite useless. Anyway, they were lost! So we did everything from scratch. Michael Crawford threw himself into the venture with pro-fessionalism and angst. He was running all over the place, although he never gave up smoking fifty cigarettes a day! We employed various top athletes as advisers including Olympic runner Gordon Pirie. The set was full of ageing Olympic runners. In the lunch hour we'd race them against each other and take bets on the result. Michael Crawford's maniacal Welsh coach was Stanley Baker who Michael had wanted in *The Jokers* as his brother. Ryan O'Neal was given to us by the studio as the American student runner, which was fine. He was a reasonable actor and had enjoyed great success in the TV series *Peyton Place*. For an ageing Czech athlete I chose singer Charles Aznavour. This concerned Richard Zanuck, who ran round Beverly Hills every morning. 'Have you seen Charles Aznavour's legs?' he kept asking. 'He's got to have strong legs.' I rang Aznavour and said, 'Charlie, if you want the part in this movie you're going to have to show us your legs.' Aznavour sent a photo of himself in his underpants standing on the bottom of a baronial staircase in his French home. He had sturdy legs! He got the part. We needed an aborigine. That was more difficult. There were no regular aboriginal actors and I didn't have time to go to Australia and conduct a search. There was one aboriginal, Athol Compton, who'd been briefly in a TV series in Australia. He was a postman. I reckoned that if he could walk round Sydney delivering letters all day he'd be fit enough to look like an athlete. He came to London and was screen tested. Thankfully he was good. He was a delightful young man and a great credit to the aboriginal people. Ryan O'Neal was another sports-mad American who ran all the time in Los Angeles. The odd man out was Charles Aznavour who never ran at all. It was a miracle he lasted the movie!

The film was budgeted at five million dollars. An enormous sum for 1970. In order to save money we arranged to shoot the very few American sequences in England as they were mainly on sports grounds and in apartments. We would go everywhere else, with the exception of Czechoslovakia, which we couldn't get into because it was behind the Iron Curtain. So we sent a second unit to Prague and shot the Czech scenes in Vienna. We had to shoot the Olympic marathon in February and March. It was meant to be the boiling heat of summer! Luckily in Rome there are lots of evergreens. The city authorities were not overjoyed at our request to close all the main Rome tourist centres including the Trevi Fountain, the Piazza Navona and the Forum, where our marathon race started. My English Location Manager in Rome, Timothy Pitt-Miller, was told by his Italian counterpart that if we wanted to close the streets twenty thousand US dollars in a suitcase would have to be given to a city official. This is not unusual in motion pictures. It's a reliable way to get results! So Pitt-Miller wandered around Rome with a suitcase full of dollar bills. Thus all the streets were closed. They even gave us a very decorative group of soldiers to line the route. Some time after we left Rome our 'helper' was arrested for taking bribes. Not ours!

Ryan O'Neal said one day, 'You know, Michael, the Olympic Games are on television and they're 98 in the top 100 most popular programmes. We're spending five million dollars making an Olympic movie. If they're not watching it free on TV, why should they pay to see it in the cinema?' In those days, track events and the Olympic Games didn't inspire the interest they do now. I was in Beverly Hills at the Twentieth Century-Fox studio sitting in Lester Linsk's office when a small aeroplane crashed into the building, strewing the pilot and the plane all over the front of the studio. Everyone thought they'd been bombed. That was my first meeting with Jack Palance whom I was later to employ. We looked at this gruesome sight together, then carried on with our business. I said to Richard Zanuck, 'We're spending a fortune on this movie. The Olympic Games are 98 out of the top 100 programmes on television. Do you really think anyone will see it?' After a second Zanuck said in a querulous voice, 'Are you quitting?' I said, 'No, I'm not quitting, Richard. I'll make this film in colour, black and white, on 8mm, whatever you say. I thought it worth mentioning.' Zanuck drew breath and came back with a classic movie line, 'It's too late now.' Which meant if he cancelled the film after we'd spent a fortune setting it up, the finger would point directly at him. If the film was made, went out and failed, there were a large number of people whom the finger could be pointed at. The principal one being me! Behind Richard Zanuck's desk was an enormous star with a picture of Julie Andrews in the middle which was about to be taken to Hollywood Boulevard where Zanuck was to put his hands in concrete to be remembered forever. Julie Andrews was pictured because he'd just released a very expensive musical with her called *Star*. 'I'm going down to put my hands in cement in Hollywood Boulevard,' he said. 'When they see the grosses of *Star*, they'll fill them in!'

Michael Crawford became convinced he was one of the great runners of history. He announced to the press that he'd run the mile in four minutes and twenty seconds. The all-time record was then four minutes and six seconds. My publicity man said, 'All our professional runners say we can't possibly tell the press Michael Crawford ran the mile in four minutes twenty seconds. It's absolutely impossible for someone who's only just started running!' I said, 'I don't care if he says he ran it in a minute and a half. It's him saying it, not me.' The statement was issued. Nobody queried it.

We started shooting in Rome on 8th February 1969. It's diverting to have a whole city at your command with thousands of extras and runners and support vehicles and flags flying and all the rest of it. We employed about two thousand extras a day, from one of the Italian extras supply groups. The weather was extremely cold. Extras would gather in their coats, hats and umbrellas and take them off just before we shot. Thus Rafer Johnson, an Olympic runner now working as a commentator, could say, 'It's boiling hot here in the Eternal City. The runners are finding the going very difficult because of the heat.'

There were other Roman extras organisations we were not using. One hit on the clever device of having their members stand among our crowd in public streets wearing fur coats and raincoats and holding up umbrellas. So I'd look at a beautifully cleared roadway with our people all looking as if it was midsummer and there'd be people spoiling the shot with overcoats with umbrellas. For a while the Assistant Directors and our extra group had fist fights and carried these protesters away. One day our runners were to cross the Angers Bridge when two hundred members of this guerrilla extras group sat down on the roadway blocking our runners! They said, 'We'd like to negotiate a deal for our group to be in the movie.' They were holding up the entire production. They were in a strong position. A negotiation took place on the bridge at 8 a.m. I had to agree to employ a number of them each day. I couldn't reduce the group I had because they'd have gone on strike. We now had another four hundred extras at substantial cost. To add insult to injury two hours later one of the guerrilla extras group said, 'Mr Winner, would you please sign this photograph of yourself. We want to put it up in our office!'

Although we had permission to block a number of streets we had great difficulty with cross streets running either side of the River Tiber. When we were ready to shoot I'd ask the English Assistant Directors to link arms across the road and stop traffic from hitting our runners. An assistant came on the walkie-talkie. 'We're linking arms across the road but the police are coming to arrest us.' I said, 'Hold firm, ignore them!' I shouted 'Action!' Our runners started off across the bridge. On my walkie-talkie I could hear the Assistant Director. 'I'm with the police now. I'm trying to argue with them but they're grabbing me, they've taken me, they're carrying me away, they're putting me in a police van . . .!' There was a click as he was cut off! But we made the shot!

Michael Crawford tells a story, doing a marvellous impersonation of me, directing in Rome when Michael was leading the race. The only thing in front of him were two open jeep escort vehicles with Olympic officials in them. We came to the end of the run and Michael Crawford said to me, 'That man in the jeep is driving much too slowly. I couldn't run properly!' So I went over to the man in the jeep – well, this is how Michael tells the story – and said, 'Listen here you fucking arsehole, how dare you drive slowly and stop the entire procession of runners?! You are a total moron arsehole. This is ridiculous of you. Now stop being a fucking arsehole and drive faster.' At which point Michael pulled at my sleeve and said, 'It wasn't that driver who was driving too slowly, it was the other one!' He pointed to the second driver. I said to the first driver, 'You're not an arsehole!' I turned to the other driver, '*You* are an arsehole!' And then gave him the speech.

During the shooting in Rome Michael Crawford decided there should be a race between our four actors who were playing marathon runners: himself, Ryan O'Neal, Athol Compton and Charles Aznavour. This would be on a track built by Mussolini with lovely statues around it. There was no point in Aznavour competing. But Michael was very keen to show he could beat Ryan O'Neal and Athol Compton. Since he was still on fifty cigarettes a day and had only recently started running, whereas the other two didn't smoke at all and were far better athletes, I didn't think Michael stood a chance. We arranged to have the race one Sunday on our day off. Ryan O'Neal was delighted. He was not happy that Michael seemed to be getting better treatment. He assured me he'd win. Michael obviously realised a few days before that he wasn't going to succeed. He suddenly decided he'd sprained his ankle and couldn't do it.

Michael Crawford and Stanley Baker shared a villa on the Appian Way to save on their expenses allowance. My driver said to me, 'That house is run by crooks. It's always robbed. They have their own people there as house staff.' I told this to Stanley Baker who was the most adorable man. He pooh-poohed the whole thing because he thought he was kind of 'in' with the mob himself.

Needless to say, the house was robbed and everything was taken from Stanley and Michael, including their passports. Stanley was known as a very tough and abrasive person, but like most people with that reputation, he was absolutely wonderful. He wore a wig. At the London premiere of *The Games* Stanley came over looking very elegant in evening dress and said, 'What do you think, Michael?' I said, 'About what?' Stanley said, 'Can't you see?' I said, 'See what?' He said, 'My wig, I've got a new wig. Do you like it?' I thought that was a wonderful remark from a tough man who was meant to be difficult.

During the course of the movie a lot of celebrities came to see us, including Julie Christie and Henry Cooper. Henry was fighting an Italian. Sean Connery was also in Rome. So Sean, Stanley Baker, Michael Crawford and I went to see Henry Cooper fight. We sat in the front row. When the Italians are not happy they throw miniature bottles of liquor, which are on sale in the stadium, hoping to get them into the ring. They normally miss and hit people in the front row! I was sitting with two of the toughest guys in English movies, Sean Connery and Stanley Baker, when Henry Cooper hit the Italian fighter a perfectly fair blow above the belt. The Italian put up a wonderful sham that he'd been hit below the belt and started doubling up and wheezing. At that point bottles whizzed through the air! 'Get under the seats!' said Sean Connery in wonderfully efficient James Bond fashion. We dived under the seats as bottles broke on the chairs above us. Eventually order was restored and the fight recommenced. I thought it funny, hiding under the seats with the tough guys!

There was a similar incident involving me and Sean in New York years later. Sean was making a movie and we arranged to have dinner at the Plaza Hotel where I was staying. When we went to the dining room they wouldn't let Sean in because he didn't have a jacket. Sean's hotel was half a mile up the road. I said, 'Don't worry, Sean, come to my room. I'll give you one of my jackets.' When we got to my room I said, 'I've forgotten the key. I'll go down and get it.' Sean said, 'Don't bother.' He stood back from the door, raised his leg and kicked the door in. It was like James Bond in super-action! I got Sean my jacket and we had dinner. After dinner, I rang Sean and said, 'I just want you to know I'm on my hands and knees picking up bits of door and paint and flushing them down the toilet so the management won't notice!'

My seventy-five thousand dummies in the Rome Olympic stadium were a triumph! It was bizarre going in at seven o'clock in the morning and seeing it apparently full of people. When we put the crowd among them you couldn't tell. Even in the still photography they looked real. Filming moved to England. On 8th April 1969 we were shooting at the Walton-on-Thames Sports Ground as a facsimile for a running track at Yale University. An emissary came from the production office holding an envelope. This missive was from a senior official at the International Olympic Committee headquarters in Geneva. It said, 'We understand you are making a film about the Olympic Games. We are sure you know the Olympic Games and the Olympic emblem are a registered trademark in 85 countries throughout the world. We have given no permission for the use of the words 'Olympic Games' or the use of the Olympic rings in your motion picture. If you require permission please send us the script so we can consider our position.'

'That's jolly!' I thought. 'We've been filming for six weeks. We have Olympic flags and Olympic emblems all over the place. Furthermore, the film is about the Olympic Games whether it's a registered trademark or not.' Because of my Cambridge University legal training (often very valuable!) I'd written carefully worded letters to the Olympic Committee in Rome who had supplied us not only with their own offices but also with Olympic flags and Olympic emblems which we'd used. We also had a signed agreement with the Olympic Committee in Australia, the next place we were due to visit. Olympic emblems and flags supplied by the Olympic Committee in Australia were now on all our sets awaiting my arrival. The letter produced panic among Twentieth Century-Fox lawyers. They said, 'You'll have to matte out [a very expensive technical process] every Olympic emblem.' I said, 'We can't do that – we may have thirty, forty flags flying in one shot!' I told them the Olympic Committee would be very hard pressed to sue us for using emblems and flags provided by their own organisation! So the lawyers took a deep breath (they'd screwed up anyway by not noticing this earlier) and we kept shooting. When the film came out, the poster didn't mention the Olympic Games, nor did it show the Olympic emblem! The poster in America showed a man getting undressed with a stopwatch behind him. I guess Americans thought it was about a race to see who could get undressed quickest.

We were shooting in England in days when the English unions were extremely bolshy. We had hundreds of extras in the White City Stadium for an athletics race in the snow. The extras' union president at the time was a wonderful Irish character, Sean Brannigan, who was continually being exposed on television for rigging elections in his own favour. I thought he was absolutely delightful! I was extremely fond of him. The night before shooting, my Assistant Directors called the union for our extras. We got four hundred. Together with our dummies, that was enough. While shooting I got word 'Brannigan's arrived. He's leading the extras out on strike!' At midday all our extras suddenly got up and left. I said to my Assistant Director, 'Where's Brannigan?' He said, 'We don't know!' I said, 'It's twelve o'clock – call an early lunch. Find Sean!' Eventually one of my assistants said, 'Brannigan's having a beer in the pub opposite the stadium.' I rushed to the pub and said, 'Okay, Sean, what do you want?' Sean Brannigan said, 'My extras are being contaminated by these dummies. They could get diseases from them! It's an absolute disgrace.' I said, 'Don't be so ridiculous, Sean, the dummies are made of plastic. You know perfectly well nobody's going to get contaminated by them. Let's talk turkey. What do you want?'

So Brannigan, in his wonderful lilting Irish voice, said, 'First of all, I want you to take any other extras we can provide during the rest of the day and pay them the full union rate.' I said, 'Sean, you don't have any more. At eleven o'clock at night your people told me they couldn't find anyone else.' He said, 'We'll find them.' I said, 'Done!' Sean said, 'You've also got to pay all my extras for summer clothing.' I said, 'What are you talking about, Sean? It's midwinter! Your people are wearing coats, scarves and hats.' Sean said, 'They must be paid for their summer clothing.' I said, 'Where is their summer clothing?' Sean looked at me with wonderful Irish wisdom and said, 'Well, Michael, it's obvious, isn't it? It's underneath their winter clothing!' I said, 'That is the most marvellous trade union negotiation! It's absolute bullshit. But I'll give every one of them two pounds for bringing summer clothing!' We shook hands. Of course, they couldn't bring any more union extras in. They sent a couple of cars around Shepherd's Bush. Anyone they could find they immediately joined into the extras union for a fee that would be deducted from the money we gave them. About twenty rather bemused people turned up at the White City Stadium and joined the crowd.

The unit then moved to Australia which we all thought at the time was going to be the penalty for going to all the other lovely countries that we'd visited. Australia had a very bad reputation in 1969. It was considered some sort of outlandish outback peopled by a strange race with funny voices. We all thought Sydney was absolutely marvellous. The food was great. The second part of our stay in Australia was in the bush. The script called for kangaroo hunters in a jeep to be driving along a dust road in the Queensland bush. The aboriginal actor ran behind the jeep at such speed that the characters in the jeep decided to promote him as a runner and take bets on him. We needed kangaroos running parallel to the jeep. I'd sent motorcycle wranglers into the Australian bush weeks ahead of our arrival to corral hundreds of kangaroos and keep them in pens. We intended to release them so they'd run out along the roadside by our jeep. This was an interesting theory. Except kangaroos do not run in a straight line and do not neatly run alongside jeeps! I was on walkie-talkies to the wranglers in the kangaroo pen and at the appropriate moment I said, 'Open the gate!' In the pen the kangaroos were going at great speed, some of them in a clockwise direction and some of them in an anti-clockwise direction. They were smashing into each other and knocking each other out for a moment! Kangaroos would fall somewhat dazed on to the ground, then get up and carry on! Luckily enough of them came out, and we got the shot we required.

I stayed in the bush during a drought with a young farmer who'd left the city and bought thousands of acres of land for two cents an acre in the hope that rain would fall and the land would be worth something. He had cattle on his land, but there was nothing for them to graze on. Unlike his rich farmer neighbours, my host couldn't afford to transport his cattle out on great trucks, which we saw going along the dusty desert roads, taking the cattle to where there was water. He had to go out every morning on his motorbike and shoot dying cattle. There was no water for washing, except very brown and dusty stuff that came out of a shower. It made you dirtier than before you went under it! The farmer's wife made me the toughest pancakes I've ever had. I said to her at 8.30 p.m., 'When did you make these pancakes?' She said, 'At midday!' But none of that mattered. It was a great experience.

We finished off the movie in Tokyo. This we'd not fully prepared for as it was only a few days at the end of the schedule. We had to run our marathon race through streets we hadn't got permission to close. In true British fashion I said to the unit, 'Stretch fifteen members of the unit across the Ginza [Tokyo's busiest street] and hold up the traffic. While the traffic's held up we'll run our runners across it from one side to the other.' My unit strung themselves out across the Ginza and we had various people positioned a few blocks away. We ran our actors, including Ryan O'Neal, across the Ginza. I was getting crackling reports on the radio that six or seven police cars were rushing towards us. At the very last minute we let the traffic go and the police couldn't find us.

It turned out Ryan O'Neal was right. There was no public interest in the Olympic marathon. Sports pictures are notoriously difficult. By the time the movie was released, Richard Zanuck had been deposed as Head of Twentieth Century-Fox. The people who took over buried the film as if to say, 'The old management was no good, what do we care?!' It's a film that I still get very heartfelt letters about. Howard Thompson in *The New York Times* described it as 'A genial, sunny and brisk entertainment package. This beautifully scenic and perceptive drama is a nice antidote for the hot weather. The real star of the picture is Michael Winner who has directed some previous British exercises with brisk adroitness. He stamps this with the same visual appeal. What makes the picture so disarming is Winner's nimble pacing, the good-natured tone and above all the off centre characterisations that make the story more than a peg for the excellent sports photography. The final 26-mile marathon race across Rome is a photographic knockout.' Margaret Hinxman in the London *Sunday Telegraph* said, 'Riveting! Director Michael Winner

is a dab hand at generating genuine tension in the training, commitment and ruthless drive that make nonsense of all the noble claptrap
about goodwill toward men and playing the game that have
decorated the last couple of Olympics like a cherry on a time bomb.
The long marathon climax is a corker.'

I was asked to show *The Games* to Paramount before it was
released because they were considering Ryan O'Neal for the lead in
Love Story. As a result of their seeing him in *The Games*, he got the
part in *Love Story*, the movie that made him. I still have the telegram
from him and his wife Leigh Taylor-Young which he sent in October
1969. 'Darling Michael, Fox dropped option. Warners dropped
option. But wonder deal at Paramount. *Love Story* with Ali McGraw.
Leigh and I will be in New York November 3rd Plaza Hotel. We
miss you. We love you. Leigh and Ryan.'

Fortunately, I had kept shadow boxing and had commissioned a
Western script from a Canadian writer living in England. This was
now to take me big time to Hollywood and the action adventure films
for which I later became famous.

15

Danger in the West

A Canadian living in London had written a Western screenplay, *Lawman*. I said, 'I've never been further west than Fulham!' United Artists said, 'You can't direct this, you're a comedy director!' Then they said, 'If you get Burt Lancaster for the lead we'll finance the movie.' This is how most pictures are made. You get the star, you get the picture. Burt was in Los Angeles. He was a legendary superstar at the time. He'd just done *Airport*, an enormous financial success. I'd been a fan for years. *The Sweet Smell of Success* was one of the great films and Burt gave one of the best performances of all time. I went to Los Angeles. Burt came to see me in my suite at the Bel Air Hotel to check me out. He's the most wonderful man. He became my greatest friend in the industry. At our first meeting he was frigid, agreeing only to go through the script with me the following day. I'd never gone through a script with an actor! You gave them the script. If they liked it they did it. If they didn't they didn't! I reported to Paramount Studios at 2 p.m. on Friday where Burt had an office. There wasn't much personal chat. Burt went methodically through every line of the script. He discussed every piece of characterisation. He challenged me on all aspects of the story. Every so often Burt looked up with a menacing grin and said, 'I'm not gonna do the

picture, Michael. I'm just getting the script right for Gregory Peck.'
I was due to return to London the next day, Saturday morning.

By 5.30 p.m. we'd got to page fifty of a hundred-page script. Burt
flipped his eyebrows to the skies and said, 'I'll have to cancel golf
tomorrow!' We agreed to meet on Saturday at nine o'clock. I then
took a stupid risk. As Burt kept saying he was just getting the script
right for Gregory Peck, I went to a film memorabilia shop and
bought three 8×10-inch glossy black-and-white photos of Peck. I
made a bubble from Gregory Peck's mouth saying, 'Thanks, Burt,
you're doing a great job!' I put the photos in an envelope with Burt's
name typed neatly on the front.

On the Saturday morning Burt briefly went out to get something. I
put the envelope on his desk expecting him to come back and open it
at once. But he put his script down on top of the envelope and carried
on going through it line by line. Since there didn't seem to be an inch
of humour around, I thought, 'Why on earth am I risking this?' The
telephone rang. Burt closed his script, leaned over and picked up the
phone. He saw my envelope. While talking, he opened it, slid out the
photographs far enough to see the bubble, put the photographs back
in the envelope and kept talking on the phone. Then he put the script
on top of the envelope, opened the script again and said, 'Now
Michael, about this line here, why does he say this?' He ignored my
Gregory Peck joke! Ten minutes later Burt looked up with a
menacing expression. His eyes narrowed and he said in that
wonderfully lilting, melodious but highly dangerous voice as he
tapped the envelope, 'Did you do that, Michael?' I said very weakly,
'Yes, sir.' Burt simply turned back to the script and said, 'Now, this
line here worries me.' Later Burt asked about a scene at the end of the
movie. 'Why do I shoot this man in the back?' he asked. 'Because
your character's a total arsehole, Burt,' I said. A week after that Burt
agreed to do the movie. I was thrilled. I now had the backing of an
American company to do an all-American Western in America. And
with enough money to buy in some other very fine artistes.

I was concerned my Western should be accurate so I employed
two of the most senior American Professors of Western History to
check the sets. The first thing I had to do was find exactly where the
sets would be. There are a number of standing Western towns where

nearly all Westerns are made. Movie companies went to the standing sets, added to them, adapted them and then left them for the next film to come in. I went to ones in Almeria in Spain and in Tucson, Arizona. Then I went to Mexico to the Mexico Courts Motel in Durango, which is in the middle of the most staggering mountain scenery, and looked at one there. On the Durango Western set Mexican peasants actually live in the buildings. They leave them when you come to film and go back when the company leaves. You had to fly to Durango in a tiny propeller plane from Mazatlan. The door flew off while I was sitting in it! It was that sort of an operation.

When I was back in London casting the film, I got a frantic telephone call from Durango from Timothy Pitt-Miller, my Location Manager. He said, 'You have to come immediately. John Wayne is making a film here now and wants to make another one directed by Howard Hawks. The Durango authorities say unless you come and personally sign the agreement they'll give the street to John Wayne who's screaming he should have it.' This in spite of the fact we'd already booked it. I flew to Mexico. Howard Hawks and his film crew were at one end of the Western street, I and my film crew at the other end. We both walked up the street, stopped in the middle and chatted and then continued on. It was like a Western gunfight without guns! I signed first and got the Durango street. John Wayne was furious with Howard Hawks for not winning because he liked living there. I visited Wayne's rented house. We chatted by the pool. It was a bungalow with what Wayne called gophers running by the wall at the back of the garden. They were large rats! I assembled one of the finest casts you could have for a Western. Lee J. Cobb was the ranch owner, Robert Ryan the weak sheriff who Burt Lancaster walks all over, Robert Duvall in a key supporting role together with Joseph Wiseman, Sheree North, Albert Salmi and many other regular Western actors who I'd seen for years and deeply admired.

As we were preparing *Lawman* I started a tempestuous affair with a well-known American actress, Susan, who was one of the up-and-coming Hollywood ladies. She was married to, although estranged from, a Los Angeles policeman who was extremely jealous. I'd look out of the back of my Cadillac limousine and say, 'Why's that policeman following us?' She'd reply, 'Don't worry, it's only my husband!' She came with me to Mexico to check locations. She said, 'My husband's just entered your hotel suite in the Beverly Wilshire Hotel with three other policemen and searched the room. He was hoping he'd find drugs!' It was kind of a jolly relationship. We parted before the movie but I was still madly in love with her. I was in Durango for two weeks before we started shooting. I phoned her every night. She'd put the phone down on me! One night I didn't ring. She rang the next day and said, 'Why didn't you call?' I said, 'Well, you haven't spoken to me for two weeks. It takes me hours to call from here!'

I discovered that for American Westerns they bought fake oil-lamps and fake Western items from Los Angeles supermarkets, dusted them down, knocked them about, and used them as the real thing. In those days you could buy genuine nineteenth-century oil-lamps in the Portobello Road for four pounds. You could buy masses of nineteenth-century stuff which looked exactly the same whether it was English or American. So all my UK crew brought antiques from Portobello Road. At the end of the movie we sold it all to John Wayne's movie that was coming in afterwards. As we led up to the start of the movie I was still pining for Susan. Timothy Pitt-Miller was in flights of hyperbole! 'It's like Tristan and Isolde! You must fly to her!' he said. I thought, 'Instead of phoning her on Friday night, I'll turn up where she lives in Los Angeles.' I rented a twin-engined propeller plane to fly from Durango to Los Angeles. It was piloted by a single Mexican. We set off for Los Angeles on Friday, which was very risky because we were starting the film on Monday. We were approaching California and my pilot said, 'Where would you like to land?' I said, 'Los Angeles International Airport.' He said, 'I'm not allowed to land at Los Angeles International Airport.' I said, 'That's where my driver's waiting. You've got to!' He said, 'I'm not allowed!' I said, 'Tell them it's an emergency, tell them I'm ill. Tell them anything! Just land.' The pilot radioed to Los Angeles Airport that there was an emergency and he landed. We were stuck on some distant runway with large Boeing 747s gliding by with people peering out of the window at us. It took us twenty minutes to get to the terminal building. I said to the pilot, 'I'll see you here tomorrow evening at eight,' and raced through the airport, into the waiting Cadillac. I was driven to Susan's apartment which was in a typical Los Angeles layout around a pool.

I got there at seven o'clock, exactly when I always phoned her. I rang the doorbell. Susan had an enormous Alsatian which started barking. She called, 'Who is it?' I said, 'Michael Winner.' She said, 'You're meant to be phoning me!' I said, 'I've come specially to show my love for you.' She said, 'Go away!' I said, 'What do you mean, go away! I've just flown from Durango, Mexico. This is a very romantic moment!' She said, 'If you don't go away, I'll call the porter!' I'm sure she was screwing somebody else there! I was so in love I hadn't twigged. I stayed ringing the bell. Susan called the porter. He had cancer and spoke through one of those squawk boxes on his throat. He asked me to leave. So I went to the Beverly Wilshire Hotel where I met Warren Beatty in the lobby and we had a long chat. Then I called Susan from the hotel. She said, 'It's absolutely typical of you. You're meant to be on the phone and you turn up in person!' She agreed to see me the next day at a Malibu beach house. It didn't rekindle the relationship. I flew back alone in my little propeller plane. I saw Susan a couple of years later when she came to London. She wanted to start things up again, but I'd kind of passed on.

Burt Lancaster arrived in Durango. He brought with him his Italian driver from Rome, Ivo Palazzi, who was a very nice person although quite what he was doing in Durango I don't know. Then he brought a wonderful old make-up man and a wonderful old wardrobe man. That was Burt's entourage of three. Which as stars go was lenient. I'd become very friendly with Burt and his girlfriend Jackie. He was tempestuous but had a wonderful sense of humour. He was the most terrific man I'd ever met. He was very helpful to me in directing because he didn't have a long attention span. Burt got very fed up if the Cameraman took too long. He'd turn to me and say, 'I think they're ready, Michael.' I'd say, 'Burt, if you go to your mark on the set they'll be ready.' Burt would walk in. My Cameraman then fiddled with three or four lights and was ready in a moment. If Burt had stayed sitting in the chair he'd have gone on for another half an hour. So Burt was my total hero. He was also the most brilliant actor, not only with dialogue but with the way he walked and the way he moved. One night we were filming in the Western street. Burt had to come out of the saloon in a very menacing manner, push open the swing doors and let them swing to and fro behind him as he stood on the edge of the boardwalk looking at someone who'd called him out for a gunfight. He got to the edge of the steps and said to me, 'How does that look, Michael?' I replied, 'All I can say, sir, is it scares the shit out of me.'

You may wonder why I called Burt Lancaster 'sir'. It's a much-used word on film sets. The unit often call the director 'sir', the director calls the star 'sir'. As a director you're a mix of butler, cheerleader, Hitler, psychiatrist and artist. The word 'sir' is used as a sign of respect. The only actor who objected was Marlon Brando. He said early on, 'I hope you're not going to call me "sir" all through the movie.' I can't remember if I did or not. Either way, we stayed good friends.

One day on *Lawman* we were filming a scene in some very rocky mountains. Robert Duvall, from a higher point in the landscape, had shot and wounded Burt Lancaster's horse. Burt now had to shoot the horse to put it out of its agony. The horse was on the ground, asleep, having been given a tablet. For the first four camera angles Burt shot the horse with a Colt '45, a short-barrelled pistol. For the fifth, Burt walked on to the set, took a Winchester '73, a very long-barrelled rifle, stood over the horse and said, 'I'm ready.' I said, 'I'm sorry, sir, you were shooting the horse with a Colt '45 not a Winchester '73.' It was a quiet remark. I thought Burt would simply switch from one weapon to the other. Instead he went berserk! For which he was famous! But I hadn't seen it before! He came up to me, stuck his face in front of mine and screamed at the top of his voice, 'You stupid cock-sucking moron, Winner! What the fuck do you know about Westerns? What the fuck do you know about anything? I've been doing Westerns all my fucking life! I was shooting this horse with a fucking Winchester '73. You arsehole! Now get on with it, you stupid limey prick.' The unit were loving this. Burt Lancaster screaming is a frightening sight! Particularly when he had a gun and I didn't! When he'd run out of breath, I said, 'I'm awfully sorry, sir, but you were definitely shooting the horse with a Colt '45.'

This drove Burt into madness such as I've never seen from anyone before or since. He grabbed me by the lapels and dragged me to the edge of a cliff. There was a thousand-foot drop below! Burt shook me over the edge of the cliff screaming obscenities: 'You cock-sucking arsehole moron, don't you dare fucking tell me what to do, you know fuck all, you prick!' and that sort of thing. The British crew were enjoying this greatly. Finally Burt said to me, 'What did I shoot the fucking horse with you arsehole cunt, Winner?' I said, 'There's no question, sir. You shot the horse with a Winchester '73 rifle.' Whereupon Burt subsided and let me down and we walked back to the set. There Burt picked up the Winchester '73 rifle. My English Script Girl, the lady who's there to make sure everything matches, whispered to me, 'It'll never cut together, Michael.' I whispered, 'Angela, I'm not going to die on a mountain in Mexico.' I called 'Action!' and we got on with it. Within an hour Burt had calmed down and was saying, 'Michael, I've had some lamb flown specially in from Los Angeles. I want you and your girl to come to my house for dinner tonight.' People later told me it was a very good sign. They said Burt only threatened to kill his friends.

Three months later we were in London doing the looping. In movies a lot of the sound has to be re-recorded, particularly on Westerns, because there may be aeroplanes overhead or other noises. For the serious American actors we not only put up where they speak, we put up where they breathe in case they want to do their own breathing. I put up the scene where Burt got up from his shot horse, took the gun and shot the horse. I said, 'Burtie dear, you'll notice in this scene that you start shooting the horse with a Colt '45 and end up shooting it with a Winchester '73. We got away with it. I cut away to a passing vulture.' Burt said, 'That's very careless of you, Michael. Why did you do that?' I said, 'What do you mean, why did I do it? You grabbed me by the lapels and threatened to kill me unless you used the Winchester '73!' Burt said very quietly, 'I don't remember that, Michael.'

Robert Ryan was an actor I'd admired nearly all my life. He was the sweetest man in the world. He came to my house in Durango to say goodbye when he was leaving. He started to cry. He said, 'Michael, you'll never know what you've done for me. I can't thank you enough.' Tears were rolling down his cheeks. I thought when he left, 'Well, it was lovely to have him and I'm very fond of Bob but why was he crying?' A few weeks later we needed him for his looping in New York. His agent said to me, 'Robert Ryan can't do any re-voicing, he's broken his leg.' I thought, 'This is odd! If he's broken a leg Ryan could come on crutches and stand in front of a microphone!' Then Bob rang me. 'I want to tell you the truth, kiddo,' he said. 'I haven't broken my leg,' he said. 'I've got cancer. I had cancer before the movie and your movie was the first movie I did after treatment for cancer. Now I've got it again. But of course I'll come to do the looping for you.' In an interview with the London *Evening News* Robert Ryan said, 'I'm kind of an authority on Westerns. I've killed or been killed in more Westerns than I can remember. But this is the first time I've ever been called "Luv" by the director. I guess that's the English . . .'

Another actor we had on the film was Lee J. Cobb whose stage performance in *Death of a Salesman* proved him one of the great actors of the century. Lee always wore a wig in movies. He carried them in a box. He was sitting on the porch of his ranch in the movie looking out over a wonderful Mexican valley. He had six wigs spread in front of him, deciding which one to wear. I said, 'Lee, do me a favour, don't wear a wig. You look marvellous without the wig.' Lee J. Cobb said, 'But Michael, I always wear a wig. If I don't wear a wig, I may never work again.' I said, 'Lee, you're doing a movie with me. You'll never work again anyway!' Lee laughed and didn't wear the wig.

The mixture of American, British and Mexican crews in Durango was a great success. It was an immensely enjoyable experience. Slightly tarnished by the fact that half the town was under the control of rebels. The students were holed up in the university and the other half of the town was free. The incoming Mexican President visited the town. Whereupon everybody shot holes in the ceiling. The President finished the revolution which at one time was going to stop us bringing any guns in because they didn't want any more guns there! Durango's probably now cleaned up and touristy. In 1970 it was a real frontier town. Just like the real Wild West. To be there with all these American actors and the Mexican population was a major change from South Kensington! I'd watched Westerns in smelly cinemas in Letchworth. Now I was in the West living it. My mouth was dry with dust. I waited around as the propmen endlessly cleared horse-shit from camera-view. It was all lovely!

We had a scene where Burt Lancaster plays the flute to the actress Sheree North who's topless. In order to help him with the fingering of the flute a young Jewish flautist was brought down who was with the Los Angeles Symphony Orchestra. Her job was to play the flute behind the camera. Burt Lancaster would mime the fingering with his flute in front of the camera. Films can sometimes be grossly irresponsible, but quite jovial. My English make-up man, Dickie Mills, said to this Jewish flautist, 'I'll have to do your body make-up soon.' The lady, we'll call her Joan, said, 'Why do I need body make-up?' Dickie Mills said to her, joking, 'Well, Sheree North is naked when Burt Lancaster plays the flute to her. So you have to be naked as well. You'll need body make-up.' Joan was confused by this. She turned to my Assistant Director who was standing next to me and said, 'Is that true? Do I have to be naked to play the flute?' My Assistant Director said, 'Of course you do. It's all right. Sheree North is naked as well.' Then Joan turned to me and said, 'Mr Winner, is it true I have to be naked to play the flute?' I said, 'Yes, dear, it's only for the one scene. Nobody minds.' Dickie Mills reappeared with a little bowl of make-up, dabbing a sponge in it, and said, 'If you'd go into that caravan and take your clothes off, let me know when you're ready. I'll come in and do the body make-up.'

Joan, now confused, but happy to be the centre of attention, walked over to Burt Lancaster's caravan. Burt was sitting under an awning playing gin rummy with Ivo his driver, his make-up man and his wardrobe man. Joan said, 'Mr Lancaster, Mr Lancaster.' Burt said, 'Be quiet, honey, I'm playing gin.' Joan said, 'Yes, but Mr Lancaster I must ask you something.' Burt said wearily, 'All right, what is it, honey?' Joan said, 'Michael Winner says I have to play the flute in the nude.' Without a flicker, Burt twigged. He said, 'Of course you do, honey.' Joan said, 'But why, Mr Lancaster? Why do I have to play the flute in the nude?' Burt Lancaster replied, 'Well, honey, it's that sort of a movie.' Then he said, 'Gin' and put his cards down on the table. Before we knew where we were Joan had taken her clothes off and was in the make-up caravan, her arm waving out of the window to tell Dickie she was ready. It was not shame that prevented me from having Dickie go in and make her up. It would have been hilarious to have her standing on the set naked playing the flute. But I thought, 'As we're in Mexico we'll probably all be arrested on some major charge. Better to play safe. So I said, 'Dickie, tell her I've changed my mind.' You might think Joan would come out in tears and be very unhappy. In fact she was absolutely delighted to be the centre of attention with this little joke. She really felt she was now one of the gang.

When you film at night you have this immense area of brightly lit houses and people, which is the set, and immediately behind the lights there are no lights at all and you go into pitch black. Around two in the morning I had to pee. The easiest thing was simply to walk into the black, past the caravans, pee on the ground and come back. Because I never have a caravan. All directors have a caravan. It's in the US Directors' Guild contract that they have to have a caravan. I believe the director's place is on the set so I didn't have my own toilet in my own caravan. I walked into the darkness, unzipped my trousers and started to pee in the pitch black. Suddenly there was a scream! One of the Mexican drivers was lying on the ground asleep! I was peeing on a Mexican! Believe me that was the quickest exit I ever did from anywhere! All Mexicans carry knives and any Mexican woken up by someone peeing on him is unlikely to be in a good mood. I never knew who it was, thank God! He never knew who I was. It was so dark he couldn't see me running off. That was the most frightening moment in my long career in cinema.

The picture was a considerable success. One of America's most senior critics, Judith Crist on the NBC *Today Show*, said, 'Another movie that I found extremely enjoyable is *Lawman*. It was made by Michael Winner, a British director who came to the United States to make a Western and he's made a very classic one. It is an exciting story, an absorbing one, very different, with some of the best dialogue I've heard in a Western in years.' Howard Thompson in *The New York Times* wrote, 'Some cutting dialogue and boiling psychological tension make *Lawman* long on sting, as sharply directed by England's Michael Winner. The acting is solid, straight down the line.' Derek Malcolm in the *Guardian* said, '*Lawman* is fun, it's a story well worth following. A well-acted, well-observed piece which thankfully relies on the medium's basic precepts rather than pulling them about in order to set some new trend.' And Alexander Walker in the *Evening Standard* wrote, '*Lawman* is outstanding. It is director Michael Winner's best film. It's a Western in the classic tradition that manages to give its theme a serious and unexpected twist to put it, like a noose, round some contemporary dilemma. Winner's direction, edgy and yet sparing time to draw the portrait of a town in depth, makes *Lawman* an out-of-the-rut movie.'

Lawman was a movie where a lot of people got shot. When United Artists saw the film, they said, 'So you can direct action, Michael! We'll find some action scripts for you!' But my next movie was to bring me together with a man I'd always worshipped and who indeed is worshipped throughout the industry as the greatest film actor of the twentieth century, Marlon Brando. It was a small picture which had been written for me by the playwright Michael Hastings as a prelude to *The Turn of the Screw*. It was unlike anything I'd ever done and the experience making it would be unlike anything that had ever happened to me.

16

Marlon the Jolly

I'd been trying to set up for years a movie one could describe in the dreaded words 'an art film'. It was written by Michael Hastings, who'd written famous plays in the sixties for the Royal Court Theatre. It was a prelude to *The Turn of the Screw* and showed the gardener Peter Quint and the nanny Miss Jessel alive, and told how they died. It was a dark, spooky film. No one was rushing to finance it. In 1970 I showed the script to a producer called Elliott Kastner. He employed Jay Kanter who'd been Head of Universal Pictures. Jay was a lowly employee of a New York agency when he was sent to meet Marlon Brando at an airport. He'd befriended Brando, become his agent and one of his best friends. Jay rang me and said, 'Do you think Marlon Brando could play the part of Peter Quint in *The Nightcomers*?' I said, 'Marlon is a genius. He could play the twelve-year-old child, he could play the nanny, he could play the old housekeeper, he could play anybody!' Jay sent him the script. Marlon liked it very much. The phone rang one day in my London apartment. It was Marlon on the line. This was another moment of great excitement for me. Everybody in the movie business was in awe of Brando's talent. He created the current style of behavioural screen acting. He took acting from the confines of theatre declamation and made it his own. Generations of actors, including current stars, have learned from Marlon and know what contribution he made to cinema in the twentieth century. I said to Marlon, 'I'm coming to Los Angeles in three days' time. Can we make a date?' Marlon hated making arrangements in advance. He said, 'I'll call you at the Beverly Hills Hotel.' I said, 'May I call you?' Marlon said, 'No, let me phone you.' I got to Los Angeles and went to the hotel.

It was now midnight to me. Four in the afternoon in Los Angeles. I had to stay by the phone waiting for Marlon's call. Eventually he phoned. We arranged to meet the next day, Sunday, for lunch at his house, high on one of the hills. People asked me, 'Where does Marlon live?' They all thought he lived in Tahiti or some strange place. Marlon lived in Beverly Hills like everybody else in the movie business.

I went up to a modest Japanese type-bungalow. There was a Tahitian lady there, Tarita, his co-star in *Mutiny on the Bounty*. He had a long relationship with her and she bore him a child. He'd also had a relationship with Movita who played the same part in the first *Mutiny on the Bounty* film! Playing ball down the hill, with an occasional shout, was Jack Nicholson. Marlon and I sat on the balcony and had a simple lunch. It was a memorable meeting. In my diary I wrote, 'Marlon Brando (1) Hates smoking (2) Very nice (3) Has island in or near Tahiti.' Then I made a couple of notes of things he wanted us to do with the script. Marlon and I were to become great friends and remained so until he died.

In London I found that having Marlon Brando in my movie didn't mean much to anybody else! None of his movies had done well at the box office for years. He was considered extremely difficult. It was said he had walked out on his last film, *Quiemada*, a number of times and they had to change location from South America to North Africa. There were a whole series of horror stories about him. None of these tied up with the gentle, witty and smiling man I'd spent the day with. The fact we had Marlon Brando in a cheap movie didn't get anyone to finance it! In order to keep Marlon interested, Elliott Kastner would, from time to time, tell Marlon he had the money. Marlon would ring me and say, 'Elliott says he's got the money. Has he?' I said, 'Marlon, until the money's in the bank, nobody's got it.

I suggest you go out on the streets of Beverly Hills with a tin can and rattle it. Maybe you could get some for us.' I've always believed it's important to be absolutely straight with people. One of the nicest things anyone's ever said about me was said by Marlon: 'Michael Winner is the only person I've ever met who doesn't talk to me in the manner he thinks I like to be talked to.' Elliott Kastner eventually found finance from a man in real estate. Strangely, the property man's company went broke when real estate collapsed around 1972. And the movie made money.

Our main location was a beautiful old house near Cambridge. Marlon got no fee, but a good percentage of the gross and the profit. I had to get Marlon insured, because every star in a movie has to be insured. This wasn't easy. Marlon's many departures from *Quiemada* had been put down to illness. The insurance company had to pay out a fortune. Similar things had happened before. So the major movie-business insurer said, 'We won't insure Brando.' I said, 'You have the greatest actor in the world. You can't prevent him earning a living. Marlon is devoted to this film. He's not going to misbehave. Let me ask you a question. How many times does a movie star turn up for his insurance medical on time for the first appointment that's made?' The man from the insurance company said, 'Hardly ever.' I said, 'Marlon Brando will turn up for his medical for this film on the dot. First time. That will show you about his professionalism with me.'

I rang Marlon and said, 'They're refusing to insure you. Please, I'm making a date with a doctor in Beverly Hills, turn up five minutes early and have the medical. Because if you don't I'm not sure we can get you insured and make the film.' Marlon turned up on time and behaved immaculately throughout the picture.

Brando had a deal with Universal Pictures. They had one picture left for which they had to pay him three hundred thousand dollars. A Universal executive rang and said, 'Will you ask Marlon Brando if he'll take the three hundred thousand dollars from us and let us count your film as our last film under his contract? Then we don't have to have him in the studio, and we don't have to see him again.' That's Hollywood! It matters not how talented or brilliant you are. If you've been difficult and you haven't made them money they're not interested. Marlon was delighted to take the three hundred thousand dollars because he was hard up. Universal even left him with a small profit percentage in the movie. Shortly afterwards Marlon did *The Godfather* and then *Last Tango in Paris* – and was very hot again! Universal could have had him for three hundred thousand dollars! Massively less than he was getting on his comeback.

Marlon came to London's Savoy Hotel. He'd decided to play the part Irish. He wanted me to find Irish people from whom he could learn the dialect. If Marlon was with someone for a while, he could get their voice perfectly. He did an incredible impersonation of me! Marlon also started dieting. He was overweight rather than fat. Marlon wanted to meet real Irishmen. I told him we'd find some in Kentish Town pubs. As I drove him there Marlon ate turkey breasts from a napkin. Marlon said, 'They mustn't know I'm there! We must go incognito!' I said, 'Marlon, the chance of your being incognito is slight.' One Monday evening we drove up to a pub in Kentish Town. I didn't know the Irish spend all their money at the weekend. There are few left with anything to spend by Monday. Marlon and I went into the private bar. In those days pubs had private and public bars. The private bar was posher. We were standing like a couple of lemons at the end of the bar. Marlon looked across the room and said, 'Is that an Irishman?' I said, 'No, Marlon, it's a Pakistani.' Eventually I said, 'Marlon let me take you into the public bar. You'll meet a lot of Irish people.' Marlon said, 'No, I don't want to cause a stir.' So I went to the public bar, got five Irishmen and said, 'Would you please come and meet Marlon Brando!' We then adjourned to a table in a large, empty back room where the pub had a band at the weekend.

It was one of the most terrific, warm evenings of my life. The Irish men were delightful. They absolutely refused to let Marlon and me get ahead of buying the drinks. They insisted on buying their own rounds. They were not impressed about Marlon Brando the actor. They were impressed that he'd married the Tahitian girl from the first *Mutiny on the Bounty* film which was made in 1935. The girl's name was Movita and she'd been married to the Irish heavyweight boxing champion, Jack Doyle. Marlon asked me to take the names and addresses of the Irishmen because he wanted to send them a bottle of whisky. The next day Marlon's driver went round to the addresses. They were all false except one! I suppose they were secretly members of the IRA! The one whose address was not false became Marlon's dialogue coach. He came down to Sawston near Cambridge and helped him. Then there was some trouble with stealing lead from a church roof, and the man vanished.

I had a contract with United Artists to make another Western, *Chato's Land*, starring Charles Bronson. By the time we got the money for *The Nightcomers*, if I made it, there would be only five weeks left between shooting *The Nightcomers* in Cambridge and shooting *Chato's Land* in Almeria, Spain. My contract with United Artists called for me to be exclusive for twelve weeks before shooting. I wasn't prepared to lose the opportunity to work with Brando. I thought, 'I'll just make the movie and see what happens.' In fact the movies were two of the best I ever did. Proof that you don't have to wait six years between pictures for everything to work.

I'd arranged a cottage for myself near Sawston Hall where we were filming and another cottage for Marlon and his entourage. The entourage consisted of a blonde American girl, Jill, who was Marlon's girlfriend, his make-up man Philip Rhodes who'd been with him since they acted on the stage in *I Remember Mama* in New York in 1944 and Philip's wife Marie. Marie stood for the Cameraman to light until Marlon came on. Normally a stand-in is the same height and hair colouring as the artiste. Marie was six inches shorter than Marlon, dumpy and had dark hair. There was also Marlon's secretary Jane.

I always have a private dining room on movies for myself and the stars so we can relax in the lunch hour. In Sawston Hall a lovely room was laid out with a tablecloth, good cutlery, china and a log fire. On the first day of shooting Marlon wasn't in the final shot before lunch. I said he could break before the rest of us. One of my Assistant Directors said, 'Marlon Brando refused to sit in the special room. He insists on sitting with the crew.' I thought, 'That's bloody ridiculous!' I went to my special room which was beautifully laid out. Then I went to the tent where the crew ate. There were big trestle tables with benches. Marlon with his entourage, Philip and Marie Rhodes, Jane and Jay Kanter sat at a trestle table. I said, 'Excuse me, sir, I have a very nice room for you in the main building.' Marlon said, 'I have to eat with the crew.' I said, 'Marlon, the crew don't care whether you eat with them or not. They'd rather not have me here and they'd rather not have you here. They'd rather get on with their lunch without the bosses sitting around. You may think it's very democratic. But the crew don't give a shit!' Marlon just smiled and said, 'Well, I'm going to have lunch here.' I said, 'It's a bloody nuisance for me, Marlon, because I've got to go and get the proper cutlery and knives and forks and everything from the other room and bring them in for you.' Which I did. As people came in, such as his co-stars Stephanie Beacham and Thora Hird, Marlon would beckon to them to sit down. They walked straight past the table. I said, 'Marlon, it's no good waving your arms about beckoning people to sit down. They're all terrified of you. They don't want to sit with you.' So at lunch on the first day of the movie there was me with Marlon and his entourage at one table and the rest of the crew chatting away on other tables. The next morning Marlon was called a bit later than anybody else. His enormous Daimler limousine had to drive down the pathway where we were filming. I said, 'Marlon, I will let this very democratic car through. Even though the unit are not driven to work in similar style!'

Later we shot in a churchyard. I had lunch set up in the vicarage. I thought, 'I don't care if Marlon comes here or not. I'm going to sit in comfort, look at my script and relax.' The crew were all my friends, they'd been with me on many pictures. It didn't mean I had to be with them twenty-four hours a day. Jay Kanter and I were in the vicarage. Marlon went to the crew tent, got Stephanie Beacham and Thora Hird and brought them back to the private room. They sat absolutely tongue-tied. It was rare for Thora Hird to be tongue-tied, bless her, because, believe me, she could talk! Towards the middle of the meal, Marlon said to Thora, 'What do you do in your acting?' because he didn't know her at all. That opened the flood gates. Thora said, 'You don't know me, Marlon, but I'm very famous in England. I do this TV series, I've done that TV series, my daughter Janette was a lovely girl and she was married to Mel Tormé. I got up this morning and I had one red sock on and one blue sock . . .' She went on and on and on! A glazed look came over Marlon's face. The Production Accountant came in with some cheques and I signed them. Later in the churchyard I said, 'Marlon, I'm arranging for Thora Hird to have lunch with you every day.' Marlon said, 'I couldn't understand her accent. I couldn't understand a word she was saying. You were no help. You just sat there signing cheques.' I said, 'I took the view that since you'd brought them in, you could have them.' After that Marlon ate in his dressing room. I ate in my private room with Jay Kanter and Philip Rhodes and Marie. And we all got on terribly well.

Marlon was the most professional, the most wonderful, the most caring and the most considerate actor I've ever worked with. He was immensely patient with the two young people who were not actually children. He was very concerned with the crew. He was always on time. He always gave of his best. He was an absolute delight to chat to in between takes. You couldn't have a nicer person to spend the day with or to have a meal with. People say to me, 'Marlon never remembered his lines.' Marlon knew every line perfectly. He knew exactly where to stand, he knew all the techniques of film-making. When acting, he'd bury scripts all over the set and occasionally write a few lines down on the back of his hand. If you got him in front of the camera and said, 'Are you ready, sir?' he'd say, 'Yes.' Then I'd say, 'Action!' and Marlon would say, 'Just a minute!' He'd rush from the camera while the camera was running and look at a script hidden under a sofa. Then he'd come back and say, 'Michael, you're in my eyeline. Could you stand out of the way?' Then he'd look at another hidden script. Then I'd say, 'Action!' again. Then he'd start acting. Brilliantly. Marlon was the only actor I knew who came to rushes. I was sitting with the Cameraman watching the rushes once. Marlon came in late. We didn't know he was there. Marlon commenced his on-screen performance of starting and stopping and looking at the script. The Cameraman and I were roaring with laughter. Tears were rolling down our cheeks. Then Marlon started acting and the Cameraman said, 'He makes a great recovery, doesn't he?'

Even though Marlon was with his American girlfriend, Jill, a whole lot of dusky maidens would turn up at his cottage in Cambridgeshire, spend the night and go away. I said to Marlon, 'How on earth do you do it? You've got a lovely girlfriend, Jill, yet these other girls come from all over the place and she's still with you.' Marlon said, 'It depends how you smile.' I said, 'I know you've got a wonderful smile, but I find that incredible!' Once somebody dropped something behind me on the set while Marlon was acting. He didn't seem to notice. Normally an actor would be put off by sudden noise, react and probably get angry! I said, 'Marlon, I do hope you weren't put off by that noise.' Marlon said, 'What?' I said, 'I heard somebody drop something behind me on the set. I hope it didn't put you off.' Marlon again said, 'What?' Then Marlon moved his head to one side and bashed the top side of his head with his hand. An earplug fell out of his ear! For filming Marlon put earplugs in so he could just about hear or understand the person next to him but he couldn't hear any extraneous noise.

Marlon was later to say publicly many very kind things about me in the press and one of them was that he thought I was the best director in the world he'd ever worked with because I let him do what he wanted. This was not strictly true. But if you have the greatest actor in the world you don't have to give him acting lessons. I try to make actors comfortable, make them happy, make them enjoy the situation, tell them where to move and stand for the camera and leave them to create the role. On one occasion Marlon had been told off by Thora Hird as the housekeeper for drinking and for putting on the master's clothes. She left the room and Marlon lifted a hip flask and said, 'Up your arse!' I let him do it his own way because I think actors should always be allowed to do it their own way. If it's fine you don't have to say anything. But Marlon said the line very loudly, even though Thora had left the room. I said, 'As Thora's left the room, Marlon, when you say, 'Up your arse!' you're saying it more meditatively to yourself. You're not shouting it out to her. Say it quietly. As an afterthought.' Marlon looked at me as if to say, 'This man has no idea what he's doing.' But because he liked me he said, 'All right.' He then did three takes my way, having done the first three takes his way. When Marlon came to rushes that night he saw the six takes, one after the other. He said, 'Michael, you were absolutely right. It was far better when I said that line your way.'

One day my Assistant Director was reading the Cambridge University newspaper *Varsity*, which I once edited. He said, 'They've got *Throne of Blood* on at the Peterhouse College Film

Society next Thursday. I may see that.' Marlon turned to me and said, 'I want to see *Throne of Blood*. It's a wonderful film, Michael. We'll go on Thursday.' I assumed Marlon would forget. The last thing I wanted was to go to the Peterhouse Film Society with Marlon Brando. In those days they didn't have videos, they had 16mm movie projectors. The reel would run out and there'd be a delay while the projector was reloaded. Also, Marlon was very against publicity. I'd seen when he arrived at London Airport how he hated photographers. He was going through a lean period so there was only one anyway! Marlon did anything he could to avoid having his photo taken. He looked down at the floor. He put his hand in front of his face. He kept walking into glass doors! When we got into my enormous Rolls Phantom car, Marlon turned his face away from the cameraman. I said, 'Marlon what do you care if you have your photograph taken?' Marlon said, 'You're right. It's silly of me. I just have this thing about photographers.' Three years later he smashed a photographer in the face in New York and broke his jaw. Burt Lancaster rang me deeply happy, because he knocked photographers about as well! 'Your pal Marlon's done better than me, he's broken some bum's jaw in New York!' he said. To prevent photographers getting into the location (in spite of the fact none was interested) we had guards with Alsatian dogs. The dogs were shitting all over the place. If I arranged for Marlon to go to the Film Society and students knew he was coming they might take photographs. Marlon would think I'd put them up to it.

On Thursday Marlon said, 'Don't forget tonight we're to see *Throne of Blood*.' I called the college and said, 'We're bringing Mr Brando. Will you arrange some extra, comfortable chairs? Please, get in a second projector so we don't have to wait while the reel is changed.' I said to my First Assistant Director, 'I want the crew on duty at the college. I want them in all the courtyards we have to pass through from the back entrance. If any of the students have cameras, I want Marlon to see them being forcibly restrained.' We got into Marlon's Daimler limousine with his entourage and drove through the wet and glistening cobbled streets of Cambridge, the yellow street lighting giving a wonderful effect on the centuries-old colleges. We ended up at the back door of Peterhouse College. As

Marlon got out of the limousine two old women were walking by. They stopped and stared in amazement. One of the ladies said to the other, 'My God, look at that! It's Richard Burton!' I said, 'Marlon, I don't know why the fuck we bother!'

I only once saw the Brando everyone was terrified of. The man who kept thinking about the script in the middle of shooting, refusing to shoot it, changing it, stopping for rewrites and generally causing chaos. Marlon had to walk from his cottage down the little lane outside and shortly thereafter was shot near a lake by Miles, the young boy, with a bow and arrow. The arrow went right into the top of Marlon's head. We were sitting in the cottage at eight o'clock in the morning waiting for them to prepare the street. Marlon said, 'Michael, if Ingmar Bergman were here, what would he say about the sociological undertones of the characters and their responses to the underlying ethos of this scene?' I looked at an empty chair. Then I looked to the door. I said, 'Ingmar has just left. He got up and left. And I'm not fucking surprised!' That made Marlon laugh. Marlon's make-up man, Philip Rhodes, who'd been with him on every film, later said, 'I've never seen Marlon behave like he did on your film. He absolutely loved it. You got him laughing from the beginning. He never stopped laughing and he never regained his balance. You saw a Marlon Brando no one else has seen.'

We went outside to shoot the scene when Marlon is walking down the lane. Before I could shout 'Action!' Marlon said to me, 'Michael, I think this scene is wrong. I don't think I should be shot by the lake. I think I should be shot in the house. I think the scene in the dining room that comes before I'm shot should come after I'm shot . . .' and he listed a whole series of things about the script he'd suddenly thought of. I said, 'Marlon, this is unfair. You've had six months to give us your views. Maybe what you say is right, maybe it isn't. It doesn't matter. We're on a very low-budget film. I'm taking no salary at all. We don't have time to do anything but get on with what we agreed to do.' I could see a flicker cross Marlon's face. Then he said, 'You're right, Michael.' We shot Marlon doing his walk.

Then I said, 'Marlon, isn't that Francis Ford Coppola standing behind the barrier with the public?' Marlon replied, 'Yes.' I said, 'Should we let him through?' Marlon said, 'No.' Coppola wanted

Marlon to play in *The Godfather*. Paramount did not. Coppola had come down to discuss the part with Marlon and to write the script. He was living with Marlon in his cottage in Cambridgeshire. The Mafia don in *The Godfather* was a part Burt Lancaster was dying to play. Burt had been brought up with Italians in the slums of New York. But the part went to Marlon after he screen tested.

In *The Nightcomers* there were some very erotic scenes. Marlon and Stephanie Beacham had to be naked. There was also some sado-masochistic stuff. Marlon suddenly said, 'I don't want any stills taken of this naked scene because I'm overweight [in fact he wasn't then] and I don't want stills because they'll be used out of context.' I said, 'This scene is part of the film. We're not ashamed to do it so why shouldn't we take stills of it?' Then Stephanie Beacham chimed in and said she didn't want stills either, which was highly irrelevant because she'd signed a contract saying she had to have stills in the nude. I thought, 'Where's Jay Kanter the great Marlon handler?' Jay was walking around the garden. He came in. I said, 'Marlon's trying to stop stills being taken of this scene. We'll need them!' Jay said, 'I'll reason with him.' I thought, 'We're going to see a great piece of diplomacy now, when Jay Kanter speaks to his old friend Marlon Brando and persuades him to have the stills taken.' Jay went over to Marlon and said, 'Don't be a pain in the arse about the stills, Marlon. Just let's have the fucking stills!' I thought that was a superb piece of delicate diplomacy! Marlon said, 'All right, Michael, I'll have the stills. But you've got to take them because I trust you not to take me from a bad angle.' I said, 'Marlon, I do not take photographs.' Marlon said, 'It's you or nothing.' I said, 'It's me.' So the stillsman set his camera and said, 'Just shoot it like this and it'll be all right.' Marlon and Stephanie then went through these enormous erotic scenes with Marlon pulling her about and faking intercourse. While Marlon was doing all this he had both underpants and wellington boots on. I don't quite know why he had wellington boots on but he did!

My Cameraman kept saying, 'I see wellington boots! I see underpants!' Stephanie was stark naked. She had the most incredible body. Marlon was going at the scene very realistically. But between the underpants and the wellington boots it was hysterical. The minute I said, 'Cut' I was on the floor crying with laughter. Marlon said, 'What are you laughing about?' I said, 'I don't know how it looks from where you are, but from where I am it's absolutely hysterical.' Then I said, 'Now Marlon, please, stand still. Karsh of Kensington is coming in. I have to take stills.' I took hundreds of photographs of Marlon and Stephanie. They were used all over the world.

There was one scene Marlon kept putting off, a soliloquy he had while sitting in a barn talking to the boy and girl. Marlon was meant to be drunk. He said, 'I'm going to have to get really drunk for this, so I want to leave it to the end.' We prepared for the scene. Marlon drank a lot of Scotch. He wasn't difficult or abusive, just drunk. What amazed me was that when he played this scene, although drunk, he remembered his lines immaculately. And it was a very long speech. He also matched his hand movements and his body movements, which is very important in movies because if you have to cut different bits of film together, if the body or hands or arms are in a different position you're in trouble. He did this scene, which was deeply moving, absolutely brilliantly while drunk. He then went home to sleep it off.

At the end of the movie Marlon made a touching speech to the crew. He talked about us being 'ships that pass in the night'. But the ship of Marlon and the ship of Winner did not pass in the night. We stayed friends through the rest of time. I've never met a nicer or straighter person. When people said to me, 'Marlon Brando is weird' or 'All these terrible things that have happened to him' or 'He's deranged' or 'He's crazy', I'd say, 'He's not.' Marlon is the most wonderful, simple, easy to talk to person and if I had to sit down at dinner I'd like to sit with him, Orson Welles, Burt Lancaster and Sophia Loren. That would be the greatest dinner party ever.

When we finished *The Nightcomers* I suggested we hold up its release. It was a costume drama which wouldn't date. The film had been bought by Joe Levine, the wonderful showman, for his company Avco Embassy. Joe absolutely adored the movie. I said, 'Wait a year, let *The Godfather* come out. Marlon will then be an enormous star and you'll have the first film after *The Godfather*.' Our picture had only cost six hundred thousand dollars. Since I was on no salary I particularly wanted to see a profit. Joe Levine thought the film was so brilliant we didn't have to wait for *The Godfather*. He released the film. It did well for an art-house film and made a profit. Rex Reed in the *New York News* wrote, '*The Nightcomers* is a genuinely gripping spooks and shivers item. Devoid of the clichés to which most such offerings fall heir to, and a movie that finally gives Marlon Brando his finest acting role in years. Brando is simply riveting as the classy, degenerate Quint. He really works in this movie and the movie deserves him.' Kevin Thomas in the *Los Angeles Times* said, '*The Nightcomers* is a film among Brando's best and most venturesome. It emerges as both a compelling tale of psychological suspense and a provocative parable. It is as beautiful as it is sinister. The picture belongs to Marlon Brando, moody and magnificent as only he can be.'

The film was an invited entry to the San Francisco Film Festival and the Venice Film Festival. At Venice the Award was picked up for me by Sir Michael Balcon who'd helped me by financing *The Girl-Getters*. When Dr Rondi, the Director of the Venice Film Festival, saw *The Nightcomers* in London, he said he loved it, adding, 'Do you think Marlon Brando would come to Venice?' I said, 'Will you give him a prize?' Dr Rondi said, 'The Venice Festival has been going for twenty-three years and we've never given a prize.' I said, 'Then Brando's not coming.' Without drawing breath Dr Rondi said, 'We'll give him a prize.' I rang Marlon and said, 'Would you like to go to the Venice Film Festival and get a prize?' He said, 'No.' At the San Francisco Festival Burt Lancaster came to support me at the screening. Afterwards Francis Ford Coppola gave a party for us in his studio and we were led through the cutting rooms where an assistant said in awe, 'This is the cutting room where Francis is cutting *The Godfather*.' Celluloid strips of *The Godfather* were there, a film which would re-invigorate Marlon's career.

If ever I went to Los Angeles Marlon was a great host. One evening we were having dinner, Marlon, Philip Rhodes and me at a restaurant in the Valley. I can't remember which Valley. All Los Angeles is either hills or valleys! We'd all ordered vanilla ice-cream. Marlon looked at his portion of ice-cream and then looked at Philip Rhodes, who'd started eating. Marlon said, 'Philip, your portion of ice-cream was larger than mine.' This confused Philip. Should he stop eating and give his to Marlon? Marlon thought about it for a second then raised his arm and said to the waiter, 'Could you bring me another portion of ice-cream?' When the bill came, I grabbed it from beside Marlon and said, 'I insist on paying!' Marlon picked up the pitcher of water from the table and stood behind me. He let a few drops go on to my head. He said, 'Unless you give me that bill at once, I'll throw this all over you!' He would have done! You really had to fight to stop Marlon paying for things.

When Marlon came to England I took him on a tour of Surrey and Sussex in my open car. He loved the thatched cottages and the leafy lanes. He rented a house in Surrey a year later. I wanted to have tea in the village of Shere, but there was a queue. I said, 'Marlon, I'll try to get you in ahead of the queue.' I went into the restaurant where there was a lovely old lady who owned it and her son, I said to the son, 'I've got Marlon Brando outside. If I put him in the queue people will start gathering round. Can you help?' Luckily four ladies were just leaving a table. The son tipped the chairs up and said, 'Get him in at once!' I said, 'Marlon, I've got you ahead of the queue at the tea shop in Shere. I consider this one of my great achievements.'

On another occasion Marlon rang me and said, 'Michael, I've just arrived. Will you pick me up at the Mayfair Hotel at 7.30 p.m. tomorrow and we'll have dinner? I'm registered under the name Charles Johnson.' I went to the lobby phone and said, 'Charles Johnson, please.' The switchboard girl said, 'We don't have anybody here of that name.' I thought, 'This is exactly like when I phoned up Orson Welles years ago at the same hotel, and they told me they didn't have anyone of that name!' I said, 'I understand that. It's not really Charles Johnson. It's a very famous person who's staying here using the name Charles Johnson.' The operator said, 'We don't have anybody here of that name at all.' I asked for the manager. A young man in evening dress appeared. I said, 'I've arranged to meet Marlon Brando to take him to dinner. He told me he was staying under the name of Charles Johnson. Perhaps I've got it wrong. Could you please tell him I'm here.' The manager said, 'Mr Winner, Marlon Brando has told me he is not to be disturbed tonight. In particular he is not to be disturbed by you. He said if you came I was to ask you to leave the hotel immediately. Will you leave.' I said, 'I'll hang around just in case.'

I knew it was a gag. I waited in the lobby of the Mayfair Hotel. Not an attractive place. The manager was pointing me out to the girls behind the desk as some kind of intruder. I looked out in the street to my Ferrari which was parked down the road. I looked all round. I couldn't see Marlon. I waited for twenty minutes. Twenty minutes in the lobby of the Mayfair Hotel is not one of life's great pleasures. I decided that Brando or no Brando I was going. I called the manager again. It was before I was writing my hotel and restaurant column, otherwise he might have been more impressed. I said, 'I'm going to leave and Marlon Brando's not going to get his dinner. In order that it be quite clear why he's not getting dinner I want your name so I can tell him about it.' The manager handed me his card with a slight flicker of fear crossing his face. He said, 'If you don't leave immediately I'll call the police.' I said, 'As I'm Chairman of one of their biggest charities this does not scare me!' I exited and walked towards my Ferrari, which had tinted windows. Marlon got out of the car, roaring with laughter, and said, 'Michael, I fooled you! I fooled you!' We hugged and kissed. The manager was standing outside the hotel and could see us. Marlon said, 'I was in the newsagent shop. When you went into the phone box, I nipped out of the door. Didn't you see any of that?' I said, 'No, Marlon.' Marlon was now taking from his pocket an enormous wodge of fifty-pound notes and heading for the manager. I said, 'Marlon don't give that man fifty pounds, he was extremely rude to me.' Marlon went up to the manager and said, 'Michael Winner is one of my best friends, a great friend. Thank you for joining in and doing as I said.' He gave the man fifty pounds.

In March 1977 Marlon came to London to play a part in the first *Superman* movie at Shepperton Studios. He was getting the biggest salary ever received by an actor until that point in time. Three million dollars for eight days work against 11 per cent of the gross of the movie. He asked me and my girlfriend Sparkle, a beautiful actress who had been at the National Threatre and in the West End, to have dinner on the Sunday at his house in Shepperton. His film started shooting on Monday. Marlon was with his son Christian, Philip and

Marie Rhodes and his secretary. If they had the hot water going, the heating for the house didn't work, and vice versa. When I hugged Marlon, he said, 'I've got newspapers under my jumper because when I was a tramp I learned that was the way you should keep warm.' I'd brought down a big chocolate cake because Marlon loved cake. He was watching Laurel and Hardy on television.

There was a Pakistani lady there, an ex-girlfriend who'd once been very glamorous. She'd come for a replay. She was talking in a fascistic way about the peasants in Pakistan and how they had to be kept down. This was very un-Marlon dialogue. Marlon whispered in my ear, 'She's a great blow job.' Then in order to stop her talking, Marlon said to me, 'How do you pronounce integral?' He said this as 'intigral', with the 'tig' as in the word 'ignore', i.e. a short 'i' sound rather than integral with the 'eg' sounding like 'egg'. I said, 'Marlon, you pronounce it integral,' pronouncing the 'egg' in it. Marlon said, 'No, you don't, it's intigral.' I said, 'It may be in America, Marlon, not in England.' Marlon said, 'Let's have a bet.' I said, 'A hundred pounds.' I went over to shake his hand. Marlon said, 'The loser of the bet has to sell French ticklers in Piccadilly for an hour.' A French tickler is a condom with bubbles on it. I said, 'Marlon, I don't want to take this bet because if you lose you won't sell French ticklers in Piccadilly Circus. I consider bets absolutely sacred. It will chip our friendship.' Marlon said, 'I promise you, Michael, if I lose I'll sell French ticklers in Piccadilly Circus for an hour.' We shook hands on the bet and then went to dinner at a local hotel and had a great evening. I left about midnight. Earlier on in the evening his son, Christian, had said to me, 'Will you talk to Marlon because I want to go to Tramp discotheque, and my father says I can't go?' I said, 'Marlon, why not let the boy go to Tramp? It's a perfectly harmless place.' Marlon said, 'I don't want him growing up meeting those sorts of people.' I said, 'What sort of people, Marlon? I go to Tramp! It's just a discotheque for young people.' But Marlon was adamant.

The next day Jay Kanter rang me from the film set. He said, 'All Marlon's talking about on *Superman* is this bet with you!' At seven o'clock I looked in the Oxford Dictionary and to my surprise the word 'integral' was only given as Marlon's pronunciation not mine! Although today it has both pronunciations. I rang Marlon and said,

'About our bet.' He said, 'Why haven't you rung me before?' I said, 'I was with you until midnight. You've been on the set.' He said, 'You could have rung me on the set. I've made all the arrangements! I'm going as a blind beggar! I'll go soon as we finish filming.' I said, 'I'm sorry to say you don't have to! You've won!' A few days later a gift came from the posh jewellery shop, Asprey. It was from Marlon. A gold medallion on a gold chain. On one side were the words, 'MICHAEL THE LOSER IS ALSO A WINNER M.B. March 1977' and on the other side was the phonetic spelling of 'Intigrəl'. Whenever I saw Marlon he said, 'You've only put on that medallion because you're meeting me.' Then he saw the gold was quite rubbed and knocked about and said, 'I see you do wear it all the time.'

Now that I had to go to Piccadilly Circus and sell French ticklers for an hour I wasn't too keen. About six months later I was speaking to Marlon on the phone. He was in Los Angeles. I said, 'I'm sorry, I haven't been to Piccadilly but I'm going soon.' Marlon said, 'You should have gone already.' I said, 'You're absolutely right.' So I got a tray made such as people sell ice-cream from in the theatre. It said, 'Purveyors of Sexual Aids to the Gentry since July 1st 1971', which was the date I was there selling the French ticklers. My chauffeur bought an enormous supply. My assistant rang the West End police and said, 'Mr Winner is going to be selling French ticklers in Piccadilly Circus for an hour. If you insist on arresting him he'll have to be arrested because it's a bet with Marlon Brando.' The police said, 'As long as he doesn't cause obstruction, we'll tell our people not to arrest him.' I arrived in Piccadilly Circus with my tray of French ticklers. I had a photographer who was discreetly photographing me so I could send the pictures to Marlon.

I had the Assistant Director who'd called the police skulking around in the background. After twenty minutes a policeman came over and said, 'You can't sell goods from a tray here like that, sir.' I said, 'We've told the police about it. They said it was okay as long as I'm not causing an obstruction.' My Assistant Director had got lost! He turned up just in time and gave the policeman the name of his superior who'd 'approved' me! I only made one sale, to a couple of people in property who I knew. They gave me one pound. When

I look at the pictures, I can see the crowds looking in awe at these French ticklers. They're talking about it, but not doing anything. Marlon said he absolutely loved the pictures. He took them out and had a laugh whenever he felt gloomy.

Marlon used to spend time with a friend who had a house in Kent near Faversham. One Sunday I was doing nothing. Marlon rang at 2 p.m. and said, 'Michael, come down to Faversham. We'll fool around.' I said, 'Where do I go?' He said, 'Just come down to Faversham railway station. Phone me on the mobile. I'll pick you up.' I left my house at two-fifteen in my Ferrari. I wanted to get the journey over. I drove like a lunatic. Down the A3. Left along the M25. Right down the M20. I was driving at 120–130 miles per hour. I was utterly irresponsible and stupid. It took me only an hour and thirty-five minutes to get from my house in Holland Park to Faversham railway station. I was in another world. There were little cottages with roses creeping up. I sat on a bench outside the station, drained. I phoned. Marlon said, 'I'll be right down.' A Land Rover duly arrived driven by a lady friend of Marlon's. Marlon got out. We embraced. As we withdrew Marlon said, 'Okay, let's go back to town!'

He didn't say, 'Have a cup of tea', or, 'Have an ice-cream' or anything, just, 'Let's go back to town!' I said, 'I'm not going on the motorway again. We'll take the scenic route through Brixton.' A year later we were talking on the phone and Marlon said, 'I still think of that drive back from Faversham in your Ferrari. It was horrific. You drove so fast.' I said, 'I promise you next time I'll drive very slowly.' Marlon said, 'There won't be a next time.' Anyway, we got back to London, had dinner in my house and chatted away. It was a very pleasant evening.

On another occasion we were sitting on my balcony. My garden backs on to Holland Park. There was some Pacific music floating in from the park. Marlon eventually said, 'Let's go and see what that is. I think that's Balinese music.' We went to the Holland Park Theatre and sat in the front row. There was a troupe of people playing and dancing. Marlon went through every island in the South Pacific deciding which one they were from, changing his mind every two seconds. He finally figured out correctly who they were. In fact there was a large sign at the side of the stage saying who they were but we hadn't noticed it.

Marlon was a very happy person. He had times when he spoke to his friends a great deal and then he didn't speak to them. Some got very upset at this. It didn't worry me. That's how he was, bless him. He'd phone me every day for a week and see me and then he'd not phone for a year. So what? When he did phone he normally started in some marvellous accent pretending to be somebody else. He once pretended to be a *Sun* newspaper reporter. He always fooled me. One particular night my girlfriend was in Miami and was going to call and tell me when I should meet her the following day at the airport. I kept getting these calls. A man would say, 'This is Baron von Stumpel' and I'd put the phone down because I get nuisance calls. The calls kept coming from about ten o'clock at night. I kept putting the phone down. Normally I'd simply transfer the calls to the local police station so someone calling would have the police answer the phone and say, 'Kensington Police'. I couldn't do that because my girlfriend was going to call. At about the ninth call I picked up the phone and thought, 'I'll just listen, I won't say anything.' A voice said in his normal voice, 'Michael, this is Marlon Brando. You keep putting the phone down on me.'

On another phone call Marlon said, 'You know, I realise now a great many of my friends were just good-time friends. I've decided I've only got five real friends in the world. I consider you to be one of them.' I thought, 'I hope you phone the other four more than you phone me!'

Marlon was also famous for the causes he adopted. I said to him on the film set once, 'Marlon, when you're walking along Beverly Hills with a placard for the Indians, don't you think that comes over rather falsely with all your wealth and position?' Marlon replied, 'Well, I can't give them the whole sandwich, I decided to give them half the sandwich.'

Marlon told me an amusing story. There was some American Indian who was involved in a very famous shoot-out in America. Marlon came over to England with this Indian who was really quite dangerous; I think he may even have killed somebody! They went to the BBC, because Marlon wanted to get the American Indian culture better known in Britain. At BBC Radio they met a lady executive. Marlon said, 'We sat there in front of this woman who was something to do with the Head of Women's Programmes on the BBC. I'm sitting there with this man who's wonderful, but quite dangerous. This woman says to him, "Do you do basket weaving?" and, "Do you do embroidery?" and, "Could we have a programme about making Indian head-dresses?"' Marlon said this woman just didn't understand that he wanted rather more from the BBC than programmes about Indians embroidering things.

On another occasion Marlon came over to see me and he said, 'You know why I'm here, Michael, it's a legal matter. You have a very good legal brain.' There was a very famous author called James Clavell. He'd had a mistress for many years who was an ex-girlfriend of Marlon's. He said he was going to leave his wife and marry her, if she had his child. She bore him a daughter. But Clavell didn't leave his wife. Clavell made a settlement on the woman in America. Marlon felt the settlement was unfair. He financed the girl to take the matter back to court in the USA. It hadn't gone well. He said, 'I've come to London because I've nailed Clavell. We found the birth certificate of this lady's daughter and on the birth certificate James Clavell put a false name. The penalty for putting a false name on a birth certificate is up to five years in prison. I'm going along to the records office in Somerset House to tell them about this. What do you think will happen?' I said, 'Absolutely nothing, Marlon. What do they care that some man put a false name on the birth certificate twelve years ago?' Marlon said, 'It says in the book the man can be sent to prison.' I said, 'Marlon, he won't be sent to prison. Nothing will happen.' Marlon went along. Nothing happened. But when Marlon got a bit between the teeth on a cause – and I think this is absolutely admirable – he was famous for pursuing it.

On another occasion, the Olympics were on. Marlon was in England. He rang me and said, 'I'm listening to the BBC coverage of the Olympic Games and they call the Chinese athletes Chinamen. It's very insulting to call someone a Chinaman. I rang the BBC Sports Department and asked for the Head of Sport. I said, "This is Marlon Brando," and they laughed and put the phone down! They've

done that three times! Can you help?' I rang the BBC and got
through to the Head of Sport's office. He was in Mexico where the
Olympics were. I said to his assistant, 'Marlon Brando keeps ringing
you and you keep laughing and putting the phone down. He's going
to phone in the next half-hour. Please deal with it properly.' I rang
Marlon. I said, 'They're ready for your call!' The next day Marlon
rang me and said, 'They're not calling them Chinamen any more,
they're calling them Chinese men and Chinese women.'

There were two standard questions Marlon always asked, which I
myself have taken up. They're quite revealing regardless of what
answer people give. The first question is, 'On a scale of one to ten,
how happy have you been during the last year?' When Tony Blair
came to my first ceremony for the unveiling of a memorial for a
police officer in the north of England, I said, 'Tony, on a scale of one
to ten how happy have you been in the last year?' Blair said, 'Four.'
I said, 'Four's absolutely terrible, Tony. You've just been made
leader of the Labour Party. You've achieved what you wanted. Why
only four?' He said, 'Well, it's absolutely dreadful, Michael. I've got
to reform the party, I've got to make them electable.' I said, 'I
thought Neil Kinnock had reformed them.' He said, 'No, I'm having
to do it all. It's really very difficult'. I asked the same question of
John Major when he was Prime Minister and he said, 'Well, I go up
and down.' I said, 'No, John, I don't want an up and down, I want an
exact number, how happy you've been in the last year on a scale of
one to ten. Ten being very happy.' Major said, 'Well, you know,
Michael, I don't need the bullet-proof car. I don't need to have all
these dispatch boxes every weekend. I don't need . . .' What he was
saying was that he didn't need the frills of power and he wasn't that
mad about being Prime Minister. He told me that he wanted to see
plays and he wanted to watch cricket and in fact he very soon got out
of the job. So these questions are always revealing. The second
Marlon question was, 'How much are you worth naked in the street!'
Marlon loved prodding into the persona of people he was with.
Nothing wrong with that. So do I!

I, too, enjoy asking pertinent questions. We were sitting by a lake
in Cambridgeshire filming *The Nightcomers* and I said to Marlon, 'If
you could live your life over again, what would you do differently?'

Marlon's answer was immediate. He said, 'I wouldn't get married and I'd kill my father.'

Marlon would telephone me frequently. He had a housekeeper called Maria Ruiz who later bore him three children. He said to me, 'You know my bedroom, I've got all that electrical equipment in it. I dropped a tiny screw on the floor. Maria bent down on all fours to look for it under the bed. That's when the relationship changed.' The relationship ended in tears. When he died, Ruiz was suing him for millions of dollars. Later Marlon had said to me, 'You know I've given up sex, Michael. I just watch the porno channel and jerk off. It's much simpler.'

Marlon was part of my life for 34 years. As an actor he changed the whole style of film performance, from stage declamation to behavioural acting where you absolutely believed in the person in the story. Generations of actors followed him and learned. He said to me once, 'You know, I seem to be a God to young actors. Apparently if I'm in a film they'll come in for less money just to be with me.' Marlon found that amazing. I said, 'You're the greatest screen actor ever. I'm sorry you're not acting much. You should be doing *King Lear* at the National Theatre.' 'I hate acting,' said Marlon. 'The only film I ever enjoyed with the one I did with you.'

Jay Kanter phoned me at 7.15 the morning after Marlon died to tell me he was dead. I rang the Press Association to pay him tribute. They'd not heard of his death. It took another nine hours before it was formally announced. The world had lost not only a great actor but a man whose conscience touched everyone. I think of him continually. Actors achieve great fame and pass on. Their celluloid persona is left. The public still see them acting. In my mind I relive my wonderful times with Marlon as a friend. The word 'unique' is over-used. But Marlon was unique.

17

Charlie Turns Up

Around the beginning of 1971 all the major American movie companies were close to broke. Most didn't have conglomerates behind them as they do today. They were simply motion-picture manufacturers and distributors. They gave away a generous amount of the movies to the producers. On my United Artists contract I had 60 per cent of the profit and UA didn't even charge an overhead, which was a common way financiers took a large amount from the producer. Also the share-out of profits was fairly honest. It was reckoned that if a film grossed two and a half times its negative cost the producers would be in profit. I was swimming once in the Caribbean Sea with the legendary Hollywood screenwriter William Goldman and he said to me, 'How is it, Michael, that I still get profit cheques on the films I made before 1973? But on the pictures I made after 1973 I never seem to get anything.' I told Bill the reason was that the companies were all near-broke in the early seventies and as a result they ferociously cut costs and started using a different set of book-keeping which basically kept the 'talent' from getting anything. It was years later that very hot talent went on a percentage of the gross. Then, if they were lucky, they got something. I was due to make *Chato's Land* for United Artists. My agreed salary was six hundred thousand dollars a picture. UA insisted on the film being made for a million and a half dollars. This was very low for a Western. The only way I could get the budget down was to defer five hundred thousand dollars. If the film made a profit, the first five hundred thousand of it would come to me. Miraculously, it made a huge profit! It was a brief period when even stars were paid less. None of these periods last for long. The industry soon went back to its profligate ways.

Chato's Land was about a posse hunting down a half-breed Indian who shot a white man in a Western saloon. The white man, a racist, had drawn first. The film had serious undertones, which the American critics saw clearly. That if you set out to destroy a nation, you end up destroying yourself. The parallel was the Vietnam War which was going on at the time. I had to cast *Chato's Land* while I was in Cambridge shooting with Marlon on *The Nightcomers*. There was a telephone operators' strike. In those days you couldn't direct-dial from outside London. I had to drive each night to The Thatched Barn pub in Elstree where I could direct-dial California. I cast the picture on the phone from The Thatched Barn. The result was as good a cast as I ever assembled. The head of the posse was Jack Palance, an ex-army figure reliving his glories. Old-time Western stars Richard Basehart, James Whitmore, Simon Oakland and Victor French were in there, as were new young actors Richard Jordan and Ralph Waite. The desert and hills around Almeria are good Western country. They have a standing Western street set. But the scenery lacked cacti which grow in Arizona. It also lacked the great finger rocks you see in some American deserts. Having had great success with fibreglass on *The Games*, we manufactured sixty different types of large cacti. We also built two great finger rocks of plaster!

This was my first picture with Charles Bronson. I've told you how we met briefly in Paris with my ex-girlfriend, Jill Ireland, who was now his wife. Every night Charlie, Jill and I would have dinner in the hotel in Aguadulce. Charlie took a great dislike to Jack Palance. This was a pity because Jack had to sit on his own at a table in the same dining room. It was only towards the end of the picture, after I kept telling Charlie what a terrific person Jack was, and when I had to go somewhere else, that Charlie and Jack Palance had dinner together.

Charlie said to me the next day 'You know, Jack Palance is a very nice man.' That was typical of Charlie. He was extremely distrusting. Jack had come from a similar background, Eastern European distant ancestry. They'd both worked in mining towns in Pennsylvania. Charlie was brought up among the poorest of the poor. He would tell stories of his life in a hut in a mining town. He and his brother had to go out with a pickaxe and some wood and cut their way into the mountain, prop up the tunnel they built, and then take coal from wherever they could find it. They were only paid on coal they delivered. Charlie would demonstrate this crawling on his back on the ground, looking up at an imaginary rock face and hacking at it with an imaginary pickaxe. It was an experience that scarred him deeply. There were thirteen people in his family living in the same hut. His father was dying of cancer. Charlie wore the hand-me-down clothes from the family member above him, a sister. So in his early years he dressed as a girl.

The Second World War saved Charlie Bronson from a life of great poverty. He might well have turned to crime because he had a very violent streak and was very bitter about the way the poor were treated in America. After the war the US government had an education programme and Charlie chose to go into acting. He plied his trade in Hollywood under the name of Charles Buschinski. When the anti-Communist hearings in the sixties were rampant he couldn't get work because everyone thought he was a Russian Commie. So Charlie changed his surname to Bronson after the name of a street in Hollywood.

On *Chato's Land* we had dinner every night, and we sat on the set together for many hours. When people said to me, 'Did you get on well with Charlie Bronson?' I'd say, 'Yes, I got on well with him. But I'm not sure how he got on with me!' He obviously got on very well! Because a few weeks after the end of *Chato's Land* he asked Columbia Pictures to employ me on his next movie as the Director. Charlie was extraordinarily fit. He claimed to be fifty-two at the time although Jill told me he was eight years older. He wore a little loincloth and moccasins and a band round his head. He tucked his pipe and tobacco in his loincloth (he was then a very heavy smoker). Chato, the half-breed Indian, was a wonderful part for Charlie. The posse would draw up in a ravine, look up and say, 'The Indian's behind the rocks.' Charlie would be at the hotel having his favourite drink, a Campari and soda. When he came to the set he was highly professional. He was also very caring of Jill's two young children from her marriage to David McCallum and his adopted child Jason, who were all with them. Charlie always looked very fierce but he had a soft side. Although he appeared taciturn he could tell a story brilliantly. One concerned how he sold talking greetings cards at Los Angeles railway station. Charlie would open the card, pull an imaginary string and, as he pulled the string, do a wonderful version of a tinny voice singing 'Happy Birthday' or other dopey messages. Even in private life Charlie didn't speak a great deal. He always said, when Jill and I were wittering away like mad, 'Good God, you English know how to talk. You never stop talking.'

It's always interesting when you meet a star you've read about to quiz them on some of the things that had been in the papers. I'd read that Charlie had been accused in court by his first wife, a Jewish woman, of putting on the vacuum cleaner to drown her cries as Jill beat her up! Charlie explained it. He and Jill were having an affair, while he was married, although he had left his wife. The wife came round to Jill's house, surprising them, and attacked Jill physically. Jill was in very good condition because she'd been a ballet dancer. Charlie's wife got the worst of it, and left. She then came back and started to fight again. This time a glass ornament was knocked from the piano. 'Jill had bare feet,' said Charlie. 'I didn't want her to get cut from the broken glass on the carpet. So I got the Hoover and hoovered up the glass.' This was typical Charlie. He was not going to get involved in the fight because he was afraid the wife might sue him for assault. But he was practical enough to hoover up the glass in case it did any damage to the girl he supported. I liked the image of the super-tough guy hoovering the floor while two women fought over him!

Charlie was a director's dream because he wanted to do his work, then get back home and relax. So he didn't get involved in too much discussion about the part. Except once. We were shooting a scene where the posse have found Chato's adobe hut and raped his young wife. They tie her to a stake and wait in the dark, using Chato's wife as bait. He'll come and save her, and the posse will capture him. Charlie's white Cadillac bumped over the dusty rutted tracks that led to our location in the Almeria hills. Bronson got out in his loincloth with his moccasins and the bandana around his head. 'What are we doing tonight?' he asked. I said, 'Tonight, sir, is very good for you. You won't be with us more than two hours. Here is your wife staked out.' I showed him a very nice mixed-race young lady I'd found in Notting Hill Gate. She was lying stark naked on the ground with her arms behind her head. Her wrists were tied by a rope to a wooden pole stuck in the ground. I said, 'You wriggle along on your stomach, sir. We'll put rubber rocks underneath so you won't be scratched. You raise your knife and cut the rope holding your wife to this stake.' Bronson said, 'I'm not doing it.' I said, 'I beg your pardon?' He said, 'I won't do it.' I said, 'Why not?' Bronson said, 'Because I never appear on the screen with a naked woman.' I said, 'But Charlie, you've had this script for months. It says very clearly you come and save your naked wife from the posse.' Charlie said, 'You put it in this afternoon!' I said, 'Charlie, scene 182, page 76, "Chato saves naked wife from posse". One of the great scenes in movie history.'

The unit were watching closely. When the director is discomfited, they're highly amused. I said, 'Charlie you have to do this scene.' Charlie said, 'I will never appear on the screen with a naked woman.' I said, 'But in *Rider in the Rain* you chased a naked woman along the beach.' 'That was in long shot,' Bronson replied. Realising I wasn't getting anywhere, I said to my assistants, 'Take this girl away immediately! Cover her with a blanket and remove her!' She was a terribly nice girl. Her name was Sonia Rangan. If she's still around I wonder where, because she was just so delightful. This was her big chance. She was very upset to be led off the set. 'Now,' I said to my Cameraman, 'raise the camera.' We raised the camera so we saw only the top of the stake with the rope. I said, 'Charlie, dear, you wriggle along through the undergrowth here and you cut the rope. Then you go back to the hotel and have a Campari.' Charlie did this. When he left we took a shot of the naked girl lying down. We panned up her body and her eyes flickered to an off-screen breaking of a twig. Then Charlie appeared and cut the rope. We achieved the same effect as if we'd done it in one shot.

I did six films with Charlie. The only one he really loved was *Chato's Land*. He was very self-conscious about his voice and about his acting. He had no self-confidence, although he was a wonderful actor and had a very interesting and unusual voice. When we saw *Chato's Land* in Los Angeles months later, Charlie said, 'Michael, you deceived me. You made it look like I was on the screen with a naked woman!' Charlie was always very meticulous. He went through every invoice and every bill. When we were trying to leave the hotel in Aguadulce to go to the airport in Almeria Charlie simply wouldn't go. He stood at the desk checking every single item on his hotel bill. He was querying everything. 'I did not call California on May 2nd,' he'd say. And then go into a long discussion with the Spanish people behind the desk. Eventually I said, 'Charlie, we're gonna miss the plane. You'll have to pay for an extra night in the hotel just to deal with the hotel bill. Bite the bullet and let's get the fuck out!' At which point Charlie gave one of his laconic half-smiles and said, 'Jeez! They're always trying to screw me!' But I did get him on to the plane.

The other great actor in *Chato's Land*, Jack Palance, had become famous as a pug-nosed, tall actor with pent-up anger. Marlon Brando told me that when he was on the stage in New York, starring in *A Streetcar Named Desire*, Jack was his understudy. Jack was full of frustration and rage that he was not playing the part. At one point Marlon had to exit the stage on one side, go down some steps and cross underneath the stage, to come up again and enter the stage from the other side. This involved him walking through an area with wooden supports holding up the stage. Marlon said, 'Jack Palance would be rocking back in his chair and throwing knives into this central wooden pillar at the time I had to get to the other side of the stage. He deliberately made it dangerous for me to pass. He looked at me with a terrifying stare. Eventually I asked the management to stop him.' I told this story to Jack who was a wonderful, quiet and gentlemanly person, but obviously capable of exploding. Jack confirmed Marlon's story. 'I was so jealous of Marlon. I really wanted to kill him. I just sat there throwing knives into this pillar to inconvenience him.' Jack was famous for his temper. He told me that on many films he took his brother with him to calm him down, 'But,' said Jack, 'my brother was worse than me! Half the time I had to calm him down!'

One night I was at dinner in Almeria with Charlie and Jill. I came back to the hotel and somebody whispered to me, 'There's been a terrible scene in the dining room with Palance.' In the dining room Jack was sitting in a corner breathing heavily with a slightly insane look on his face. I said, 'Jack, they've just told me you've been throwing tables and chairs all over the place! You've been screaming, shouting and hitting people! You choose the one night I'm not here! It's very unfair! I'd like to have seen it!' This lightened Jack up a bit. He'd been very pleased that a real estate developer was putting up new villas near Almeria. They were going to give Jack a house so they could use his name as an inducement to buyers. Jack said, 'These cock-suckers came to dinner and,' he continued, 'you know what, Michael? They were unbelievably anti-Semitic. They spent a lot of time insulting the Jews. Eventually I completely lost my temper, I got up, I turned over the table, I threw things at the wall, I grabbed one of them by the throat and threatened to kill him and they both left.' I said, 'Very noble, Jack! I'm proud of you. But please, if you do it again, be sure I'm around to watch.'

Chato's Land became a major cult film in France. Pierre Mazars in *Le Figaro* said, 'Michael Winner's talent is so strong that his story attains universal relevance. Here is a Western which treats suffering like human tragedy, or like Faulkner in his war novels. The director's style, always varied, never degenerating into the ordinary, is of the same quality as the work.' In *Le Monde* Claude Fleouter wrote, 'Like other young American directors, observation of the Vietnam War and the atrocities committed there have led Michael Winner to see and discover the same violence in the old West. *Chato's Land* is a remarkable Western, told and filmed with skilful precision.' Michel Duran in *Le Canard Enchaîné* wrote, 'Michael Winner, who last year gave us the exceptional film *Lawman*, succeeds now in surprising us, astonishing us, even riveting us for two whole hours. In *Chato's Land* the escalation of violence is exceptionally well put across. The film is breathtaking. Winner does not go in for Grand Opera like the Italian Leone, there is no bravura, but instead a subtle de-mystification of the Western and its heroes.'

On the whole the British missed the point! Although Eric Shorter in the *Daily Telegraph* called *Chato's Land* 'intelligent, taut, imaginative and handsome with terse, sometimes even lyrical, dialogue'. The Americans certainly understood it. Norman Maclean Stoop in *New York After Dark* wrote, '*Chato's Land* is an unusually satisfying Western. The parallel to Vietnam is almost impossible to ignore. There is a convincing attempt at realism with the dialogue avoiding both the mindless "frontier talk" of standard Westerns, and the cutesy modernisms of some more recent ones. Bronson's inscrutable brand of heroism combines anew the-Indians-win morality with an old-fashioned John Wayne-like strength, and Jack Palance is very good as the indecisive posse leader who sees everything in terms of past glory – for which, I'm afraid, read: Johnson or Nixon.' Frances Herridge in the *New York Post* wrote, '*Chato's Land* is a thoroughly satisfying Western. The character-isations are fascinating to watch as are the gradual change in viewpoints. And if you find any likeness to our war in Vietnam, the film-makers would probably not object. The entire cast is excellent.'

I gave a lecture at the Arnolfini Cinema in Bristol shortly after *Chato's Land* was released. I said that it reflected the war in Vietnam. The audience roared with laughter as if this was ridiculous! Well, the French and the Americans saw it! In Bristol they're not very bright!

When *Chato's Land* finished my agent got a call from Columbia Pictures who were making a film called *The Mechanic* starring Charlie as an assassin. They said, 'Bronson insists on having Michael Winner as the director which is fine with us.' Because of budget problems the picture moved to United Artists and became my first Hollywood picture. I switched the end of it to Naples and the Amalfi coast because (a) I thought it was good for the picture and (b) I'd never been there and it would be an interesting trip. I started shooting *The Mechanic* at the end of 1970. This meant I shot two and a half major films in one calendar year. Normally people wait a year or two between movies. *The Mechanic* introduced me to Hollywood where they have the most professional and speedy crews in the world, with the possible exception of New York. In England we have on every movie a 'Standby Painter'. He comes in the morning and sets out endless pots of paint. Then he sets out brushes. He sits there until he's required to do something such as touch up a bit of paint on the set, or paint the end of the track (the hardboard that's put down for the camera to run across) so it matches the ground. On the first day of *The Mechanic* the end of the track was coming into picture. I called, 'Standby Painter!' The Propman said, 'We don't have a Standby Painter in Los Angeles, Mr Winner!' He took a spray can from his van and said, 'Here, Mr Winner, you spray the track.' I took the can from him and said, 'It'll be a pleasure.' They said, 'No, no. We'll do it, Mr Winner.' I said, 'No, I'll do it. You've asked me to do it. I'll do it.' On my next UK film I said, 'We're not having a Standby Painter, we'll just have some spray cans on the prop truck.' This caused consternation, because the unions were very strong in those days. And extremely stroppy. My Production Manager said, 'Who do we put on the unit list as the Standby Painter?' I said, 'You put at the head of the unit list "Producer, Director and Standby Painter: Michael Winner". If there's any painting to do I'll do it so as not to embarrass any of you.' That's what we did. I never employed a Standby Painter after that.

The script of *The Mechanic* by Lewis John Carlino had been around for a long time. It initially concerned two homosexuals, a Mafia assassin and a young apprentice who becomes very friendly with him, learns from him and eventually kills him. The homosexual element was taken out. If Charlie thought there'd ever been one, he'd not have made the movie. He was no liberal! I was particularly impressed by a young actor called Richard Dreyfuss, who'd just had a big hit on television. I said to Charlie, 'We should have Richard Dreyfuss as your assistant.' Charlie had seen him and didn't like him. So I couldn't get Richard Dreyfuss past Charlie Bronson. Instead we got another boy who was very hot from television at the time called Jan-Michael Vincent. Jan was very beautiful and later went on to a very chequered career in which drugs and alcohol featured heavily. But he was very pleasant in 1971. Charlie hated him. Jan came in one day and sneezed. Charlie said, 'You've got a nasty cold there, Jan.' Jan said, 'Thank you, for caring about that.' Charlie said, 'I don't care about it at all. I just want to make damn sure you don't pass it on to me!'

Charlie was not an enormous star at the time. This was to be his first Hollywood movie. It was produced by Robert Chartoff and Irwin Winkler, two of the biggest producers of the day, who were, at the same time, making *Rocky*. Charlie insisted that Jill Ireland play the part of a Los Angeles call girl. Irwin Winkler said, 'This is ridiculous.' He had a very good actress in mind. He said, 'I'm going to have breakfast with Charlie. I'll tell him he's not casting the picture. He can't force his wife on us. He's there as an actor and that's it.' Irwin Winkler went to breakfast with Charlie in the Beverly Hills Hotel. I said, 'How did it go, Irwin?' He said, 'I told Charlie I didn't want Jill Ireland to play the part of the call girl. Charlie simply put his knife and fork down and said, 'Okay, I'm quitting the picture,' and got up to go.' Irwin said, 'At that point my only concern was to save the picture. Because without him we didn't have one. If he'd asked for his father to play the call-girl part, I'd have agreed!' So Jill played the part. It wasn't a catastrophe. It did show the intense loyalty Charlie had.

Early in 1972 the unit moved to Naples and Amalfi with my British crew. I visited a famous shop called G. Appa. They do the most wonderful carved coral, carved rare stones and cameos. The chief carver, Professor Notto, carved a seashell that I bought where you can see the fingernails on the girls, the carving is so immaculate. I told Charlie about the place. He said, 'I'd have liked to have gone there. I'd have bought something for Jill.' A few days later we were having lunch in Ravello in a wonderful restaurant overlooking the hills and the distant Mediterranean sea. I had six staff come from G. Appa. They set up a trestle table in the dining room and laid out their goods. They had tortoiseshell, they had combs, they had highly expensive jewellery! The salesmen stood there in dark suits as Charlie, Jill, me and my girlfriend ate lunch. After the first course Charlie got up, walked over to the trestle table, picked up a ring with a stone in it, looked at it, threw it back on the table and said, 'This is rubbish.' Then he walked away. The director of G. Appa said, 'This is disgraceful, I'm taking everything back.' I said quietly, 'You've just made a major sale! My advice is wait.' The Appa director looked confused, but stayed. After the next course, Charlie got up again. I knew this would happen. He went to the trestle table and picked up something else and said, 'This isn't bad.' Like he was the expert and he knew what was good and what was bad. In the end Charlie spent three hundred thousand dollars there. A lot of money in 1972! He bought Jill the most beautiful coral necklace, brooch, bracelet and ear-rings. He bought me something, I forget what now. He bought my girlfriend a present, he bought my assistant, Stephen, a present. And he bought things for his staff in Los Angeles.

The Mechanic was an enormous success. I still get profit cheques from it. Kevin Thomas in the *Los Angeles Times* wrote, 'Michael Winner has come up with another winner in *The Mechanic* which reunites him with Charles Bronson. It's a hard-edged, brutal yet absorbing contemporary gangster movie. *The Mechanic* is a suspense entertainment for all its strong existentialist undertones. There's a hard-boiled hero, lots of highly evocative authentic locales and much breath-taking action. Performances are top notch.' Frances Herridge in the *New York Post* said, '*The Mechanic* is ingenious, even amusing and directed by Michael Winner with his usual sizzling tongue in cheek style.' Charlie was very big in France where Claude Fleouter in *Le Monde* wrote, 'Action film-maker Michael Winner has already shown in *Lawman* and *Chato's Land* his ability to get the desired effect with his accuracy of observation, the same qualities we find in *The Mechanic*. The principal characters are well defined by a series of small touches, and Charles Bronson is remarkably well directed. The film is further graced with a number of touches of humour.' Sheridan Morley in *Films and Filming* wrote, 'You'd be ill-advised to miss *The Mechanic*: it's crisp, cool, clear and when they start Winner's seasons at the National Film Theatre (as they undoubtedly will 20 years from now) it will still be looking good.' I'm not holding my breath for the National Film Theatre to start a Michael Winner Season!

While I was filming on *The Mechanic* in Italy my father had a heart attack. His doctor rang me from London and said, 'You should come back immediately.' I said, 'I can't come back – I'm directing a film.' The doctor said, 'But your father is going to die in the next few days.' I said, 'You don't understand. This is a movie.' This is typical of how utterly gripping movies become. It would have been very difficult for me to leave an entire motion-picture crew leaderless and rudderless in Amalfi. So I didn't. As it happened my father lived and in 1970 he and my mother moved to the South of France to take up residence there. They had been living in the mansion in Melbury Road in a raised ground-floor and basement flat. The basement was extremely damp and, my mother said, would never be anything but damp. Above them were two rent-controlled tenants. The lease was only seventeen years so I was able to buy it quite cheaply. The matter was investigated thoroughly by the district surveyor and I had to pay an arm's length price as in those days they had a gift tax. One of the tenants left and I bought the other tenant out. I've spent a great deal of time restoring this house to its Victorian splendour. It was the home of a very famous artist called Sir Luke Fildes whose main painting, *The Village Wedding*, hangs in Lord Andrew Lloyd Webber's dining room. It was designed by a well-known Victorian architect, Norman Shaw, and is on many of the tours of London.

When you live in rather grand surroundings you attract the burglar fraternity. There was a time when burglars were queueing up to break into my house. They would wander in during the day through the French windows even when the house was fully occupied. Once there were fourteen people in the house at one o'clock and the table was laid for lunch. My bedroom was on the raised ground floor next to the living room. One of the maids saw a burglar at my bedroom desk. He must have thought he'd entered burglar heaven. In the right-hand drawer of my desk were forty watches from Rolex to Patek Phillipe. What he didn't know was that most of them were fake except for four Patek Phillipes. The maid who saw the burglar screamed. A young man who was working for me as an assistant and Jenny Seagrove, my then girlfriend, chased the burglar out of the house, down the street outside my house, and left along Kensington High Street yelling for people to help them. Nobody did. They eventually tripped the burglar up outside the Commonwealth Institute in Kensington High Street and sat on him! Again nobody came to help! They went through his pockets and took back the watches, whereupon their hands were full of watches so they could no longer restrain the burglar. He got up, said, 'Fuck you,' and ran off. They came back to the house and poured these watches on to my desk. Unfortunately one of the Patek Phillipes was missing. I said to

Jenny Seagrove, 'You'll have to go back every day until you find it.'
That was a joke! I got the insurance company to give them each a
thousand pounds. That was a miracle!

I'd already protected the house with an enormous number of
grills and bars and solid metal doors with bullet-proof glass which
cannot be broken and steel door frames so they could not be
knocked open. This applied to the front door and various doors
within the house. It particularly applied to my bedroom door. One
night I was there and I realised I hadn't locked the door. I said to my
then girlfriend, who had the wonderful name of Sparkle, 'Would
you go and lock the door?' She said, 'I can't be bothered.' I thought,
'Nothing's ever happened.' So I went to sleep. At three in the
morning I heard a noise outside the bedroom. I went to the door
which was closed but not locked. I opened the door and facing me
less than two feet away was a burglar. He had in his hand a rusty
steel prod with a wooden handle for picking up leaves. Seeing me
naked, not a pretty sight, the burglar was more taken aback than me.
I slammed the door and locked it. I screamed out to Sparkle, 'Call
the police!' She said, 'What's the number?' The burglar, instead of
running off, started hurling himself against the door. I knew it was
likely to cave in because the door had fallen somewhat on the hinges
and the lock only went in about a sixteenth of an inch. It then
became a total French farce. I ran round the bed to get to the panic
button that set off the alarms. Sparkle ran in the other direction to
lock herself in the bathroom. We collided at the bottom of the bed.
I got to the panic button. The alarms went off and the burglar went,
having taken very little. In fact there's nothing worth taking in my
house. Only a few bits of porcelain they could sell for three pence if
they're lucky on the burglar market.

About four nights later burglars came in through the bars which I'd
placed too far apart and took a few bits and pieces. Three weeks later
I was woken up again around three in the morning. I could hear noises
from the living room next door. I went to the bay window of my
bedroom and looked through. On the balcony outside the living room
were three black men trying to break in. They wore white bobble hats
and long, light grey suede coats. I thought, 'This is ridiculous! At least
they could wear balaclavas and look like burglars!'

I walked back into my room thinking, 'If I press the panic button again my staff will quit. They're all uptight already about all these burglaries.' So I went back to the window and knocked on the glass. The burglars looked round, couldn't see me and carried on trying to get in. So I drew back the curtains and waved a handkerchief at them screaming, stark naked, 'Cooee!' That would have scared anybody! Off they ran. A short time later a very small lady policewoman and a very fat male policeman arrived. I said, 'What would you have done if the burglars had still been here? There were three of them and they were very tough.' The policeman said, 'We'd have called for help.' I said, 'That wouldn't have been much good. You'd probably have been dead by then.'

Another time a very respectable Scoutmaster-looking man came to my front gate, which we now keep locked, and said, 'I'm collecting for The Friends of Holland Park.' (That's the local Holland Park society.) He had a clipboard and asked for ten pounds for my year's subscription. I gave him the ten pounds and off he went. A year later he came back. He said, 'Remember me?' I said. 'Yes, you were collecting for The Friends of Holland Park.' He said, 'It's still only ten pounds.' I said, 'Last year I asked you for a receipt. I didn't get one.' He said, 'I'll see the secretary sends you one this year.' I gave him the ten pounds and off he went. I got no receipt, so I phoned the secretary of The Friends of Holland Park. He said, 'That's a well-known confidence trickster. He walks round Kensington collecting ten pounds for The Friends of Holland Park. He's a crook.' I thought he deserved to get away with that, it was such a cheek. I suppose if you live in a house with nine toilets, seven bathrooms and about forty-six rooms you can expect to have occasional problems. I now have more than one hundred and sixty-eight lights outside the house. Blackpool illuminations have nothing on me. The entire house and gardens are brilliantly lit with cameras and burglar alarms all over the place. Since then nothing has happened. Or maybe word got out from the burglars who came in that everything they took was rubbish and they couldn't get any money for it. Either way things have been quite peaceful lately.

18

Spying and Dying

My next movie reunited me with Burt Lancaster. United Artists had a CIA spy picture, *Dangerfield*, to be produced by Walter Mirisch, an important, old-time Hollywood producer with a number of Academy Awards. My regular writer Gerald Wilson re-wrote the script. The story concerned an ageing CIA agent, an ageing Russian agent – who I got Paul Scofield for – and a young French hired assassin for the Central Intelligence Agency, played by Alain Delon. Early in the proceedings I resigned from the film because of differences of opinion between myself and Walter Mirisch. To the surprise of the Hollywood community, United Artists backed me and handed over the movie, leaving Walter with a credit but no active participation. The title *Dangerfield* had been registered by somebody else, so we needed a new name. I'm a Scorpio and fairly typical. Burt Lancaster is a Scorpio and very typical! Flashes of great temper but very kind underneath. Alain Delon was a Scorpio and Walter Mirisch, the deposed chief, was a Scorpio. So we gave Alain Delon's spy character the code name Scorpio and called the film *Scorpio*.

It was set in Washington, Paris and Vienna. Quite a lot in the CIA headquarters. My American Location Manager said, 'What sort of building do you want for the CIA?' I said, 'The real CIA!' He said,

'What if I can't get it?' I said, 'We'll get another Location Manager.' In 1972 the CIA was very secret indeed. No one was meant to know where it was. It hadn't been investigated and criticised. Richard Helms was the Director, Angus Maclean Theurmer was his Assistant and Howard Osborne was in charge of Internal CIA Security. My American Production Manager got on to Burt Lancaster who, in turn, reached Senator Tunney who, in turn, got permission from the CIA for us to shoot in their 'secret' building. This was a major coup. I went to Washington and turned up at the CIA one Saturday. We were met by Howard Osborne and shown round. I was with my girlfriend, who'd recently been a major American beauty queen, Miss Rhinegold Beer. She caused great excitement among the CIA agents. We took some Polaroid pictures of the agents with her and threw in the waste-basket the used Polaroid covering, which at the time kept an image on it. These were examined by agents the following Monday and caused consternation as to why this beautiful girl was posing with CIA agents!

In my passage through the building I took photographs of everything, including signs that said, 'No photography' and 'No tape recording permitted'. I also tape recorded all the details I could see. I photographed the badges the agents wore to get in and out of the building, all the entry and exit signs and everything. I took the photographs in case anything adverse happened and I needed to recreate it elsewhere. I went back to the Watergate Hotel in Washington and telephoned David Picker, the number two at United Artists. I was excited I'd got permission to shoot in the CIA.

A couple of days later Picker rang me and said, 'Arnold doesn't want you to take up your permission to shoot in the CIA.' Arnold Picker was the distinguished Chairman of United Artists. He worked on a number of committees in Washington. He was obviously nervous that having a movie showing the CIA assassinating people would compromise his position in Washington. I said, 'David, I beg of you, have Arnold reconsider. Because we have this very great location success. We'll be the only film ever to shoot in the CIA.' David Picker rang back and said, 'Arnold says if you show the CIA the script and get their approval, you can go ahead.' I said, 'If the

CIA want to see the script they could have it secretly photographed. They could steal it! They haven't even asked for it! They gave permission on a synopsis of the story.' But Arnold was adamant. I was in the interesting position of having to send the CIA a script showing them involved in a great many nefarious activities and on top of that written by a Canadian who was barred from entering America as a suspected Communist. I sent the script to Angus Maclean Theurmer, the Assistant CIA Director Richard Helms. To my amazement Angus wrote back, 'It was your side that cancelled the arrangement to shoot here, not us. We have read your script. We have kept a copy of page 53 and 97 [neither had anything remotely interesting on them] and if it is all right with your people we can return to the status quo ante.' That's Latin for meaning we can go back to where things were. Namely we still had permission. The letter was extraordinary because the CIA didn't have to tell me they'd photographed two pages of the script.

They could photocopy the whole script without telling me! I sent the CIA letter to David Picker and said, 'Here's the letter Arnold wanted.' So we used the real CIA.

The shooting of *Scorpio* commenced in Washington in June 1972. I was staying at the Watergate at the exact time President Nixon and the Republican Party arranged to have their subversives break into the offices of the Democratic Party in the Watergate building. I later said, 'They may have robbed it, but they certainly wouldn't have stayed to dinner.'

The CIA took no particular precautions about my bringing in a two-hundred-strong British and US film crew with local extras. We went on a Sunday when it wasn't too busy. None of us had to take passports or any identification, which is often required when you go into sensitive areas. I turned up ahead of the crew. Howard Osborne, the Director of Security, was there with a nice CIA lady who had what looked like an ice-cream tray. In it she had a lot of badges. She said to me, 'This will show we've got a sense of humour, Mr Winner!' They'd made a special CIA guest badge with a scorpion on it! I said, 'How many of those badges have you got?' She said, 'A hundred.' I said, 'You have got a sense of humour. I'm bringing in two hundred people!' My crew lined up to get in and CIA agents were saying, 'What's your name?' and then they'd say to the person next to him, 'Can you verify this is the real person who's just given his name?' And the next person would say, 'I've no idea who he is. He's English, I'm from Washington.' Howard Osborne saw the badges my actors were wearing. They were almost identical to the real badges, blue with a space for the photograph of the agent. Around the agent's photograph were a number of small red squares with white lettering on, indicating areas of the building the agent was allowed to enter. Howard Osborne said, 'Where did you get those?' I said, 'I had them printed in London, Howard. You were with me when I photographed them on my reconnaissance.' Howard said, 'They look exactly like our badges.' He asked if he could keep three of them.

I was sitting with the crew at lunch outside in the CIA grounds when there was suddenly a terrible wailing of police cars. I said to Alain Delon, who was under investigation because his chauffeur had been found with a body in the boot of his car, 'They've come to get you, Alain.' Alain was extremely amusing. He was born two days earlier than me. He was an enormous star in France but he'd never made it in America. He had a problem: he spoke very fast. I said, 'Alain, French accents are difficult to understand anyway. Please don't speak so quickly.' He said, 'But they told me I had to speak fast so it looked like I understood the language.' I said, 'Yes, well, don't speak fast, Alain. Speak so we can understand you!'

We were sitting in Washington one day. Alain and I were on our chairs and Burt Lancaster was a few yards from us. The public were besieging Burt for autographs. Nobody was taking any notice of Alain. They didn't know him in America. Alain said, 'Michael, you know when we go to Vienna, it will be different. Because I'm very famous in Vienna. For many years I took out Romy Schneider who is the Queen of Vienna. When we're in Vienna they'll all know me.' A few weeks later we were sitting in a Viennese street. It was exactly the same! I was with Alain and Burt was a few yards away. Hundreds of Austrians milled around Burt to get his autograph and to be photographed with him. Nobody took any notice of Alain Delon. I said, 'Alain, when we were in Washington and Burt was getting all the attention, you told me that when we came to Vienna I'd see something quite different. Crowds would all be around you, because you were very famous in Vienna.' Alain smiled. 'Not in this quarter of Vienna,' he said.

I asked one of the agents working with us in the CIA, 'Why do you think we were allowed in?' The agent said, 'I understand Richard Helms wanted to make the CIA more accessible.' I never understood this remark. When I got to London I received an extraordinary letter from Howard Osborne. He said, 'Dear Michael, It was a great pleasure to have you. You all behaved very well and we very much enjoyed you being in the CIA with us. When you left we gave your movie CIA identity badges to three of our agents and they all got into the building wearing them the next day. So could you please not show the badges in close up on the screen. Will you also be sure to destroy them at the end of the shooting.' This was a careless letter. Luckily I was not anti-CIA. I was very pro-America. I didn't use any of these letters to embarrass the institution which had helped us. I wrote to Howard, 'It would be very difficult not to show the artists wearing the badges in close up because that's how we make a film. We've already established the badges on them and we're now filming scenes in England some of which are supposedly in the CIA. But if you'd like to nominate a time and place I'd be very happy to burn the badges after the film in front of a CIA agent.' I never heard from Howard again. It was only when the Watergate robbery and investigation came to the front of American politics that all those people – Richard Helms, Angus Maclean Theurmer and Howard Osborne – entered the news when they gave evidence. I was reading about old friends.

We used England as America for some interiors because it meant we didn't have to keep the whole crew in hotels in Washington. I was amused by a later review in the *Washington Post* which said, 'It was wonderful to see Washington's old Madison Hotel on 61st Street captured on the screen shortly before it was pulled down.' It was the British Railways hotel near King's Cross!

One of the great pleasures of working on *Scorpio* was to be with Paul Scofield. We became great friends. Paul is the only man I know personally who turned down a knighthood. He said, 'But you wouldn't want a knighthood, would you, Michael?' I said, 'I'll take anything, Paul.' Now I'm not sure I would. The first day of shooting, with Paul playing an ageing Russian agent, was in an Edwardian building in Holland Park. We used it as the interior of the Russian Embassy in Vienna. I said to Paul, 'You start here, sir. Then you say the line up to this point and then you piss off and walk over there and say the rest of it from there.' I called 'Action!' and Paul did the scene. I went over to Paul at the end, and said, 'I'm terribly sorry, sir . . .' Paul said, 'I know, Michael, I forgot to piss off!' He was a man of immense humanity and terrific wit. I used to go to his cottage in the country and he came to my house in London to have dinner with Sophia Loren. I put him on in *The Tempest* in London, having brought the show down from the Playhouse in Nottingham. Paul had a wonderfully naughty side. We were having drinks after the first night – it was amazingly a show that made a profit, which is very rare for the theatre. At the reception a man came up and talked to me and Paul and then walked away. It seemed a perfectly normal conversation. Paul said, 'Did you hear that fucking cunt?' I said, 'What, Paul?' He said, 'He's an absolute shit, that man. He's the theatre manager. I can't stand him, he's a real arsehole.' It was wonderful to hear Paul using those words in that beautiful Shakespearean tone of voice.

While we were filming in Washington two representatives came from Britain's National Film Theatre to ask Burt Lancaster if he'd give a lecture at the National Film Theatre. They were then called the John Player Lectures. They'd had less starry people, I'd done one myself. Burt was to be their first major star. They asked if Burt would let it be televised. Burt agreed to do the lecture and to have it televised. Back in London I reminded Burt. He said, 'I don't want it televised, Michael. I get paid for television. I thought it was just a talk to a few students.' I'm sure that's what Burt genuinely remembered of the meeting. But it wasn't true. I told the National Film Theatre that Burt didn't want the television cameras there. This upset them greatly because it was a big opportunity for them. It would be the first one to be televised. They asked if I'd have him reconsider. Burt thought about it and he said, 'You know, Michael, I often use bad language. I don't want that to be caught on television.' I said, 'I'll ask them to let you edit from the tape recording up to five one-minute sections. Would you then do it?' He said, 'Yes.' So I wrote to the BBC, whose Producer was now calling me about the televising of the lecture. The Producer said to me, 'The BBC can't agree to have anyone else edit their material. But I'll give you my word that we'll let him take these five minutes out.' I said, 'That's not good enough. You have to put it in writing.' I'm sure today the BBC would put this in writing. But in those days the Producer, or the BBC, or both, were very up their own arse. They said, 'No, it concerns the BBC Charter and we can't put it in writing.' I said, 'Fine, then there's no television.'

On the day of the lecture my publicity man went to the National Film Theatre in the morning and rang me on the set. He said, 'The National Film Theatre is surrounded with television equipment. The BBC are bringing in their cameras and their cables. They're televising this lecture without Mr Lancaster's permission.' I rang the BBC Producer and said, 'My publicity man is going to be in the National Film Theatre at seven o'clock tonight. Mr Lancaster and I will be having dinner. When I'm telephoned and told there's not one piece of TV equipment in the National Film Theatre, only then will I arrange for Burt to come at seven-thirty for the reception, followed by the lecture at eight-fifteen.' At seven o'clock my man rang and said, 'All the television equipment has gone.' So Burt and I turned up in the lobby of the National Film Theatre. I'd made the mistake of conducting all these arrangements myself. So the staff and the organisers were looking at me with a deep and massive disregard. They blamed me for Burt not having the television there. I've never been in a place where people hated me so much. Someone said, 'Mr Lancaster, why did you object to the television? Why didn't you want the BBC to tape your lecture?' Burt Lancaster said, 'Television? I wouldn't have minded television at all.' He turned to me and said, 'You never told me anything about television, Michael. I'd have been very happy to have this televised.' At that point the hatred directed to me went totally off the Richter Scale. I've never known anything like it!

In those days at the National Film Theatre you went from the lobby into a very narrow corridor which led to a spiral staircase up to a big reception room. This is where they were having drinks for 'important' people before Burt's lecture. For a short time Burt and I walked side by side, in front of everyone. I said to Burt in a low voice, 'Burt, you've just stabbed me in the back. You've left me in a pool of blood with what you said about the television.' Without dropping his pace Burt said, with his wonderful smile, 'You've got to remember one thing, Michael. The star always has to look good.' That's why Burt was so absolutely marvellous. He could do these things and you just had to forgive and love him.

After that the BBC put out an internal memorandum, the sort of thing they did in those days, saying that neither Michael Winner nor any of his films were ever to be on British television again. I was due to do an important film programme and they suddenly phoned me and said, 'We can't have you on.' We were sneaked a copy of this memo and my solicitor wrote to them and said if anything was against the BBC Charter, this was. It was victimisation. The BBC caved in. In order to show that I was not banned they asked me on to some gardening programme!

Scorpio went on to shoot in Vienna. There was a big chase scene through the new subway that was being built. Burt, although he was fifty-five years old, was determined to do as many stunts as he could. Alain Delon was game for anything. In one scene we'd kept the Viennese traffic held up. Burt was to chase Alain across the road. They both had guns in their hands. We should have had only stuntmen driving the cars. But the real traffic had been held up! The drivers were irate and in a hurry! Their cars came tearing down! Burt and Alain ran across it. When I see that scene my heart misses a beat. Burt is going in front of members of the public, running in front of the cars, pointing at them as if to say, 'Don't you dare run me over.' The end of the film was in Paris and involved a big shoot-out at Orly Airport. There had been a number of plane hijackings shortly before. Originally Orly had said we could come. Now they said we couldn't. Alain Delon heard me discussing this. He said, 'If you want to get into Orly Airport, I know who you have to bribe. Just give me thirty thousand dollars in a suitcase.' Alain got the thirty thousand dollars. We suddenly got permission to shoot wherever we wanted at Orly. They even let us bring in real guns and real blank bullets. It was interesting to note the contrast between the CIA 'precautions' before letting us into the CIA and the far stricter way Orly Airport acted. We all had to bring our passports. We all had to have badges with our pictures on them. The security was immense.

In Vienna, shooting on this huge underground construction that went down a hundred feet or more, there was a scene where Burt was running up scaffolding ladders and along wooden platforms with wooden railings. One of the baddies fired a gun at him. There was an enormous divide between the film crew and Burt on his wooden walkway – a 'moat' a hundred feet deep. We had three cameras on our concrete ledge. As Burt ran along his walkway three bullet hits slammed into the wooden rail, just missing him. I did these bullet hits myself. I held a metal rod and touched nails sticking out of a box. As I touched each one the bullet hits went off. I called 'Action!', Burt ran up the steps then along the walkway, and the bullet hits went off perfectly, just 'missing' him! I called 'Cut'. The Camera Operators said, 'Got it, Mr Winner, that's fine.' I saw Burt walking back along the walkway. I knew I was in trouble. Burt screamed at the top of his voice, red in the face and apoplectic with rage! 'Hey you pricko Charlie! You stupid fuck English moron pig! You piece of scum! You shit-head idiot! What the fuck do you think you're doing?! You couldn't direct fucking traffic, you couldn't direct anything! Why the fuck can't you get it right?!' I was confused! There was nothing wrong! I said in very gentlemanly fashion, 'I'm terribly sorry, sir, I don't know what you're talking about.' Burt went even madder. He yelled, 'You fucking arsehole! You limey cunt! I'm talking about the fucking bullet hits. You stupid prick! They went off at the wrong time. You cock-sucker! Now we've got to do the whole fucking thing again!'

I looked round at the cameramen who were as bemused as me, because they knew it was perfect. I said, 'I'm terribly sorry, sir, the bullet hits went off just as you passed, just missing you. So when you were there [I pointed], the bullet hits went off, there!' Burt said, 'You fucking idiot!' I said, 'Excuse me, sir, where do you think the bullet hits should have been?' Burt pointed to an area well behind him. It was ridiculous! You'd have had to see him run by, hold on the wooden railing and wait for the bullet hits. He said, 'That's where they should fucking be, you cock-sucker!' I thought, 'I'm not going to argue.'

It took about forty-five minutes to lay these bullet hits. You had to wire them in, you had to put explosive in them, you had to wire them back to me on the other side of this great divide. I said, 'I'm terribly sorry, sir, we will redo the shot.' The Camera Operators said to me, 'We can't get Mr Lancaster and the bullet hits on the screen. We've got to go to a wider angle.' I said, 'Do anything you like. This one's for Mr Lancaster.' We eventually re-set it and I called 'Action!' Burt ran along and the three bullets went off just where he wanted them. They were miles behind him and completely useless. Burt walked up after the shot and said, 'How was that?' I said, 'Fine, sir.' Burt screamed at me, 'Well, you see you fucking idiot! If you listen, you learn!' I'll never forget that. It was absolutely magical. My assistant whispered to me, 'It was two weeks before the end of *Lawman* he had a go at you last time. It's obviously something about the time in the schedule.' Within a day Burt was asking me to dinner again and bought me the most enormous present at the end of the movie. Burt was famous for his temper. It was quite irrational. I didn't give a damn. He was the most terrific person. If I occasionally shout at someone today, they say, 'This is terrible, you mustn't do that.' I say 'Please! A number of people in my life have shouted at me. They were the best people. Who cares!'

The movie finished. Jay Cocks in *Time* magazine said, 'Burt Lancaster has the proper cunning and just the right kind of careful menace and restrained violence. There is a very clever, quietly brutal assassination, some estimable supporting players and even a certain obtuse symmetry to the carnage that closes the film.' Kevin Thomas in the *Los Angeles Times* wrote, 'Handsomely mounted and deeply cynical, Burt Lancaster is a staunch figure of dignity even sympathy. Alain Delon is well cast as a cool yet not unprincipled killer. Paul Scofield dominates as a warm, full-blooded man who has faced all the evils of Communism squarely but still believes in it.' In the *International Herald Tribune* Thomas Quinn Curtis said, 'Burt Lancaster agilely dodges bullets in Washington, Paris and Vienna. There is an especially well-acted scene in a Viennese hide-out in which he discusses the profession with an old Soviet spy, Paul Scofield. Michael Winner has directed maintaining a tense pace and the required suspense throughout.' Harry MacArthur in the

Washington Daily News said, '*Scorpio*'s a rousing spy thriller. It generates a lot of excitement. The performances are excellent. Burt Lancaster's risk of life and limb is incredible. Alain Delon is a chilling killer.' Margaret Hinxman in the London *Sunday Telegraph* wrote, '*Scorpio*'s Michael Winner's most accomplished film. It is never out of control. It's a tough, exciting, cloak and dagger adventure, the plot exudes a fortuitous whiff of Watergate with something more than mere panache.'

I remained close friends with Burt. If ever I went to Los Angeles he'd lay on dinners for me. If he came to London I'd be with him. He was always accompanied by his girlfriend Jackie although in later years they parted. Once Burt came to London and introduced me to his wife-to-be, Susie. He said he was thinking of marrying her. He asked me what I thought. I said, 'I definitely think you should marry this lady. She seems a very, very nice person.' He married her shortly thereafter. It was not long after that I heard Burt had suffered a stroke. In June 1982 I was in Los Angeles and went to his apartment in Century City. It's a place I'd been to many times. It had a large Mexican door and looked out over Beverly Hills. It was evening and his wife Susie said to me, 'If you don't understand what Burt says at first, ask him to repeat it.' She took me into a dimly lit room. Burt was lying on a bed that could be wheeled about. It was without question one of the most terrible moments of my life. Burt couldn't speak at all. He grunted or he said, 'Lo-lo-lo-lo.' You felt he could hear everything. At one point he raised his eyebrows in that wonderful dismissive 'My God, what am I having to go through?' gesture which he did when someone said something he didn't like. He was paralysed. He could just about raise one arm. I knew he could hear what I was saying. I held his hand and talked to him. He cried and I cried. I told him I loved him. That was the last I saw of this incredible athletic, witty, full-bodied man. He didn't die for a number of years. People came and took him out in a wheelchair, pushed him around and brought him back. Susie stayed by him and looked after him. But what a tragic ending. An ending everybody fears. Not death, which is simple, quick and clean. But a living hell. A mind trapped in a useless body. It was a terrible way for such a superb man to end his life.

19

Death Wish Explodes

My next picture was *The Stone Killer*, in 1973. It starred Charles Bronson. It was from a book by John Gardner, the man who'd written to me many years back telling me I had rave reviews in *Time* and *Newsweek* for *The Girl-Getters*. His book, *A Complete State of Death*, dealt with the Sicilian branch of the Mafia doing a multiple bank heist in Stratford-upon-Avon in order to finance a massacre of the old Mafia in New York. By the time Gerald Wilson finished with the script Stratford-upon-Avon was gone! It was a Mafia cop story with Bronson as a tough cop following up a killing that led him from Los Angeles to New York and back. The movie was financed by an Italian, Dino de Laurentiis. He was planning to re-locate from Rome to Los Angeles. *The Stone Killer* was his first all-American movie. I opened offices for Dino in the old Goldwyn Studios in Hollywood. From there I ran the film. Dino was a wonderful character. Very enthusiastic. Sometimes a little late paying bills, but always upbeat. The movie also gave me a chance to direct one of Hollywood's finest character actors, Martin Balsam, and many other American actors I'd admired over the years. It was a major action picture with cars crashing through windows and into each other in mammoth chases. In those days there were no digital effects to help you. If a car came out of a window, there was a man in it. After it crashed to the ground everybody waited to see if he was still alive. On the first day of *The Stone Killer* I was directing on location in Los Angeles. A very beautiful blonde girl wearing white hot pants, a white blouse and white boots came up to me holding a red rose. She said, 'I'm a present from Joe.' Joe was our Casting Director. His present was the rose and the girl. She was a young Hollywood actress who enjoyed being promiscuous. There are girls like that in every town in every country in the world. There's nothing wrong with them. They want to get out and enjoy life. We have serious and lengthy relationships. And we have fun affairs. Life would be very tedious if we were restricted to only one!

I was now very friendly with Charlie Bronson and often visited his palatial home in Bel Air and spent evenings with him as well as being with him during the day. Because Charlie had suffered so much in his youth he felt he'd given already. He was not deeply sympathetic to the world. He was particularly fond of the extreme right-wing American Vice-President Spiro Agnew. He'd come on the set each day and read Spiro Agnew statements from the *Los Angeles Times* and say what a wonderful man he was. During the movie Spiro Agnew had to resign over irregularities in his financial life. I said, 'It's a terrible day, Charlie! Your hero Spiro Agnew has been forced out of office for being dishonest.' Charlie said, 'Jeez, that always happens to the good people!' When we booked Charlie into a hotel in New York for the shooting, he said, 'I don't want to be above the second floor because if there's a fire, I won't be able to get out.' In America a second floor is the floor immediately above ground level. That means you're often above the noise of reception rooms. But Charlie was adamant. In view of what has since happened it was not unintelligent!

Charlie was very conscious of the fact that he'd come to stardom late. He dieted carefully and exercised all the time. I found it droll that he'd be shooting everybody with an eagle eye, then we'd go to lunch together in a restaurant, he'd forget his glasses, and I'd have to read him the menu! One of the things Charlie most hated was when members of the public came up to him to shake his hand. He usually refused. 'I might catch something from them,' he said. Charlie always believed people were out to cheat him. There was a magic moment on *The Stone Killer* when he said to me, 'Steven is watering down my Yuban coffee.' There was a rather dreary American mass-produced instant coffee called Yuban. Charlie loved it so I made sure there was a good supply for him. My personal assistant, Steven, would make the coffee in Charlie's caravan and bring it to him on the set. I said, 'Why would Steven water down the Yuban, Charlie?' Charlie said, 'He thinks if he doesn't use so much coffee the company won't have to buy so many tins of coffee for me.' I said, 'I tell you what, Charlie, I'll send my driver now to buy a hundred tins of Yuban from the nearest supermarket. I'll donate them to the Charlie Bronson Yuban Trust.' That got half a smile from him until he sipped the coffee again and said, 'Jeez, this is watered down!'

I was on a run. *The Stone Killer* got rave reviews. Roger Greenspun in *The New York Times* wrote, 'I like Michael Winner's latest *The Stone Killer* very much indeed. It keeps turning into exciting cinema, crude but often funny and sometimes quite brilliantly idiomatic. It may come as close to inspired primitivism as we are likely to get in the movies these days.' Roger Ebert in the *Chicago Sun-Times* wrote, 'Michael Winner's *The Stone Killer* is a superior example of its type, tough cop against the mob. It offers stylish escapism at break-neck speed and it gives us a chase and a gun battle that surpass themselves.' Roy Frumkes writing in the *US National Board of Review* said, 'Some of the year's most lucid headlong narrative film-making – entertainment with all the aesthetics and complexity of art – flow through Michael Winner's latest story. Story telling is the core of successful film-making be it Bergman or Ford, and Winner spins a tale on a level with the best of the heavyweights. Social muddle emerges as an honest portrait of America's divergent nature. Winner's two previous films, *The Mechanic* and *Scorpio*, were heavy with themes of social, political and criminal paranoia. The present climate in this country is laden with mistrust and Winner seems in retrospect to have been intellectually very close to all of it.'

At the end of *The Stone Killer* we were to shoot a scene in Kennedy Airport. Then I'd board a plane for London where I edited the films myself. When other directors took a holiday after shooting a movie, I'd sit hunched over the Moviola for ten weeks, marking up the celluloid myself with a wax pencil and making the Sellotape joins. On our last day of *The Stone Killer*, Charlie said, 'What shall we do next?' I'd been traipsing around for a few years with a script called *Death Wish* which nobody wanted. I said, 'The best script I've got is *Death Wish*. It's about a man whose wife and daughter are mugged and he goes out and shoots muggers.' Charlie said, 'I'd like to do that.' I said, 'The film?' Charlie said, 'No. Shoot muggers.' That's how *Death Wish* got made. It was from a novella by a writer called Brian Garfield. I think the original book sold three copies. Brian Garfield's mother bought two of them. It had been picked up by two producers, Hal Landers and Bobby Roberts, who'd got United Artists to finance a screenplay. United Artists showed it to me. I thought it was marvellous and wanted to do it. But they said, 'We can't make this film, Michael, nobody will accept a citizen who goes out and shoots other citizens as a hero in movies. It just can't be done. Also, it's uncastable. If we get Charles Bronson to play the hero [he was at the time an accountant], no one will believe he's an accountant, but they'll believe he's a killer. If we get Walter Matthau to play the hero, they'll believe he's an accountant but they won't believe he's a killer.' I said, 'Fellas, this is ridiculous. Killers don't go around looking like killers. Killers are frequently the nice man with spectacles and a cat who lives next door.'

United Artists gave up on the movie and said I could offer the script to any other company. If I sold it they'd want their money back plus interest. So for three years I offered the script of *Death Wish*. All the movie companies said the same thing. 'You can't make a film where a citizen kills other citizens.' And, 'It's uncastable.' Dino de Laurentiis was not conventional like the American majors. He adored the script of *Death Wish*. He had a contract with Bronson, and he immediately put it into 'go'. In recent years *Death Wish* has been dismissed in Britain, but in America it's considered an important watershed film in the history of movies. It was in many of the American critics' Ten Best of the Year list. The English critics on the whole liked it when it came out. They've since written it off as exploitative nonsense, which it isn't. It became the most imitated film in history. After *Death Wish* showed that you can have a citizen killing bad guys and be a hero, practically every American action film ever since took that theme. *Kill Bill* is *Death Wish* with Jap swords. Revenge films abound now. Before *Death Wish* it was only in Westerns that a citizen could gun down nasty people and be applauded.

Dino de Laurentiis sold *Death Wish* before we started shooting to Paramount for release in America. The Head of Paramount, Frank Yablans, was very worried we shouldn't show too many black muggers. Statistically most of the muggings in New York then were done by blacks and Hispanics. Yablans was concerned we shouldn't appear anti-black. I thought that was anti-black in itself. Because he was saying that blacks were so debauched a race that they'd support black muggers and not wish to see them killed by Charlie Bronson. When the film came out the black people, who were massively mugged in their own communities because the muggers don't have to go so far, cheered loudly whenever Charlie Bronson killed muggers. Black or white. I saw 'muggers' in groups of seven young actors and picked out the most likely ones. Then I had them play a scene where they had to rape a chair. In one of these office auditions there was a young man with a knife and dark glasses who looked very odd. Suddenly he took out the knife as if he was going to attack me. One of the other actors jumped on top of him! A major scuffle ensued in my small office. It was very silly because the fellow with the knife was only play-acting, but you don't draw a knife in a crowded office in New York. There was one young man who was particularly loose and brilliant in the auditions. I went to Frank Yablans and Dino and said, 'You don't have to worry about the blacks. I've just chosen the chief mugger in the film. He's a Jew! You won't have trouble from them!' They said, 'Who is he?' I said, 'You've never heard of him. Jeff Goldblum.' That was Jeff's first film. I did another film with him soon afterwards. Later *Death Wish Two* had Laurence Fishburne, the African-American actor who became a big star playing the chief mugger. And in *Death Wish Three* Alex Winter, who starred with Keanu Reeves in the *Bill and Ted* movies, was the main mugger.

I was waiting for Charlie Bronson to tell me he wanted Jill Ireland to play his wife in the movie. I didn't think she was suitable for the part so I kept quiet. Finally I said to him, 'Charlie, do you want Jill to play your wife in *Death Wish*?' Charlie said, 'I don't. I don't want her humiliated and messed around by these actors who play the muggers.' Charlie thought for a moment and then he said, 'You know the sort of person we want, someone who looks like Hope Lange.' Hope Lange was the very nice-looking typical American lady who had starred in the *Dick Van Dyke Show*. I said, 'Well, Charlie, the person who looks most like Hope Lange is Hope Lange. So I'll get her.' And I did. It was a terrific idea of Charlie's. She was perfect for the role.

The first *Death Wish* was shot in New York in freezing weather. It was so cold at night the water of our eyes froze. We wore face masks. I think Bronson's job in *Death Wish* is a very fine piece of acting. The script had been written by Wendell Mayes, a distinguished old-timer who'd written for Gary Cooper and Otto Preminger. I added a scene at the beginning where Charlie is on holiday photographing his wife in Hawaii. Then his wife is murdered and his daughter raped. Later the photographs come back from the laboratory after he's been down to Tucson and been given a gun by an architect. It's the emotional impact of the photographs that makes him go out and kill his first mugger. There's also a wonderfully bizarre scene which I had Wendell put in. Charlie has done a number of murders and is now very happy. He's found a vocation. He's fulfilled. He's fighting back against those who murdered his wife and made his daughter catatonic. He's painted his apartment red and he's got very loud music playing and his son-in-law comes in and says, 'Please Dad, I've just been to see Carol in the hospital' and Charlie says, 'Well, we can't worry for ever, we've got to get on with life.'

Most films need a coda at the end. I wrote one for *Death Wish* which nobody liked! It turned out one of the most effective scenes in the film. One people remember. Bronson has been caught in New York but the police won't arrest him because he's become a national hero and muggings were down 60 per cent as a result of his cleaning up the streets. So they tell him to get out of town. He ends up at the railway station in Chicago, where he sees some louts roughing up a young girl. He goes down on one knee and raises his finger like a gun, smiles and does a click with his finger as if he's going to shoot muggers in Chicago. This was considered far too outrageous to put

Above: With Alice Faye on the set of *Won Ton Ton The Dog Who Saved Hollywood* in Los Angeles in 1975.

Left: With James Caan when he visited the standing New York set on the lot at Warner Bros. Burbank studios during the shooting of *Won Ton Ton* in 1975.

Right: Greeting Richard Dreyfuss in New York when he appeared as an unpaid extra in *The Sentinel* in 1976.

Left: In the Central Intelligence Agency, Langley, Virginia, on *Scorpio* in 1972.

Below: With Charles Bronson during the filming of *Death Wish* in New York in 1974.

Left: With Burt Lancaster and Alain Delon in Vienna on the set of *Scorpio* in 1972.

Above: Directing Ava Gardner on *The Sentinel* in Brooklyn in 1976. Ava was the most beautiful, insecure and lovely person. We remained friends until she died in Kensington, London, in 1990.

Bottom left: On the set of *Won Ton Ton The Dog Who Saved Hollywood*.

Bottom right: With Robert Mitchum and Joan Collins on location for *The Big Sleep* in Kensington, London, in 1977.

With Sophia Loren in St Lucia for the filming of *Firepower* in 1978. It was Sophia – whose oft repeated phrase was 'What's the discount?' – who taught me how to save money everywhere!

Sophia serves me spaghetti with her own sauce in St Lucia during the filming of *Firepower*. Anthony Franciosa is on the left and on the right are James Coburn and Lynsey de Paul.

With O.J. Simpson and Nicole (who later became his wife) in Bridgeport, Connecticut, during the filming of *Firepower*. I always thought that, as alleged double murderers go, O.J. was extremely pleasant!

With Faye Dunaway in Hertfordshire, England, in 1983. 'Faysie' (as I called her) was a total and cheerful delight. Not, in any way at all, the wicked lady I'd been warned about!

With Charles Bronson in east New York during the shooting of *Death Wish Three* in 1985. Repeat visits to the plastic surgeon had changed Charlie facially from the man I first met. He was also getting a bit chubby, but still terrific to work with. I, on the other hand, look marvellously thin!

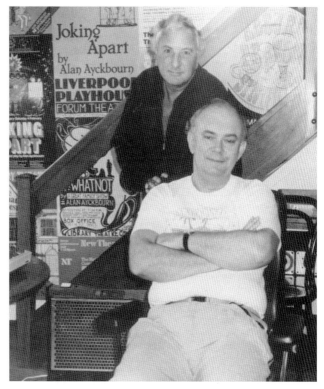

Right: With Alan Ayckbourn
at his home in Scarborough
when he was showing me
the locations he wanted us
to use for *A Chorus of
Disapproval* in 1988.

Below: With Lauren Bacall
in Israel during the shooting
of *Appointment with Death*
in 1987.

With Sir John Gielgud, Peter Ustinov and Jenny Seagrove in Israel for the shooting of *Appointment with Death*. It was here that Jenny and I became an item.

On the set of *A Chorus of Disapproval* with Anthony Hopkins, the most marvellous and amusing professional I've ever worked with. He's a great actor, too!

in a movie in 1974. Dino de Laurentiis said, 'It is well over the top, people couldn't possibly accept it.' I said, 'What do you mean, Dino? Either they accept that Charlie's having a nice time killing muggers and they're glad he's killing them, or we're dead anyway. It won't matter what we put at the end of the movie.' Wendell Mayes took the same view, that mine was a deeply immoral end to the movie and couldn't possibly be done. We shot at Central Station in New York, which was doubling for the railway station in Chicago. Charlie said, 'I will not do this scene, Michael. It means that I'm enjoying killing people. I can't possibly have my public think that.' I said, 'Charlie, of course you're enjoying killing people! That's what the movie's about! You're enjoying doing away with thoroughly evil people!' What saved me was that Charlie always wanted to go home to dinner and have a rest. He either had to sit in Central Station arguing with me forever or do the scene! Very reluctantly, and under protest, he did it. Later when the scene was a great success and critics and public loved it, Charlie went round telling everybody he wrote it!

Death Wish was a mould-breaker in a number of ways. It was the first film that permitted a citizen to kill other citizens and be a hero. It was also the first film for many years to have the word 'Death' in the title. In 1974 it was thought to have the word 'Death' in the title would put audiences off. Dino de Laurentiis was determined not to call the film *Death Wish*. He said the book hadn't sold at all so we weren't cashing in on a popular book. And the word 'Death' was a deterrent. I edited *Death Wish* at home in my London house. We also did all the sound recording in London except for the music. It was the first film score by Herbie Hancock, the brilliant jazz musician. I chose him because Dino wanted a cheap band and at the time I was having an affair with one of the actresses in the movie who was very into jazz music. She said, 'Herbie Hancock is a new genius.' I listened to his record *Head Hunters*, thought it absolutely brilliant and persuaded Dino to take him. To go back to the title, *Death Wish*, which Dino refused to have. He and Paramount came up with a ghastly title, *The Sidewalk Vigilante*. They instructed me that was what the film would be called. They sent me over posters with that title on it. I made the movie titles in London. I sat in my cinema at home with my editing assistants when up came the titles of the film: 'Dino de Laurentiis presents Charles Bronson in a Michael Winner film *The Sidewalk Vigilante*'. You could feel the displeasure and sympathy from my staff when this dreadful title came on the screen. I telephoned Dino de Laurentiis and said, '*Death Wish* is a wonderful title. *The Sidewalk Vigilante* stinks. I have the film here in London. You're going to have to come and take it away from me forcibly, because I'm changing it back to *Death Wish*. That's what I'll deliver!' Dino could have used his legal rights and taken the film back, but my passion in defending the title won him over.

Three weeks before the film opened Dino rang me in London and said, 'Michael, you've got to help me. Tell me you'll do me a favour.' I said, 'What is it?' He said, 'Michael, I cannot sleep. You can't use 'Death' in the title of the film. You've got to take away the title *Death Wish*.' I said, 'Dino, take sleeping pills! It's a great title and it's coming your way!' In a stroke, when the film was released and was an enormous success, the word 'Death' crept into titles all over the place. It suddenly acquired considerable magnetism!

Death Wish became the phenomenon of the motion-picture industry in 1974. That summer the two big hits were *Death Wish* and a compilation of old American MGM musicals called *That's Entertainment*. The same people went to both movies. The psychos and action freaks did not go to *Death Wish* and the sweet people to *That's Entertainment*. The same people like different types of movies.

When *Death Wish* opened in New York I was sitting in Dino's office. At 1 p.m. the phone rang. A man asked for Mr De Laurentiis. I said, 'He's not here.' The man said, 'I'm the manager of the 83rd Street East cinema. Are you Michael Winner?' I said, 'Yes.' He said, 'I want you to know the cinema's full.' I said, 'How can the cinema be full at one o'clock in the afternoon on the first day?' He said, 'It's phenomenal.' Audiences can smell out what they want to go to.

I was very nervous about *Death Wish*. It was a dark film. Not a massive action film as my other films with Charlie had been. Comparatively few people were shot and they were shot at night in dark clothing, so there was no leaping about or blood or car chases. Yet not only in New York, but all over the world, whenever Charlie Bronson shot a mugger the audience burst into applause. We went to the Loewe's Astor Plaza, a very big cinema on Broadway, with Frank Yablans of Paramount on the first night of the movie. It was besieged. So much so that Yablans had them put the price up! One person bought the ticket for three dollars and the next person bought it for four! The cinema exploded with cheering every time Charlie shot anyone. This happened all over Europe. At that time New York was the mugging capital of the world. Everyone there was getting mugged. In London very few people were getting mugged. It was as if people in Europe were saying, 'Kill them in New York, Charlie! Don't let them get over here!' It was a film that hit the spirit of the times. Rex Reed in the *New York Daily News* wrote, 'Rarely in screen history has a movie caused so much violent controversial reaction from both audience and critics as *Death Wish*. It is a powerful, explosive audience identification movie. I found myself rhapsodising in its vicarious sense of urban justice. In the final and most shattering scene the audience burst into applause that sounds like rifle fire. *Death Wish* is a startlingly original film.' Judith Crist in the *New York Magazine* wrote, '*Death Wish* is a first rate suspenser set and filmed in New York City, that provides, with bristling topicality, more empathy and Aristotelian purgation for the beleaguered city dweller than a month full of lone rangers or a legion of Shanes in our innocent Western-orientated past. The breath-stopping denouement and tidy twist resolution will satisfy every basic instinct we liberals are heir to! What makes this fantasy work is the superb performance of Charles Bronson as the protagonist, complemented by Vincent Gardenia as the detective and the entire cast. Winner's fast paced exquisitely detailed direction supplements the authenticity of Bronson's creation.' And thus were nearly all the reviews, including most of the English ones. I was hot again! I had a hit! But I was about to waste this opportunity.

20

Dogs and Ghouls

In 1975 movie executives were gripped with the mindless belief that audiences would be fascinated by stories about old Hollywood. They were churned out with irrepressible optimism. There was *Gable and Lombard*, *W. C. Fields and Me*, *Day of the Locust*, *Nickelodeon* and others. They all collapsed at the box office. I didn't know that when I accepted what I still believe was a very funny script, *Won Ton Ton the Dog Who Saved Hollywood*. It spoofed the story of a German Shepherd dog star, based on the life of Rin Tin Tin, the famous canine star of the thirties. The film was to be produced by David Picker, who'd been Chief Executive at United Artists, but had left to become an independent producer. He now had an office at Warner Bros. There's a very big difference between being a buyer (holding a position in a distribution or studio company where you could put a picture into 'go') and being a seller. Picker was amazed at how long people took to ring him back now that he was no longer a buyer. He was further outraged that Warner Bros were not keen on his script of *Won Ton Ton* and rejected various re-writes. They'd announced Picker's contract with a fanfare. As things got more and more sticky, Picker said to me, 'What do you think they'll say if I say to them, "Unless you make this movie I'll quit the studio?"' I said, 'They'll say, "Goodbye!"' Picker looked amazed. That's what happened. Barry Diller had recently moved from television to movies. He'd just been made Head of Paramount. He wanted Picker to guide him through the wiles of Hollywood movie production. So Paramount took over Picker's deal from Warner Bros.

The main star of *Won Ton Ton* was an extremely bad-tempered German Shepherd dog who bit practically everybody on the set. I was nervous I'd have to take a course in dog directing but I was assured that (just as with *Hannibal Brooks*) the trainer did everything. I would speak to the trainer, the trainer would speak to the dog. The dog would then do as we wished. The trainer would go on all fours and perform whatever actions the dog had to do while the dog looked on bemused. On the human side of the cast we had Madeline Kahn who was a good comedienne; Art Carney (who'd recently won an Academy Award) played a studio chief; Phil Silvers, who as Sergeant Bilko was one of my all-time favourites, was past his prime but still brilliant; and a very good actress called Teri Garr, who went on to some success. The male lead was Bruce Dern who had been with David Picker on his previous picture. He's a good actor but always has an air of menace. He would not have been my choice for a light comedy lead. But Picker had been my boss at United Artists. I was not about to fall out with him. I don't think anything would have made *Won Ton Ton the Dog Who Saved Hollywood* a box-office success, but I don't think David Picker's idea of having endless old-time stars in small parts helped the movie. Although it was great fun on the set!

In order to get more than a hundred of these people in, we had to keep building up tiny parts, so they were good enough to attract some has-been to do a cameo. They were has-beens who'd been the most enormous stars! I'd watched them entranced as a child in the smelly cinemas of Letchworth, Hertfordshire. My phone list each day read like I was one of the greatest producers in the 1940s. We had Milton Berle, Walter Pidgeon, Fernando Lamas, Zsa Zsa Gabor, Cyd Charisse, Yvonne de Carlo, Joan Blondell, Rudy Vallee, George Jessel, Johnny Weissmuller, Victor Mature, Virginia Mayo, Peter Lawford and dozens more. If I'd had all these stars sign my script it would be one of the greatest pieces of cinema memorabilia ever. On top of everything, the two script writers (one of whom insisted on being a producer) were not talking. One of them refused to sell his rights in the script unless the other one was thrown off the movie!

David Picker was a delight. The atmosphere on the set was amusing. And for me to see these old-time stars coming, often five or six in one day, was a movie-buff's dream. I sat on a sofa and said to Virginia Mayo, 'May I hold your hand, Virginia? I adored you from the stalls of the cinema when I was at school.' She was a lovely person. Zsa Zsa Gabor played a guest at a major Hollywood premiere which we filmed at Grauman's Chinese Theater on Hollywood Boulevard. All the old stars worked for five hundred dollars a day. Zsa Zsa said to me, 'I want my own make-up man.' I said, 'Darling, we've got a wonderful make-up man. He was with Marlon Brando for years.' Zsa Zsa said, 'But is he good?' I said, 'He's so good you'll end up looking like Marlon Brando!' Zsa Zsa was down there at night at Grauman's Chinese Theater. She's very cheerful and chatty. She said, 'That's my husband in the crowd behind the barrier.' I said, 'Do you think we should bring him through and let him sit with you?' She said, 'No, darlink, he's on the way out!'

We were shooting a big premiere scene all night at Grauman's Chinese Theater. It's a lovely custom in Hollywood that when an actor finishes on a film, the Assistant Director or the Director says, 'This is the last day of so and so,' and everybody claps. It was now three-thirty in the morning. We'd been filming since eight o'clock at night. The extras were asleep in the cinema seats. Seven or eight big stars were asleep. We carried on lighting the film. Then everyone came to life for the shooting. We were doing a scene with the brilliant comedian Phil Silvers. I thought, 'This is Phil's last shot in the movie. But we're all so tired there's really no point in announcing it.' Then I thought, 'No, I can't let this man go quietly.' So I held my hands up and said, 'Everybody, I have a very important announcement to make. The shot we have just taken is the last one on our movie for one of the greatest comedians in the history of the world. A man for whom we all have the most enormous admiration. May we please give a rousing send-off to Mr Phil Silvers.' Everybody went mad. They all stood up! They shouted! They applauded! They cheered! Phil was in an aisle seat. I was standing next to him. While everyone was clapping and cheering Phil pulled at my arm. He said, 'That wasn't my last shot. I'm with you again next Tuesday.' I said, 'Phil, don't tell them. You'll never get another send-off like this!'

The film finished and the studio were not happy. By now they'd seen a number of 'old Hollywood' films flop disastrously. Strangely enough, our sneak previews were amazing. The cinemas were jammed to capacity. The preview cards were very good! The publicity was gargantuan. The dog was shopping at Cartier. The dog was eating in the best restaurants. It was a movie that lent itself to magazine and newspaper attention. None of this helped at all. The movie illustrated the Hollywood maxim: 'Every film's a great success until it's released.' *Won Ton* got tepid reviews and died a death. I thought then, and still think, it's a very funny film. I was buoyed in this view when Peter Falk rang me in London ten years after its release and said, 'Michael, I've just seen *Won Ton Ton* on television. It's very funny. I don't know why it didn't get better reviews.'

The film had a few devotees. It was named Best Comedy of the Year by the British magazine *Films and Filming*. Judith Simons in the *Daily Express* wrote, 'It's great to have a film in which the whole family can excitedly participate. Director Michael Winner has really scored!' The London *Evening News* wrote, 'This film is a marvellous treat. Michael Winner has given his delicious farce a touch of sadness combined with brave gaiety.' Joe Baltake in the *Philadelphia Daily News* said, '*Won Ton Ton* is so persistently ingratiating that it may very well be this year's most huggable flick. The whole thing is ginger-snappy, colourful and brainless – and downright impossible to dislike. Michael Winner seems to view his new film as a breath of fresh air and is enjoying it to the hilt. It's a joy that's contagious. You'll have to look long and hard for another movie that's half as nice as this one.' I was disappointed that my aim in making the movie had not succeeded. I was not director of a hit! Now I'd be stuck with blood-thirsty shoot-em-ups after the success of my action pictures. I'd wanted to use my moment as a hot director to switch to comedy. But you pick yourself up and carry on.

I was at a Beverly Hills party given by my friend Herb Jaffe who'd been number two at United Artists. Ned Tanen, the Head of Production at Universal Pictures, was there. The next day he sent me a paperback book, *The Sentinel*. The book had come out some years earlier in hard cover and not done well. Universal bought it and gave it to a number of directors and writers, none of whom produced a script they liked. Now the paperback of *The Sentinel* was high on the best-seller charts. I said I'd be happy to do it. A deal memo was produced within a couple of hours with a good fee for me to write the script. If Universal approved the script, I'd produce and direct the movie. I was about to go back to London when Ned Tanen's assistant, Raphael Etkes, rang. He said, 'We forgot to ask something before we gave you the job of doing the screenplay. Can you write?' That was typical of Hollywood! I said, 'Yes, Rafi. I've written a number of screenplays. You've seen some of them. Anyway, you can decide if I can write when I hand the script in!'

The Sentinel was the normal hocus-pocus horror film. There's always a girl in a spooky house who hears strange noises and goes out of her apartment in a negligée and climbs the stairs holding a carving knife. Any sane person would have locked themselves in, called the police and moved out the next day. But if you do that in a horror film, there's no story. I sent the script in after six weeks and within a couple of days I got a call from Ned saying, 'You've cracked it. We'll make the movie at once.' I said, 'Do you want big stars?' Because if a studio says they'll make the picture as long as you get whoever the hot star is at the moment, your chances of making it are slight. The hot star of the moment always has a hundred scripts on offer and needs enormous money. Ned said, 'We'll take who we can get.'

There were some wonderful parts for famous older character actors; the leads were a young girl and a young man, she a New York model, he a lawyer. I'd always been a fan of Martin Sheen. I assumed, as on all my other pictures, that if I put someone forward they'd be accepted. Martin came to lunch in my London house. I said, 'You've got the part. I have to get approval from Universal but they'll accept you. Take it as done.' We shook hands and I thought what a nice person he was. To my surprise, Ned Tanen said, 'Martin

Sheen's done too much television.' I said, 'Who's he done the television for?' Ned said, 'For us.' There used to be a very 'them and us' attitude in Hollywood. There were people in movies and there were people in television. Never the twain should meet! They accepted a girl for the lead who was very hot on television called Cristina Raines. She'd played a small part in *The Stone Killer* as Charlie Bronson's daughter. We'd cut the scene out of the film. Not because of her acting but because the scene didn't add to the movie. Ned suggested an actor called Chris Sarandon to play the lawyer. He'd been nominated for an Academy Award for a wiped-out drug-addict homosexual in *Dog Day Afternoon*. He had only one scene as Al Pacino's boyfriend, in which he was startlingly good. I'd seen Chris on the Broadway stage in a Shakespeare musical five or six years earlier. I remember thinking, 'This is a very good-looking young man but he just doesn't have it. He'll never be a star.' But since Ned was keen on him, I went along.

We got a wonderful group of people for other parts including Christopher Walken (who should have played the male lead) Beverly D'Angelo (who should have played the female lead) in her first movie, and old-timers Ava Gardner, Martin Balsam, John Carradine, Jose Ferrer, Arthur Kennedy, Burgess Meredith, Sylvia Miles, Eli Wallach and Jerry Orbach. It was also Tom Berenger's first film. He played a tiny part towards the end. We were still in pre-production when Cis Corman, our Casting Director, who later became Barbra Streisand's partner and co-producer, said to me, 'There's a private screening of *Lipstick*. Don't you think you should see it?' *Lipstick* was a female version of *Death Wish*. Dino de Laurentiis had offered it to me. I'd turned it down. Chris Sarandon was the star. I went to the movie and came out convinced that Chris Sarandon was not a very good actor unless he played nut cases. He was absolutely wrong for our straight part of a New York lawyer. I rang Bill Battliner, Head of Universal Casting. I said, 'Have you seen *Lipstick*?' He said, 'No.' I said, 'I saw it this afternoon.' Bill said, 'What did you think?' I said, 'I think Chris Sarandon is never going to make it as a major actor. I don't think he's right for our movie.' There was a pause and Bill Battliner said, 'Are you going to tell Ned that?' I said, 'No, I'm not, Bill. If the film relies on

Chris Sarandon I'm not going to bring it down. I'll hope we can make him better.'

The movie shot in New York in the summer of 1975 where it was as hot at one end of the scale as it had been freezing while we shot *Death Wish* on the other. New York crews are the best in the world. They're the sharpest, the wittiest and the fastest. They also make the most noise. On a good day they shut up just long enough for you to get through the take!

On this movie I became very friendly with Ava Gardner. We stayed friends for life. She lived near me in Kensington in a converted Victorian house in an immaculate apartment. She didn't gossip much about her life. She'd been married to Mickey Rooney, the bandleader Artie Shaw and Frank Sinatra. She'd been the mistress of Howard Hughes. We were having dinner one night, when Ava said: 'You know, Michael, there was one day in the fifties when I learnt how powerful Howard Hughes was. I'd just departed from a lover in America. Howard Hughes always used to have me followed. The minute a romance broke up his people would come to me and say, "Howard would like to see you at his home in Florida." So I went to him in Florida and we had a brief revival of the relationship. Then I decided to go to Cuba where I had a friend I wanted to see. I went to Miami Airport with Renée, [a black lady assistant who Ava had with her on *The Sentinel*] and my flight at eleven o'clock in the morning was suddenly cancelled. I transferred to the next flight to Cuba which was at two in the afternoon. That was cancelled. Then I transferred to the flight at four in the afternoon. That was cancelled. Howard was cancelling all flights out of Miami to Cuba. It was particularly annoying because in those days they had segregated toilets and Renée, being black, had to go to a toilet miles away from the airport in a hut. We had to walk in the hot sun to get her there. I was determined to stick it out. I stayed at Miami Airport. I slept on the sofa. I kept transferring to other flights to Cuba. It wasn't until three o'clock in the afternoon of the second day that Howard couldn't stop the flights any more and I got to Cuba.'

I have no doubt that story is true. Ava told so few stories that she wouldn't invent one. When she came to write her autobiography I said, 'Ava, you've had the most incredible life. Now you can tell everybody the truth about it.' Ava said to me, 'Darling, that's the one thing I'm not going to do. I'm going to put forward the view of me I want people to remember me by.' Later she was going to be in my film *Appointment with Death* even though she'd just had a stroke. The part in the movie was that of a cripple. Ava insisted on coming to my house to tell me personally that the doctor had advised she just wasn't well enough to do the movie. She apologised profusely for pulling out.

After that I'd see her from time to time. She'd phone me regularly, often a bit drunk. Many times to ask me to help her with clues on a crossword puzzle. She had an album which was full of photos of her corgi dog. When the dog died she bought another corgi that looked exactly the same and filled another album with photos of that dog. She called me one night and said, 'My film *Pandora and the Flying Dutchman*'s on television. I'm watching it. You know, I looked pretty good damn good in those days.' Ava was without doubt one of the most beautiful women in the world. I said, 'Ava, you looked absolutely sensational. You're a great beauty and you always were.' 'I never realised it,' she said. 'I just realise it now, looking at this film. I was a pretty good-looking broad, wasn't I?' Her lack of self-confidence was sad and endearing.

At the end of *The Sentinel* script there was a line which read: 'The denizens of hell come through the walls of the house and besiege our heroine.' It was a reasonably budgeted film but we didn't have enough to make up fifty people every day in prosthetics, which takes about six hours for each person. We'd have needed twenty make-up men. So I decided to use genuinely deformed people. My assistants gathered a group of the most amazingly deformed people. They were all very, very nice human beings. Later on I got press cuttings when many of them went back to different parts of America and the cuttings all had one theme. That the person who was deformed said, 'How wonderful it was to be on the movie and to be in the company of other people who were deformed, because we realised we were not alone in the world.' We were filming at a large house in Brooklyn overlooking the Hudson River when I sensed something odd going on. There seemed to be additional people on the set. And gossiping. I said to my Assistant Director, Charlie Okun, 'What's happening?' Charlie said, 'Trade union representatives from the camera union, from the Directors Guild and from the IATSE are here. The crew phoned them because they object to having lunch with the freaks. They want a screen put up outside so they don't have to look at them during lunch.' I said, 'I've never heard anything so disgraceful in my life. These people have been disadvantaged by God. They're terrific people. We're working with them all day on the set. Don't tell me these brawny New York technicians are so frail they'll fall to pieces if they have to see them for an extra hour during lunch. I'm ashamed of everybody.' Charlie said, 'Be that as it may, Mr Winner. I've got a screen going up. The freaks will eat on one side of the screen. We'll eat on the other.' I said, 'Charlie, do you realise how disgraceful this is? I want to tell you something. I'm coming to lunch today and I'm going to sit with the freaks to show my view of this matter.' Charlie Okun said, 'What are you complaining about, Mr Winner. You never even eat with the crew! You eat in your own private air-conditioned room in the house. I'll bet you that's where you'll have lunch today.' To my endless and great shame Charlie was absolutely right. Come lunch time it was ninety-five degrees outside. It was cool and air-conditioned in my little room that I had for myself to relax in. That's where I had lunch. Disgraceful.

In one scene Chris Sarandon is lying dead and Beverly D'Angelo and Sylvia Miles are stark naked, taking out his brains with their fingers, and eating them. It was a jolly picture! Beverly D'Angelo was the most wonderful girl, on her first film. We became very close. She came back to England and lived with me for a while. Later she became a star and married Al Pacino. In a number of interviews they said to her, 'What about that eating-the-brains scene?' Beverly said, 'Michael Winner, the Director, said to me, "Darling you'll be with two Academy Award-nominated actors, so don't worry about it."' Beverly had just opened in a musical version of *Hamlet* in New York. In my movie she played the part of a lesbian living with her girlfriend Sylvia Miles. In the movie Beverly had to masturbate. She said, 'Michael, will this masturbation be done in good taste?' I said, 'Beverly, darling, there are those who would not consider any masturbation on the screen to be good taste. All I can say is, you're going to do it and I'm going to photograph it. So whether it's in good taste or not depends on you.'

There was another star in *The Sentinel* who was not credited on the screen. Richard Dreyfuss came down while we were shooting in New York. He was visiting someone on the set. For a gag he was prominent in the background as an extra.

When *The Sentinel* was finished Ned Tanen and I took it to the home of Sid Sheinberg, the boss of Universal Pictures. When the head of a studio sees a director's film the director is very concerned it should be shown properly. Sid and his wife sat in their lounge and the film was projected. After twenty minutes the door to the room opened, casting a shaft of light upon the screen and a large German Shepherd dog came in, sat down and looked at the movie. Someone outside eventually pushed the door partly closed. Ten minutes later a second German Shepherd dog came in and sat and looked at the movie, leaving a beam of light on the screen. This time nobody shut the door. For the duration of the film the dogs walked in and out and light from the door shone upon the screen. That struck me as poor behaviour, Sheinberg's, not the dogs. Whether the head of the studio likes the film or not is irrelevant. People have taken a great deal of time and effort making a movie. For a studio head to show it in his house with dogs walking in and out is tacky. Sid Sheinberg is no longer the Head of Universal. He produced a couple of dud movies and vanished.

The Sentinel was a box-office success. Every time I see it I think what a pity we didn't have Christopher Walken and Beverly D'Angelo in the leads instead of in supporting roles. But nobody always makes good choices. Often you're influenced by the studio. The reviews, on the whole, were very good. 'The dark shenanigans are eerie, unnerving and suspenseful. A smoothly-wrought shocker that rivets attention right up to the last reel,' said Bruce Williamson in *Playboy*. Rex Reed in the *New York Daily News* said, 'There's enough here to keep you screaming for days. This bone-chilling nerve-frying Halloween epic is about a haunted house in Brooklyn Heights. The special effects will have you shrieking with terror. Half the fun is watching the horror mount at a neck-breaking pace without knowing too much at any premature point in the plot. It's effectively blood-spattered nonsense, extremely well made and always eager to do what a good horror movie should do which is send you into shock.

If you have a soft heart for things that go bump in the night, be sure to take along someone with an even stronger heart who can carry you home.' I think he summed the movie up rather well.

21

Sleep and Sophia

My next movie, *The Big Sleep*, was with another 'bad boy' who turned out to be a gent. Producer Elliott Kastner showed me the book and asked me to write a script. I'd never read Raymond Chandler before. I was struck with the poetry of his rhythms and choice of language. I'd always thought he was a street writer dealing with the seamy life of Los Angeles. But he did it with a cadence that was almost like Oscar Wilde. The project was taken up by Lord Lew Grade. Lew had been a friend of my family when I was a child. He was an immensely loveable, marvellous character. He always answered his own phone. He always made his own calls. I was put on the phone list to be called at 7 a.m. I said, 'Lew, who do I have to fuck to get off the seven o'clock list and get on the 9 a.m. phone list?' I never achieved that. Robert Mitchum played Phillip Marlowe. For other parts we had Richard Boone, the wonderful American action heavy, Sarah Miles, Joan Collins who was going through a very raw period, Edward Fox, John Mills, Oliver Reed making a welcome return to my life, and the marvellous Hollywood actor James Stewart. We sent Stewart the script to play the part of Colonel Sternwood. The slightly nervous voice of Jimmy came on the phone. 'I'm afraid I can't play this part, Michael. It's written in such an

English manner.' The film had been re-set in England, but the family
remained American. I said, 'Jimmy, every word of your dialogue in
this movie is untouched, unchanged by so much as a comma, from
that written by Raymond Chandler.' It didn't surprise me when I
read that Raymond Chandler had been to Dulwich College, and
before his strange death was planning to re-locate to England.

The Big Sleep was made on location in and around London. I
deliberately chose locations that had not been seen. We ignored
tourist London. Mitchum and I got on very well. Before the movie
started we were going to the theatre together to see John Mills who'd
acted with Bob in *Ryan's Daughter*. That afternoon some nude
models had come to my office to shoot a cover for the supposedly
pornographic book that was to be found in Geiger's bookshop. This
played a leading part in the movie. For such photos you have to shoot
your own material in order to be sure of copyright. On *I'll Never
Forget What's'isname* we needed a dirty picture for the young Oliver
Reed and his schoolboy friends to gawp at behind a cricket pavilion.
A crew member bought a photo at a sex shop in Soho. It showed a
lady with large bosoms. When the movie came out we got calls from
a man who claimed to be 'Miss Appel's agent'. Apparently Miss
Appel was the lady in the picture and she hadn't given permission for
it to be in *I'll Never Forget What's'isname*. I suggested Miss Appel
came to the office to show us her bosoms so we could positively
identify her. Eventually the 'agent' gave up. On *The Big Sleep* I took
no chances. So we took some photos of four nude girls for the cover
of the book. When I met Mitchum in the theatre in Shaftesbury
Avenue that night, one of the girls, a blonde, Lindy Benson, was
Mitchum's date. She stayed Bob's girlfriend throughout the movie.
Except for one moment when another girl on the film, who was kind
of stalking Bob, and having an affair with him as well, came to the
apartment we'd got for Bob in Arlington House in St James's. The
girls had an enormous fight in the corridor while Bob and his friends
egged them on. Lindy won. The other girl was dispossessed.

The movie went exceedingly well, even though it rained a lot and
we went massively over schedule. Bob was an immense professional. He was known to be a heavy drinker and difficult. Most of
the time he was like a college professor at an American university.

He was very quiet. He spoke with great dignity. He read a lot and had a very droll sense of humour. He gathered round him a fairly rough group of friends. He'd say to me, 'I don't know why these people keep putting themselves upon me. They came into my apartment last night and stayed till three in the morning. All I wanted to do was go to sleep.' I said, 'Bob, you're six foot three, you're built like a brick shit-house. Let me get this clear. They ring the bell. You open the door. And these people simply push you aside, leaving you flattened on the floor like in a comedy cartoon. It's very simple. If you want to go to sleep, Bob, you say "No".' Bob said, 'Yeah, I must remember that.' One day Bob was complaining about how much his son was costing him. I said, 'Bob, I hate to tell you, but it's normal for a father to finance his son.' Bob said, 'When he's forty years old?' I said, 'Bob, you just won the argument.'

One of Bob's co-stars was Sarah Miles, who's the most brilliant actress but can be difficult. Employers are frightened of her, which is a great pity because she's an enormous talent. In our movie she played Camilla Sternwood, the daughter of the ageing, dying General. We were shooting in Knebworth House near Luton as the General's house. When Sarah saw the room which was to be hers in the movie she went ballistic. 'The room has to be white!' she said. 'Why?' I asked. She said, 'Because in the original film the room's white.' I said, 'Well, this isn't the original film. You don't get white rooms in a kind of English castle.' Sarah was adamant. So, ever wishing to keep the artiste happy, I rang up the Art Director in Sarah's presence and said, 'Miss Miles will go out with you over the weekend. She will choose every piece of furniture for her room and you will go with her with three empty trucks. Whatever she chooses from the hire houses, you take.' So the room was decorated all in white. When Sarah came in four days later I said, 'Sarah, I'm going to blindfold you and lead you to your room.' When I took the blindfold off I said, 'You see, just as you wanted!' Sarah looked around the room and said, 'Fantastic!' Then she saw one cushion and said, 'That cushion! It's red!'

It was wonderful to work with Oliver Reed again. It was our sixth film together. Oliver was drinking more than before. He'd never be drunk on the set, but sometimes he'd be so drunk the night before that he'd come on the set a bit gone. We were filming in a house in the staid suburb of Chorleywood. It was summer. We sat on the lawn. Oliver suddenly stood up and said, 'You know, Bob, last night I was playing this game where two people have their legs astride a pole and they're naked and they hit at each other to see which one can knock the other off the pole. It completely did in my bollocks. Would you like to see them?' Bob said, 'Not really.' I kept silent. Oliver said, 'I'd like to show you.' There were a few members of the public watching us over the low wall of this suburban house. They had the pleasure of seeing Oliver Reed take his trousers down, revealing a very sore genital area. He exposed it closely to Robert Mitchum, although, thank God, not to me! The residents of Chorleywood took it very well. They kept watching as if nothing was happening. Oliver then put his private parts away and resumed the role of perfect gent!

Joan Collins was, as ever, extremely professional. She was famous for wearing wigs. I said, 'Joan, I don't want you to wear a wig on this picture. I hate wigs.' Joan said, 'I promise you, Michael, I will not wear a wig.' The hairdresser, Stephanie, had been on a number of my movies. I said, 'You see that Joan doesn't wear a wig.' The first day Stephanie came on the set and said, 'Pull at Joan's hair. You'll see it's real.' I pulled at her hair. It was firmly on her head. Joan came every day with her real hair. When she'd finished on the film Joan kissed me goodbye. Then she wandered to the edge of the set and called out, 'Michael!' I looked round. Joan took the wig off her head and waved it at me. It had been a wig all the time! I was glad this part helped Joan get *Dynasty*. Because when *The Big Sleep* was shown in America, the producers of *Dynasty* saw it and decided she was playing just the type of person they needed in their show.

Richard Boone was a famous American actor who'd starred in many Westerns. He was also known as a drinker. He brought a bottle of Scotch with him to the set each day and probably more. But Richard never appeared drunk. He drank all day, but he stayed totally together. Mitchum didn't drink during the day. He loved his food. We had special stuff brought in for him for my lunch area with the stars. But there was a danger of Mitchum drinking at night. We were doing a scene in an alley at the side of the Savoy Hotel. Mitchum had been inside with me having dinner. He came out drunk. Sarah Miles rose to the occasion and did all she could. But as Mitchum wobbled down the alley it seemed unlikely we'd use the material. A German TV crew was there to interview him. It ended up with Mitchum screaming they were all Nazis, doing a Hitler salute, yelling he wanted them all dead and running up the Strand to catch a taxi home! We arranged to go back two nights later. I said, 'Bob, please, this time don't drink. Because we're having to re-shoot a night's work and that's not right.' Bob took it seriously. When we got there just before the dinner break, the little roadway down the side of the hotel now had an enormous gaping hole in the middle. There were piles of earth all round, flashing lights and trestles to stop people falling in. The gas board was digging up the area! I said to my people, 'When I come back after dinner I want to see no hole!' The hole was filled in. The earth-moving stuff was pushed out of the way. The barriers and lights were pushed down a side street. The next morning six Irish navvies turned up and couldn't believe their hole had gone! The gas board were very good about it. I offered them compensation, but they declined.

On another occasion while we were shooting in Knebworth House, Barry Norman came down for his BBC television pro-gramme at ten o'clock in the morning to do an interview with Mitchum. Bob is not crazy about interviews. Every time I said, 'Bob, would you like to take five minutes with Barry Norman?' he said, 'No.' I'd look out of the window and there would be Barry Norman with two chairs facing each other and his camera crew. He'd sometimes move a chair an inch one way or another. This went on from ten o'clock in the morning until six o'clock at night. Then we finished and Bob came out of the building. Barry Norman went up and said, 'Mr Mitchum, I'm Barry Norman, from the BBC.' Mitchum said, 'Fuck off,' kept walking to his limousine and drove away. Barry Norman said to me, 'Where's Mitchum going?' I replied, 'To the Letchworth Hall Hotel, Barry.' Barry Norman said, 'Are you telling me he'd rather be at the Letchworth Hall Hotel than be interviewed by me?' I said, 'Looks that way, doesn't it?!' Mitchum's car disappeared in the distance.

Towards the end of *The Big Sleep* there's a gunfight between Mitchum as the good guy and Richard Boone as the bad guy.

Mitchum had a revolver and Richard Boone a machine gun. Both Mitchum and Boone were drunk. Guns were going off when they shouldn't. They were firing in the wrong direction. It was a nightmare. I said to the crew, 'This is the gunfight at Alcoholics Anonymous.' I don't know how we ever managed to get enough good stuff to put that sequence together. The irresponsibility of Mitchum and Boone for being pissed on that particular evening was nothing to what I'd done in the afternoon. We'd finished shooting our daytime work and to fill in time we took a shot which was meant to be at night, of a string of burning handkerchiefs tied together, soaked in petrol, hanging from the petrol tank of a Rover car. Mitchum later set fire to them and blew up the car. We built a large hide of canvas around the front door of a house and put the Rover car in it so it was dark. Then we took all the petrol out of the car so when we lit our handkerchiefs it wouldn't blow up the car. I was standing on the gravel forecourt and said, 'Tell these people to stop messing around with the car. Let's shoot, otherwise it'll be dinner time.' Somebody said, 'They haven't got all the petrol out of the way.' I said, 'Of course they have.'

At that time I smoked cigars. I lit a match and threw the match on to the ground. An enormous burst of flame came up because there was petrol still there! The flame roared along to the canvas hide and inside to the unit with the camera. They rushed out screaming! The canvas hide caught fire! Flames roared up on the outside of the house! It looked like the entire house would go! At that exact moment, coming up the lane at the side of the house, were three members of the Thames Valley Fire Brigade in full uniform. One was holding a chocolate cake, one was holding a vanilla blancmange and the other was holding a fruit salad. They were bringing them up for our imminent dinner break. When I saw the flames leaping up around the house and three uniformed members of the fire brigade holding these bowls of dessert, I collapsed in hysterical laughter. My Cameraman Robert Paynter also roared with laughter. We have photographs of this to prove it! Everyone else was terrified. Luckily they put the flames out and there was no damage to the house. One of the cameras was burned but we had three with us so it didn't matter. A small bit of a tree was burned, which deeply annoyed the owners of the house. They were paid a fortune anyway. They were living at the Connaught Hotel running up unbelievable bills while we were in their house. It was my most reckless and stupid moment. Luckily no one was hurt. If they had been, I hate to think of the trouble I'd have been in.

I got to know Mitchum very well. We went out most weekends together and I saw him for years afterwards. I'd see him when he came to London. I'd see him when I went to Los Angeles. He was a very quiet man normally. He had a happy marriage to Dorothy, a lady who had been his childhood sweetheart. On one occasion I was having dinner with Mitchum in Claridge's when Jack Lemmon came by. After dinner he joined us for coffee. Mitchum was on the wagon. He'd been to the Betty Ford Clinic to dry out. He said to me, 'I didn't want to go to the Betty Ford Clinic. But my whole family came and told me I had to go there.' His wife was also in the clinic. I never realised Dorothy drank but she went to the clinic, dried out, and stayed sober. Mitchum wasn't drinking but Jack Lemmon was absolutely pissed. Jack Lemmon was the most wonderful drunk. Not one piece of angst or bitterness came out. He was a total delight. He was witty. He was like an inebriated pixie. Jack said, 'Do you think we can get into Tramp?' Tramp is a well-known London discotheque. I said, 'Of course, I've been a member since 1966.' So we went to Tramp, Jack Lemmon, Robert Mitchum and me. We stood in front of the desk. The girls are very severe there. They looked up and I said, 'Michael Winner.' The girl at the Tramp desk said, 'He's not here.' So there I am standing with Jack Lemmon and Robert Mitchum and the girl can't recognise them, and she doesn't recognise me! I said, 'Come on, let's go down.' For the rest of the evening everyone tried to pretend it hadn't happened or that the girls had thought I was somebody else. The evening in Tramp was one of the funniest of my life. Bob was sober so he looked a bit glum. Jack Lemmon was on terrific form. His eyes swivelled and popped out of his head as each girl came in with a skimpier dress and bigger bosoms! It was like a scene from a comedy movie.

The next day I was to drive them down to the French Horn at Sonning, one of my favourite spots to take movie stars. Jack and Bob came to my house. We went down in my Bentley. Jack had a large vodka in his hand as we drove. Bob was in the front with me, my girlfriend and Jack in the back. My driving was not very good. The terrified comments everybody made only had me roar with laughter and I became more dangerous! We got to the French Horn, had a wonderful meal and took a lot of Polaroid photos. When we got back I spread the Polaroids out on the bonnet of the Bentley. To my amazement both Jack and Bob grabbed at them. Here were two major stars who are photographed all the time. Yet they're seldom photographed in their private lives, so they wanted these pictures. Six weeks later Bob visited again and I took him down to lunch. The waiter said, 'Our speciality this morning is champagne and peach juice.' I said, 'I'll have one.' My girlfriend said she'd have one. I didn't look at Bob because I knew he wasn't drinking. Bob said, 'I'll have one, too.' I said, 'I thought you were on the wagon.' Bob said, 'I've given it up.' I said, 'How long did it last?' He said, 'About six weeks.'

On another occasion Bob came to town to film an American TV series. They were shooting in the Surrey village of Shere. Bob had a habit of falling madly in love with girls at very short notice. He'd write them poetry. There was a girl behind the barrier watching him who he took a shine to. He'd invited her to lunch at Claridge's and asked me to come, too. I said, 'I'll look in after lunch, just to see how you are.' I went into Claridge's. The girl had obviously been thrilled to accept the invitation. She'd been thrilled to be part of a group in the village of Shere watching Bob Mitchum. But now she was alone with him. Communication was quite difficult. She realised she was going to be asked to sleep with him. I could see this was worrying her. When I and my girlfriend got up to go, the girl said, 'Please don't go, Mr Winner.' I thought, 'If you accept invitations from a film star with a major reputation it's no good freaking out.' So I left. Around seven o'clock that evening I phoned Bob. He was staying at the Athenaeum Hotel in one of the private suites at the back. He said, 'I sent her off, she wouldn't do anything. How do you get laid in this town?' I said, 'You go to the lobby and get a magazine called *What's On*. It's full of adverts for call girls. Phone one up.' Bob said, 'I'll go right now.' I rang Bob back about an hour later. I said, 'Did you get fixed up?' Bob said, 'No, I rang one of the call-girl numbers and I got an answerphone! So I gave up!' If you want to know what the real big-star movie life is, that's as good an example as any. Bob lived a very full life but sadly died of cancer. Before he died this enormous man seemed to shrink and fade away. At my last meeting with him I looked at the tragedy of it all. But he'd had a bloody good time.

The Big Sleep was particularly well received in America where I had expected it to be murdered. Noel Carroll of the *Soho Weekly News*, which was a very 'in' paper in New York, said, 'Winner's version of *The Big Sleep* will be remembered as one of the most consistently Expressionist films of the late 70s. He forges a new conception of the original story.' Walter Spencer, a famous radio critic on *WOR New York* said, 'This is the best *Big Sleep* I've seen, it's the best of the Raymond Chandler films.' Rona Barrett on ABC Television, one of America's most famous television critics, said, 'It's more faithful to Chandler's original than the Bogart starrer. Michael Winner has assembled a superior cast. Mitchum is nearly perfect as Marlowe. Candy Clark as a whacko drug addict acts with fiendish delight. Sarah Miles is intense and sensual. Oliver Reed is suitably sinister as a casino owner, John Mills is elegant as a police inspector and Richard Boone's scary as a hardened killer.' The film did fine and played with great success all over the world. It's still continually shown on television.

After I finished *The Big Sleep* a friend of mine rang from Rome, where he was working for Carlo Ponti, the husband of Sophia Loren. He said, 'Carlo's desperately looking for a film for Sophia and Lew Grade wants to finance it. Have you got anything?' The only script I could think of had been given to me four years earlier. It was originally by a famous screenwriter, Bill Kirby, who'd written it as a *Dirty Harry* sequel for Clint Eastwood. Warner Bros kept a supply of scripts ready for Clint. So the minute one *Dirty Harry* finished they could offer him another. Clint had not chosen this one, but it was good. Warner Bros gave it to me to produce and direct. I went for the first time to reconnoitre the Caribbean where it was set. Later Warner Bros decided not to make it. I showed the script to Charlie Bronson, who Lew Grade was sure was going to make a movie for him. I went to Loren's luxurious apartment on the Avenue George V to meet her and Carlo Ponti. After about fifteen minutes Sophia, who

I later got to know very well and absolutely adore, crossed those beautiful legs of hers, sitting elegantly in an eighteenth-century French chair, looked at me with her piercing brown eyes and said, 'Tell me about our movie. What is my part?' 'Well,' I said, 'your part is a black girl in Martinique and she has seven lines of dialogue.' There was a silence. After a second Sophia slightly raised an eyebrow, pursed her lips and said, 'Oh!' Then looked as if to say, 'We can cancel lunch.' I said, 'Sophia, I've studied the script with the writer. In four weeks' time the part will be a white Italian lady and the co-star of the picture.'

Lew Grade went to the Cannes Film Festival, stood between Charles Bronson and Sophia Loren, and announced the production of *Firepower*, its new title. Lew asked me to employ O. J. Simpson, whose agent was a friend of his, in the third part. I was later to become extremely friendly with him. I knew, which Lew Grade did not, that Charlie Bronson would not do the movie. Charlie never did a movie with a star leading lady. He liked to be the only star in the picture. He was insecure. He didn't want competition. Lew was surprised when Charlie suddenly pulled out! By this time I had a great many technicians, art directors, set designers and location managers in three Caribbean islands, St Lucia, Antigua and Curaçao. I said to Lew, 'We'll replace Bronson with somebody else. We've still got Sophia.' Sophia had not wanted to act with Charlie Bronson. She thought he was inferior. Lew rang me a bit later and said, 'Michael, I don't think we can find anyone of the size of Charlie Bronson to take this role. I know we can get James Coburn but that's not enough. I'm going to cancel the picture.' I said, 'You mean I should bring everyone back from the Caribbean?' He said, 'Yes.' Lew said this on Monday. You couldn't give a unit notice until Friday. So I delayed giving them notice, hoping something would happen to save the movie. I could never in my wildest dreams have guessed what did.

At 6.30 a.m. one morning, half an hour ahead of schedule, came a phone call from Lew. He said, 'Are you listening, Michael?' I said, 'Of course, Lew, but you're calling me half an hour early!' Lew said, 'Never mind that! I want you to listen very carefully. We are going to make *Firepower*. Have you sacked everybody?' I said, 'No, I was waiting until Friday.' He said, 'Keep them there. This film is going to be made. Nothing is going to stop it being made. We'll get the best actor we can to replace Bronson. Do you understand me?' I said, 'Yes.' I thought, 'What on earth has happened?' Later I read the newspapers. In Nigel Dempster's *Daily Mail* column the headline story concerned *Firepower*, Lew Grade and me. It said, 'Everyone is quitting this picture!' Lew Grade, it reported, was going to have to face an enormous bill for pre-production on a movie for which he hadn't properly secured his stars! If the picture was cancelled Lew would look an idiot. I don't know who told Nigel this, but I now realised this was why Lew had called me. So we signed James Coburn and went off to make the movie.

Firepower was a story of a Howard Hughes-type figure living secretly in the Caribbean. Coburn, a bounty hunter, is out to get him. Sophia switches sides and becomes the villain. Carlo Ponti said to me when he saw the script, 'Sophia will not shoot the villain.' I thought he meant she wouldn't gun down the villain in the movie. I said, 'Carlo, she doesn't shoot the villain. The villain gets away to live happily ever after.' Carlo meant Sophia would never play the role of a villain. In fact she did. She enjoyed it, and was very good. She was the secret mistress of this multi-billionaire Howard Hughes-type recluse. The movie started in Antigua, which is definitely the most corrupt place I've ever visited. It is in the hands of a family who have been accused endlessly of rigging the elections and various other devious things. We went in all innocence and were clobbered massively, as other film companies had been before. We stayed in a posh hotel called Curtain Bluff.

Sophia had a suite in a house overlooking the sea. O. J. Simpson and I were in suites in the main hotel. O. J. had his friend Al Cowling as his stand-in. He later drove the getaway car before the famous trial. Al was a fellow football player. O. J. was going to join the Forty-Niners, a San Francisco team. He was past his peak, but he trained like crazy. He and Al Cowling would run down stairs backwards, which was apparently particularly good training! James Coburn was shacked up with Lynsey de Paul, so he didn't speak to anybody else in the evening, Sophia Loren was with her female secretary. She went into her suite every night and cooked spaghetti.

I sat for ten weeks with O. J. Simpson and Al Cowling and later with his girlfriend Nicole who became his wife. At that time O. J. was married to a black lady. After three days on the movie O. J. said, 'I'm going to bring this girlfriend down. Her name's Nicole Simpson. She's pretty but very dumb. She won't last the picture.' As we all know, Nicole went through the picture, became Mrs O. J. Simpson and lasted until, it is believed, he murdered her. This doesn't affect my liking O. J. After his first trial I was on a serious, political discussion with Adam Bolton of *Sky News*. The Attorney-General and some MP were there. Adam Bolton introduced me. 'And Michael Winner who was a friend of O. J. Simpson's.' I said, 'No, not *was*, Adam. *Am* a friend of O. J. Simpson's.' Adam Bolton said, 'But he's murdered two people.' I said, 'What's two dead bodies between friends?' Nobody took this up! The programme just carried on! I think the first O. J. Simpson trial showed clearly that the LA police fabricated so much evidence that the jury were right to find him innocent. I wasn't about to re-try him. The second trial put him in a worse position, but it doesn't alter the fact that he was not convicted of murder, whether people believe he did it or not.

James Coburn was mad about Ferraris and because of him I bought one. It was a disastrous car and kept going wrong. Other than that, Coburn was boring. O. J. was continually saying, 'You know, Michael, blacks can't swim.' I'd say, 'O. J., we're in the Caribbean and there they are in the sea! Swimming!' O. J. said, 'You've never heard of a black athlete who's a swimmer. Blacks excel at all other sports. We've measured their bone density. There's a reason why blacks cannot swim.' O. J. was haunted by this. Three months after the movie his two-year-old daughter drowned in his swimming pool. He had an extraordinary premonition. In the meantime Nicole arrived and was fatuous, but pleasant. O. J. was a delight and Al Cowling was a delight. I stayed very friendly with them for many years after the movie. I went to O. J.'s house, which became the centre of the court case. I spent a New Year's Eve at a party given by Bob Cardashian who became OJ's lawyer halfway through the trial – some say to stop him giving evidence about where the black bag went. The black bag was seen on TV exiting O. J.'s house, held by Cardashian. It was believed to contain O. J.'s bloodstained clothes, which it was alleged he was wearing on the night of the murder of his wife and her male friend.

I knew many people involved in the proceedings. I was an O. J. trial groupie. I came to the conclusion he was guilty. I hadn't spoken to O. J. for about four years when, shortly after the trial, the phone rang and a funny voice spoke in greeting. I said, 'Marlon! You're putting on a funny voice!' A voice said, 'It's not Marlon, it's O. J., man!' O. J. was coming to England to speak at the Oxford Union and be on television. Should I say, 'O. J., I think you've killed two people, I'm certainly not going to talk to a double murderer' and put the phone down? Or should I say, 'Hi, O. J., what you been doing?' In the split second I had to make that decision I chose version two. I took the view that O. J. had always been very nice to me. I'd also been riveted by his trial. Now I had an opportunity to talk to its main participant.

O. J. came to London. I was with him every day. I said, 'I saw your trial and I was driven to the conclusion that you were guilty.' O. J. said, 'Well, the way it was presented, man, I'm not surprised.' We then discussed the trial at great length. We discussed his life with Nicole. O. J. maintained his innocence. He also maintained his outrageous sense of humour. When we took some photos at his suite in the Hyde Park Hotel, I said, 'Stand behind me O. J. because if I'm sitting I don't look so fat.' When the photos came out O. J. was pretending to strangle me! We were driving around Hyde Park Corner, a crowded and dangerous spot. I nearly hit two people. O. J. said, 'Watch out, man! They'll say O. J. killed another two!' As far as I'm concerned O. J. went through the justice system of a civilised country and came out the other end. His life is destroyed. He was the most incredibly popular man I ever walked the streets with. Blacks and whites adored him. He is now a forlorn, broken man. He might well have been worse off in jail but he still paid a severe penalty. I don't wish to make it any worse by turning away from him. He came back to London in 2003. I saw him then. He was crippled with arthritis. O. J. was extremely pleasant during the shoot of the movie, very relaxed, always going to help local charities on the islands we visited, always prepared to go to hospitals and see people who were unwell.

Sophia was the most wonderful, dedicated artiste I ever met. She was always on time. She always knew her lines. She never made trouble. On our first day the scene was on a boat. Filming on boats is always a bore. I got to the quayside in Antigua at 6.30 a.m. Sophia was not due until seven. I said out of curiosity, 'Any sign of Sophia?' They said, 'There she is.' Sitting on a bollard was Sophia Loren, early and ready to work. When we got on the boat we shot in sequence. The scenes were between Coburn and O. J. Sophia had to wait and walk from one side of the deck to the other to get out of the way because there wasn't much room. When we were finally ready for her, three hours later, I said, 'Where's Sophia?' She came up from down below, went to her place and started to act. Somebody said to me, 'You know where Sophia was? She was being violently seasick in the toilet downstairs.' Sophia never mentioned it. She's the ultimate professional.

One day Sophia came to me and said, 'You know, Michael, a very famous member of the Italian paparazzi has come to the island. He's caused me a lot of trouble before. I think he's going to get shots of O. J. and me talking and put it about in Italy that we're having an affair. I don't want that. He's staying at the Le Toc Hotel.' I said, 'Don't worry, Sophia, I'm very friendly with the Prime Minister. I'll fix this.' I rang the Prime Minister and told him. An hour later the Chief of Police of St Lucia rang and said, 'Mr Winner, we've broken down the door of this man's room in the Le Toc Hotel. He's now in prison!' I said, 'That's very kind of you. But on what charge?' The Chief of Police said, 'He came here without a work permit and he came to work.' I rang Sophia and said, 'The man's not going to photograph you with O. J. because he's in prison.' Sophia said, 'I didn't want him in prison! I just wanted to make sure he didn't come near the set. That's terrible! He'll take it out on me when I get back to Italy. Can you get him out?' I said, 'I only just put him in, Sophia! I'll phone the Chief of Police and do my best.' I couldn't get him, but the Chief of Police, the Prime Minister of St Lucia and his wife were all due on the set the next day.

We were filming in a beautiful setting called Marigo Bay. It was just incredible in 1978. A typical tropical island bay with palm trees and hills around it. Sadly it's now a yacht basin. It looks like a car park. That's what's happened all over the world as tourism and wealth encroach. Down to this lovely setting came the Prime Minister, his wife and the Chief of Police. The Chief of Police looked like a commissionaire at a major European hotel. He was full of epaulettes and medals. I said, 'It's very kind of you to put this photographer in jail, but Miss Loren and I would appreciate it if you'd now get him out.' The Chief of Police said, 'Don't worry Mr Winner, we're deporting him.' I said, 'When's he going?' The Chief of Police said, 'The problem is, we can't get him on a plane to New York. He's waitlisted for next Wednesday.' I said, 'He didn't come from New York! He came from Italy!' The Chief of Police replied, 'Yes, but there are no flights from St Lucia to Italy.' I told Sophia the situation. She kind of rolled her eyes skyward and smiled. After the movie she rang me and said, 'That paparazzo caused me terrible trouble once I got back to Rome. He follows me everywhere. I was stopped for speeding and he took photographs like I was being arrested. We had a press conference for a movie and he stood up at the back of the hall and started shouting that I'd had him thrown into jail in St Lucia!'

Sophia was not in all the scenes in Antigua. I said to her, 'What do you do when you're not filming? Sophia replied, 'I go with my secretary and we sunbathe naked on a beach.' I said, 'I don't believe what I'm hearing! Antigua's full of people with cameras and you're stripping off on public beaches!' Sophia tapped her nose with her right forefinger and said, 'Michael, I'm from Naples.' The tapping of the nose was meant to indicate some extraordinary skill. Combined with the words 'I'm from Naples.' She was basically saying, 'Shut up, Winner, I'm cleverer than you at these things.' Weeks after the film was over I was at home and the telephone rang. Sophia said, 'Have you seen *Paris-Match* this week?' I said, 'No, Sophia. What's in it?' Sophia said, 'Nine pages of me in the nude on the beach in Antigua. In France we have *droit moral* which means I can sue them. Do you think I should?' I said, 'Sophia, how do your tits look?' She said, 'They look very good, actually.' I said, 'Don't sue. Send them a thank-you letter.' Sophia could often appear very grand. When the film started I was occasionally using very bad language! Sophia said, 'Oh, Michael, I do hope I'm not going to have to hear that language throughout the film!' I cut it down as much as I could. We flew from St Lucia to Curaçao. As we came down the steps of our private plane, walking towards us were the Mayor of Curaçao and various dignitaries. The Mayor was holding a large bunch of flowers. Sophia said, 'Oh my God, look at that arsehole, I'm going to have to fucking put up with all this now!' I said, 'Sophia, dear, you've learned very quickly!'

It was after the movie that Sophia had to face prison in Italy on charges of tax evasion. I was impressed by how very shrewd Sophia was when she said, 'I'll go to Italy to give myself up in the summer because I'm sure it's very cold in the prison in winter.' I read the newspapers which gave a glowing account of her having a beautifully decorated cell with a television and being treated in a very special way. I mentioned this to Sophia when she told me how dreadful it had been. She'd served seventeen days of a one-month sentence. She said, 'The press were quite inaccurate. I had a tiny little cell. I had a very old small black-and-white television. I had to stay in my cell the whole time because when I walked about the first day the prison wardress said to me, "It's very dangerous for you to walk about Sophia. Any of these women would get a lot of attention and esteem in the prison if they cut you with a knife or a razor." So after that,' said Sophia, 'I stayed in my cell.'

The *Sunday Times Magazine* used a young freelance called Tina Brown who'd just left Oxford. I was not aware at the time that she was the girlfriend of the Editor, Harry Evans. The magazine asked us to pay all the expenses for her to come out. Flying someone to Curaçao and back and putting them up in a hotel is no mean expense. I said to Tina Brown before she came, 'On no account must you talk about Sophia Loren's supposed sex life and affairs', which were rampant in the press at the time. Tina said, 'I won't, I give you my word.' I told Sophia, 'I think this lady's safe. She's not going to ask you about what the other press are talking about at the moment. She'll just talk about your career.' After the interview with Tina Brown Sophia said, 'She didn't mention anything. She was fine.' I had dinner with Tina Brown that night. I was already friendly with Harry and later I became very friendly with both of them. When the article appeared the first lines were 'Michael Winner took me aside and said, "Whatever you do, don't ask Sophia Loren about her affairs or her sex life because otherwise you can't do the interview!"' I thought to myself, 'That's a stab in the back. This girl will go far.'

Firepower was an enormous action film. Everything got blown up. We were in St Lucia and we'd blown up five jeeps which James Coburn was putting limpet mines underneath. We were in a rain-forest jungle. We had a little time still to shoot. I said, 'Let's blow up another jeep.' They said, 'We haven't got one.' I said, 'What's that jeep over there?' pointing to a jeep owned by a local doctor who'd lent it to the sound crew just for the four weeks of filming in St Lucia. They used it to carry their equipment. I said, 'Get the equipment off. We'll blow it up!' This jeep was driven along a riverbed. We put all our explosives in it. It was then pulled the last couple of yards on a wire, a remote control switch would be pushed and the whole thing would blow up. By chance the doctor, his wife and his family came to visit us that day. They were pointing with pride at their jeep which was featuring in the movie. A second later – and I will never forget the look on their faces – the whole jeep blew up and bits of it fell all around them! They just couldn't believe it! We paid for a new jeep! On another occasion we had to blow up a helicopter. That's done by having a perfect model helicopter which you fly by a remote control. It has explosives in it and again by remote control the helicopter is blown up. We had seven cameras on this because you can't afford to miss. We set the helicopter off from a beach at the unit hotel. A man had come from California with these helicopters. The helicopter hadn't really yet got into the air when someone on the beach turned on a radio. The radio set the explosion off! The helicopter blew up about four feet from the ground. None of the seven cameras got it! Luckily we had another helicopter and no one turned on the radio!

As well as Loren, Coburn and O. J. Simpson, *Firepower* featured some of the most famous character actors of Hollywood, including Anthony Franciosa, Eli Wallach, George Grizzard and Vincent Gardenia, who'd played the detective in *Death Wish*. I wanted Victor Mature to play a little scene at the end as a millionaire Sophia Loren is about to go off with. Victor had been my hero from the days when he was pushing over pillars in *Samson and Delilah* and bringing down the temple. Victor had to have five thousand dollars in cash in a carrier bag because he was on a pension and if he had an income it would have destroyed the pension. I'd had him with me on *Won Ton Ton* but he only got five hundred there so it didn't matter. Lew Grade agreed the five thousand dollars' cash in a plastic bag. Victor was the favourite on *Won Ton Ton*. He was the only star who tipped the drivers generously. He was famous for the line when he was a big star when they said, 'Victor, in this scene you have to swim across the river and although there may be crocodiles, don't worry, because when we fire a gun the crocodiles go away!' Victor said, 'What if one of them's deaf?' Victor had a very bad motorcycle accident on his first movie so he wouldn't do stunts of any kind. He thought getting out of a car was a stunt. I met him outside the Pierre Hotel, in New York. I said, 'Victor, you've got green hair.' He said, 'I think something went wrong when I dyed it. It's normally white.' I said, 'We've got Sophia Loren who insists on making herself up. She has an orange face! Our last scene will be orange-faced woman meets green-haired man!' Nobody noticed!

We were shooting with Mature and Sophia Loren in a very posh town house in New York. There were beautiful models dressing the set. Everyone was in evening dress. In a lull, just before a take, when there's absolute quiet as everyone waits for the director to say 'Action!' Victor said, 'Michael, can I keep this dinner suit?' Victor lived in Rancho Santa Fe. He led a very rustic life playing golf. I said, 'What on earth do you need a dinner suit for in Rancho Santa Fe?' Victor said, 'It'll come in handy for funerals.' I said, 'No one wears a dinner suit at funerals.' Victor said, 'I do.' I said, 'Victor, you've just won the suit. Have it.' Victor and I corresponded and spoke on the phone for years afterwards until he died. Another superb person.

While we were in New York, the actor Robert De Niro asked if he could meet Sophia Loren. The request came through our Casting Director, Cis Corman, who'd been a long-time friend of De Niro and later became the President of Barbra Streisand's production company. Cis said to me, 'Nobody must know Bobby's there. So when he comes he's going to say his name is James Thomas. You must greet him as James Thomas.' At the appointed hour Bobby De Niro came to the set. All the New York technicians knew him well.

He was greeted with a hail of 'Hiya, Bobby!' 'How are you, Bobby?', 'How's things going, Bobby!' De Niro came round shaking hands with the crew. When he reached me Cis Corman said, 'Michael, this is James Thomas.' I said, 'Very glad to meet you, Mr Thomas. I'll see if Miss Loren is ready!' I went to Sophia's caravan, checked it was okay, came back and said, 'Yes, Mr Thomas, Miss Loren is ready.' I took de Niro to her caravan, opened the door and in he went. About twenty minutes later he came out and said goodbye to Cis Corman and me. I said, 'Goodbye, Mr Thomas. Very nice to meet you.' And Bobby went off through the crew, all of whom were saying, 'Cheerio!', 'See you, Bobby', 'Good to see you, kid', 'How are you Bobby', 'Keep well, Bobby!'

We had a scene in Miami where James Coburn and O. J. Simpson were trying to get into this millionaire's house and German Shepherd/Alsatian dogs attack them. One of the dogs turned out to be the dog star of *Won Ton Ton the Dog Who Saved Hollywood*. He was now so vicious that he had to wear a muzzle at all times. He was living the story of *Won Ton Ton*: a dog star who went to pieces and ended up a nothing. Knowing him as I did, I was bloody glad he wore the muzzle.

Firepower was a major action film. London's *Time Out* magazine said, 'Gaudy and accomplished. Loren and Coburn have never looked better.' In *The New York Times* Janet Maslin wrote, 'There's a nice chemistry in the teaming of Sophia Loren, James Coburn and O. J. Simpson, each of whom has an unusually physical presence on the screen. Together they generate an air of friendliness and cooperation.' *Films and Filming* wrote, 'The old energy that made Michael Winner's *The Mechanic* a cult classic is here in abundance. There are some of the most technically expert action scenes I can remember. It is good fun and genuinely exciting and entertaining. Loren is as good as she's been for years.' It wasn't an important film. It was a pleasant meat-and-potatoes action movie. It did okay, and was fun to make. I enjoyed it!

22

Enter the Nosh Brothers

Dino de Laurentiis, the Italian producer who'd made *Death Wish*, was in London in 1981 making a movie at Pinewood. He said, 'Let's do another picture!' He had in mind a book he'd once optioned called *Space Vampires*. He asked me to call the agent to see if it was still available. The agent said a new option had been taken by two Israelis, Menahem Golan and Yoram Globus. They were going to start a company in Hollywood and make movies after minor success in Israel. Dino rubbed his hands together as if clearing dust from his palms and said, 'Buy it from them.' That was how I met Menahem Golan and Yoram Globus. Two of the most amazing characters I ever came across in show business. They were called, in movie-world, the Nosh Brothers. Even though they were cousins. They were staying with other Israelis in a house in London. Yoram and Menahem looked like they'd been sleeping rough on a student outing. Menahem was very large. Yoram was rather small. They sat in my antiques-filled living room and I treated them like youngsters entering the industry. 'We'd like to buy your option on *Space Vampires*,' I said. Menahem looked up and replied in a guttural voice, 'A million dollars!' The option was worth twenty thousand at most. I said, 'Is that your final say on the matter?' Menahem said,

'Yes. Come and make the picture for us.' I said, 'I'm negotiating on behalf of Dino de Laurentiis. You're telling me there's nothing you'd accept under a million dollars?' 'No,' said Menahem. 'What about $999,999?' I asked. 'No,' said Menahem. I said to Dino, 'They're a couple of nut cases!'

Shortly thereafter I saw the start of what became the Cannon Empire when Menahem and Yoram took full-page advertisements in *Variety*, the show-business trade newspaper. One of them announced that Menahem was to direct Charles Bronson in *Death Wish Two*. Dino had the rights to make further *Death Wish* movies but we'd both decided in 1975 that it was a one-joke picture. There was a poor second book which Brian Garfield, the original author, wrote. Golan and Globus hadn't bought that book. But they had the rights to create their own sequel to *Death Wish*. I got a call saying Charles Bronson insisted I direct the movie. So I set off for the Cannon offices on the 23rd floor of a building on Hollywood Boulevard. They were besieged by creditors. People walked in threatening to kill anyone in sight because they hadn't been paid! A young and loyal staff were holding the fort. Menahem was in the Philippines directing a karate film. Yoram was in New York trying to raise money. I was shown into a dirty office. I spent the first morning cleaning it with damp paper towels. I rang up friends and said, 'It's bizarre!' It seemed Cannon were unlikely to hang in the offices much longer, let alone find the money to make *Death Wish Two*. They'd agreed a rich two-million-dollar deal with Bronson. They'd agreed a good deal with me. One of their junior executives, Danny Dimbort, came in shaking. He said, 'We sent Dino de Laurentiis a hundred and fifty thousand dollars per contract to pay for the rights of *Death Wish Two*. He's just sent our cheque back saying he won't sell!' I rang Dino. I said, 'You've just fired me! I came over here to make this movie. Now you've taken the rights away.' Dino said, 'Come and make it for me, Michael.'

It would have been much better for my career to get back with Dino de Laurentiis, a major producer, than stick with a couple of Israeli newcomers who, according to all visible signs, would shortly be broke. I said, 'No, Dino, you've got to sell it to them. Go through with the deal.' So Dino agreed to accept their cheque and sell. Menahem eventually appeared from the Philippines wearing a bright shirt with guitars and palm trees on it and with the publicity lady, a young American girl with long blonde hair, in tow. He assured me how valuable the company was going to be and offered me two dollars' worth of Cannon shares for every dollar of salary I was due to receive. The offices were still besieged by creditors. Cannon shares were $1.25 at the time. I thought they'd never ever be anything. They went to $145 each before they collapsed again and the company went down the tubes. In between times Menahem and Yoram were the most wonderful firework display the industry had seen.

At the beginning things were a bit rough. They managed, somehow or other, to let me take on a pre-production crew, and the crew were paid. They were a top union crew. Not a non-union crew that works for much less. As we got near shooting the money began to run out. Menahem and Yoram were somewhere else. In the office of Chris Pearce, their Associate Producer, sat Willie, the Eastern European book-keeper. They were discussing how they could make the down payment needed for the Screen Actors Guild. Chris had arranged to meet Kate Crone, the Screen Actors Guild lady, for lunch that day and bring a banker's cheque. But they had no money. 'I know,' said Chris, 'I'll say the motorcycle messenger was killed in an accident on Sunset Boulevard as he was bringing the cheque.' Then, realising the fatuousness of this, he said, 'No.' Willie suddenly rose in his seat and said, 'I have an idea, Chris! I have an idea!' Then he thought for a minute and said, 'No, Chris, I don't have an idea.' I said, 'Chris, go to the lunch. She's not going to pull the actors off the film when we haven't even started shooting because you don't have the down payment for the Screen Actors Guild. You'll have a few days, if not weeks, of grace.' Willie the book-keeper mortgaged his house to pay for a couple of days' shooting. Then Danny Dimbort, the junior executive, mortgaged his house to pay for a couple more days. Somehow or other Menahem and Yoram found money to keep the film going.

The story was much the same as the first *Death Wish* except on this occasion Bronson went out and shot the muggers who'd actually raped and killed his daughter and his maid. It was a premise that still worked. Revenge against absolutely awful people. As in the first film, when we discovered Jeff Goldblum as one of the muggers, in this second film I discovered Laurence Fishburne, who played one of the muggers. In *Death Wish Three* Alex Winter, also playing a mugger, later became famous as the star of *Bill and Ted's Big Adventure*. We shot a lot of *Death Wish Two* on location in downtown Los Angeles, which has now been cleaned up. Then it was a spectacularly interesting and beautiful place. It was full of rundown brothels, places for male prostitutes and hermaphrodites, drug dealing, places where people could hire a bed for two dollars a night and live in a dormitory. It was the absolute pits of LA. Charles Bronson had an alcoholic brother who lived there. Occasionally Charlie brought him to his house and gave him a job as a handyman. But his brother always went back to these debauched streets of downtown Los Angeles. He was killed when somebody tried to cut some money from his back pocket and cut off a large slice of his bottom. Bronson's brother died in a tiny, smelly room, lying there for many weeks before anyone knew he was dead. Charlie told me his brother came up to him for money while we were shooting *Death Wish Two*. He said, 'Don't give me more than twenty dollars or they'll kill me for it.'

On the first day of shooting the bus came with our extras from a casting agent. They were dressed as they believed down-and-out tramps, prostitutes other low-life people would dress. Behind the barrier, where the road was cordoned off for us, were the real local down-and-outs. Drunks, alcoholics, prostitutes. But marvellous people. I always enjoyed coming early to those locations, putting my director's chair down in the middle of the street where everybody said you couldn't possibly sit safely, and talking to the locals. I said to my Assistant Director, 'These people from the bus look ridiculous. Behind that barrier we have real people. I'll use the real people as extras.' He was outraged. He said, 'You can't possibly use them. They're all drugged. They're alcoholics. None of them will stay.' I said, 'Send the bus back. I will personally go and get the real people.' I picked about forty people from behind the barrier. They were absolutely marvellous. Each night we'd pick them and give them some money. They stayed with us. They had something to do they thought was worth while. It was a pleasure to work with them. Their clothes were perfect!

I didn't realise how cold it was in Los Angeles at night, so the first night I went into a local secondhand shop. There was an old nylon jacket padded with goose feathers. I still have it! It had a zip-up front. It was five dollars. I knocked the man down to three. The shopkeeper said, 'If you leave it around, Mr Winner, I'll sell it back to you tomorrow.' We'd come at six at night. By eight the hermaphrodite prostitutes would be going out in their high heels and dresses. At five in the morning they'd be coming back. They got on with their lives and we got on with ours. One night two gunshots rang out. A policeman came to me and said, 'That was your girlfriend,' meaning one of the cross-dressers I'd chatted to. 'Her girlfriend just shot her in the arse!'

Filming at night in the worst slum areas is fascinating. Talking to the people and hearing their stories is riveting. The film itself ran smoothly. Jill Ireland had a big part. That kept Charlie happy. Working in Hollywood is always fun. The executives show films every weekend in the private homes. Actors I'd already befriended, such as Mitchum and Brando and Burt Lancaster, were delighted to have someone they could feel comfortable with. And of course there were the girls. Endless girls. Bachelor heaven. I started an affair with the girl who played Bronson's daughter. It didn't last because she kept finding other girls hiding in the Beverly Hills Hotel walk-in closets when she came round to surprise me.

At the end of the movie I edited it myself in London. I was sitting in my house when Menahem Golan rang. He said, 'We've got Isaac Hayes to do the music. We've done a deal with his record company, Elektra. They're giving us the music free and we get a small share in the album as well.' I was a fan of Isaac Hayes but I was enraged that Menahem had chosen a composer without consulting me. I was to go to Los Angeles in two weeks to meet with Hayes. I said, 'Menahem, I'd like to think about that. Maybe I can suggest somebody better.' My next-door neighbour, who I'd never ever seen, was the legendary rock guitarist and leader of Led Zeppelin, Jimmy Page. I telephoned the house and spoke to the housekeeper. His agent, Peter Grant, rang me. Grant was one of the great characters of the music industry. I explained what I wanted. He said, 'Jimmy's on a boat at the moment but he can come and see you in ten days' time.' I said, 'That'll be too late, Peter. We have to have a decision now because Isaac Hayes is prepared to do the music free, with Elektra paying him. If I'm going to replace him, I have to know Jimmy's available.' The next day Grant rang me and said, 'What's happening?' I said, 'Nothing's happening. Jimmy's not free to see me. I'll go with Hayes.' Peter Grant said, 'All right, I'll do a deal for Jimmy. What are you offering him?' I said, 'Isaac Hayes is doing the music free and Cannon films are getting a share of the album and a share of the publishing.' Peter Grant, who was known as a very tough negotiator, then said the most amazing thing. 'Well, how do I beat free?' I said, joking, 'Jimmy Page has to pay to do our music!' To my amazement Peter Grant said, 'How much?' I said, 'A hundred and seventy-five thousand dollars.' Peter Grant said, 'I'll call you back.' He rang back a quarter of an hour later and said, 'We'll pay a hundred and seventy-five thousand dollars and we'll give a better percentage than Elektra are giving you from the album.'

I told Menahem I'd got Jimmy Page on a better deal. Then I sent a contract letter down to Peter Grant's house in the country with a driver. I said, 'Peter, you have to sign this letter because the deal means nothing unless the letter's signed.' I knew the music industry well. They'd say anything. Do less. That was the last time I spoke to Peter Grant for five years, until he rang me out of the blue to wish me a happy birthday. Every time I rang Peter's house to ask if he'd signed the contract and say my driver was sitting outside I was told, 'He's just having breakfast,', 'He's having a bath,', 'He's gone for a walk.' A whole series of young cockney voices relayed to me why Grant was unavailable. Finally, having kept a car outside Grant's house nonstop for forty-eight hours, I said, 'Tell Peter Grant unless he signs this letter of agreement and it's back with me by 6 p.m. this evening, the deal's off. I'll go with Isaac Hayes.' The letter was signed and I got it back.

Jimmy did the music. At that time Jimmy Page was said to be a terrible drug addict. Incapable of doing anything. Led Zeppelin had broken up because the drummer had died and a member of the entourage, the man who designed the band's record covers, had died in Jimmy Page's house. Jimmy was supposedly in a very unstable state. None of this worried me because I'd continually been told I was dealing with people who were unstable and impossible and they'd all turned out to be very nice. One evening my doorbell rang. A thin and slightly wobbly Jimmy Page had come to see the movie in my private cinema. He seemed very pleasant. We later became good friends.

Jimmy is the most wonderful musician. He did impeccable music for *Death Wish Two*. It hit every music cue it had to hit. Music for a film has to be written to a twenty-fourth of a second to coincide with things happening on the screen! He was also a very together person. He lives in a famous Victorian house. It's on many of the tours of London, as is mine. Except that Jimmy knows far more about Victorian art and architecture than I do. He's a genuine expert. He had another house in Windsor, which he bought from Michael Caine, which was full of fine Victorian paintings and immaculately kept. His music for *Death Wish Two* was so good that when I made *Death Wish Three* later we used it as a temporary music track. It fitted so well that I rang him up and said, 'Jimmy you can have a music credit for another film without doing anything!' So Jimmy got the music credit for *Death Wish Three* which had the same music we'd used on *Death Wish Two* re-cut by me. In both cases we added a string orchestra to play Jimmy's beautiful melodies.

Death Wish Two was a great financial success. It was not a film likely to set critics alight, but it didn't do badly. Writing in the *Guardian* Derek Malcolm said, 'The action is as fast and furious as Winner can make it. The film has narrative drive, excitement and credibility.' In the *Evening Standard* Alexander Walker said, 'A thrill of vicarious satisfaction . . . Michael Winner has stripped away all non-essentials from the story leaving just motive and action.' The *New York Daily News* said, 'The formula's great and it still works.'

The most amusing press report came from the *International Herald Tribune* in September 1983. Richard Munro, the President of Time Inc., who owned Home Box Office, the leading US cable movie network, announced their research. It showed that 'HBO viewers preferred *Death Wish Two* over the Academy-Award winning *Chariots of Fire* by a 4 to 1 margin.'

Later the same year I was in the Concorde lounge on my way to New York when I bumped into my old friend Terry O'Neill, the photographer. He was now living with Faye Dunaway. Faye was anxious to find something to do in England. I said, 'I've got the ideal script for you, *The Wicked Lady*. It's about a noble lady who goes out at night as a highwaywoman and gets mixed up with the criminal crowd at the end of the eighteenth century.' Faye was interested. This had been a favourite film of my youth starring Margaret Lockwood and James Mason. I'd telephoned Pinewood Studios a few years earlier and said to their Chief, Cyril Howard, 'You have a film I'd like to buy the re-make rights of.' He said, 'What's it called?' I said, '*The Wicked Lady*.' He said, 'Never heard of it.' I said, 'Of course you haven't, Cyril.' He said, 'What are you offering me?' I said, 'Fifty pounds.' Cyril said, 'How can you offer me only fifty pounds for the rights to re-make a movie?' I said, 'I'll pay you thirty thousand pounds on the first day of shooting if it's made. For the moment I'll pay fifty.' Cyril said, 'That's ridiculous.' I said, 'No one else has offered you fifty pounds for it. You'd never heard of it until I rang up. So as it's the best offer you've got, you may as well take it.' Thus I bought the rights to re-make *The Wicked Lady* and had an appalling script done by Edna O'Brien. I then wrote another script myself which I showed to Edna. She said my script was absolutely terrible and she wanted nothing to do with it. When the film was finished she went to the Writers Guild and claimed I'd copied her script. They arbitrated the matter and decided I hadn't nicked a word of her script. Therefore the credit should read that the script was by me and the people who'd written the original movie.

Yoram and Menahem wanted Faye at the Cannes Film Festival so they could make a big splash. I went to Cannes as the guest of Cannon Films. They had practically the entire Croisette and the entire Carlton Hotel plastered with Cannon Films posters. I arrived at the airport and a young man met me with a car. He said, 'I'm sorry, I can't go on the motorway, Mr Winner. As I was leaving the hotel Menahem Golan took all my change. We'll have to go on the coast road, which is free.' I went to the Carlton Hotel to some tiny room they had for me. It was only for two nights so it was okay. Cannon gave a press conference announcing the movie with Faye Dunaway. It was held in a downstairs room at the Carlton. The room was partitioned off with a concertina wall on tracks. Faye Dunaway and

I sat on a podium in the back area of the room. The journalists came in from the much larger front area where they'd been having canapés and drinks. Then they'd exit this back room through a door which led out through the kitchens. Thus another lot could come in.

The first lot of journalists entered the room. Questions were asked and answered. The partition heaved with other journalists wanting to get in. Menahem Golan, who'd been in the Israeli Army and was extremely strong, eventually decided that the first group had been there long enough. He said, 'Ladies and gentlemen, will you now please leave the room to make way for your colleagues who are waiting. Go out through this door at the back.' None of the journalists moved. This did not amuse Menahem, who had a fiery temper. He repeated, 'Would you please leave the room. We have to accommodate your journalist colleagues who need to come to this conference area.' Still nobody moved. At this point Menahem stood in front of them screaming at the top of his voice and grabbed a journalist by the lapels and shook him. He said, 'I tell you, you fucking arseholes! If I ask you to leave the fucking room, you leave the fucking room! If you don't leave the room I'll fucking kill you because I'm an Israeli and we don't stand for any shit!' A journalist stood up at the back of the room and said, 'I've been coming to the Cannes Festival for twenty-three years and I've never heard such disgusting language or seen such a disgraceful press conference.' Menahem replied, 'You're a fucking arsehole, get out!' I was on the platform roaring with laughter. I looked at Yoram Globus who was at the side, and said, 'I want Menahem to run all my press conferences!' The journalists eventually left the room. The next day in the *Nice-Matin* paper Faye and I were on the front page. Faye was looking absolutely terrified. I was roaring with laughter. But the next group of journalists came in and then went out and the whole thing went very smoothly. It's sad that Menahem and Yoram's company went under some years later. They were fun people.

Cannon now had a whole chain of cinemas in America. Shortly before the beginning of shooting *The Wicked Lady* they bought what was the second-biggest circuit in England, ABC. They also bought Associated British Studios at Elstree. This produced a furore in the British press including some highly anti-Semitic observations.

Menahem and Yoram were painted as vulgar aliens contaminating the purity of British cinema. They were also accused of intending to sell the studios for property development. In fact the non-Israeli, all-English group who were their rivals for the studios had exactly the same plans. Menahem and Yoram kept the studios for a very long time. Far longer than they should have done.

I'd just got Faye Dunaway a wonderful house in Belgravia for the duration of the film. I sent Cannon's first month's rental cheque plus a security deposit totalling thirty-five thousand pounds. The estate agent phoned me and said, 'The cheque's bounced.' I rang Menahem and said, 'I don't like to trouble you, because I know you're very busy, but your leading lady is about to be thrown out on the street. The rent cheque's bounced.' I could hear Menahem screaming at the book-keeper at the other end for daring to issue a cheque they couldn't meet. I said, 'Menahem, it's nothing to do with him. It's to do with you!' Menahem said, 'Tell them to present the cheque again!' This was a standard line of Menahem and Yoram. They reckoned that if a cheque was re-presented it would take four days to go through and in the four days they might get some money into the account. I said, 'What if the agent wants to present it on special clearance?' (a way of getting a cheque cleared in one day). Menahem said, 'Tell him he can't.' I told the estate agent, 'The money's been delayed coming from America, but you can re-present the cheque.' The agent said, 'Can I re-present it on special clearance today?' I said, 'Not if you want any money! Give the money two or three days to get in.' The cheque was re-presented and went through.

Menahem and Yoram were sending cars around the ABC Cinemas and collecting the cash from the ice-cream and sweet kiosks. How much money was spent at the ice-cream and sweet kiosks dictated how many people we could pay on *The Wicked Lady*. One day everyone's cheque bounced. I offered to buy the crew's cheques for 90 per cent. That shut them up. I told Faye to get on with it because if she pulled out she certainly wouldn't get paid. In fact everybody got paid (as they did on all my Nosh Brothers movies) and the film was finished.

During the production Menahem and Yoram arranged an enormous loan from Franz Afman at the Schlavenburg Bank which was later bought out by Credit Lyonnais and was the subject of great scandal in the banking community! All Faye Dunaway's cheques were made up, the units had been made good, the only person with unpaid salary was me. Menahem and Yoram came on the set very excited, saying, 'We've got the money!' I said, 'That's wonderful, Yoram! But I'm still owed eleven weeks' salary.' Yoram and Menahem said, 'Don't worry – you're in the family!' I replied, 'Who do I have to fuck to get out of this family and get paid!' I stayed in the family and got paid!

The Wicked Lady was a wonderfully camp story of this regal lady of the manor who became a highwaywoman. Faye played it to the hilt. *Time Magazine* said, 'Her eyes looked like Darth Vader. It seemed as if she had the entire costume budget of the film on every time she entered the screen.' I brought out of semi-retirement a famous cameraman called Jack Cardiff who was doing films for the Children's Film Foundation. Faye annoyed him greatly by talking directly to the Chief Electrician and telling him to re-position the lights. Jack, who was a superb cameraman, got very over-excited about this. I said, 'Jack, you've been making films for the Children's Film Foundation. Your career is in the doldrums. Nobody's going to fire Faye Dunaway from this film. If you come up against her, you'll be fired and another cameraman will be here in two seconds. I suggest you do the film and get the benefit of having made it.' Which he did.

As her co-star we had Alan Bates as a highwayman. John Gielgud played an old retainer she poisons. A wonderful cast included Prunella Scales, Denholm Elliott and other stalwarts of the English cinema. It was my first film with John Gielgud who was without question a most magical man. He became a dear friend. Johnnie was the ultimate professional. He was always the first person on his mark. The first person on the set. He was immaculate in everything he did. Once we were working late and there was a big hush with this crowd of people in costume. It all looked terribly regal. Suddenly Gielgud's voice was heard. 'You know, Michael, this is the time I'm normally watching *Starsky and Hutch*.' Another day I was having lunch alone with Johnnie in my little room for the stars. Terry O'Neill came in with a photograph he'd taken of Gielgud and Faye

Dunaway. He said, 'Sir John, I'd like you to have this photo.' Gielgud looked at it and said, 'Oh Terry, it's so wonderful. I love the way the light falls on the lace. And the way it touches Faye's hair. Could you please sign it for me? And would you please have Faye sign it for me?' Terry practically walked out of the room backwards bowing, saying, 'Yes, Sir John.' When the door shut I said to Gielgud, 'Johnnie, when they both sign this photograph, where will you put it?' Gielgud half looked up at the ceiling and made a little sniff. 'Up my arse!' he said. Johnnie would sit down every lunch time and say, 'Who shall we destroy today?' He was not really malicious. He loved show business. He had a great interest in everything going on, particularly in the theatre. I'd often visit him at his home in Oxfordshire. I took lots of photos there. When one of his books was coming out he referred the publishers to me for photographs of him to go on the cover. My house is full of little gifts from Johnnie. Gilt-embossed messages on leather address books, things like that. I even bought his *Spitting Image* puppet at a charity auction so he stands, robed, in my private cinema. I hate to think what Johnnie would say about that!

When I took Faye Dunaway on everybody warned me, 'You've had Brando and Bronson and Mitchum and stars who are meant to be difficult. You charmed them. But your luck's run out with Faye Dunaway. On *Mommie Dearest*, where Faye played Joan Crawford, the only thing that came out of her caravan for the first two days of shooting were the wigs. They were cut in four pieces and thrown out the window!' I never take notice of these stories. I found Faye to be absolutely charming, very ladylike and immensely dedicated. She's a Capricorn, so she goes into everything with enormous vigour. Terry O'Neill said to me, 'Faye never turns up for the first day of a movie so we'll have to have a fake first day.' I said, 'A fake first day will cost just as much as a real first day. The first day of this movie is on the bridge at Ecton in Derbyshire. Faye's going to be there. We start the movie.'

We had a pre-production day to shoot doubles riding across the skyline. Faye, who'd been horse-riding like mad, said, 'Let me do that myself.' I said, 'But Faye darling, we'll do it with doubles. It's just tiny figures on the brow of the hill.' Faye said, 'I'd like to do it myself.' So instead of having a couple of extras, we had this enormous caravan and Faye had to come along and get dressed in the costume when all she was was a silhouette on a hill about an inch high on the screen. Faye was choosing from twenty hats. She did the riding very well. She rang me at eleven o'clock that night and said, 'Michael darling, we'll have to shoot it all again!' I said, 'Why, Faye?' She said, 'I chose the wrong hat.' I said, 'Faye, at the distance you are away from the camera no one would know if you were wearing a bowler hat, a jockey's cap, a flower hat! It doesn't matter.' Faye was deeply caring. That was not being difficult.

On the first day of the movie we were shooting on the bridge at Ecton in Derbyshire. It rained. I have a photo of Faye sitting on her horse. She wouldn't even get off the horse to go to her chair, let alone to her caravan. She had an enormous plastic bag over her head to keep her dry. I thought, 'This really is one of the great professionals of all time!' She was never late. She was always quick getting changed from one costume to another. I consider her the most impeccable worker. She did seem to have her own personal worries. I recall Faye sitting in an arbour of the most beautiful rose garden dressed as a late eighteenth-century lady of the manor, with a deep, worried frown on her face. I said, 'Faysie dear, is something wrong?' She said, 'Yes, I have a serious drama in my life.' I said to her, 'Could we relegate it to a minor problem?' Faye said, 'No, darling, it's a serious drama.' I walked away. But she was always enchanting. She was always pleasant. She was always good for a laugh. I called her 'Faysie'. As far as I was concerned it was just another case of all the stories about her being nonsense.

Faye said to me, 'Darling, do you know if I have a day off next week?' or 'Do you think I might have a day off the week after next?' I said, 'Why do you keep asking me about whether you have a day off or not?' Faye said, 'Don't tell anybody, but I want to go to the local registry office. I need half a day to get married.' I said, 'Why didn't you say that? We'll arrange it!' I was sworn to secrecy. Faye married Terry O'Neill in a small town in Hertfordshire. The film finished and I was still sworn to secrecy. No one knew they were married. I said, 'Faysie, let's announce your marriage just before the premiere and get some publicity.' Then Faye gave an interview to the *Daily Express*. During the course of it she admitted that she'd got married, which they didn't even give much space to. I said, 'Faye darling, you've wasted my big publicity opportunity by letting this sneak out.' If only the marriage had lasted!

The Wicked Lady probably garnered the most praise from the English press of any of my movies. It was very camp, very kitsch and brilliantly performed by an incredible cast in the most beautiful locations. It was an invited entry at the Cannes Film Festival. It was the only film I ever made that the British critics liked more than the American critics. 'All's as it should be . . . ravishing photography . . . sumptuous costumes . . . dazzling Jezebels, romantic clinches, spirited tongue-in-cheekiness. Mr Winner shows how zestfully he can stand and deliver,' said Alexander Walker in the *Evening Standard*. 'A jolly period swashbuckler with a cynical contemporary edge. It achieves a nice sense of everyone being after his or her ends first,' said Derek Malcolm in the *Guardian*. 'The cinema devoid of serious purpose is a marvellous thing – *The Wicked Lady* is intensely watchable. The film is an elaborate joke, and often a very funny one. There are few directors who could carry it off with the verve of Mr Winner,' wrote Peter Ackroyd in the *Spectator*. Even Barry Norman, who hated me, spoke very well of the movie: 'Miss Dunaway makes an attractive, flashing-eyed villainess, Mr Bates is a dashing rogue. Winner fills his canvas with nice touches. It's encouraging to see him throw himself wholeheartedly into a piece of light entertainment. An agreeable tongue-in-cheek Restoration romp it is, too.' Jack Pittman in the show-business bible *Variety* wrote, 'Sex, humour, and style distinguish Michael Winner's entertaining comedy drama. It goes at a typically brisk pace. Nudity, passionate love scenes, a number of good jokes, Faye Dunaway performs with satisfying conviction, Bates makes a charming rogue, Gielgud has a marvellous deadpan time of kidding himself.'

Just before *The Wicked Lady* was shown in the West End in London there was an altercation with the then Film Censor, James Ferman. When Ferman came to the job in 1976 he announced he didn't want any local council in Britain to over-rule his decision and ban films passed by the British Board of Film Censors. Some of the local councils – Leeds in particular – were very censorious. The only way Ferman could stop them was to censor all films as strictly as the most censorious local council. He was a disaster. Whereas his predecessor, John Trevelyan, had attempted to keep freedom of expression and a sensible line in censorship, Ferman made us the most censored country in the free world. He delighted in making ridiculous cuts all over the place that no other civilised country would have considered. So films that were shown uncut throughout Europe and in America were cut to ribbons here.

In the case of *The Wicked Lady* we had a whip fight between Faye Dunaway and a gypsy girl which was a diversion to permit Alan Bates to be saved from the gallows at Tyburn. It was a comedy movie and the whip fight, although a little severe, was also comedic. Even though the gypsy girl was whipped until her top came off! Nobody believed anyone was seriously hurt. Ferman demanded that the scene be cut from the film. In America you can challenge the Censor's decision by going to a board consisting of cinema owners, distributors and producers and they vote as to whether or not the Censor should be over-ruled. They over-ruled the American Censor on *Death Wish Two*. There is no appeal against British censorship. So I created my own appeals board. We showed the film to fifty leading members of the film industry and other important people in England. Without exception they praised it to the skies and told Ferman he was ridiculous in wishing to cut this scene. I look at their views with some amusement now, considering how feminist we have become. Today the chance of getting fifty of the most distinguished people in the country to support the retention of a scene where two women whip each other is slight!

Kingsley Amis wrote, 'I very much enjoyed *The Wicked Lady*. In my opinion it contains no offensive material and I see no objection to it being shown uncut to persons over 15.' The distinguished director Lindsay Anderson wrote, 'I think the picture is a first-class piece of genuinely popular entertainment, colourful, vigorously romantic with its tongue beautifully in its cheek. I don't understand on what grounds the censor could possibly want to cut the film for an adult audience.' Even the old school of Great Britain headed by Percy Livingstone, the President of the Society of Film Distributors, wrote, 'My view is that *The Wicked Lady* should be shown uncut with an 18 Certificate.' John Mortimer QC said, 'It's a sort of romantic spoof or pantomime and the duel with horse whips between the two ladies seems to be in the spirit of the piece and quite undisturbing. I would have no hesitation in allowing my 11-year-old daughter to see it.' The director Sir Alan Parker wrote, 'Both my wife and I enjoyed *The Wicked Lady* very much. The scene in question seemed innocuous enough to me considering the tongue in cheek romp of the rest of the film. I hope you get a reprieve.' The director John Schlesinger wrote, 'I thought *The Wicked Lady* was a most enjoyable romp done with great gusto. I'm astonished that you've run into censorship problems particularly with the scene at the gallows when Faye Dunaway gets her comeuppance. I cannot imagine any teenager being in the least adversely affected by it.' Fay Weldon, at the time Chairman of the Booker Prize Committee, wrote, 'I frequently stand in front of the TV screen to guard my children to their disgust from images I consider disturbing and indecent. I would not worry if my 12-year-old saw *The Wicked Lady* in the uncut version I saw yesterday and I think my elder children would positively benefit from it. The explicitly sexual scenes are surprisingly optimistic and romantic.'

James Ferman, presented with fifty of the most distinguished people in the land taking the view that the scene should be passed uncut, decided he hadn't actually seen it before! Only his committee had! Ferman then saw the film and passed it uncut! It was, of course, perfectly all right for an X Certificate and probably for a lower-grade certificate. Unfortunately the current version on TV and video is a covered-up one done specially for prudes! The 'gypsy' whipped naked was a cockney Greek from Crouch End. A very nice girl who I would never have expected to reach stardom. But Marina Sirtis, who I also employed in *Death Wish Three*, went to Hollywood. There she became a regular in the *Star Trek* TV series, not movies. Good luck to her! I'm glad I helped!

23

Cut-Price Casanova

In 1983 Lorimar, the successful producer of American TV series, offered me a cleverly written movie thriller, *Scream for Help*. They didn't want stars. It was set in the New York dormitory town of New Rochelle where a seventeen-year-old girl was under threat from her stepfather. We filmed it partly there and partly in England. We were building the seventeen-year-old girl's room in a studio in England as it had to catch fire and have a lot of special effects involved. I went round houses in New Rochelle to take reference photos of rooms of seventeen-year-old girls. I'd knock on doors in this highly respectable community and say, 'Excuse me, do you have a seventeen-year-old daughter? If so, I'd like to look at her bedroom!' Half the people we approached called the police to tell them a child molester was on the loose! The others showed us the rooms and were very pleasant. The Chief of Police of New Rochelle rang me and said, 'Michael, please tell us when you're going out on these reconnaissances. Then we can assure people we know about it and it's all right.' On the first day of checking out New Rochelle, I had my one and only meal in McDonald's. I ordered a Big Mac, which I was looking forward to. I was terribly disappointed. I found it soggy and tasteless. I greatly enjoyed the milk shake. When I spoke to the Head of Lorimar, Lee

Rich, he said, 'How did it go today, Michael?' I said, 'It was disastrous, Lee. I had this terrible lunch at McDonald's.' Lee said, 'I've never eaten in McDonald's.' I later spoke to his wife, a once famous actress called Pippa Shaw, and she said, 'Of course he's eaten in McDonald's. He takes the children there every Saturday.' The film played in Leicester Square and in theatres throughout Britain. In America it went straight to television.

I followed this with the third *Death Wish* film in 1985. The series had been described by many critics as black comedy and I thought *Death Wish Three* was particularly black and particularly comic. Bronson was dealing with gangs plagueing East New York which at the time was the toughest area in the city. It was a mass of dilapidated mansion apartment blocks which had been lived in by middle-class Jewish people. These were now crumbling and inhabited by Hispanics and blacks. We'd find mattresses on the floor where they'd shoot up. Drug needles were everywhere. It was the sort of area I absolutely love. Half the film was shot there and half in the old Lambeth Hospital in London. Strangely, the Victorian architecture of England and the Victorian architecture of New York are very similar. The police station I photographed in East New York was exactly the same type of architecture as the Lambeth Hospital, which had enormous grounds on which we built New York streets. One apartment building location in East New York was where our gangs would run out of the cellar. I checked it out. Two weeks later when I went back the building had fallen down! This ten-storey block had just collapsed because it was so decrepit!

Jill Ireland had suffered from breast cancer, had a breast removed and was now in remission. She believed she'd beaten the disease. Her birthday was on 24th April. I gathered with Jill and Charlie and their daughter Zuleika at Tavern on the Green in New York to celebrate her birthday and the end of the cancer. We'd started filming in New York a few days earlier. Jill wasn't in the movie, but accompanied Charlie. Her cancer had a terrible effect on him. He knew that although cancer went into remission, it was likely to return. Charlie was deeply in love with Jill and I sensed on *Death Wish Three* that her illness still weighed heavily on him. I later learned that halfway through the movie Jill's cancer began to return.

Charlie was his usual professional self, except his age was beginning to show. He'd had plastic surgery, shortly after the first *Death Wish* and from time to time a great deal more of it. That wonderfully lined face became increasingly bland.

On *Death Wish Three* Charlie was fighting the gangs of east New York who'd killed an old buddy of his and raped a girl he knew. Charlie, most unlike the man I knew, was complaining rather a lot. He said, 'The gun's too loud. It hurts my ears.' He was referring to an old machine gun he used. One day I said to Charlie, 'You chase the mugger, sir. You run down here and turn right round the corner.' Charlie said, 'Jeez, my doctor told me not to run without warming up for an hour beforehand.' I said, 'Charlie, you can't run because your doctor told you not to. You can't fire a gun because it hurts your ears. You've still got to kill thirty-six muggers! You'll have to open a hot-dog stand and food-poison them!' That got half a smile out of Charlie. Of course, he did everything he had to do.

Jill was very happy in London because it was her home town. Charlie was keen to get back to the life in California. The UK locations were 'authentic' New York. When a British TV crew shot us filming a scene in Lambeth where a garage is blown up and the 'New York' Fire Brigade come and put it out, the TV footage was later shown on American television. The head of the Teamsters in New York, which is the tough drivers' union, rang Michael Tadross, my New York Production Manager, and said, 'That arsehole Winner and you have sneaked into New York without using Teamsters and done more shooting on *Death Wish Three*. We're going to get you.' Michael Tadross said, 'It was shot in England.' The Teamster captain said, 'I've lived in New York for fifty-seven years. I know New York when I see it! Don't bullshit me!' That was the greatest compliment I had about the authenticity of our New York streets built in Lambeth. I'd photographed cracks in the east New York pavements, I'd photographed doorways and other details for the Art Director to copy.

It was the last movie I was to work on with Charlie. Cannon offered me further *Death Wish* movies, but the series had run its course. The three *Death Wish* movies I directed were done with proper crews and sizable budgets. They all did very well. Cannon then cut them down to ridiculously low budgets and they went straight to video. I'd see Charlie and Jill if I went to America. After Jill died I spoke to Charlie regularly on the phone. He told me he'd met a girl, Kim Weeks, who was the first person since Jill's death he felt really keen on. This was the lady he was later to marry. He met her because of me. I had an actress on *Death Wish Three* called Deborah Raffin. Her then husband, Michael Viner, was a publisher and a manager. He befriended Jill, took her on and represented her two books. Kim Weeks was his secretary. That's how Charlie met her and eventually married her. For the last years of his life Charlie was totally out of it with Alzheimer's disease. He remembered no one. There was considerable conflict between Kim and Charlie's children. He died in September 2003. I was not asked to the funeral.

Shortly after *Death Wish Three* Menahem Golan and Yoram Globus sent me a script of an Agatha Christie book, *Appointment with Death*, set in Palestine in 1935. I'd never wanted to shoot in Israel. All the Israelis I'd met seemed guttural and arrogant, even though I greatly enjoyed Menahem and Yoram. Nevertheless, we assembled a remarkable cast. Peter Ustinov was again to play Poirot. Lauren Bacall, who hadn't worked much for a long time, was to be the villainess, Carrie Fisher, Piper Laurie, Hayley Mills and David Soul were also in the movie and I brought in my old friend John Gielgud. It was also the movie on which I met the girl with whom I was to have my most publicised relationship, Jenny Seagrove. After she came into my office I rang her agent and said, 'I have two offers. Firstly, I wish to marry Jenny Seagrove. Secondly, I want her in the movie, but for that I have to get approval.'

It was 1987 and probably the last time anyone could film in most of Israel without there being any serious problems between Arabs and Jews. It was extraordinarily beautiful. The Arabs were very friendly. The restaurants were staggeringly good, particularly the Arab ones. Even the Jewish food was good. When I said, 'Don't you have a Jewish restaurant here?', meaning an Eastern European delicatessen-type restaurant, they all looked at me as though I was mad. Because they were all Jewish restaurants! To them a Jewish restaurant was the old Sephardic-type Arab-Jew restaurant which was more or less identical to the Arab restaurants. To tread the streets of Acre, the old crusader fortress port, or go into the alleyways of Jerusalem or to the Dead Sea and the Red Sea was absolutely fascinating. The Israelis thought I was mad. I'd walk through the alleyways of Jerusalem at night and the crew would say to me, 'You're crazy, you'll be killed.' Far from being killed, Arabs would offer us coffee and honey cake and ask us in. They are the most hospitable people. When we filmed in the narrow alleyways of Acre the Israelis looked up to the roofs for fear of snipers. I'd be going round the Arabs thanking them for having us in their area and having coffee and honey cake with them. It's a pity these two groups can't get on, because beneath their rough surface the Israelis are extremely amusing and the Arabs are an absolute delight.

I'd always been told how hard-working the Israelis were. I found them rather lazy. In England and America we always shoot a full six-day week. In Israel the crew absolutely refused to work past lunch-time on Friday. They worked a five-and-a-half-day week. Saturday was off as it was the Shabat or Jewish Holy Day. I'd say to them, 'Fellows, what's all this nonsense about stopping at lunch time on Friday?' They'd say, 'It's the Shabat.' I said, 'Shabat starts at sunset. The sun doesn't set at two o'clock. It sets at seven-thirty.' They said, 'Ah yes, but we have to get home to go to synagogue.' I said, 'None of you go to synagogue! Furthermore, home is only about forty-five minutes away from almost all of our locations.' My greatest triumph in crew handling in my life in motion pictures was getting an Israeli crew to work until three-thirty one Friday afternoon. They never forgave me for it. I said in frustration to one of the Israeli crew members, 'I don't understand you people. You fought six wars and you're absolutely dynamic. Yet you need more people to do the job than I need in London or America. And you want to clock off every Friday at two o'clock.' He replied, 'Yes, Mr Winner, but you know fighting all these wars has quite exhausted us. We're very tired now. We need more rest!'

All the actors on the film, with the exception of David Soul, who I found a total pain, were very pleasant people. Betty Bacall was famous for being extremely difficult. She certainly wasn't to me. But she was rough on the crew. Six of her drivers quit and she went through four wardrobe assistants. One day the wardrobe assistant who carried her bag had walked out. I said, 'Don't worry, Betty darling, I'll carry your bag until we get somebody else.' We were sitting by the Wailing Wall in Jerusalem and I said, 'Betty, you know I love you and I think you're terrific. But you hardly work at all now. People are going to go off this film telling horror stories about you and about the way you treat the drivers and the lower-down-the-line people. Can't you just keep quiet? It will affect your bank balance.' She said, 'No, Michael darling, that's the way I am and that's the way I will always be.' So good luck to her. In fact this film helped her a great deal because she hadn't worked in movies for a long time before it and it got her back in the game. She is now rightly acclaimed as one of the grand dames of American cinema.

Any film with Menahem Golan and Yoram Globus also involved temperamental producers. There was a memorable telegram sent to me in Israel by Menahem which said, 'This is an irreversible instruction from the Chairman of the Board of Cannon Films. You are to fire immediately six people in the Art Department . . .' and he listed a whole number of other crew members who were to be fired immediately. It finished saying, 'This is an order and I expect it to be carried out at once.' The Israeli heads of departments came to me very worried and said, 'What shall we do? Menahem's sent this telegram and he wants so many people fired!' I said, 'Don't do anything!' They said, 'But what if Menahem calls us up and asks us if we fired the people?' I said, 'Tell Menahem that Michael Winner told us to carry on.' So we kept all the crew. At the end Menahem rang and said, 'Be sure to congratulate the English Art Department I think they did a brilliant job.' If I'd listened to him half of them would have been fired and they wouldn't have done a brilliant job!

It was during this movie that I started up with Jenny Seagrove. Before our relationship commenced I was with another girlfriend in my hotel suite and we were looking at still photographs that had been taken on the set, including some of Jenny Seagrove. Jenny has since admitted that she went through a period of anorexia and bulimia. And she was still somewhat affected by this. She looked thin beyond belief. She looked haggard. She was certainly not looking as good as she should. Jenny was staying at another hotel. I rang her immediately. It was around ten o'clock at night. I said, 'Jenny, I'm looking at stills of you and you really are ridiculously thin. You're looking almost aged. Haggard. You've absolutely got to put on weight.' Jenny responded as if I was requesting the most difficult thing in the world. 'How do I put on weight?' she asked nervously. I said, 'It's very easy. You ring room service and order six vanilla ice-creams and a chocolate cake!'

Jenny was married but had left her husband. Her previous boyfriend, a theatre director called Peter Coe, had just killed himself and his mother in a car crash on the M25. I already had a girlfriend with me in Israel who was kind of temporary. She was due to leave on Friday and another one was arriving on Wednesday from England. Jenny Seagrove always seemed very nervous and uptight and troubled. I asked her to dinner on the Friday night and said to Lauren Bacall and Carrie Fisher, 'I'll be with you on Saturday at the Dead Sea.' They were staying there for the day. I took Jenny to a lovely Arab restaurant in the old town of Jerusalem. I was rather like Sammy Davis Jnr. They always used to say of him that when he opened the fridge and the light came on he did his act. When I was with a girl I invariably did my act. I was sitting with Jenny in this Arab restaurant. I put my hand on her arm, looked in her eyes and said, 'Darling, if we don't make love tonight it will be too late.' As I said it I could see she was going to accept! I thought, 'What on earth will I do with the girl who's coming out on Wednesday!'

Jenny moved into my hotel that night and into my life for six and a half years. We certainly loved each other. But we both behaved quite appallingly at times during the relationship. This made a change. Normally I behaved appallingly and the girls behaved very well. Later Jenny said in an interview that she was drawn to me because of my bee impersonation! I used to have a gold-and-black-striped T-shirt. I would bend my arms so that my hands were shoulder level and flap them up and down. I would then walk into glass shop windows and bounce off and go forward again and bounce off again. I was very proud of my bee impersonation. Unfortunately I'm now too fat for the T-shirt!

After a couple of nights at the King David Hotel in Jerusalem, where Jenny and I were now living, I said to her one evening, 'I'd like you to go stark naked into the corridor and I'll let you back in very quickly.' Jenny said, 'You promise you'll let me back in?' I said, 'Of course.' She was a game girl, Jenny. She was not the frosty, cold person she sometimes appears to be. She ventured into the corridor without any clothes on! Only about three people by the elevator saw her for a few seconds. The next day I told John Gielgud the story on the set. He said, 'Good for her. She always seemed such a glum girl.' I was not the most faithful person in this relationship. I don't know why, but throughout my life I've been consumed with taking anything that was available. Be it a chocolate, a piece of cake, potato crisps or girls. But I certainly loved Jenny. On the first birthday she had when she was living with me in London I got the band of the Welsh Guards in full ceremonial uniform – thirty of them – and smuggled them into my garden early in the morning. I got up, pulled the curtains back and the band of the Welsh Guards played 'Happy Birthday to You'. Jenny knew of my infidelities and stayed with me. Funnily enough it was only when I stopped all that and was faithful that she left! There's a moral there somewhere but I can't be bothered to work it out.

When we started Jenny said, 'You'll never stay with me because my husband, who's dreadful, will pursue me. He'll phone you a hundred times a day.' I said, 'I'll just put the phone down.' That's what happened. Jenny's husband, an Indian actor, Madhav Sharma, would telephone incessantly, wait, not talk, and put the phone down. If we came back from the theatre and had been in the house half an hour and her husband hadn't called I said, 'Jenny, what's happened, is he upset with me? He hasn't called!'

It was the relationship with Jenny that put me even more into the public eye in England, because her husband refused to give her a divorce. Jenny had to fight one of the very few contested divorces ever in the history of the English legal system. I helped her with it. All court cases are debilitating, none so more than a divorce. One night Jenny was crying in bed. I asked, 'Why are you crying?' She sobbed, 'Why is my husband putting me through this? Why won't he just let me go?' The next day I said, 'Jenny, you've been apart for almost two years. After five years you can just send a letter and get a divorce automatically. There's no need to fight. Why are we bothering?' Jenny replied, 'Because during the marriage my husband made all the decisions. He insisted he decide everything. I'd just like to make one decision regarding the marriage myself.' That was a very human and reasonable thing to say. It took a long time and a lot of stress but when it came to court Jenny won the case and was granted a dissolution of the marriage on the grounds of her husband's unreasonable behaviour. The headlines read 'Jenny Freed From The Spider's Nest'.

I also learned what happens when you get a vast amount of publicity – people come out of the woodwork. A couple of years earlier I'd had a brief affair with a young model/actress with the extraordinary name of Sandy Grizzle. She'd also had an affair with Peter Cook. She sold to the *Daily Star* newspaper a 'Those I have fucked' story in which I figured in a mild way. Jenny was now living with me. I used to buy the Sunday papers outside the Odeon Kensington on our way home from the theatre on Saturday night and read them in the kitchen. I was with Jenny having a cup of Earl Grey tea. I flipped through the *News of the World*. Filling the two centre pages the heading read 'Michael Winner whipped *EastEnders* girl and used her as sex slave'. Then there was a main headline: 'Jenny's Movie Mogul Said No Sex, No Part'. Then another which said, 'With tits like that I can make you a star' and another, 'He called me his black bitch'. A final headline along the bottom right, concerning a girl I'd never even met, read 'Get your clothes off, he said.' I sat paralysed with rage. Miss Grizzle had been a casual visitor to my place a year or so earlier. She'd watch television, have a 'do', be given dinner and then go off to Stringfellows to carry on the good work. She'd seen a chance to make some money and sold this absurd story to the papers. She'd not been a sex slave. She'd been an extra in *Death Wish Three*. She was a jolly participant in what had been a pleasant affair. I felt particularly frustrated because it was a Saturday night and there were no lawyers I could call. The next day I spoke to a friend of mine who was Deputy Editor of a Sunday paper. He roared with laughter. He thought the whole thing was extremely funny. He said, 'Excellent, Michael! You now end your life a sex symbol!'

On Monday we instituted proceedings against the *News of the World* which would have been extremely easy to win because the whole thing was untrue. I had dozens of postcards from this girl saying how much she loved me and was looking forward to seeing me. I had presents she'd given me. The day I had supposedly ordered her to come to the house for some mammoth sex session and was with her all night I'd been at a wedding with another girl and three hundred people. I wrote a serious article about press responsibility in the *Independent* a few days later. I sent it to some seven hundred of the most important people in England saying that the *News of the World* was behaving extremely badly. The Editor shortly thereafter 'departed', blemished by a whole series of stories, including one the week before mine which said that Arnold Schwarzenegger was a Nazi and had a shrine to Hitler in his living room! Arnold's a lovely fellow! His agent was Jewish. His friends are Jewish. He knows more Yiddish than I do!

The letters I got back when I sent out my *Independent* article were hilarious. Nobody gave a damn about my predicament! My friend Sir Peter Imbert, the Commissioner of Police, wrote a long letter about what the press had done to him reporting he'd taken the mascot off police cars or some nonsense. Alan Ayckbourn wrote, 'I personally think all Eastenders should be whipped regularly.' A journalist called Clive Hirschorn said, 'As Frank Sinatra remarked, "Hell hath no fury like a whore with a press agent."' The best reply came from the then Shadow Home Secretary Gwyneth Dunwoody, who wrote on House of Commons paper, 'Dear Michael, I assure you when the Labour government gets in at the next election, we intend to pass legislation preventing the press from inflicting this sort of dishonesty on innocent people. This will be part of the Labour policy. Yours sincerely, Gwyneth Dunwoody.' Then she wrote by hand at the bottom, 'PS If you are doing these wonderful things, why don't you ask your friends round?' Letters of support came from people as varied as Stanley Kubrick, John Schlesinger, the head of the British Film Producers' Association, plus half the Shadow Cabinet and half the Cabinet. The matter was settled with an Apology in the High Court and a payment of damages by News International to my charity, the Police Memorial Trust.

My fear that I would be alienated by right-thinking society proved unfounded. When I was walking around Scarborough looking for locations for my movie *A Chorus of Disapproval* women would stick their heads out of windows and say, 'Hello, Michael! You can come up and whip me any time.' The only person who took it all extremely seriously and was deeply distressed was me. Of course I hadn't whipped Miss Grizzle, although in retrospect I wish I had. It was quite funny because I'd had a coachman's whip on *The Wicked Lady* made out of paper to use in the whip fight between Faye Dunaway and one of the other actresses. The propmen had brought it back to my house at the end of shooting and left it in my hall. Anyone who came into the hall saw this coachman's whip as though I had a coach and horses outside. When the article came out I said, 'Get the whip out of the hall!'

The movie was typical Agatha Christie. Innocuous and pleasant. Vincent Canby in *The New York Times* said, 'Like a month in the sun with old friends. The scenery is exotic, the unravelling of the murders most perplexing, and the actors in enthusiastic form.' Rex Reed on his TV show *At the Movies* called it, 'Solid entertainment, one appointment you'll be glad you kept.'

I had acquired the rights to Alan Ayckbourn's play *A Chorus of Disapproval*. I'd seen it at the National Theatre and thought it was perfect for a movie because it was set in so many different locations. I was very keen that Alan should do the screenplay. He was busy so I turned his play into a screenplay, keeping faithfully to it but re-setting the locations all over Scarborough to places Alan personally showed me. Then Alan, who writes very quickly, spent two solid days at the computer and came out with the final script. I also gave Alan casting approval. We'd pretend we were at the Eurovision Song Contest. Alan would say, '*Le jury belge dit cinq points.*' I'd respond, 'Five points isn't enough, Alan. If you only like the actor five we've got to find somebody better.' Thus we cast the movie with great actors headed by Anthony Hopkins and Jeremy Irons and featuring Prunella Scales, Jenny Seagrove, Richard Briers, Patsy Kensit, Lionel Jeffries, Sylvia Syms, Barbara Ferris and Gareth Hunt.

I'd never worked with Anthony or Jeremy before. Though I had a link to Jeremy Irons. Years before he met her I'd tried to screw his wife, Sinead Cusack. I'd taken her out a few times and got her into the bedroom. This was shortly after she'd been shacked up with George Best with half the British press around George's apartment in Chelsea. When I'd tried to get Sinead's clothes off she said to me, 'I don't do this sort of thing, Michael, I'm a nice Catholic girl.' I was having dinner with Jeremy and Sinead. Jeremy said, 'Michael, I understand you tried to get into Sinead's knickers.' I said, 'That's true, Jeremy. But she said, "I don't do this sort of thing, Michael, I'm a nice Catholic girl."' Jeremy said, 'But she'd just been shacked up with George Best for six weeks.' I said, 'I know that, Jeremy! I meant to say that to her but I never did. I've rehearsed saying it to her in my mind ever since!' When Jeremy and Sinead came to my enormous mansion in Kensington and looked around admiringly I said, 'Sinead, think darling, if you'd said "yes" all this would have been yours!'

The movie was about an amateur dramatic group joined by a nervous young man trying to get laid who ends up screwing nearly everybody in the group, including the wife of the producer, a solicitor played by Anthony Hopkins. We were rather like this group of actors in the far-flung North East of Yorkshire in Scarborough. There were no star caravans or attitudes. It was just before Jeremy and Anthony became major international stars, so everybody was working for tiny money.

Anthony Hopkins is without question the least starry person I've ever worked with. Once he found out where Alcoholics Anonymous was in Scarborough he was happy. He was also immensely professional in every aspect of production. We went to Marks & Spencer in High Street Kensington to get his clothes. I chose an enormous amount of stuff, which was laid out on the counter. Jackets, trousers, shirts, underwear, everything! I said to Anthony, 'Would you mind if I played a little game and tried to get a discount?' Anthony said, 'Of course not. Have a go.' I said to the assistant, 'What's the discount?' The assistant said, 'We don't give discounts at Marks & Spencer.' I said, 'This is a very large amount of stuff here – surely it's worth a discount?' The assistant said, 'No discounts!' I said, 'Would you get the manager, please.' The manager came over and I said, 'I'd like a discount on this lot here.' The manager said, 'I'm terribly sorry, Mr Winner, we don't give discounts.' I pointed to Anthony Hopkins, who could hear me. I said, 'Look, that's Anthony Hopkins. That's not chopped liver. Anthony

Hopkins, one of our most distinguished actors, is going to wear these clothes in a movie. Surely that's worth a discount?' The manager said, 'I'm not authorised to give a discount.' I said, 'Well, you are authorised to put the whole lot back on the shelves, and that's what you can do.' At this point the manager came to his senses and said, 'Well, I'll give you three pairs of trousers and six shirts free.' I said to Anthony, 'Thank you, Anthony, you've just saved us enough money for one violinist to add to the orchestra at the end.' Jeremy Irons tells a story of when we went to Bata, the shoe shop opposite Marks & Spencer in High Street Kensington, and bought him about three pairs of shoes and I asked for a discount. They gave me three tins of shoe polish and four cleaning cloths. He regaled a Critics Circle dinner with the incident!

Anthony felt that once he got the costume right everything would be okay. He eventually found a beige coat. Before he started his first scene he walked off with it. I said, 'Where's Anthony?' They said, 'He's round the corner jumping up and down on his coat.' Anthony was wearing down the coat to how he thought it should be. He put ink on it, he scraped it against a wall. He semi-demolished this coat! Then he came back and said, 'Now I'm ready to play the part.' He proceeded to give the most brilliant performance.

Jeremy Irons is a highly mercurial, brilliant, very likeable actor with flashes of appalling temper. This didn't worry me! My best friend in show business, Burt Lancaster, had the most dreadful temper and exhibited it frequently on the film set. Who cares? Actors are actors. They're not meant to be perfectly controlled and sedated people. If they lose their tempers, it's often about something quite different from what they are supposedly losing it about. We were shooting in a rehearsal room in Scarborough. It was very quiet. The Cameraman was doing the lighting and the cast were sitting around chatting quietly. Suddenly Jeremy Irons screamed at the top of his voice, 'Winner, get over here!' A silence fell on the room. Jeremy shouted again, 'Winner, you heard me! Come here!' At this point I always think it's best to revert to the role of butler. Be the perfect English servant. I walked over. I said, 'Yes, sir, what can I do for you?' Jeremy was apoplectic. He waved two pieces of typed paper. 'How dare you issue this!' he said. I asked, 'What is it, sir?' Jeremy said, 'It's the biography of me that you and your stupid company are giving out to people.' I said, 'With respect, sir, the biography was given to us by your agent.' Jeremy continued, at full pelt, 'My agent is there to get me work! She's not there to issue biographies!' I said, 'This biography has only been given to the *Scarborough Evening News*. I'll personally arrange a raiding party to get it back. Here's a pencil. Please write whatever you want changed. I'll have it sent to the production office, re-typed and re-issued.' Then I wandered off. After ten minutes I went back to Jeremy's chair. I said, 'Do you have the changes, sir?' Rather sheepishly Jeremy handed me the two sheets of paper. The biography was 1,200 words long. Jeremy's only change was the addition of three words. To be put into a section about plays he starred in which had transferred from the Royal Shakespeare Theatre to the West End. We had only put *The Rover*. He added 'And *Richard II*'. Thus a mini-crisis passed by!

Two years earlier Patsy Kensit had made a film, *Absolute Beginners*, which was one of the great disasters of English cinema. She was not the star, but it had seriously damaged her career. I thought she was perfect for the part of Richard Briers's daughter. I suggested her to Alan Ayckbourn. I thought he might be influenced by the general feeling that she was blonde and tacky, which I did not think true. She was a good actress and a nice person. Alan had seen her on television and also thought she was very good. He approved her. Patsy asked Jenny Seagrove and I if she should get married. We both told her she was too young at twenty-one. She told us her boyfriend was a photographer. I was sitting on the set one night, shooting outside a local theatre. Somebody came up and said, 'Patsy Kensit got married this afternoon.' I said, 'Who did she marry?' They said, 'A singer in a rock band.' His name was Dan Donovan. He was the son of a photographer and presumably did a bit of photography. I phoned the hotel where Patsy was staying. She answered the phone, heard my voice and slammed the phone down! I phoned back and her friend Alexandra Pigg, another actress in the film, answered. I said, 'Patsy's just put the phone down on me.' Alexandra said, 'Yes. She's terrified! She thinks you're going to tell her off for marrying Dan Donovan.' I said, 'I've phoned to congratulate her. He's a very nice boy and I hope it works out.' Patsy came on the line and said, 'I'm so relieved that you're not going to tell me off.' I said. 'Patsy, darling, Dan's terrific. I want to congratulate you.' Later Patsy and Dan joined me in Barbados for their honeymoon at my suggestion. Patsy lay topless on the beach, which is not allowed in Barbados. I said, 'Patsy, I'm sorry, would you mind putting your bikini top on because I'd like to take a nice photo of you and Dan for your mantelpiece.' She also came to my New Year's Eve party that year. She wore exactly the same dress as Jenny Seagrove! They were both delighted and posed for photographs together! It was a joy making *A Chorus of Disapproval* in Scarborough. It's a very interesting town. It had some wonderful fish and chip shops. A couple of very good restaurants and the best ice-cream parlour in England. It also offered farting cushions and fake pats of shit. Perfection!

Critics on the whole loved the movie. It won first prize at the Cologne Film Festival and played many other festivals. Kathleen Carroll in the *New York Daily News* wrote, 'A perfect cast. Jeremy Irons is delightfully funny as Guy. Anthony Hopkins is wonderfully eccentric as the irascible Dafydd. A giddy, buoyantly witty British comedy.' Jami Bernard in the *New York Post* wrote, 'Michael Winner imbues the film with a boisterous theatricality befitting the story's origin. The characters bounce around with gusto and are disarmingly amusing.' Mike McGrady in *Newsday* wrote, 'Sterling performances by Anthony Hopkins and Jeremy Irons and direction by Michael Winner that is deft and light-hearted as the prize-winning play it's based on.' Michael Lasalle in the *San Francisco Chronicle* wrote, 'Laugh-out-loud funny, sweet and touching with an extraordinary cast. Anthony Hopkins gives an example of perfect character acting. Jeremy Irons is hilarious.' In England Derek Malcolm wrote, 'Michael Winner does understand that Alan Ayckbourn is quite a cruel writer so there's a bit of blood which is absolutely necessary.' Dilys Powell in *Punch* wrote, 'Action, jokes and spirited and experienced players: you are promised a good evening.' Margaret Walters in the *Listener* wrote, 'The one-liners are deliciously funny, the anatomy of suburban cheating is never less than shrewd; the acting is excellent.'

24

Variety is the Spice

As the last decade of the twentieth century rolled in I had to face a career choice. I'd already made twenty-seven feature movies involving many of the biggest stars in the history of cinema. I'd not only produced and directed most of these, and written many of them, but I'd edited nearly all of them. Sitting in the cutting room for weeks of back-breaking work at the Moviola at a time when shooting's over and most directors take a holiday. I'd also directed and produced a great many second feature movies and short movies. I realised that if I was to stay massively in the game I'd have to spend far more time in America purchasing scripts, promoting scripts and being in Los Angeles where the action truly is.

England has always been a backwater as far as movies are concerned. We have very fine technicians and very fine actors. But we've made very few successful films. If you look at the history of British cinema, all the great periods of British film-making ended up in bankruptcy. Alexander Korda in the thirties and forties and Ealing Films in the forties and fifties. Ealing Studios did not close down because the rightly acclaimed and brilliant films were a success. It closed down because they ran out of money! Sir Michael Balcon, a genius of British cinema, then went on to Bryanston Films which also ran out of money. Rank in the forties lost seven million pounds in movie production and had it not been backed by a flour-mill conglomerate it would have closed down. Later on we saw other production companies such as David Puttnam's Goldcrest, and Nick Powell and Stephen Woolley's Palace, run out of money. Even though they produced some good films. It's no good pointing to occasional British hits. In between are hundreds of movies most of which get shown, at best, only on television or video. The world has been lured by the glamour and showmanship of American pictures. I was brought up on them. They're made by people whose object is to show a profit. In England profit is a dirty word. You're meant to say something significant. You're meant to send a message. Movies are two hours of light relief in a dark room at the end of a heavy day. The public want to be amused and entertained. They don't go to be educated.

I knew, as the nineties came, that unless I went back to California, where I had lived for so much of the seventies and eighties, and plugged away, going round the studios, meeting people and generally promoting myself and my scripts, I'd be in for a thinner career in England. There comes a point at which you have to choose life. It was no longer essential I worked every single day. I've seen important actors and actresses, and very distinguished directors, trembling with fear at the thought they may never work again. Fear is an over-riding factor in show business. The public don't see it. They see actors, actresses and directors when they're working and successful. Promoting a movie, appearing on TV talk shows. They don't witness the financial decline and the career decline that happens to nearly everybody. I became one of the chiefs of the Directors Guild of Great Britain which represents directors in all media. When I joined them for their first Council in 1980 I realised how many directors, who had been household names, had been out of work for years. They were running restaurants, doing other jobs, or working very occasionally on television. I decided to stay in England. I didn't want to live in hotels or rented houses in California any more.

I knew I'd pay a penalty. But I'd passed through the fear barrier. There's something very refreshing about that. I no longer woke up trembling if I didn't have a movie to start. So in the nineties I continued to make movies, but less than before. The first one was a strange script called *Bullseye!*, which was originally written by a dear friend of mine from Cambridge, Leslie Bricusse. It had been around for many years with Michael Caine and Roger Moore attached to it. No one wanted to make it. Menahem Golan had left Cannon, which had gone into liquidation. He'd split from his partner Yoram Globus. He was starting a new company, 21st Century. He was keen to have a movie to announce with stars in it. I offered him the script of *Bullseye!*, which he hated. I said we'd update it and change it and he could announce at Cannes that he had Michael Caine and Roger Moore. That was enough lure for Menahem to enter very rich deals for the two actors, probably giving them more than they'd ever had. There was also a nice deal for Leslie for his script, and myself for directing and producing.

It was a silly story of two scientists who discover the source of endless energy and are impersonated by two crooks in an attempt to get the secret from them. The script was set on the Orient Express going from London to Venice with stops all over Europe. I sought help from some of the finest comedy writers in Britain. We were doing reasonably well, and the film was in pre-production, when Menahem said he couldn't afford to take the Orient Express train to Venice. It could go no further than Scotland! Also, he'd employed the co-scriptwriter of *Honey I Shrunk the Kids* to write a new script in five weeks! This was difficult for me because I was trying to find locations and now I didn't know what they were! Everything was taken out of my hands while this American genius wrote a script. Perhaps he wasn't concentrating. Perhaps he didn't care and just took the money! When his script came in everybody, including Menahem, agreed it was useless. We were now three weeks from shooting. We had to go back to the script we had and improve it as best we could. That sort of situation happens many times in motion pictures.

Nevertheless, we had great fun making the movie. Michael Caine and Roger Moore are wonderful people and very professional. I think some of the scenes are extremely funny although overall it's a bit of a mess! Strangely enough, I get very supportive fan letters about *Bullseye!* It's like a *Carry On* movie with two rather distinguished elderly actors, who in a way go against the grain of the slapstick humour. At least on *Bullseye!* I had one of my most memorable lunches. We were shooting in Syon Park, owned by the vastly rich Harry, Duke of Northumberland. An emissary said, 'The Duke would like to invite Michael Caine and Roger Moore to lunch.' I knew the last thing Michael and Roger wanted was to be an entertainment for the Duke and his friends over lunch in the middle of a working day. I negotiated that the Duke would bring only one person, his girlfriend. On the day of our lunch I went into the immensely plush and historic dining room of Syon Park to seek out the Duke's equerry. I said, 'What are we having for lunch?' The equerry said, 'His Grace thought we'd get the food from your location caterers.' So the invitation turned out to be an invitation only to sit in the grand dining room! Many of our junior staff had to forgo their lunch hour to carry our location food from the catering wagon into the grand dining room. I thought this unbelievably mean. A few weeks later I met the Duke in the bar of a London theatre during intermission. He borrowed two pounds from me to buy a cup of coffee and never gave it back. He died a few years later. I must have told the story somewhere, because his brother, who is now the Duke, sent me a cheque!

We were shooting at a school in Richmond. It was our base and we shot many of our scenes there. Film units believe that because they're in the movie business they are not heir to the travails of normal folk. This was demonstrated when three of our unit cars were in the forecourt of the school by the artists' caravans. The unit were eating lunch in rooms behind the main school buildings. With abandon which defies common sense, the drivers left their keys in the cars! The caravans were left open! Nobody was there to guard anything! Thieves ransacked the stars' caravans, ransacked the wardrobe and make-up truck, nicked handbags and a great deal of personal items, and then got in the unit cars and drove off in them! The unit returned from lunch to find this blatant robbery. It was just kind of insane.

Later in the nineties I acquired the rights to a first novel, *Dirty Weekend*, by a strange, possessed Jewish writer named Helen Zahavi. The book was highly controversial. We got it enormous publicity. It was a female *Death Wish*, where a woman, threatened by a sicko neighbour, first kills the man persecuting her with obscene phone calls and then induces men to come to her and kills them. It was poetically written. Sadly, Helen has written nothing since to capture the public imagination. Nor did *Dirty Weekend* do so, really! In spite of us getting the book so much attention, it sold less than two thousand copies in hard cover. But I raised some money and went ahead to make the movie. It was set in Brighton where Helen Zahavi had lived and claimed to have been threatened herself.

To star in it I chose two unknowns I'd admired in the theatre. I'd seen Lia Williams in an Alan Ayckbourn play. The villainous young man, whom she bashes to death with a hammer, was Rufus Sewell. I saw him playing a Hungarian in a strange play at the Criterion Theatre. Rufus went on to become very successful. Lia won the London Critics' Award for the Best Screen Newcomer for the movie but never did much in films. She did okay on the stage.

This film was also beset by robbery. We were filming in Brighton quite close to one of those wonderful squares that lead down to the sea. We went round the corner to film somewhere else. When we came back, the trestle tables where our tea had been laid out, and the tea urns, had all been nicked! Later, in Notting Hill Gate, our catering kitchen with its generator attached was parked under the Westway. Suddenly there was a bang and all the lights and electricity in the catering truck went out! Thieves had harnessed the generator to another vehicle and driven off, breaking all the cables connecting it to the catering truck! Lunch was late! I was sitting one day with Rufus Sewell in a street in Brighton. I said, 'Rufus, what's your ambition?' He said, 'To get out of Isleworth.' I thought that was funny. He had a tiny room in Isleworth at the time. Rufus deservedly got out!

Dirty Weekend made people uncomfortable. A young girl blatantly going out to murder baddies didn't have the same allure of Charles Bronson in *Death Wish* or Clint Eastwod in *Dirty Harry*. The book became a feminist cult tale. The film, like the book, received a mixed reception.

William Leith in the *Mail on Sunday* called it, 'A black comedy, fast and entertaining. Bella kills perverts, we are supposed to like her for doing it, and we do.' Julie Burchill in the *Sunday Times* described the film as, 'Martian, almost surreal. We all know Michael Winner is gifted with quite a sizeable sense of humour. Lia Williams is excellent. In the moments before she kills a witchy little smile transforms her face from thin-lipped rigidity into something wolverine and savage.' *Company* magazine called it, 'The most empowering vision of femininity since *Thelma and Louise.* Great entertainment. The most important release this year.'

My final film in the twentieth century was another twist on *Death Wish* called *Parting Shots*, where a young man who learns he is going to die decides to go out and knock off five of the people who most damaged him during his life. It was an out-and-out comedy with Bob Hoskins, Ben Kingsley, Joanna Lumley, Oliver Reed, Diana Rigg, Felicity Kendal, John Cleese and the lead played by the singer Chris Rea. It came out just after the Dunblane shooting massacre, which was not the best time for a comedy showing people getting shot. By then I think my fame in my newspaper columns and my general exposure in Britain was turning many critics to give their opinion of me, even though they didn't know me, and not the film! Alexander Walker in the *Evening Standard* summed it up. He wrote that critics would be disappointed that the film was rather good. He described it as 'A soft-boiled *Death Wish.* It's tastefully done. Fans of "Winner's Dinners" will be gratified to note the patented table-napkin waving scene.' Brian Pendreigh in the *Scotsman* called it, 'A mixture of the *Carry On* films, the Ealing comedies and *Death Wish.* It's easy viewing. Joanna Lumley is hilarious. Oliver Reed is quietly amused and amusing.' Most of the other reviews were not nice! At the time of writing I am working on a horror movie called *Madame Celeste* about an evil clairvoyant.

I was kept in the forefront of Britain's national psyche by two accidents. In the spring of 1993 I was having lunch with the then Editor of the *Sunday Times Magazine.* I'd written for the *Sunday Times* since the late sixties. The Editor said, 'You must do an article for me.' I said, 'I've just had the most terrible meal at Le Pont de la Tour. Everything went wrong. The service was terrible. We got the wrong food. Some of the food was off. When I wrote very nicely to Terence Conran telling him what had occurred he wrote a snotty letter back saying, "I've received your film script, I will investigate!"

I'll do an article about my life in restaurants just to get revenge on Terence Conran.' I wrote detailing some dozen incidents in restaurants. A couple of weeks later the magazine Editor was fired and a girl took over. When someone takes over they seldom want anything commissioned by the person before. For the first time, I'd not done this article directly through the Editor of the paper. I had always worked through Harold Evans and after him directly with Andrew Neil. This new lady was going to bury my article. She did a poor job on the magazine and 'moved on' shortly thereafter. I said to Andrew Neil, 'I've written this article but your woman is letting it rot!' Andrew said, 'I'll call you back.' He rang a few minutes later and said, 'It's absolutely brilliant! It'll go in this Sunday.'

My article took the full front page of the Style Section, which was then a broadsheet, and half of the next page. It caused an enormous furore. Hundreds of people wrote in. Many other newspapers wrote about it. It was the talking point of May 1993. One of the restaurants I slated in the article was L'Ortolan in Berkshire. I'd been there a year earlier with Jenny Seagrove, had a terrible meal and been given an awful table. As I left, the chef's wife said, 'How did you like it?' I said, 'Fine.' Whereupon she produced the guest book. I wrote some pleasant platitude and left. When I slated the restaurant John Burton-Race produced the guest book in which I'd praised the place. Andrew Neil said, 'You've really let me down.' I said, 'No, I haven't, Andrew. If you read the *Ronay Guide* the editorial makes the point that when anybody in a restaurant is asked whether their meal is good, they nod "yes". They've been complaining about it for hours beforehand. They go home and say how awful it was. But still, the head waiter comes along and says, 'Everything all right?', and they all nod 'wonderful'. No one wants to make a scene and everybody's fed up anyway.' So I wrote a second article.

Andrew Neil, seeing the enormous response from the readers, decided to start a new page called 'Restaurant Watch'. He said, 'Would you write a column on the side of the page just to tie it in to your articles?' I thought, 'This will last two or three weeks and then I'll bow out.' Andrew asked actors and actresses to review restaurants. That was a mistake! They want to be loved. They're not going to criticise anything. After a very few weeks Andrew rang me and said, 'I'm not paying these luvvies to eat at my expense and say everything's wonderful. What are you doing on the page?' I said, 'I'm doing three hundred words at the side.' Andrew said, 'Do six hundred. It's your page.'

Thus I became a food writer! Andrew Lloyd Webber, who wrote a food column in the *Sunday Telegraph*, is highly qualified. I'm not. I had the good fortune to be born to comfortable parents and I ate very well all my life, often in highly important places. But I couldn't tell you the constituent elements of the sauce or indeed of any dish. I don't think the public want a chemical analysis of the ingredients. They want an opinion they can rely on. They want an entertaining read. Since I'm not paid any expenses by the *Sunday Times* I'm punting with my own money. People trust me. If I praise a restaurant, even if it's in a foreign country, it's full up by lunch time the day the paper comes out. And it's full up for the next two or three weeks at least. Maybe forever.

I began to learn the bizarre side of the restaurant business. When I started, the doyenne of restaurant critics, Fay Maschler, was going to have lunch with me. She said, 'Whatever you do, don't book in your own name. I never do.' I said, 'What's the point of not booking in your own name, Fay? All the restaurateurs know who you are. The minute you come in you're known anyway.' She said, 'If I book in my own name they may buy food in specially for me.' I thought this was ridiculous until, on quite a few occasions, restaurateurs would say to me very pointedly, 'We couldn't have bought that food in specially for you, could we?' Which means they had!

I also came into contact with chefs galore. The idea of the celebrity chef is absolutely ridiculous. Chefs should stay in the kitchen and cook. I've never met any chef who had anything interesting to say in print. They are a group of people who make the most arrogant, temperamental and ridiculous actor look like a saint. I'm not surprised they're all completely nuts because having to go out and buy food at six in the morning and then be in the hot kitchen all day preparing immaculate plate decoration and laying carrots out in little squiggles would drive anybody mad. I'm quite fond of some of them because I like crazy people. I don't care at all if restaurants buy in food specially for me. I like the thought of it. I'm very careful in a restaurant to look round and see how everyone else is getting served. I often chat to other punters on the way out. Although everyone says restaurants must be on red alert when I come in I can only ask, 'Why do I frequently get served cold food? Food I didn't order. Burned food and a general load of old rubbish.' If that's red alert I hate to think what normal conditions are!

The column remains immensely read. People come up to me all over the world and talk about it. The readers' letters at the side are better than the column itself! People get deeply over-excited about me and about matters which are really of no great concern at all! My most constant critic was Terence Conran. He endlessly wrote nasty things about me and I endlessly wrote nasty things about him. A year or so ago I was sitting by the pool of the Cipriani Hotel in Venice and I saw someone a couple of sun-loungers away who looked like Terence. Public tiffs are one thing. But I know from my long experience on the radio programme *Any Questions* that politicians who hammer each other on the air are often very friendly behind the scenes. So I wandered over. I can't say Sir Terence looked happy to see me coming. The sight of me naked but for my cut-off jeans is not too appetising anyway! I could see Terence thought I was going to start a major row! But we shook hands, had a chat and became friendly. That night his wife rang me and said, 'Terence has made a booking at Harry's Bar but he can't get in downstairs, which is the best place to be. He can only get in upstairs. Can you help?' I was happy to get them into the best area of Harry's Bar. About a year and half after I'd started with the *Sunday Times* column I was asked to take over the political column in the *News of the World* while Lord Woodrow Wyatt was on holiday. I'd already done this on the *Sunday Express* for two or three weeks a year earlier. The first column I wrote got the most enormous reader response. Some four hundred letters came in, which is a staggering amount for a journalist. Piers Morgan, the Editor, was delighted. He said, 'If we get three letters a month on Woodrow it's a lot.' He asked me to write the column for the second week of Woodrow's absence. Then he suggested I write a political column regularly.

My *News of the World* page was consistently shown in MORI polls to be the most-read column in the paper by a long way. It was also the most-liked column. Sometimes we got more than a thousand letters. I adapted it to have some items about consumer matters. When anything went wrong in my own life I'd call the head of the company 'Twit of the Week' if it wasn't dealt with quickly. The readers loved the fact that I'd buy things that collapsed or go to places that let me down. Just as happened to them. Although I continued in the movie business, these two columns had a readership of around sixteen million people every Sunday. The *News of the World* column was terminated after nine years even though MORI polls still showed it to be far and away the most-read and most-liked column on the paper. I thought that strange. But I didn't have to sell the house to make up for loss of income.

At this point an odd thing happened that took me in yet another direction! I'd become friendly with Peter Wood, the founder of Direct Line insurance. A brilliant man who changed the whole concept of insurance by cutting out the broker and selling direct to the public. Peter was a fan of my *Sunday Times* column. We met after he wrote to thank me for having praised him in the *News of the World* for reducing my car insurance premiums when I moved to Direct Line. We had lunch about once a year. Peter then sold out Direct Line and Privilege Insurance and opened his own company called esure with the Halifax Bank of Scotland.

I'd seen absolutely dreadful advertisements for esure on television. They were computer-generated rubbish which didn't put over any clear message. I said to Peter at one of our lunches, 'Are those commercials of yours selling any policies?' Peter raised his eyebrows to the ceiling and pulled a face. I took that as 'No'. I said, 'I've thought of a commercial for you, Peter. I didn't bring it to lunch to present like a schoolboy but I think it's very funny.' Peter said, 'Tell it to me.' I told him my commercial, which has since become legendary in the world of commercials. I'm driving a car and keep hitting people, the basic line being that esure don't want to insure drivers like me, they only want to insure careful drivers and thus they can save the customer a lot of money. It was also a piss-take on commercials because a lady whose car I hit pursues me screaming and I say, 'Calm down, dear, it's only a commercial.' This became a national catchphrase with all the top comedy impersonators doing it on their programmes from Rory Bremner up, down and sideways. At the lunch Peter said, 'We'll make it.'

A few weeks later Peter turned up in my house with his advertising agency chief, Greg Delaney of Delaney Lund, Knox Warren and the Chief Executive of his insurance company. Greg Delaney hated me! He hated the idea that anybody, other than someone in his organisation, should write a commercial. He was rude, boorish, offensive and stupid. Peter rang me afterwards and said, 'Greg Delaney told me in the car he thought your commercial was dreadful and he didn't want to make it.' I told him, "If you don't make it you'll be fired."' I said, 'Peter, you keep telling me you don't like this man and about all the dreadful things he's done for you. Why you don't just fire him now?' Delaney Lund, Knox Warren stayed with the project. But when they saw Peter Wood was actually making my commercial and we were in active pre-production, they resigned the account rather than have anything to do with me. I continued making the commercial through my own company. Thankfully, it became the most enormous hit both with the public and with people buying car insurance. So much so that the Chief Executive said to me, 'Because of you we've had to open a new office in Manchester for four hundred staff.'

So suddenly I was back in commercials – not having directed one since 1955 – although I'd starred in a few since then. For the first commercial we needed an elderly lady to pursue me and shout that I'd damaged her car. I was looking through all the casting directories and photographs that agents had sent in and I suddenly thought, 'What am I doing? The girls I employed in the early sixties are all elderly now. There were some marvellous actresses there! I know them and I like them.' So I rang up Julia Foster who had starred in *The System* in 1963, the film that got me going in the movie business in a big way. She came over and was in a couple of these commercials. Later we did one where I dressed as both a fairy and a witch and my ex-girlfriend Vanessa Perry, who'd been a dancer in *42nd Street* in the chorus with Catherine Zeta-Jones, starred in that! I'm still doing these and they're still getting a lot of attention.

So between the odd movie, newspaper articles, directing and starring in commercials and endless appearances on television I've kept in the public eye. I could spend my entire life doing television shows, largely for very little money, or going on the radio, for even less money. We get at least five calls a day requesting that. I do things as varied as *Question Time* and *Shooting Stars* with Reeves and Mortimer. I was asked to do a programme called *Celebrity Sleepover* where they put you with an unknown host for the night and see how the so-called celebrity reacts to being with a member of the public. I hate staying with people. Marlon Brando asked me to spend Christmas with him on his island in Tahiti. I said, 'How's the hotel, Marlon?' He said, 'There isn't one.' I said, 'Where do I sleep?' He said, 'In a tent.' I said, 'I'll wait till you build the hotel.' I've turned down time away with very famous people in very luxurious surroundings because I'd much rather be in a hotel and free to do what I like. The *Celebrity Sleepover* programme seemed to change a lot of people's view of who I was. I had a wonderful time. I stayed with a cockney flower seller on the Essex/Herts border. A delightful man with a wonderful wife, a very beautiful and hard-working daughter who ran her own beauty salon, and a very nice young son. They were marvellous hosts and I enjoyed it greatly. A lady journalist who'd slated me regularly saw the programme and decided I was not the person she thought I was. All I was doing on the programme was being myself. I still see my hosts. They've come to my house for dinner. I've been down to the wonderful Columbia Road market in London where my host has a flower stall.

I'm actually a very quiet and well-behaved person, contrary to the views of some people. I suppose I've encouraged the view that I'm eccentric and difficult. I'm not really difficult. I go into restaurants, I eat very quietly. If I know the people in the kitchen I go and thank them and the waiters. Then I go away. This disappoints many people who see me there. They're desperately hoping there'll be a scene. Michael Caine, when I did *This Is Your Life*, said I was a complete fraud because I was nothing like my public image! And he's known me very well for forty years! The only person whose view I really have to care about is my own. If I can go to bed at night satisfied that I haven't hurt anybody, that I've made some contribution to society however minor, and that I behaved decently, then I can rest easy.

Sometimes, like everybody else, I overstep these boundaries. I hope not too often.

I realise I've told you a great deal about my movie activities and stories concerning famous stars, but I've really told you little about myself. I'm probably the worst person to write about myself. I'm not even sure if I know myself. But my life has been extraordinary. It's extremely unusual for someone to reach my age without having been married or having had children. Girlfriends say this is because of my mother, who was a bit nutty. I've been in love with girls. I've had many girlfriends. They've been and are a wonderful family for me. I stay friendly with nearly every girl I took out. Many of the significant ones I'm still in touch with and help. Although, sadly, Jenny Seagrove won't talk to me, even though she walked out when I was so ill with heart problems that I couldn't walk thirty yards. I was distressed when Jenny left me three weeks before my triple by-pass operation. Forty years of smoking twenty large Havana cigars a day, starting at nine in the morning and finishing around eleven at night, with my heart beating so fast I thought I was going to explode, caught up on me. It's bizarre that I went through the sixties and seventies seeing all these people on major drugs from cocaine to heroin. I thought how silly they were. Yet all my friends who were on drugs seem very healthy now and I was on a drug called tobacco that did me enormous damage.

After the operation, Alyce, the wife of John Cleese, thought I was particularly distressed at Jenny leaving me and suggested I see an analyst. She recommended a friend of hers a couple of blocks from my house. A very nice young man. I went to see him and he said, 'Why are you here?' I said, 'Because Alyce Fay said I should come.' He said, 'Do you intend to come regularly?' I said, 'Why don't we, at the end of the session, stop ten minutes early and if you can tell me why you think I should come regularly I'll be very happy to come again.' Ten minutes before the end we stopped the session. I said, 'Okay. Why should I come again?' The analyst thought for a minute and said, 'I don't think you're ready for me yet.' I could see he was somewhat distressed at the loss of a fee-paying customer. But, of course, he was right. Shortly after that I met a lovely young dancer called Vanessa Perry and we had the most delightful five-year relationship. So, stress or no stress, you carry on. And things that seemed important diminish with the passage of time.

I am not going to list for you the various famous actresses with whom I had affairs or relationships. I was not remotely the perfect boyfriend. I was invariably unfaithful. That did not mean I was not seriously in love with the principal person I was with at the time. But I realise now this was very hurtful and selfish of me. Many relationships broke up because of it. If I'd had the sense to stay totally loyal, they could have ended in marriage and a happy life. As it is, I've had a happy life by another route. I'm now much more settled than I used to be. And faithful! I have left behind my rather pathetic seduction techniques. Trying to get a girl into bed is always hilarious. They invariably say, 'But I hardly know you.' To which my standard reply was, 'Believe me, when you get to know me better you won't like me at all. I'm at my peak now. I suggest we do it before things go downhill.'

I'm pleased to have set up Britain's only charity ever organised to honour the police for the work they do by placing memorials to the police when they die on duty. In 1984 I was deeply moved by the death of policewoman Yvonne Fletcher, who was gunned down from the Libyan Embassy in St James's Square one April morning. I was chatting to my old friend and associate John Fraser who's worked for me since we were at school together when he used to make my bed and do my washing-up. I said, 'There's all this fuss about this girl dying. But who remembers the name of the last police officer killed on duty? We ought to put memorials to them.'

John said, 'They do in France – for the Resistance they put up little plaques.' I wrote a letter to *The Times* thanking the police for what they did and saying we should honour them by the placing of memorials at the spot where they died. I got about twenty letters as a result, ten of them enclosing money. One was from the television personality Katie Boyle. I had no intention of putting up any memorials! I simply thought it was something that should be done. A couple of days later my old friend David English, who'd fired me from the *Daily Sketch* in 1958, rang me. He was now Editor of the *Daily Mail*. He said, 'Will you do something like your letter to *The Times*, only longer, about Yvonne Fletcher and the police for the day of her funeral?' I did a full-page article in the *Mail* and more people sent money. I had about three hundred pounds in about thirty cheques. I decided to send all this money back and enclose a letter from the Charity Commissioners telling people how to set up a charity. I'd say, 'When you form the charity count me in for five thousand pounds.'

I wrote to the Charity Commissioners asking how to set up a charity to honour policemen slain on duty. At ten o'clock the next morning the phone rang and a Mr Rao said, 'I am a Charity Commissioner. I have your letter. Are you telling me you want to put up memorials to mere policemen?' He actually used the words 'mere policemen'. I put my hand over the telephone and said to my Mr Fraser, 'Fuck it, we'll have to do this!' I returned to the phone. 'That's right, Mr Rao, I'd like to put up memorials to police officers slain on duty.' He said, 'We're not going to allow you to form a charity to do that. Are you telling me if a policeman is killed you're going to put a memorial up to him?' I said, 'Yes.' He said, 'We won't allow it.' I said, 'Have you ever allowed memorials as a charity before?' He said, 'We allowed one for Mountbatten and one for President Kennedy but we're certainly not allowing one for policemen.' I said, 'I'll tell you what, Mr Rao. You may not be aware of it, but Yvonne Fletcher died recently and there's a great swell of sympathy for her. I want to collect for her memorial while she's still remembered. I'm going to ring off now, but you stand by because I'm going to tell the press what you've said and the phone will start ringing. It will be every television station, every newspaper and every radio station in the country. Tomorrow you'll be the most famous person in the land.' Mr Rao said, 'I don't like your attitude.' I said, 'We're not in conflict.' He said, 'Yes we are, you're trying to bully me.' I said, 'You're absolutely right, Mr Rao. I'm trying to bully you. If this charity is not formed by 1 p.m. today, I shall call a press conference at 3 p.m. and play the tape of this conversation [which I didn't have!] where you say that the police are not worth honouring and that Yvonne Fletcher is not worth a memorial and you don't intend to allow it as a charity.' Mr Rao started to get flustered. He said, 'Well, I can't deal with it that quickly. I have to get Revenue permission and I have to . . .' I interrupted him, 'None of that's my responsibility. It's yours.' And I slammed the phone down.

At midday Mr Rao rang and said, 'The charity's formed, you can start collecting.' I said to Mr Fraser, 'I'm Chairman of the Police Memorial Trust!' If I were going to make a film and cast the head of the Police Memorial Trust I certainly wouldn't pick somebody like me. I'd cast some old colonel or retired civil servant. But I'd created the job! I had to do it.

Questions were asked in the House of Commons about whether a memorial would be placed for Yvonne Fletcher and for the victims of the Harrods IRA bomb. A Home Office Minister got up and said, 'We're very pleased that a British citizen, Michael Winner, has formed a charity to place these memorials. He has the full support of Her Majesty's Government.' The only people who were a real pain were the local police in St James's. They believed any memorial put up to the police would be desecrated and cause them embarrassment. They wrote ridiculous letters to one of the police magazines saying, 'St James's Square is a well-known place for tramps and drug addicts and the Winner Memorial would be vandalised instantly.' If there's any place in London that is not a place for tramps, vandals and drug addicts, it's St James's Square. I had the fullest support of Yvonne Fletcher's parents. They were wonderful. They supported me 100 per cent. They've come to every single memorial we've put up in London since. I had the support of Scotland Yard and the police in general. I met with Assistant Commissioner Geoffrey Dear. He said, 'Wouldn't it be wonderful if we could get the Home Secretary to unveil the memorial?' I said, 'Geoffrey, we're not having the Home Secretary. We'll have the Prime Minister. The Home Secretary will sit behind her. We will have every single political leader on the platform. Every Shadow Home Secretary as well as the Home Secretary will be here to honour the police.' That's what we got.

Before getting it, however, I had some lessons in the ghastliness of some people in this country. We asked Westminster Council for permission to place the memorial on the pavement. Westminster Council didn't answer. Finally I got Dame Shirley Porter, leader of the Council, at home one Saturday morning. I said, 'We've applied to put a memorial up to Yvonne Fletcher and we're getting no response from your Council. I'd like this matter dealt with.' Dame Shirley came back quick as a flash, 'What's the deal?' she said. I couldn't believe it! She was talking about a deal like we're selling clothing! 'If she wants a deal,' I thought, 'I'd better give her one.' I said, 'We're asking for the memorial to be nine inches thick. We'll cut it down to six inches thick.' Dame Shirley said, 'Done.' She may have considered herself a loyal Conservative and the leader of a wonderful Council but Shirley Porter didn't have the decency to turn up to the ceremony when Mrs Thatcher unveiled the memorial. A lot of police did turn up. But none from the local police station where Yvonne had worked. They should be thoroughly ashamed of themselves. I'm sure, now, they are.

The Police Memorial Trust took off splendidly. We put up a memorial to the Harrods bomb victims. We now have thirty-six memorials in place all over the country and are placing a National Police Memorial in the Mall designed by Lord Foster. This should be up soon. The Queen has agreed to unveil it. The police and the families are unbelievably grateful. People who have lost a young man or a young woman, a son or a daughter, are traumatised for the rest of their lives. When they see a memorial they feel that their son or daughter did not go in vain, that their courage is recognised by the nation. Mrs Thatcher unveiled another memorial for us, and so did every Prime Minister and every Home Secretary. Tony Blair has unveiled six of them.

As we came to planning a National Police Memorial it was felt I should meet the Police Associations, the Police Federation, the Association of Chief Police Officers and others. So they came to lunch at my house. After lunch, where they had a lot of wine, following spirits beforehand, we were having brandy in my lounge. Leslie Curtis, then Chairman of the Police Federation, the union for the police constables, sergeants and inspectors, crossed his legs and said, 'What my members want to know is whose hand is in the till?' I said, 'I can tell you, Leslie, exactly whose hand is in the till. My hand is in the till. It's in the till of my property companies and it's putting money into the Police Memorial Trust. It's in the till of my personal account and it's putting money into the Police Memorial Trust. It's in the till of my motion-picture companies and it's putting money from there into the Police Memorial Trust. Please send accountants round tomorrow to go through our books. Because you'll name me the greatest hero in the history of the British police force.' Leslie became a good friend. The next day he sent us a donation!

25

I Lose £35 Million and Smile

My mother was lying naked on the floor of her room at the Grosvenor House Hotel. I'd asked the maid to open the door when there was no reply. Mumsy had been very ill. Now she was just about breathing. For a fraction of a second, I thought, 'Shall I leave her there to die?' It was only a split second. Then I called the doctor. He later told me had I not done so she'd have died. What extraordinary emotion, hatred, angst, call it what you like, had me even think of leaving my own mother to die in a hotel room? What I most remember about my mother is that I loved her. And her smile. She had a smile that was quite the most beautiful thing I've ever seen. It exuded happiness, mischief and pleasure. It was as infectious and all-consuming as her anger.

She was a beautiful woman, was Mumsy. White-haired from an early age, elegant, well spoken. She was the most frightening person I've ever known! She reduced highly professional and distinguished men to jelly. When her mood turned, the crisp venom of her remarks, her total fearlessness, cut deeply through everyone who got in the way. When people speak of my parents, Helen and George, they usually say, 'Your father was an angel. What a wonderful man. Your mother was . . .' This is followed, after some thought, by 'unusual . . .

difficult . . .' or '. . . a character'. She was also wonderful. Although there were times I thought the opposite. Girlfriends are apt to say that's why I never married. I know people who spend years in psychoanalysis to get mothers out of their system. I wouldn't dare do that. When I was a child she was a caring mother. Sometimes over-caring. She embroidered blankets and cushions. She sewed on name-tags. She cooked very well. Her meat loaf with a hard-boiled egg going through it and her lockshen soup and kneidlech were some of the great taste sensations of my life. We weren't well off at the time. In Letchworth, Hertfordshire, where we had a semi-detached house, my nanny had taken me for a walk once. When we returned my mother was running up and down outside, distraught, between groups of embarrassed neighbours. She thought we'd been gone too long. She turned sharply on the nanny. It was a display of a neurosis that discomfited me, and was to do so in the future.

What interested her most was gambling. Bridge, gin rummy, poker, she was extremely good at all of them. When not playing at home she was a regular at Crockford's gaming club in St James's. When the wartime sirens went off, she and her friends would go down to the shelter. The card game would continue. By the time I was fourteen I had a column in seventeen local newspapers. I met the stars of the day. I came home, excited, and said, 'I had dinner with Louis Armstrong last night, just him, me and his wife.' 'Oh yes, dear,' my mother replied, then, turning to another guest, 'you know what Mrs Cohen had last night? A three of clubs. Mrs Bijou had an ace . . .' It was around that time that I had my Bar Mitzvah, my con-firmation in the Jewish faith. I was never religious but I looked forward to the party. Mumsy decided it would be a poker party. Baize tables were set up throughout the house. Little gold chairs were hired. My bedroom was used as a cloakroom. I sat on a mountain of mink coats piled up on the bed. Alone.

Later I had my own life, meeting the stars, writing more and more for national papers, going to Cambridge. And then making movies. Mumsy was mostly jolly, loving, eccentric. My parents lived increasingly in the South of France. I can see her eyes now, alight with fun, as the fat restaurant owner in La Napoule sang with his two musicians at her check-cloth table. She was a genuinely sophisticated woman. Rules meant very little to her. I recall the most startling meal of my life. We were in Claridge's, Mumsy, George and me. For years Mumsy had said at nearly every meal, 'George, you must give Michael more shares in the family business. He's young. We're old.' Afterwards she'd whisper to me, 'Why didn't you support me?' I said, 'It's not important, I really don't need any extra financial help.' At this particular lunch Dad said, 'I've done something that will please you, Helen.' 'What?' she asked suspiciously. 'I've re-allocated the shares in favour of Michael,' said George. The blood drained from Mumsy's face. She looked down. She gasped. After a while she looked up in horror. 'You mean Michael's got more shares than me?' she said.

Shortly after that George died. In 1970 they'd gone to live in the South of France. This was to be fatal. Mumsy was within a few minutes' drive of the Cannes casino. I was busy making film after film. With typical perversity, however many hits I directed my mother revelled in saying to people, 'You know my favourite film of Michael's? His nudist film *Some Like It Cool*!' My mother felt, with justification, that I spent too little time with her. Her gambling went berserk. People who've never been close to a congenital gambler can't realise the extent to which it is an addiction. No less consuming than drink or drugs. Like all 'habits' it has to be fed. With money. Mumsy was a legend in the Cannes casino. She was there almost every night. She was feted and fawned on. She would go up to famous people and say, 'Do you know my son, Michael?' Thus Fellini, Roger Moore, Yul Brynner and many more would greet me, 'How's your mother?' 'You don't know my mother,' I'd say. 'Met her in the Cannes casino . . .' was the reply. After she lost her first million pounds the casino let her have the gala dinners free.

Years after she died I went into the Cannes casino with Jenny Seagrove. We were ushered in as guests. 'Anything you like, Mr Winner. Your mother was a good client of the casino,' the manager said. She'd been dead for years. Mumsy always used to play on zero or zero-trois, that is on the line between zero and three. So I said to Jenny, 'Go on zero. We'll see if Mumsy's watching us.' Jenny put ten pounds on zero and it immediately came up. She was very excited; she wanted to play more. I said, 'Take the three hundred and sixty pounds' winnings and run. Otherwise you may be trapped like my mother into believing you can make your fortune here.'

My father had a highly important collection of paintings, furniture and jade. It was left to me, but for my mother's use during her lifetime. It decorated the penthouse in Cannes. The penthouse was also left to me. To pay her gambling debts Mumsy would remove a painting from the wall, take it in a taxi and sell it to a local shop. Thus went the jade, the paintings and the furniture. At least, I thought, I'd get the penthouse itself, at the top of a remarkable building. It had enormous roof terraces overlooking incredible gardens and the Bay of old Cannes and La Napoule. My mother became agitated about this. The shares and deeds of the apartment were kept in a Swiss bank, in Geneva. My mother kept saying to me, 'We must go to the bank manager and sign a piece of paper telling him the apartment is mine for life and then yours.' I said, 'But he knows that, Helen. That was in Dad's will.' But my mother kept referring to this visit we had to make to the bank. One day I was at the bank and I said to the bank manager, 'I know it's strange but my mother insists on coming here and signing a second piece of paper saying the apartment is hers for life and then mine.' The bank manager said, 'I know that already, Mr Winner. Anyway, the money is in the account and the apartment is owned on bearer shares. Both you and your mother can sign independently.' A bearer share means that whoever holds the share owns it, no questions asked. I phoned my mother from a phone box in Geneva Airport telling her I'd just been to the bank. She said, 'Darling, we must go there together, you and I. I want a piece of paper signed so the bank manager knows for sure that the apartment's mine for life. Then it goes to you.' I said, 'He knows that! Anyway, the apartment is in bearer shares and the cash is there and either one of us can sign on our own.' Mother said, 'I'm far too ill, I can't go at the moment. When I'm better we'll go and get a signature that the apartment is mine for life and then yours.'

A few weeks passed and I was at the bank in Switzerland again dealing with my parents' affairs. I said to the bank manager, 'I know this is silly but my mother still insists on coming here to sign a piece of paper saying that the apartment is hers for life and then mine . . .' The bank manager interrupted, 'Mr Winner . . .' I continued, '. . . but she's ill. She just can't move at the moment.' The manager said, 'Mr Winner, the day after you came last time, your mother arrived. She took everything out of the safe, the bearer shares, the deeds of the apartment, the money, everything. There's nothing left!' I went back to the same phone box in Geneva Airport and phoned my mother. I said, 'I'm in Geneva.' My mother said, 'Oh darling, I must go with you to the bank. We must have the manager see this piece of paper signed by you and me saying the apartment is mine for life and then yours. But I'm too ill.' I said, 'Mother, what are you talking about? After I phoned last time you came the next day. You nicked everything!' Without drawing breath, my mother said, 'Yes, darling. Things haven't been too good between us. I had to protect myself.' Thus I lost the apartment. Mumsy sold it to pay the gambling debts. She ended up in a small room overlooking the central well of the Carlton Hotel in Cannes. A hotel where she'd previously stayed in the grandest sea-view suite. She probably flogged off eight million pounds' worth of stuff at seventies prices. Thirty-five million pounds at least today.

People would say to me, 'Sue!' I'd say, 'How can you sue your white-haired old mum?' Anyway, she was threatening to sue me. Determined to get money at all costs, she went through ten firms of lawyers, all of whom she fired and took to the Law Society because she thought they'd charged too much. She claimed that the shares issued to me by my father had been done improperly. Even though she signed her agreement to all of it. But drug addicts need money. They will break into their son's or daughter's piggy bank to take it to get a 'fix'. Thus Mumsy had to have money to get her fix at the casino. Yet during all this, the threatened lawsuits, the difficulties, I continued to speak to her and visit her. We dined together. It was an extraordinary double life. Like all addicts she protested she was no longer involved. 'I don't gamble any more darling, I just go for a coffee,' she'd say. I said to her one day, 'You did well last night, Helen. Mrs Rose saw you with an enormous pile of chips.' 'Just looking after them for someone else,' was Mumsy's reply. Desperate to win more money, she often bet on four roulette tables at once. A beautifully dressed white-haired old lady running excitedly from one table to the other.

Her first demand for money with a threat of litigation came to me in 1974. I promptly got a blocked artery. When Mumsy flew to London to be with her hospitalised son, the doctors said, 'You can't go anywhere near him. You're the one who caused it.' She phoned me amazed and indignant! For ten years firms of lawyers would come in to see me holding a small file. 'Look what you've done to your mother!' they'd say. 'Er . . . this is the full file,' I'd reply, producing one six times the size. 'And she's going to fire you anyway and refuse to pay your fees.' When a famous QC gave a written opinion that she had no case for action against me whatsoever she told her solicitor, 'Sue him for libel.' She was a card, was Mumsy.

It's funny how images, often of things you never saw, haunt you. One I think of is one of the saddest I can imagine. Mumsy had decided to reciprocate hospitality to a dozen of the English contingent in Cannes. The best table had been booked in the grand dining room of the casino where a sixteen-piece orchestra still played every night. She was always beautifully dressed with lovely jewels. I can see her now stepping out of her taxi, smiling, ready to be the perfect witty hostess. She fell over heavily in the mud, breaking her hip. She rang me later from the hospital to tell me about it. She didn't deserve that. That was terrible. Eventually the money and her health ran out. She couldn't afford to gamble. She couldn't afford to live so well. But she was too ill for it to matter. Years of chain smoking and drinking coffee all day took a toll on her. She would fly from England to France and France to England not sure whether to come back and live here or not.

She had settled again in France when my then girlfriend, Catherine, who had come over from Poland like my mother, phoned her. Catherine said to me, 'I've asked your mother to come and live with you at Melbury Road.' I couldn't believe she'd done that. I knew it would lead to nothing but trouble. But my mother duly arrived one Saturday night with her suitcases and she retired to bed around eleven o'clock. The next morning, Sunday, at six o'clock in the morning, the internal buzzer rang next to my bed. I answered it and my mother said, 'Oh, hello darling. Is everything all right?' I said, 'What do you mean, "Is everything all right?!" It's six o'clock in the morning. You've woken me up.' 'Oh dear, I didn't realise,' my mother said. Mother was a Capricorn. She was also nuts. When Capricorns want something they buzz or demand it immediately. My mother felt like talking to someone at six in the morning and that was the end of it.

Her stay was a beyond-belief disaster. She lay upstairs in her room most of the time. When my domestic staff came in she told them I had cheated her out of everything, the property, the lot! She also told them, 'You know Michael's homosexual really, don't you!' She was also phoning poor Catherine's mother, starting at six in the morning and finishing at midnight, although I didn't know that. Until one evening Catherine rang me. She said, 'Your mother's driving my family mad. She phones at six in the morning and phones again until midnight.' Then she told me what Mother was saying to my staff.

I was absolutely furious. I went upstairs to where my mother was lying in bed – it was around ten o'clock at night – and she said, 'Oh hello, darling.' I said, 'Mother, you are driving everybody completely bonkers. You are the most horrible person. You're phoning Catherine's mother day and night. You're telling the staff lies about me. You are absolutely evil. I hate you. I want you out of this house tomorrow morning and if you're not out of the house I shall personally come and throw you through the window.' I was screaming hysterically. To say that I was overwrought is to put it mildly. It's a miracle I didn't have a heart attack. My mother simply lay in the bed, her breathing getting more and more laboured, looking up at the ceiling. I kept screaming abuse as long as I could and then went downstairs to bed. My bedroom was underneath hers. I thought, 'That's done her in! She can't possibly live through that and it's a miracle if I will.' I waited in the morning for the staff to knock on my door and tell me my mother was dead in the room upstairs. Instead I heard her footsteps upstairs walking from the bed to the toilet. I heard the taps turned on. I heard the toilet flush. I thought, 'A silver bullet wouldn't kill her.'

When I came out she was sitting in the hall in her fur coat, her bags were packed and she was leaving. She moved into a hotel and I continued to see her there. She would change her will almost daily, according to who came or did not come to visit her. She always carried with her a small holdall in which was her jewellery. If she was pushed in a wheelchair from the airport she was holding the jewellery. On one hotel visit in London she called for the staff to bring the jewellery from the safe. She handed it all to me. 'I want you to have this,' she said. I said, 'I really don't want your jewellery, Mother.' She said, 'No, I insist.' I said, 'Would you write this down as well?' because I was fearful of what might happen. She wrote a note saying that she wished me to have the jewellery. A couple of days later a friend of hers rang and said, 'Your mother's going to the police. She says you stole her jewellery!' There was no question her mind was going. But this was still very hurtful. I rang her and said, 'I understand you think I've stolen your jewellery.' 'Of course not,' she said, 'you wouldn't do such a thing. Whoever said that? I'll sue anybody who claims I said such a thing.' There was a pause. Then she added, 'But do you know where my jewellery is?' I said, 'It's in my shoe cupboard in the suitcase which you handed to me two weeks ago at the Churchill Hotel.' She said, 'Do you think I could possibly have it back?' I said, 'Of course you can. I'll bring it in this afternoon.'

All this became extremely debilitating. For the last few months of her life I could no longer visit her although we spoke regularly on the telephone. When I was told that she'd died, the first thing I thought was, 'Well, at least she never caused any real trouble.' That's a terrible thing to think about your own mother's death. I have photos of her all over the house. Her smile is still with me. She once said as she lay in bed ill, 'You know, the only thing I wanted in life was to be loved.' I did love her but I never told her. Now it's too late.

I also think of my father a great deal. He was, as everyone who knew him said, 'the most wonderful man'. He was quiet, smiling and elegant. He was totally supportive. He was very witty. A friend of his once telephoned and said, 'I'm having trouble with my son. He lives in a penthouse in Bayswater and he keeps threatening to throw himself out of the window. What should I do?' My father said, 'Move him to the basement.' Dad wasn't as flamboyant as my mother. He was more conventional, more conservative. But in his own way he was every bit as unique a character because he was so utterly good. His volatile wife was a burden which he bore bravely. I don't think they were a perfect couple.

When my father was sixty, he came to me and said, 'I hope you don't mind, Michael, but your mother and I are going to get divorced.' I said, 'That's ridiculous. You're sixty.' It was many years ago, when divorce was less acceptable than now. I said, 'You can't possibly get divorced, George, what are you talking about?' He said, 'Well, I manage a certain amount of property for Helen and she's had a lot of money from it. She's found out that if a husband doesn't register for a separate tax assessment from his wife he's responsible for his wife's taxes. She owes a hundred thousand pounds [probably two million pounds in today's money] and she's saying I have to pay it.' Throughout their marriage, my mother was highly critical of my father, most unfairly. He would not hear any criticism of her. She was absolutely devoted to me. I said, 'Don't worry, George, I'll fix this. Why don't you split it down the middle? Pay half.' My father said, 'Why should I pay half? She's had all the income.' I said, 'Just to settle the matter.' George agreed.

I went to my mother. I said, 'Helen, would you do me a favour.' 'Anything, darling,' she said, 'anything.' I continued, 'I understand there's a little problem with your tax and you want George to pay it.' 'Don't let it worry you,' said Mumsy, 'you keep out of it.' I said, 'I'd greatly appreciate it if you'd settle the matter. I've spoken to George and he's prepared to pay half the tax.' 'He'll pay it all,' she said in an icy voice that I'd never heard before. It was then I realised how utterly consumed she was with money. And how very dangerous she could be.

George did pay it all, bless him and continued to live with her. I'm sure that's what killed him. It would have been far better if they'd got divorced. I remember Mumsy saying to me, 'I don't mind getting divorced, darling, I don't need anything to live on. I'll just take a small flat somewhere.' If the divorce had happened she'd have slaughtered him. She'd have taken him for everything. Perhaps that would have killed him anyway! They were an odd couple, Mum and Dad. I didn't give them enough time or love while they were alive. I was consumed with writing, producing and directing movies. It was a full-time occupation. I regret now that I didn't give them more attention and a clearer show of affection. I have to live with that.

When my mother finally died in a nursing home, there was the matter of such possessions as she had left. She'd placed them in twenty-seven tea chests with a storage company in Cannes, together with some furniture. I'd been paying heavy insurance on it, the same insurance as if she'd never sold anything! I arranged for it to be transported to my house in London. Would I find there any of the paintings which my father had shown me with pride when he bought them and said, 'One day, this will be yours,'? Would I find any of the jade, which were museum pieces? We started to open the tea chests. They were beautifully packed. There were light bulbs. There were toilet rolls. There were old bars of soap carefully labelled by Mumsy. There was some linen and a couple of dinner services. A few bits of unimportant silver. As we unwrapped each piece I thought, 'Maybe this will be a significant memory of what was once in the house I was brought up in.' But there was not one. It was all trivia. The detritus of life. My family heirlooms went to the Cannes casino. I don't begrudge that. If it gave Mumsy respite and pleasure, then it doesn't matter. I have some cushions she embroidered. I have some photographs. But above all, as I go from room to room, I can see her bustling about. I can see her smiling. I can see her excited and happy. I can also see the kindness that shone in my father's face every day of his life. I was blessed to have parents like that.

26

Who Am I?

I gave a lecture at Oxford University. One of the students asked, 'Are you planning to make any more movies with Burt Lancaster?' I replied, 'That would be quite difficult as Mr Lancaster's been dead for ten years.' As we were returning in the car my girlfriend said to me, 'You know, the students didn't know who half the people were you were talking about. They haven't heard of those stars. They're gone. They're not on television any more. They're not in movies. They were most interested in hearing about you. Whenever you spoke about yourself, I could see how alert and interested they became.' I suppose it must have been true. She was an observant girl. The people with whom I've lived my life are legends among those who follow movies. But 'following movies' is a meaningless term. We see our first movie at a certain age and that's when we join in. What happened before is comparatively irrelevant.

As for not telling that audience at Oxford more about me, perhaps I've not told enough in these jottings of memory. We all live inside ourselves. There is somebody there. But that somebody is more apparent to those watching from outside than to us living on the inside. We live our lives through the eyes of others. In my case through the eyes of those I've worked with and those I've spent my private time with. There I've been particularly fortunate. When I look back on the years, months, weeks, hours and minutes of my life, the movies were an incredible and exciting experience. But each movie ends. Everybody thinks they've made at least a dozen new best friends. Most of them fade away. Only a few hang on through the years ahead. On the other hand, the girlfriends I've enjoyed being with have been an immense source of pleasure. Their company, their problems, their wit, their tantrums, their fury at my indiscretions or downright philandering. All these are treasured moments. People say, 'Don't you miss having a family?' They are my family. Some I still see, many I speak to regularly. They're friends. The passion of the moment has long passed. The girls, some now very old, remain a valuable and continual part of my life. Some days as many as six or seven phone up for advice or just for a chat. I think that's very nice. Some, of course, I help. I'm always there. I'm a Scorpio. We never forget those who were good to us. Or those who were bad.

I've behaved most appallingly in my life to the girls who loved me and trusted me. I was besotted with a burning desire to have new sexual experiences. To leave no girl untouched. The ones who loved me and who thought at first that I was faithful, I let down. The relationship became chipped, and although I remain friends with them settling into a married life with them became impossible because of my frivolities. Or my refusal to commit. Perhaps I did it deliberately because I was afraid of commitment. Perhaps I wanted to wander from person to person, sometimes staying for years, sometimes for hours. Like a traveller endlessly journeying across the earth, spending more time here and less time there, but never stopping the journey.

The sum total of life is what we do and who we meet and who we are. What we do and who we meet are very clear. Even if memory fades they were clear at the time. What is never clear is who we are. We're a different person to each person who sees us. I remember how years ago when I made my first speech at the John Player Lecture Series at the National Film Theatre in 1970 the distinguished film critic Margaret Hinxman introduced me as 'The man you love to hate'. I thought, 'Why should anybody want to hate me? What have I done to cause any resentment or dislike among my fellow citizens?'

Years later my Producer, David Picker, on the movie *Won Ton Ton* said, 'Everybody says you're impossible, Michael. But the minute Hollywood technicians heard you were coming back to do another movie, I was bombarded with calls from unit members you'd employed before dying to be with you again.' None of this matters to me. The only person I have to answer to for my behaviour, my attitudes and my activities is myself. If I've been honourable and behaved with kindness and decency, I can say at the end of the day, 'That's it!' If there are those that don't like it, I can wake up in the morning, look in the mirror, say, 'Fuck 'em!' and get on with life. One thing I cannot possibly do is complain. People say, 'Ah, but you never got an Oscar. You never had a three-hundred-million-dollar-grossing movie.' I can live with that. I started as a child hypnotised by light on a screen, which cast images of people I never expected to associate with. As years went by, I met them, befriended them, worked with them and became part of that disparate community. And parallel to that I met and was accompanied by and loved by some of the most beautiful women. I mean beautiful in the sense of spirit as well as physical beauty. Thus it has continued throughout my life.

And then you say, 'But is there a meaning to it all? Is there some greater purpose?' Some of us delude ourselves that there is and that we know the secret of it. I remember walking along the beach with John Cleese one day in Barbados. We had our feet in the lapping sea water. The sun was shining and the flowers were blooming. There were golden sands and a slight breeze. The surroundings were as near perfect as you could get. As we walked John Cleese said to me, 'You know, Michael, there must be more to life than this.' I told that story to Bjorn Ulvaeus of Abba many years later in Portofino. He was a very nice person, but always looked glum. He said, 'Swedes are always glum.' I said, 'You remind me of John Cleese,' and I told him the story. It was the best laugh I saw him have during the week we were together.

Is there more to life than simply living it? Should we be frustrated if we can't find it? Should we spend our lives searching for it? I don't think it's necessary. I think it's important to get on with it. Having fun is no crime. Trying to live among people you like and doing what you like is no crime. I'm always suspicious of the do-gooders. We say, 'Wasn't Mother Teresa wonderful?' She was wonderful. But she was doing what she wanted to do. Nobody forced her to do it. She did it because that's what she enjoyed doing. She enjoyed saving the poor. I enjoy making movies and being with girls. Although I'm now faithful and happy with Geraldine. Mother Teresa and I were both doing what we wanted. Someone who's really heroic is somebody who's doing something they desperately don't want to do and are doing it for the good of the community. I've never met anyone like that. It's probably true of soldiers going to war, who are forced to fight and do so with great valour. They're conscripted. They don't choose to go. Yet many become heroes. I admire that greatly. Most people do what they want to do and either make a success of it or make a mess of it. Most of us make partly a success of it and partly a mess of it.

My story told in these pages is of just such a person. I suppose you could read them and think, 'He was a great success.' Or you could read them and think, 'He was a failure.' You can read them and think he was a very nice person. Or read them and think he wasn't. Since I've no confidence in those who judge me, it doesn't matter much. What I hope most of all is that you've had some pleasure reading my anecdotal life, had a few laughs, been slightly surprised here and there, and can put this book down with a smile. If I've achieved that, if I've passed a few hours with you and you've had some enjoyment from it, then I'm happy. I may not know you've done this. I may have to guess you've done it. But either way I'm happy. There's no point in not being happy unless you have some really dreadful reason not to be.

Life is a compilation of minutes, hours, days, months and years. You live through them Then you die. I view each day as a small mosaic tile. The tiles stretch out through childhood, adulthood and old age. The gold ones are days of pleasure. The grey ones are days of unhappiness or despair. We should all gather as many golden tiles as possible. When you get grey tiles you can never go back and change them. You can't re-play the grey day. It is logged, irrevocably, as failure. To which some people say, 'You have to suffer to be a real person.' Possibly. But it's best to suffer as little as possible. Looking back on my life I see mostly golden tiles. They were coloured by the pleasure of working in the movie business, by the people I met both professionally and personally and, perhaps, by a little skilful navigating through the corridors of existence.

So now I sit in this enormous house where famous people of the Victorian era gathered to have their portrait painted by the man who built it, Sir Luke Fildes. As I look out of the window at the variety of green leaves waving on a summer night I also see the faces of those I shared my life with. Almost without exception they made me happy. They gave me so much. They were terrific people. How lucky I was to get their time and in many cases, their love. I am leaving the house – already on many of the tours of London – to the nation. People will wander through it. Maybe in fifty years they'll say, 'Who was Michael Winner?' I don't know the answer to that. So why should they?

Stars on Winner

MARLON BRANDO

'Another picture I enjoyed making was *The Nightcomers*, a 1971 thriller based on Henry James's *The Turn of the Screw*, directed by Michael Winner, an Englishman who, like David Niven, had an arch sense of humour as well as a stout characteristically British sense of class.'

In Marlon Brando's autobiography, *Songs My Mother Taught Me*, 1994.

Written on a best-seller about ecology Brando gave to Michael Winner – 'Dear Michael, this may be the butt end of our days if we cannot embrace the spirit of this book. At least it is a comfort to know that you will contribute to the laughter as we exit. Warmest remembrances. Marlon.'

Interview with Peter Noble, *What's On in London*, 14th June 1974.

'I never knew you could make films like this. It's so fast. No one troubles you. You can keep the flow of what you are doing. I'm really enjoying it.'

Interview with Tom Parkinson, *Oldham Evening Chronicle*, 7th August 1971.

CHARLES BRONSON

'He's the only European director I know who ranks with the best of Hollywood. He cuts the film as he shoots it. That takes great concentration and he has it.'

Photoplay, London, March 1972.

'It's all simpatico, we get on well together. I admire particularly the way he gets things done. He's intelligent and he's cheerful. A lot of people find it difficult to understand him, but . . .'

Interview with Des Wilson, *Observer*, London, 7th July 1974.

'Winner is an intelligent man and I like him. I don't ever talk to him about the philosophy of a picture. It has never come up. I don't like to over-talk things.'

Interview with Roger Ebert, *Esquire*, August 1974.

ORSON WELLES

'Most films I've been in have been bad. I don't think this one is [*I'll Never Forget What's'isname*]. It's very funny. Michael is a very talented young man with a big future ahead of him.'

Interview with Hunter Davies, *Sunday Times*, London, 27th February 1967.

BURT LANCASTER

'He's sharp, bold, without respect for convention. *Lawman* could be one hell of a Western.'

Interview with William Hall, *Evening News*, London, 22nd May 1970.

'Michael Winner is a very fast and intelligent director, always in command.'

Interview with John Williams, *Films Illustrated*, London, October 1972.

SOPHIA LOREN

'Michael Winner is very stimulating, very easy to work with, because he always knows what he wants. He creates the right

atmosphere for the actor. He allows the actor to get on with it and does not stop until he gets what he wants.'
> Interview with Albert Watson, *Edinburgh Evening News*,
> 30th September 1978.

'Michael is so sweetie, a little noisy, OK! But I can forgive anything if he is funny.'
> Interview with Tina Brown, *Sunday Telegraph Magazine*,
> 12th November 1978.

FAYE DUNAWAY

'Michael's got wonderful taste. I think the production of *The Wicked Lady* is beautiful – it has merriment. He's a wonderfully pleasant man with a great sense of humour. I never expected to enjoy myself so much. This is the only film I've ever truly enjoyed making. Everything in the past has been so full of anguish. Anguish. That's partly my fault. It's been years since I really had a good time making a film. Michael Winner made the whole thing seem like fun. So I was very relaxed throughout the picture. That hasn't happened before.'
> Interview with Roderick Mann, *Los Angeles Times*,
> 26th October 1982.

'Making *The Wicked Lady* was a lot of laughs. People say tension is necessary to make a good film, but I disagree. I think the happier you are the better you work.
> Interview in the *News of the World Magazine*,
> 5th December 1982.

SIR ANTHONY HOPKINS

'It was a huge change coming from long Shakespearean speeches for The National Theatre to Michael Winner's short, sharp shooting in fragments. I've rarely worked this way before and I find it exciting, because I don't really know where I'm going to end up in any scene. I don't need to build up to a line any more. And if I want I say, 'Let's take it back to so and so' and no one objects.'
> Anthony Hopkins interviewed in *Bradford Telegraph & Argus*,
> 7th May 1988.

'My character in *A Chorus of Disapproval* has no sense of humour; that's his problem. But Michael Winner has.'
Interview with Sheila Johnston, *Independent*,
5th May 1988.

'If you start looking for meaning in the part you are dead. Fortunately Winner just shoots it. He's brisk and I like his speed.'
Interview in the *Yorkshire Post*, 10th May 1988.

'Winner's rough and ready approach to film making suited my temperament because it was fast. This endless talking in the theatre – I can't stand it. Michael cuts through all the nonsense. He's a great showman. A lot of Alan Ayckbourn's characters are not very subtle. They are like cartoon, Gogol-esque – and Michael directs accordingly.'
Interview with James Rampton, *Independent*,
27th October 1989.

SIR MICHAEL CAINE

'Michael, you've been a friend to me for a long long time. But whenever I read a newspaper I never recognise the person who is my friend. So I am here to tell everybody you are a complete and utter fraud. You come on like this bombastic, ill-tempered monster. It's not the side of you I see. I see a man who has a tremendous artistic eye, you have one of the greatest collections of illustrations from children's books that I have ever seen. You are an incredible legal brain. Before I even go to my own lawyer I talk to you first. You are extremely funny, very sensitive, very kind and very generous. I hope everyone believes me when I say you are a kind, gentle, wonderful person. And I'm not kidding.'
Michael Caine on Winner's *This Is Your Life*, Thames TV,
17th October 2001.

ROBERT MITCHUM

'I saw *The Big Sleep* in San Diego and liked it. It's the perfect movie equivalent of Raymond Chandler's literary technique. Things pop out all over each other. You just have to forget about the plot and examine the characters and the dialogue. Michael Winner is consistent, although he considers himself superior to the rest of humanity and fancies himself a ninetenth-century rake.'

Interview with Philip Wuntch, Dallas Morning News,
19th March 1978.

JEREMY IRONS

'I like Michael Winner. He makes me laugh a lot. As a director he works in a very specific way, very fast, very short takes, always moving the camera around. I'm not sure it's my favourite way of working, but it is the way he works and as an actor you have to adapt.'

Interviewed in Photoplay, August 1988.

ALAIN DELON

'I can't say for certain why we got on so well, perhaps it's because we're both Scorpios. Or whether it's because we have respect for each other's work and person – maybe it's a bit of both. Certainly I enjoyed making Scorpio and I enjoy the people I'm working with.'

Interview with Gilda Archer, Your Stars Weekly, London,
4th November 1972.

ROBERT RYAN

'I'm kind of an authority on westerns. I've killed or been killed in more than I can remember. But this is the first time I've ever been called "Love" by the director. I guess that's the English . . .'

Interview with William Hall, Evening News, London,
22nd May 1970.

'I am enormously impressed by several things about Winner. His technical knowledge is considerable. He knows what he's doing. He knows what he wants. Also Winner creates really electric atmosphere on the set because he's an unpredictable man. That's good because the repetition and boredom of making movies can have its effect on the whole picture, and nothing like that happens when Winner's around.'

Interview in Films and Filming, London, March 1971.

MICHAEL CRAWFORD

'It seems to me that a producer/director like Michael Winner is a very good idea. There can't be all those daily rows and at least they see rushes at the same time that way. You work with a man like that not for him.'

Interview with David Castell, *Films in London*, 5th April 1970.

CHARLES AZNAVOUR

'Michael Winner is a very thrilling director because he lets the actor play, he lets you absolutely free, and he has a great sense of humour. He's young in every way and you also feel absolutely comfortable.'

Interview with Tony Bilbow on BBC *Late Night Line Up*, London, 12th July 1970.

PAUL SCOFIELD

'I've had plenty of opportunity to admire Michael Winner as a director from the audience point of view, that is with myself sitting in the audience watching his films. I found them to be extraordinarily outgoing and sympathetic. Full of the kind of energy which I find very exciting in a director.'

Interview in *Photoplay*, London, May 1973.

OLIVER REED

'I think Michael has a reputation for being difficult. I like him because he's very honest and there's nothing phoney about him. As long as you're honest and straightforward and don't cower around and you're honest to him, I've always found he's OK. I've worked with him many times and had no trouble. We've always got on very well. Michael and I joke around a lot because he's got a good sense of humour. Behind Winner's megaphone, voice, cigar and chair there beats a heart of gold – sort of!'

Interview with Robin Bean, *Films and Filming*, London, June 1967.

SARAH MILES

'Now there's my friend! I love Michael Winner. He's surrounded in shit with a heart of gold – true! Always been a friend of mine, Michael.'

> Interview with Barry Norman on BBC television,
> 15th September 1977.

SIR STANLEY BAKER

'Michael Winner has impressed me as much as any director I've ever worked with. Some directors I regard as directors: some as film-makers. Michael Winner I regard as a film-maker. The difference being that he is more than capable and very adept at forcing a production along. Michael Winner makes things happen on the floor in all stages of production. When it comes to directing, he knows exactly what he wants. It's very rare to find a director like that. I'm terribly impressed by him.'

> Interview with Kevin Gough Yates and Margaret Tarratt, *Films and Filming*, London, August 1970.

SIR JOHN GIELGUD

'*The Wicked Lady* is great nonsense, directed by a mad nut called Michael Winner, a foul-mouthed director with a certain charm – at least very respectful to me, though most unpleasant to underlings – a restless maniac mixture of George Cukor, Harpo Marx and Lionel Bart.'

> Quoted in Gielgud's *Letters*, edited by Richard Mangan, 2004.

SIR ALAN AYCKBOURN

'Michael Winner's a nice man, very honest, sort of Yorkshire in the sense that he doesn't pussyfoot around. He just says it with sometimes brutal frankness.'

> Quoted in the *Yorkshire Post*, 10th May 1988.

RICHARD BRIERS

'Michael is unique. He's a great professional – rather like Hitchcock, he's worked everything out in advance, and if you don't co-operate and do what he wants he gets very annoyed! He has of course a very clever mind. You know he did a law degree. And he's totally star struck. I find him delightful.'

Interview with Victor Olliver, *Woman's Journal*, December 1989.

JENNY SEAGROVE

'Michael Winner behaves like a three-year-old. I remember him once wearing a yellow and black shirt and doing an extraordinary bee impersonation. I thought anyone who can do that is worth getting to know better.'

Quoted in the *Independent*, 14th September 2000.

Others on Winner

'One of Michael Winner's early school reports told him not to keep going to see Warner Bros Gangster films or he would grow up to be a gangster. There are some in the film business who would say that he has.'

Sunday Telegraph, 25th September 1988.

'I can think of no other public persona that is so utterly divorced from his private originator as Michael Winner.'

A. A. Gill, *Sunday Times*, 5th December 1999.

'Before our meeting people had warned me Winner was a feisty egomaniac whose first love was self-promotion. If Winner has an ego it makes good copy. He's not one of those deadly dull directors who go around eating humble pie and boring the press to death because they don't know where their next job is coming from. He is witty, opinionated, quick and after twenty movies still full of enthusiasm for the business.'

Rex Reed, *New York Sunday News*, 20th February 1977.

'When you look at British film Director Michael Winner one thought asserts itself: he has the look of a born mischief maker. If you were going to make a film about the Gods of Teutonic mythology it wouldn't be necessary to look any further than Winner's elegant house to find the casting for Loki. A hell of a thing to say about the forty-two-year-old Director who has made some of the best and worst films of recent years and worked with almost every big star here and in Europe.'

Tom Sullivan, *Dover Daily Advance*, New Jersey, 30th July 1978.

'Winner suggests a certain wild and wooliness. In fact he looks as though he just fell out of bed. His flowing mane of frizzy grey hair and brown hair obviously has had few encounters with a comb. His shirt is untucked, his jeans have a droopy seat, on his feet are a pair of velvet slippers and no socks. His ever present Cuban cigar resembles a Con Eddison smoke stack. One senses that even if Winner's cigar won't explode, he just might.'

Jim Wright, *Hackensack New Jersey Record*, 3rd September 1978.

'Michael Winner at 42 with nineteen films behind him is buoyant, abusive and dazzlingly shrewd.'

Tina Brown, *Sunday Telegraph Magazine*, 12th November 1978.

'Michael was a quiet and obviously very sensitive man, who, in between blasts of the inevitable cigar, flashes sudden and engaging smiles. Undoubtedly he is a very nice man.'

Interview with Frank Barrett, *Fuse*, March 1975.

'The celebrity Tina Brown has enjoyed meeting the most is Michael Winner. Everyone says, "Oh how can you like him? He's awful!" But I loved him. He was directing a film with Sophia Loren and had fixed up for me to meet her and everything went like clockwork. He took me out to dinner and was very funny and best of all knew exactly what I wanted because he'd been a journalist himself. Oh, I worship efficiency, I just adore it.'

Tina Brown, interviewed in *Over 21*, February 1979.

'Winner rarely stands still. He prowls like a caged bear as he talks and illustrates his point. His booming voice is more suited to the set than to intimate surroundings. One would not be surprised if he suddenly shouted "Camera!" in the middle of a discourse.'

Thomas Quinn Curtiss, the *International Herald Tribune*, 6th January 1981.

'Winner continues to pace among the crew and public. A tall bearded young man follows him on his left and two paces behind. This is his assistant Daniel. On the other side a heavy set bodyguard with glasses keeps close by. This assistant is singing quietly to himself. "I do wish you wouldn't sing, Daniel," says Winner, loud enough for the unit to hear him, "it makes me think you may be happy in your work." A minute later Jim Thalman, one of the twenty off-duty police working for the unit in full uniform with guns to match, returns from investigating two gunshots. "You know that black transvestite, the one built like a marine, the one who was shouting at us from the hotel window?" "Yeah," says Winner. "Her boyfriend just shot him in the ass," says Thalman. "You're kidding," says Winner. "No, taken him to hospital: says Thalman.'

Mark Weinberg, Films, October 1981.

'Winner's films are typically well-paced and visually appealing, if at times slick in style and slick in contents. On the set he uses an unusually large number of setups, but shoots relatively few takes. His films are always shot on location, never in a studio. When the shooting's over Winner edits all the films himself using the pseudonym Arnold Crust.'

Lowell Goldman, US Film Journal, March 1984.

'All the *Death Wish* movies were directed by this elegant man with the millionaire suntan and the grey hair curling artistically over his turned-up collar. Mr Winner is a scholar and a gentleman but here today he's bossing around the most villainous looking crew since Bluebeard broke up his first team.'

Daily Record, Glasgow, 14th June 1985.

'Winner, an intense man, has maintained that despite the violence of the *Death Wish* pictures there is a comic book edge to the films, "A certain winking at the audience going on". He described *Death Wish* to us as "a horror comic rip off" and defended the sociological gestalt of the pictures by noting that the *Death Wish* pictures identified that the villain of the past has changed from the wicked king or the American Indian to the mugger.'

Lewis Beale, Los Angeles Times, 23rd June 1985.

'After forming the Police Memorial Trust suddenly the irrepressible Winner – so often caricatured as little more than a cigar chewing movie director – finds himself something of a public hero. "It certainly is unexpected," he says quietly. In fact it is one of the public signs that Michael Robert Winner MA has long been a more complex figure than many reports have suggested.'

The Times, 17th September 1985.

'At fifty, glossy-grey, comfortably rounded, Michael Winner is a man of furious, almost intimidating energy and several legends – only some of which are anything like true. Michael Winner is quoted as saying, "Anyone who complains in my position is a total moron. I've been granted an extraordinarily pleasant life." '

Nigel Pollitt, *City Limits*, 10th January 1986.

'Winner is a complex character: one might reasonably assume this enthusiasm for the thriller genre constitutes a kind of Rosebud (Winner roaming his labyrinthine realm endlessly wreathed in cigar smoke like the ageing Orson Wells) the key to which remains eternally inviolate to outsiders.'

John Kemp, *Artseen*, December/January 1986.

'Dark and sometimes affectionate accusations of schizophrenia or madness abound – among the cast that is, just as in any normal touring group of thespians. They are mostly directed at Winner who, stomach bulging, Monte Cristo No 1 cigar flourished in one hand and megaphone in the other, is shadowed everywhere by a hang-dog personal assistant wilting under the weight of a bag full of note books, portable telephone, spare cigars and other bric-a-brac essential for coping with hysteria.'

Andrew Duncan, *The Times*, 20th July 1987.

'There is a great sense of mischief about Michael Winner, but his boyish enthusiasm has put many egos out of joint. A carping rival once remarked "The trouble with Winner is that he's made three *Death Wishes* and none of them have been fulfilled." '

Robert Moore, *Daily Express*, 7th May 1989.

'With the face of a cherub, the force of a whirlwind, the reputation of a maverick, Michael Winner revels in controversy.'

John Sweeney, *Observer Magazine*, 1st October 1989.

'A self-confessed cross between a holiday camp host and Hitler, Michael Winner also describes himself as moderately intellectual.'

Victor Olliver, *Woman's Journal*, December 1989.

'Life is quite miserable enough as it is. Without Michael Winner, our Jester Laureate, it would be nothing short of unbearable.'

Matthew Norman, *Evening Standard*, 5th November 1993.

'Michael Winner sits behind a red mahogany desk of gratifying grandeur. The horizon on which his silver head bobs is so far away it is difficult not to cup the hands around the mouth and shout "Haloo". Smaller than one would expect, he calls you "Darling" even though, as far as you can remember, you're not married to him. He's funny, he's clever, he is abrasive. He's dated actresses for forty years, one went to the *News of the World* to tell of frolicking in his jacuzzi and swimming in his pool to Frank Sinatra records. How can he protect himself from such scurrilousness? "By going into a monastery or not having sex, or spending all day playing with yourself. The alternatives are worse than the risk." '

Jessica Berens, *Tatler*, September 1994.

'Michael Winner has the appearance of a benign Jewish grandmother. You could imagine him making chicken soup for you after a family bereavement.'

Peter McKay, *Evening Standard*, 31st August 1994.

''Behind that fat cigar and plump physiog, the bombast and the incredibly loud laugh, lurks a rather different gentleman riddled with contradictions.'

Sunday Telegraph, 3rd October 1993.

'Michael Winner's impression of a pantomime version of Lady Bracknell was aided by his use of pince-nez on the end of a stick to peruse the menu. His table manners, I was interested to note, owed less to the plays of Oscar Wilde than to the *Alien* series of science fiction feature films. When an item of food on the end of a fork comes within a foot or so of him, his head leaps forward, his mouth opens wide, and within a split second the item has disappeared into the Winner stomach never to return.'

Craig Brown writing of being in the same restaurant as Michael Winner, *Sunday Telegraph*, 30th July 1995.

'Michael Winner's desk is, by his own admission, very untidy. Although he insists that this never stops him laying his hands on something the moment he needs it. Should his study catch fire, he wisely says he would endeavour to save himself first, followed sharply by his diary. And difficult as it is for a man who has been spotted escorting some of the world's most beautiful women to admit, nothing has ever taken place on the top of his desk other than his usual business practices.'

Samantha Taylor, *Men's Health*, December 1995.

'Britain's most reviled man (. . . with his friend O. J. Simpson)'

Daily Mirror headline over a picture of Michael Winner and O. J. Simpson, 15th May 1996.

'I tried everything to get him to lose his temper but he never did. He's a hopeless old sweetie really and quite clever enough to see me coming. He laughed at my attempts to needle him.'

Lynn Barber, *Observer*, 24th May 1998.

'He looks like a homicidal grandmother who has just been released into the community after a lifetime weaving baskets in a high security mid-west prison.'

Peter McKay, *Evening Standard* quoted in the *Sunday Times*, 30th August 1998.

'Michael Winner is not the monster some claim but is, in fact, quite a laugh at an interview, and certainly it's easy to see why so many like him.'

John Naughton, *Empire*, May 1999.

'He may be all the things that people say and more – peevish, querulous, testy and unctuous but he can also be devastatingly charming. Unless slighted, or badly fed, he has a marvellous sense of humour, roaring with laughter at the smallest joke, his eyes disappearing in merriment.'

Jane Kelly, *Daily Mail*, 22nd October 1999.

'Michael Winner is a man who you'd just love to hate if only he wasn't so charming.'

Harriet Lane, *Observer*, 6th May 2001.

'The dawn of the age of the blistering restaurant review in London was most likely 1993 when Michael Winner, a wealthy Londoner who directed the *Death Wish* films in the 1970s and 80s was invited to write a piece about his dining experience for the *Sunday Times*.'

The New York Times, 9th November 2003.

'Lunch with Michael Winner is always fun but never relaxing. He gets upset so easily. One minute he's sitting there beaming, telling anecdotes and hooting his great ha-ha-ha laugh, next he's grieving and keening over some perceived catastrophe.'

Lynn Barber, *Observer*, 24th January 2004.

'Michael Winner. Mr Winner the bully. The babe magnet. The director of *Death Wish*. The scourge of sloppy waiters. The man who could explode at the drop of a frozen éclair. This man is a comic creation, a wonderful piece of pantomime in our dull lives although he says he's a quiet man. The *Winner Guide* is one of the finest pieces of comic writing and Michael Winner has no fear in laughing at himself.'

Victoria Mather, BBC Radio 4 *Loose Ends*, 12th October 2002.

Winner Talking

'A team effort is a lot of people, doing what I say.'
> Alix Palmer, *Sunday Times*, London, 5th April 1970.

'When other producers warn me you meet the same people on the way down that you meet on the way up, I can't think of a better reason for staying on top.'
> Hank Grant, *Hollywood Reporter*, 7th November 1972.

'When I came down from Cambridge I was a very bad assistant director. I was an idiot. You should do whatever you're doing well. I did it badly. So I became an out of work director. Well, it was better than calling myself an out of work assistant director, wasn't it?'
> Hunter Davies, *Sunday Times*, London, 22nd May 1966.

'On my first films we had a crew of two. Me and the cameraman. We went on the bus because the budget didn't run to a car. We'd stick the light-wires into the wall sockets using matchsticks. If you got away with ten electric shocks a day you did very well.'
> Arthur Steele, *Birmingham Evening Mail*, 7th August 1971.

'I tried for any job that was advertised and usually invented an experience of that job I didn't have. I remember the first time I was in a cutting room, they said to me: "Do you edit?" I said "Edit? Marvellous editor!" They said, "Alright, take this film and edit it." Of course I had no idea what you did, but I learnt. I now edit all my own films.'

> Charles MacLean, *Vogue*, London, September 1973.

'In the old days you could make a film for $250,000. You could reckon on getting your money back from people sheltering from the rain.'

> David Lewin, *Cinema Today*, London, 21st September 1970.

'After making Britain's first Twist film – *Play It Cool* – I thought everyone would want to employ me. I sat in my office to horrendous silence. If the phone rang and it was a wrong number, it was a big event.'

> John Player Lecture, National Film Theatre, London, 13th September 1970.

'On the pictures I've made for American companies one has had total freedom. On *The Jokers* the rushes were in one day and Universal Pictures said: "We don't remember that scene in the script." I said, "That's right, it wasn't in the script. And maybe to-morrow you'll get another scene that wasn't in the script. You should be very thankful you're getting something extra." '

> Robin Bean, *Films and Filming*, London, February 1968.

'The great thing in this business is that disaster is always around the corner. If you don't believe that you're a fool.'

> Michael Billington, *Illustrated London News*, 10th May 1969.

'The only time the director has to be judged is when the picture is out. It's very easy for a director to be a hero during the period of shooting, because he only has to finish on time and do everything everybody tells him. But the minute the picture comes out and is not successful, or it's no good, it's no good the director saying: "But don't you remember on Wednesday evening you told me to do that and you thanked me for doing it." Then the director is a villain and demoted and useless for the rest of his life. So I'm never interested in being a hero during the course of the picture. I'm quite happy to be whatever I have to be – to get what I want. Because I'll only go on the end result. I've made the mistake of acquiescing, and it's a terrible mistake.'

Robin Bean, *Films and Filming*, London, February 1968.

'Producing and directing, they're part of the same function. A sculptor has to understand all about his stone, the hardness of it and the grain. If a painter wants red he goes and mixes his own colouring, he doesn't call "give me red". Film making is just the same. Making a film is like painting with money.'

David Castell, *Films Illustrated*, London, April 1972.

'Who says that actors are cattle? Show me a cow who can earn a million dollars a film!'

David Lewin, *Cinema Today*, London, 1st July 1970.

'I never plan shot by shot at all. Particularly when you work on location you have to be able to learn from the first hour's work what you should put into the second, and from the first two hours what you should put into the third, and so on down the line. And although I get the script as right as possible, and we don't make that many changes in it, we certainly don't shoot it in such a way that the actors are forced into a scheme that the director has worked out three or four weeks ahead.'

Gordon Gow, *Films and Filming*, London, August 1973.

'I don't think that film-making has to be a miserable event. I think you have to run your set according to the atmosphere required by your leading players, who take the brunt of the picture.'

Gordon Gow, *Films and Filming*, London, August 1973.

'I film like modern guerrilla warfare. I go out into the streets and shoot. If I get into trouble in one place, I can move somewhere else. If I need ten more extras I just pull them out of the watching crowd. Yesterday in Washington I pulled out four, found they came from London, and had to put them back again.'

Jeremy Campbell, *Evening Standard*, London, 14th June 1972.

'At the time of the Watergate robbery we were staying in the hotel. I didn't think much of the place. They may have robbed it, but they certainly wouldn't have stayed for dinner.'

Jane Cobey, *Honolulu Advertiser*, 24th January 1974.

'You can't make a picture every year that has a major statement to make. They just don't come along.'

Sue Clark, *Cinema Today*, London, 18th March 1972.

'I think you can often direct an actor by saying very little. If he gets it the way you want it you needn't tell him anything at all. You're telling him where he has to move, so immediately you're tying him to a certain pattern. You put him in a scene at a certain pace which is going on around him and he livens up to that. A director certainly doesn't make the film on his own. The actors make an enormous contribution.'

Photoplay, London, August 1970.

'Remember, a writer of talent only needs a typewriter and paper, a painter only needs brushes, canvas and paint, but I need a million dollars or more to be in business. That's a hell of a business to be in.'

Des Wilson, *Observer*, London, 7th July 1975.

'This is a changing business and experience is of yesterday. You have got to have knowledge of today.'

Arthur Sandeles, *Financial Times*, London, 22nd December 1969.

'Look at me, I'm the best known director in England – mind you I didn't say the best liked. But you mention my name to the public and nobody cares.'

David Castell, *Films Illustrated*, London, August 1972.

'What is the hardest part of directing? Keeping awake for ten weeks at a stretch.'

John Player Lecture, National Film Theatre, London, 13th
September 1970.

'I went around the city with my location managers and I said: "Well now, we'll close the Forum, we'll close these two miles of road by the Colosseum, we'll close the Trevi Fountain, we'll close the Piazza Navona, and we'll close the St Angelo Bridge." They turned to me and said: "Fine, but what are your alternatives?" I said: "There are no alternative streets, but there are alternative location managers." The streets were closed.'

Mirror Magazine, London, 25th April 1970.

'I always work with a script-writer. They're all bone idle. I've often locked them up and told them: "You're going to get fed, but you're physically locked up." Ultimately, of course, the writer must be happy with what's happening, and I always stick with one writer. I think it's immoral to bring in another.'

Marina Warner, *Vogue*, London, March 1970.

'I just go home at night and eat my cornflakes. I phone up my friends in the business who are doing worthwhile things, and they're at home eating cornflakes too.'

Ivor Davis, *Toronto Globe*, 2nd February 1972.

'I rarely do more than two takes. And I don't rehearse. The first take is the rehearsal. I found that I used to be saying – okay, now let's do it the way we did it in rehearsal And it was never that fresh again. So instead we shoot the rehearsal.'

Don Saffron, *Dallas Times Herald*, 25th July 1968.

'The main thing is not to duplicate work, not to shoot the same speech or situation from ten angles and sort it out later. I make my decisions on the spot. Nor do I shoot a film that's half an hour too long. All my films have wound up within five minutes of their original length.'

Variety, New York, 2nd June 1971.

'I think Los Angeles is a very sad place. The world dreams of this city and here it is with its neon signs and telegraph poles. As Orson Welles said: every street looks like the road to the airport.'

Dick Lochte, *Los Angeles Free Press*, 27th April 1973.

'I always do my own editing. If someone else edits you will never get it all back again. You wind up adapting someone else's adaptation.'

Dick Lochte, *Los Angeles Free Press*, 27th April 1973.

'My films are saying you're unlikely to win, but it's still worth trying.'

Dick Lochte, *Los Angeles Free Press*, 27th April 1973.

'To-day's revolutionaries have a habit of becoming to-morrow's establishment. Society changes, or fluctuates, or ebbs and flows at much the same rate. The number of really good revolutions in the world, or in any section of its enterprises, seems severely numbered.'

Variety, New York, 2nd June 1971.

'I think lunacy is a very important quality for a successful director. And caring, and keeping alive. I think having an organisational ability is under-rated. You have to prepare your own ingredients. Because if you rely on other people you'll be absolutely stabbed to death.'

Variety, New York, 26th October 1970.

'What are films for? For a number of people, a small minority, they're a serious way of life, a very serious social statement. Though in general, it is a fact, films are for entertainment. For me they're not. They're something that gives one a chance to say something, that I would not otherwise have.'

Variety, New York, 26th October 1970.

'I often don't say "Cut", I keep the camera turning, and the actors laugh, or look confused, or walk away. I've often used those shots too in the film.'

Marie Hoy, *London University Magazine*, 8th November 1973.

'Thank God I'm extremely interested in everything around me. I'm fascinated by people and things wherever I go.'

Charles MacLean, *Vogue*, London, September, 1973.

'It's very difficult for a mass medium to be an art. Shakespeare wrote for a minority of sophisticated city dwellers. Da Vinci painted for aristocratic patrons. A mass audience does not call for art. It calls for entertainment.'

Jane Cobey, *Honolulu Advertiser*, 24th January 1974.

'It's no good sitting around waiting to be anointed with work: you've got to create it for yourself.'

John Player Lecture, National Film Theatre, London, 13th September 1970.

'Lunacy is a very important quality for a successful director. Most top directors are quite a bit batty. That's what makes them great. They can conceive fantasies beyond the normal mind. Another quality is just keeping alive. It is quite remarkable that no director has been murdered in cold blood on the set.'

Dorothy Manners, *Los Angeles Herald Examiner*, 30th September 1970.

'Generally I'm dealing in my films with people who pursue an extraordinary path and achieve whatever it is they wanted to achieve – and find it was not worthwhile. I'm fascinated with people who dream of an alternative life. But people find no escape. You can't change yourself. You can't run away from yourself.'

Charles Champlin, *Los Angeles Times*, 28th January 1972.

'I'm getting so mellow I can hardly get out of bed in the morning.'

David Waterson, *Cambridge Evening News*, 27th February 1971.

'I think the producer's role is to keep quiet and service the director, and keep out of the way.'

Variety, New York, 26th October 1979.

'You have to set an Englishman's house on fire to get him out to the cinema.'

Mark Shivas, *The New York Times*, 17th February 1974.

'Any of us who talk about future plans is a fool, because the future for us is so changeable. One is here today and gone tomorrow. Quite likely I'll be gone tomorrow. So I'll say goodbye now, in advance.'

Dick Lochte, *Los Angeles Free Press*, 27th April 1973.

'Before I accept any invitation I make telephone calls to find out who the other guests are. If there is anybody coming I don't like, I say no. That's only sensible. Why should I allow myself to be trapped in a small room for several hours with people I dislike intensely?'

Roderick Mann, *Sunday Express*, 8th October 1974.

'If I go to an awards dinner, I'm lucky if I get my dinner let alone the awards.'

Steve Demorest, Andy Warhol's *Interview* magazine, October 1974.

'I've never located a script which was a conventionally beautiful love story. I'm not sure that if I did I'd be the best person for it. Because I think all my films have been cynical or twisted. I say twisted in the best sense of the word.'

Steve Demorest, Andy Warhol's Interview magazine,
October 1974.

'I shoot exclusively on locations. Never in a studio. Life is lived in real places and I shoot in real places.'

Mark Carducci, Asprey Park Press, New Jersey, 18th May 1975.

'I think you have to say that a film star like a barrel of oil or a piece of bread or anything else, is worth its market price. Its rarity value. Just as a postage stamp goes up if there's only a few of them, a human being goes up if there's only a few of them.'

Tony Crawley, Game, June 1975.

'The only fact that helped me and helps anybody is tenacity. The race is not to the fleet of foot it is to the person who doggedly refuses to accept rejection and keeps working hard even when nobody is asking him to.'

Music Plus, May 1975.

'Hollywood's a town of sick, over-ambitious, nervous people of whom creative people are only the tip of the ice-berg. Seven-eighths of the people there are rubbish living off the creative ones.'

Roderick Gilchrist, Daily Mail, 16th June 1976.

'There are things that would move everybody to irrational violence, but I would think I would be one of the last to be moved to violence because I am (a) a devout coward and (b) quite weak. But I could easily be moved to flight.'

Alexander Stuart, Gallery International, September 1976.

'Hollywood is good only for alcoholics, tennis players and short distance swimmers. Since I don't drink, can't play tennis and swim rather feebly there is nothing there for me.'

Roderick Mann, Sunday Express, 21st November 1976.

'The only film I ever thought would be a hit was my movie *Won Ton Ton the Dog Who Saved Hollywood* and it proved my greatest failure. In America reviews were terrible and it did no business. In England the reviews were much better and it did even worse.'

Roderick Mann, *Sunday Express*, 21st November 1976.

'My mother gave me a gold cutlery service – hundreds of pieces. It was very ostentatious, to put it mildly, so ridiculously opulent and decadent that I rather liked it. I've only used it twice. Last time I put it in the dishwasher and it came out all scratched.'

Woman's Journal, December 1976.

'If a cheap film comes out of Mesopotamia or East Bengal showing an Indian person climbing 206 steps to get from A to B, they call the shot one of the greatest camera movements in cinema history, when all it is is five minutes of a man walking upstairs. It's all nonsense and if these films attract an audience of five it's a big day. Meanwhile the people in East Bengal don't go to see these bores. They're all going to see American horror movies.'

Rex Reed, *Sunday News*, New York, 20th February 1977.

'The masses are all looking for entertainment and not art. All they want is an hour and a half of light relief in a dark room and if you don't give it to them you find yourself down the toilet.'

Rex Reed, *Sunday News*, New York, 20th February 1977.

'They're all too fucking mean, all these critics who love these art films and say they should all get a showing. But if you said, "well if you love them so much put £10 a week of your salary into financing them" they'd go white and fall on the floor.

David Litchfield, *Ritz*, 1977.

'There's nothing wrong with making popular entertainment. You have to say something about society at the same time. Some people see it, others don't. If fifteen per cent see it I'm happy, that proves it was there.'

Bart Mills, *Los Angeles Times*, 23rd October 1977.

'When Victor Mature arrived to do *Firepower* he told Winner "I don't do anything active you know." Said Winner afterwards "It was only later I found out he classified getting out of a car as a major stunt.'' '

Roderick Mann, Sunday Express, 2nd July 1978.

'Our society is in a state of supreme technological advancement but there is a huge leaning on spiritualism, mysticism, the zodiac and so forth. We worship superstition. We look around at our comforts, totally reject them and turn to a series of things that would have been pooh-poohed in mediaeval times. It's all a form of opting out. People want to get out of this society, not participate in it. They don't want to rely on the forces that are around them because they don't like the things around them. We have a psychotic need to believe something else in our very shallow and commercial surroundings.'

David Sterratt, Christian Science Monitor, 24th May 1978.

'If a movie runs too long everybody thinks he knows how to trim it. The producer says what should go out. The distributor says what should go out. Some half-wit at a preview writes something on a card and they say "My God you know that man in the stalls with the big hat he didn't like that bit, take it out", it's madness. But if your film is only 95 minutes long nobody can say anything.'

Chris Chase, The New York Times, 24th April 1981.

'In the sequel to Death Wish Bronson's daughter is once again attacked and raped. This time she is thrown out of a window and killed. Wasn't that stretching coincidence a bit far? "Oh I don't know," said Winner dryly. "Perhaps the poor girl is just accident prone." Winner says he had only one problem with Death Wish Two. He couldn't find an actress to play the daughter who winds up going out of the window. "I must have seen more than a hundred actresses before we found Robin Sherwood," he said. "You see we were looking for a nice, simple-looking girl. And need I tell you very few actresses in Hollywood look either nice or simple." '

Roderick Mann, Los Angeles Times, 11th May 1981.

'Charlie [Bronson] is a dream to work with,' Michael Winner said, 'like all actors he is not outgoing – rather shy in fact. Not at all like his reputation. But then I found that the real sweeties to work with are the ones I was warned against: Bronson, Lancaster, Brando.'

Bob Thomas, *Philadelphia Enquiry*, 20th June 1981.

'I mean what are movies? They are a couple of hours' relief from life in a dark room. A tiny dot on the tapestry of life. But those of us who love them, we remember movies we see with some pleasure. That can't be bad, to provide pleasure can it? We don't do miracles you know, we make movies.'

Mark Weinberg, *Films*, October 1981.

'I don't use real extras any more,' Michael Winner explained. 'We just take them off the streets. Can't beat these faces. Look at them, their clothes, their attitude, it's unique. I was talking to one the other night. He has all his belongings in a small box, shoes, towels, bits of soap, that sort of thing. Totally down and out, slept in a doorway. He said to me, "I want to live in Rome, Italy, that's what I want." I said, "Why? Have you ever been there?" He said, "No, I just want to live in Rome, Italy." Then he stubbed out his cigarette for the take. It couldn't have been more than an eighth of an inch long and he put this tiny bit of cigarette back in his coat. I gave him a pack at once. I took the pack from my assistant of course. I only smoke cigars.'

Henri Bollinger, *Weekend Hong Kong Standard Sunday Magazine*,
13th September 1981.

'All the mistakes you make when you're 18 you continue to make throughout the rest of your life. We all have certain built-in mal-functions which we are led to believe experience will cure. But it doesn't.'

Sunday Express Magazine, 17th April 1983.

'Film directors are voyeurs. We observe, but we are frightened to join in. It gives me some pleasure to create the macho man on celluloid to make up for the total lack of it in my own life.'

Geoffrey Wansell, *Sunday Telegraph Magazine*, 17th April 1983.

'I take home a script and cut it down to the point where I find it's not boring me. I've never heard anyone say a film was too short.'

Brent Lewis, *9 To 5*, 25th April 1983.

'Did you know that four to one people preferred watching *Death Wish Two* to *Chariots of Fire* on Home Box Office? People have a right to enjoy what they want. That doesn't mean they just want violent films because when *Death Wish* was a big hit one of the others was *That's Entertainment*. I don't believe that both films had totally separate audiences. People went to both films because people like different types of movies concurrently.'

Alan Jones, *Starburst*, May 1984.

'We made *Death Wish* in 1974. Eleven years later Bernard Goetz shot people in the subway. He's a very slow learner if it took him eleven years to follow this film. He must be mentally retarded. I don't approve of what Mr Goetz did. But I have to say that if he has to shoot anybody on the subway I wish he'd do it on the week we're opening.'

Brian Case, *Melody Maker*, 13th March 1985.

'The idea that people come as rational sane human beings to a cinema and they are turned into depraved morons in the course of seeing a dramatic reconstruction of things they know go on anyway, is absurd.'

Winner letter in *Video Trade Weekly*, 3rd February 1986.

'I can see us doing *Death Wish Twenty-four* when Charlie Bronson is in a wheelchair shooting cripples and I'm directing by telephone from my hospital bed.'

Annabel, February 1986.

'I went to the First Night of the worst play in the history of the West End, *Top People*, by the people who did *The Rocky Horror Show*. This woman said to me after the First Night, "Did you have good seats?" I said, "Yes, they were wonderful dear, but they were in the wrong theatre."'

David Litchfield, *Ritz*, February 1986.

'I'm not in the least bit interested in having a title, although let's put it this way, I think it's very suburban to want a Knighthood or to think on those lines. People who are insecure want something

pinned on them to make them a human being. I am not that insecure!'
David Lewin, *Mail on Sunday You Magazine*, 16th February 1986.

'In *Appointment with Death* there are only two deaths – which compares with a body count of sixty-three in Michael Winner's last *Death Wish* movie. "It's the first time I've been under budget on blood," he says.'

David Lewin, Daily Mail, 20th July 1987.

'I don't think violence on the screen has any effect whatsoever on the people on the street and there are no studies to prove that it does. If it were true people who watch comedy shows would become funny and those who saw love films would become amorous.'

Broadcast, 23rd October 1987.

'Being bored is the one thing I detest above all else. If someone invites me to dinner I ask exactly who is going and exactly where I shall sit because I'm not prepared to risk spending four hours with people I find boring.

Angela Levin, *Mail on Sunday You Magazine*, 15th May 1988.

'Success has gone to my stomach.'

Evening Standard, 19th May 1988.

'I usually get on very well with the stars. It's when they say someone's a real sweetie that I get worried. It usually means that they're a sweetie on the surface but ghastly just a fraction underneath.'

Tim Ewbank, Celebrity, 1st June 1988.

'They talk about the body count in *Death Wish*. You count the bodies in a John Ford Western! I was brought up on John Wayne shooting hundreds of Red Indians. I was brought up on John Wayne mowing down the Japanese in the Pacific. People say "Oh well it's more realistic in your films." But it was very realistic to me when I was a child, very realistic indeed. It's all nonsense.'

Tew, July 1988.

'I opened my bedroom door once at 3 in the morning and there was a man standing there with a knife a foot away from me. By a miracle I got the door, slammed it and locked it before he came to. Then he tried to break the door down. But I don't believe the chap was in my house just because he'd been watching television.'

Sunday Telegraph, 25th September 1988.

'Women have more brains than men. I really do think that when women have to chose a husband or a boyfriend they are in terrible trouble.'

Best, 27th January 1989.

'Dickensian areas always interest me. I love the American slums. When I'm filming on location all the film bosses say Jesus Christ don't go down there, don't talk to anyone. But I go and talk to them all, the prostitutes, the pimps, the drug addicts, they all love the *Death Wish* films. When the Bronx gangs won't move and threaten to cut up the film crew's faces I walk over and within seconds I have them all working for me. I genuinely care for them. American film crews treat them like sub-humans. But the truth of the matter is that muggers are very interesting people.'

Robert Moore, *Daily Express*, 7th May 1989.

'Michael Winner says people are always coming to him with Michael Winner stories. "I wish most of them had happened because I come out of them as wondrously monstrous."'

Sunday Sun, Newcastle, November 1989.

'It's easier when there's no one roaming around like a producer to spoil things. When Titian was famous for his red he didn't say to an assistant give me a red. He'd mix his own colour and he knew where the chalk and the oil came from. It's the same with a film – you have to mix your own ingredients.'

Millimeter New York Magazine, October 1989.

'A man who was charged with rape said he'd seen *Death Wish* and was so excited he went and raped. They found out he'd raped eight times before. Was he saying he'd seen eight films?'

Victor Olliver, *Woman's Journal*, December 1989.

'British films tend to be made for a few friends of the producer's in Hampstead.'

Video Camera, January/February 1990.

'I've always found religion rather suspect – killed off more people than eating airline food.'

Interview in *Woman's Journal*, February 1991.

'As a film director you're acting, putting on a show to keep everyone alive, treading a line between jolly uncle and fascist dictator.'

Fiona Cumberpatch, *Sunday People Magazine*, 10th February 1991.

'Michael Winner is asked which historical figure he most identifies with. Answer, "Mickey Mouse because he keeps cheerful and never gets older." What makes you most depressed? "Having someone with a large head sitting in front of me in the theatre." What is your most unappealing habit? "Farting." What do you consider the most overrated virtue? "Pride." How would you like to die "In a manner that permits me to return." How would you like to be remembered? "Accurately as a wonderful, witty and all over marvellous person."'

Guardian, 6th July 1991.

'Historically in film and in stories the heroes knock off the villain. John Wayne did not go up to the wicked cattle barons and say I hereby arrest you, you're going to be given a trial, you're going to be given free legal aid and nine months hence you will appear in court and have the right to three or four appeals. The whole pith of drama is that people get on with it. It is smoother and cleaner than life.'

William Leith, *Independent on Sunday*, 14th June 1992.

'Winner is asked if screen violence doesn't cause actual violence. Answer: "Look nobody is going to see Hannibal Lecter in *Silence of the Lambs* and go out and eat their grandmother. We see a film, we see people getting shot, we say 'There you are, they got shot.' Then we go and have dinner. It doesn't encourage anybody to do anything. The whole argument is quite honestly pathetic."'

William Leith, *Independent on Sunday*, 14th June 1992.

I asked Michael Winner would he describe himself as an irascible man. "No, I would not. I would describe myself as a very patient man."'

John Preston, *Sunday Telegraph*, 7th June 1992.

'Hunter Davies was asked by Michael Winner "Why did you ask me to do this interview?" Answer, "Well, I have this theory that you're an eccentric." Winner, "Of course I am, who wants to be normal?" '
                    Hunter Davies, *Independent*, 24th November 1992.

'Declining an early morning reception for the *Good Morning Television* [programme] Michael Winner instructed his business partner John Fraser to decline on his behalf. "Mr Winner rarely attends breakfast meetings unless he has slept with the person the night before. Although I am sure you are prepared to make very many sacrifices for the cause of *Good Morning TV* we quite understand this is unlikely to be one of them." '
                    Evening Standard Londoner's Diary, 23rd December 1992.

'The idea that people are full of blood lust just because they go and see a gangster gun fight is absolutely ridiculous. I was brought up on the Warner Bros. Gangster films, James Cagney shooting Humphrey Bogart or vice versa. My headmaster used to say in my school reports that they were a very bad influence and I shouldn't go to see them. Now these films play in cinemateques all over the world. We all went to see them at school and I can't recall any of my school associates or myself becoming murderers.'
                    What's On, 27th October 1993.

'I survived the operation but I think I did better surviving the food.'
                    Independent, 20th November 1993, after Winner left hospital
                    following a triple by-pass operation.

'I enjoy the company of girls. They're nicer, kinder than men. They've a better sense of values, are less arrogant and more giving. Probably because they have all been pushed around and have watched men and decided they don't want to be like that. I don't blame them.'
                    Woman's Journal, May 1994.

'I was always out of place as a child. I had a few very good friends, because I was always eccentric. I don't know if I was a likeable child. Some people liked me and some people didn't. I never gave a shit either way then or now.'
                    Melody Maker, 28th May 1994.

With Jeremy Irons, mercurial and magical, and looking very serious in this picture from the set of A *Chorus of Disapproval*.

With Jenny Seagrove, adorned with the blonde wig and sexy outfit that she wore for her role as a suburban swinger in *A Chorus of Disapproval*. She also wore black underwear, suspenders and high heels on the set. A newspaper copied the framed photo of her with me in my living room and said this was an 'at home' scene shot for sexual pleasure!

With Michael Caine and Roger Moore, fully kilted, in Inveraray, Scotland, in 1989 during the filming of *Bullseye!* It rained every day. I'm not going back!

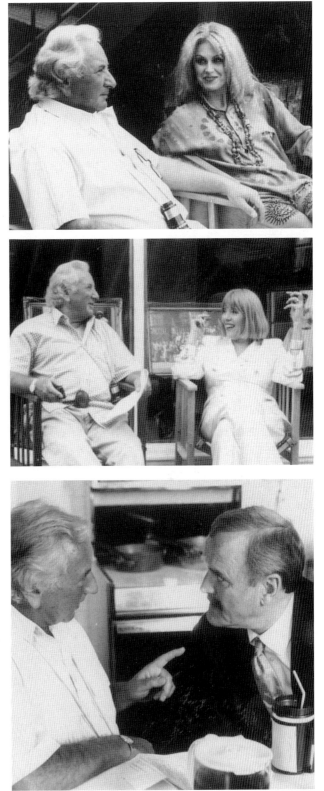

With Joanna Lumley on the set of *Parting Shots* in 1997. Joanna used to live next to me in Kensington. We'd meet in the park. When she moved to south London, I asked why. She said, 'I can't afford Kensington any more.' I said, 'But you're doing very well, Joanna.' She said, 'I give all my money away, don't you?'

With Diana Rigg on the set of *Parting Shots*. Diana and I have been friends for over thirty years, and if there's any better friend, I don't know one.

With a rather intense-looking John Cleese on the set of *Parting Shots*. I arranged for John Cleese's honeymoon and accompanied him and his new wife on it! Miraculously the marriage survived.

With my mother in the South of France, circa 1974. She was at the height of her gambling enthusiasm at the time.

With ex-girlfriend Vanessa Perry, an absolute delight, who has now found stability with someone else and has a beautiful baby, Marlon. She appeared in three of my commercials. This photo was taken in Barbados.

With lovely actress Sarah Alexander, another ex! When I knew Sarah she was eking out a living working in a flower shop. She has since rightly and justifiably become an enormous success as a star on British television.

With ex-girlfriend Georgina Hristova in Portofino. It greatly amused the press that Miss Hristova was on state benefits while flying in private planes to exotic places with me. But this was absolutely legal! She was not in any way abusing the benefit law. She needed benefits for herself and her son in case we split up. And we did!

With Geraldine Lynton-Edwards somewhere in Italy, I forget where. She looks just as great as she did when I first met her 132 years ago. Which proves cryogenics really work. If only they'd worked on me!

Top: With Tony and Cherie Blair at one of my police ceremonies. Tony has been an immense supporter of the Police Memorial Trust charity, which I run.

Right: With the bust of Sir Robert Peel, founder of the modern police force. I bought him in an auction and he now sits in my swimming pool. He's forced to suffer seeing me swim naked. We let him out for this photograph.

Left: In my reincarnation as the esure fairy. I wish my parents had lived to see me doing my commercials. They'd have liked me as an insurance salesman. They always thought I should have a proper job.

Bottom: With actress and dancer Giselle Wright in a commercial for First Alternative, esure's sister company for less careful drivers with posher cars.

I'M <u>NOT</u> HIS SISTER!

'It's quite simple, instead of wasting time blaming film and television for the evil in society, just double or treble all criminal sentences and you will clean up the crime rate in seconds.'

Edinburgh Evening News, 4th June 1994.

'If you were ever to meet yourself what would you think of Michael Winner? Answer "I think if I met myself when I was in my courteous mood I'd think I was rather dull. If I met myself in my rumbustious mood I'd think I was rather pushy. But I can from time to time be extremely funny. If I met myself in my funny mood I would think I was absolutely marvellous."'

Loaded, August 1994.

'I think one of the great myths and untruths put about is that power and money attract the opposite sex. I think people with power and money, which I suppose includes myself, have to get over that hurdle in order to get laid. I think most women want to feel they're with someone who desperately needs them, to whom they can contribute. They like lame ducks. I'd love to find these girls who find power and money attractive throwing themselves at me. But I really haven't. I've had to work very hard for them.'

Loaded, August 1994.

'The thing with journalists is that you spend an hour talking to them and then they pick out ten minutes of the hour and give the impression that was the balance of the meeting.'

Ed Perkins, *Varsity*, 10th February 1995.

'The first girl I ever slept with was a Rabbi's daughter. I've actually slept with two Rabbis' daughters – one from London and one from Brighton. They were both ravers.'

Sharon Garfinkel, *Shalom*, 5th April 1995.

'I'm often asked if I regret not marrying and having children. That's rather like asking a man who's never had vanilla ice-cream if he regrets not having vanilla ice-cream. He doesn't know because he's never had it. He's seen it. He's aware it exists. But he's never experienced it. And as he's led a happy life it doesn't trouble him.'

Sharon Garfinkel, *Plays and Players*, April 1995.

'I think revenge is a very good reason for doing anything. Anyone who's charged with rape, murder, robbery, it's like everybody who's driving over the speed limit down the motorway is taking their crippled mother a takeaway meal. Everyone charged with an offence says, "Well, I went to the cinema and that's why I did it."'

In the same article Michael Winner is asked, 'What would you like to be remembered for? "Well, I'd rather be remembered for the films because that has been my main life. If you broke my life down on a time and motion study then far and away the most part of it would be films. And for having observed accurately parts of society which others didn't dare reveal. I think the social history of a country has to be recorded by the Arts. You can't say that is so awful – rape or whatever – that we must not record it. Let's pretend these times were a lot nicer than they were. But I have to say that when you go, you go. And to put it bluntly everyone can fuck themselves."'

Mark Taylor, *Oxford Independent*, 2nd March 1996.

'When I look back on life the only thing I regret is that I didn't spend enough. Every time I was at an airport being shoved around like cattle I asked myself why haven't I got a private jet which is something I could well afford. If you've got money you may as well enjoy it. I do enjoy it but I wish I'd spent more of it. I guess there must be a puritanical streak in me which prevents me from doing so.'

Sunday Business, 2nd June 1996.

'I certainly was a workaholic. I never took a holiday. And don't forget that when I did the main lot of my movies from 1963 to 1985, I did sometimes two and a half a year. I not only wrote them. I produced them, directed them and edited them. So when the director at the end of a movie says, "Well, I'm off for a three week holiday. I'll come back and see a rough cut," I was breaking my back in the cutting room. I did it at the exclusion of everything else.'

Miscellany, Trinity College Dublin, November 1996.

'I'd rather listen to the advice of a friend who I respect who's gone out and paid for his meal than to a restaurant critic. There's only one food critic in the country who pays for all his meals and that's me. I'm the only food critic in the world who goes where he wishes to go and pays full price. Nobody else does that. They may pay but they get it back from the newspaper. I get none of it back from the *Sunday Times*. I pay for the hotels and the food and I like it that way.'

Phil Robinson, Eat Soup, 1997.

'I'm the greatest law and order freak in the world. I believe in shooting rapists. I believe in shooting child molesters. I believe in putting people in prison. If someone hits an old lady with an iron bar he ain't going to hit another old lady with an iron bar if he's in prison. And as for blaming screen violence for everything, it's a witch hunt. Can anybody seriously believe if you remove 20 per cent of violence from all films and television a mugger would wake up in Brixton the next day and say I'm not going to mug anybody?'

Sabine Durrant, Guardian, 10th January 1998.

'I got a Third in Law and Economics at Cambridge. If I had not been able to maintain a career in show business I suppose a Third in Law and Economics would have made me a senior biscuit salesman.'

Yorkshire Post, 5th June 1999.

'What would it surprise people to know about you? Answer: "That I am very quiet and shy. The public Michael Winner is all an act." '

Mail on Sunday You Magazine, 16th May 1999.

'I know I'm overweight and aware of what I should be doing. But like lots of people I diet between meals.'

Sophie Rena, Daily Express, 23rd October 1999.

'Every director has his own vision, right or wrong. All directors are egomaniacs there's no question.'

Celluloid, July 2000.

'There's nothing more tedious than those pompous tired old buffs who moan films today aren't what they used to be.'

Daily Mirror, 26th April 2001.

'I stopped stealing when I was 17. Now although I take towels, soap and cutlery from hotels and airplanes I ask permission first.'

Harriet Lane, Observer, 6th May 2001.

'My mother was charming but could be a monster. I know I'm like her sometimes.'

Jennifer Selway, *Daily Express*, 26th July 2001.

'I hate being a guest. People who ask you to stay want you to amuse them. You're a slave to the host's whims.'

Sunday Times, 29th July 2001.

'Women like to be treasured for themselves. They don't get taken in by men with money. In fact I did far better when I was an assistant director.'

Aberdeen Press and Journal, 18th August, 2001.

'The media are desperately short of celebrities so they make stars out of people who previously were background workers. Soon we'll have celebrity plumbers. Nearly all celebrity chefs are a bore, even though some of them are my good friends.'

Reader's Digest, November 2001.

'This is carrying democracy to ridiculous extremes. If you and I can get in the same carriage in a train as his Tonyship [the Prime Minister] what's the world coming to?'

Belfast Telegraph, 5th November 2001.

'People think, "What the fuck's he doing leaving his house as a museum – who the fuck does he think he is?" But that's not the point. It doesn't matter who I am. If a butcher left his house and it was absolutely untouched by human hand for sixty years it would be interesting. It gives something back to the town where I lived.'

GQ, June 2002.

'I can't think of anything worse than owning a restaurant. I might turn up!'

GS, Autumn 2002.

'Restaurateurs on the whole are utterly ghastly, untalented, no, they're untalented ego-maniacs. There are exceptions, but most of them are utterly damaged.'

GS, Autumn 2002.

'I would be quite ferocious and there would be mass death. I would kill muggers, rapists and child killers for a start and then people who park illegally.'

Winner saying what he would do if he were God, *Daily Mirror*, 1st March, 2003.

'For more than forty years I looked like an elegant film director. Now I look like an unsuccessful drug dealer.'

Winner on his new passport photograph, *Daily Telegraph*, 8th August 2003.

'Bending down to pick something up from the floor was a major effort and I had endless chest pains. But my thirty minutes of Pilates every morning and enforced one hour walk each evening have transformed me.'

Daily Telegraph, 12th November 2003.

'I am always approached when they want to put ten idiots into a confined space.'

Winner on being asked to participate in reality TV shows, *Aberdeen Press and Journal*, 23rd December 2003.

'There is only one sin: to be boring.'

Sunday Times, 6th June 2004.

'The inspiring young film director, Michael Winner, died yesterday while in his fifth year of being twenty-nine years old. He was killed on his film set by a large arc lamp dropping on him from a great height. The police investigating the accident have had confessions from all one hundred and thirty-six of the unit wishing to take credit for the event. Mr Winner leaves behind him a number of significant films all much enjoyed by his mother. He will, of course, return.'

Michael Winner's self-penned obituary, *Sunday Telegraph Magazine*, 20th July 1973.

Michael Winner
Curriculum Vitae

1950–57 Show-business columnist Middlesex and West London Newspapers Limited. Film critic for *Films and Filming*, *New Musical Express*, *The Motor*, etc. Freelance writing in the *Spectator*, *Picturegoer*, *Showgirl Glamour Revue* and others. Editor and film critic of Cambridge University newspaper *Varsity*. In Fleet Street on the *Sunday Express*, *Sunday Mirror*, London *Evening Standard*, *Daily Sketch*

from 1960 all British national newspapers.

1993 hotel and restaurant columnist *Sunday Times*.

1994–2003 political columnist *News of the World*.

Books: *Winner's Dinners*, 1999, revised edition 2000; *Winner Guide* 2002; autobiography: *Winner Takes All*, 2004.

Television

Call boy BBC Television 1956. Assistant Director on filmed TV series: *Dick and the Duchess*, *Mark Sabre*, *The White Hunter*.

Films

1956 *The Square* (short) starring: A. E. Matthews. Director/Producer/Writer; *This Is Belgium* (short). Associate Producer only;

Floating Fortress (Rank). Associate Producer.

1958 Screenplay *Man With A Gun* (Anglo-Amalgamated). Starring: Lee Patterson, Rhona Anderson, John Le Mesurier.

1957–61 Various short films and thrillers as Producer/Director/ Writer, including *Girls, Girls, Girls* (United Artists), *It's Magic* (United Artists), *Danger Women at Work* (United Artists), *Behave Yourself* (United Artists) and *Haunted England* (Columbia).

1960 *Shoot to Kill* (New Realm) Producer/Director/Writer. Leading Players: Dermot Walsh, Joy Webster; *Climb Up The Wall* (New Realm) Second unit only. Leading Players: Jack Jackson, Russ Conway, Craig Douglas, Cherry Wainer.

1961 *Out Of The Shadow* (New Realm) Producer/Director/Writer. Leading Players: Terence Longdon, Donald Gray, Diane Clare, Dermot Walsh, Robertson Hare; *Some Like It Cool* (New Realm) Producer: Adrienne Fancey.

1962 *Play It Cool.* Production Company: Independent Artists. Distributor: Anglo-Amalgamated. Producer: David Deutsch. Director: Michael Winner. Script: Jack Davies and Henry Blythe. Music: Norrie Paramor. Photography: Reg Wyer. Editor: Tristam Cones. Leading Players: Billy Fury, Helen Shapiro, Bobby Vee, Dennis Price, Michael Anderson Jnr, Richard Wattis, Anna Palk, Peter Barkworth, Bernie Winters, Lionel Blair, Frederick Jaeger, Max Bacon, Jeremy Lloyd, Jill Mai Meredith, Hugh Lloyd, Ray Brooks, Maurice Kaufman, Danny Williams, Marianne Stone.

1962 *The Cool Mikado.* Production Company: Harold Baim. Distributor: United Artists. Producer: Harold Baim. Director: Michael Winner. Script: Michael Winner from the opera *The Mikado* by W.S. Gilbert and Arthur Sullivan. Music: Martin Slavin and John Barry. Photography: Dennis Ayling. Editors: Fred Burnley and Frank Gilpin. Leading Players: Frankie Howerd, Stubby Kaye, Tommy Cooper, Mike and Bernie Winters, Dennis Price, Lionel Blair, Kevin Scott, Dermot Walsh, Jill Mai Meredith, Glenn Mason, Pete Murray, Jacqueline Jones, Peter Barkworth, Tsai Chin, Marianne Stone, Carole Shelley.

1963 *West 11*. Production Company: Dial Films. Distributor: Warner-Pathé. Producer: Daniel Angel. Director: Michael Winner. Script: Keith Waterhouse and Willis Hall from the book *The Furnished Room* by Laura Del Rivo. Music: Stanley Black. Photography: Otto Heller. Editor: Bernard Gribble. Leading Players: Alfred Lynch, Kathleen Breck, Eric Portman, Diana Dors, Kathleen Harrison, Freda Jackson, Finlay Currie, David Hemmings, Ha Hemmings, Harold Lang, Marie Ney, Patrick Wymark, Una Stubbs, Virginia Weatherall, Francesca Annis, Peter Reynolds.

1964 *The System*. (US title *The Girl-Getters*). Production Company: A Kenneth Shipman–Michael Winner Production. Distributor: Bryanston Films/BLC. Producer: Kenneth Shipman. Director: Michael Winner. Script: Peter Draper. Music: Stanley Black. Photography: Nicolas Roeg. Editor: Fred Burnley. Leading Players: Oliver Reed, Jane Merrow, Barbara Ferris, Julia Foster, Ann Lynn, Guy Doleman, David Hemmings, Harry Andrews, Andrew Ray, Mark Burns, Derek Nimmo, John Alderton, Clive Colin Bowler, Iain Gregory, Roy Hudd.

1965 *You Must Be Joking*. Production Company: Ameran Films. Distributor: Columbia. Producer: Charles Schneer. Director: Michael Winner. Original Story: Michael Winner and Alan Hackney. Music: Laurie Johnson. Photography: Geoffrey Unsworth. Editor: Bernard Gribble. Leading Players: Michael Callan, Lionel Jeffries, Terry-Thomas, Denholm Elliott, Bernard Cribbins, Wilfrid Hyde-White, James Robertson Justice, Leslie Phillips, Gabriella Licudi, Patricia Viterbo, Irene Handl, Peter Bull, Miles Malleson, Arthur Lowe, Lee Montague, Tracy Reed, James Villiers, Stanley Meadows, Richard Wattis, Peter Barkworth, Peter Gilmore, Richard Caldicott, Lance Percival, Norman Vaughan, Clive Dunn, Graham Stark, Jon Pertwee, Jill Mai Meredith, Marianne Stone.

1966 *The Jokers*. Production Company: Gildor-Scimitar. Distributor: Universal. Producers: Maurice Foster, Ben Arbied, Michael Winner. Director: Michael Winner. Original Story: Michael Winner. Screenplay: Dick Clement and Ian La Frenais.

Music Johnny Pearson. Photography: Ken Hodges. Editor: Bernard Gribble. Leading Players: Michael Crawford, Oliver Reed, Harry Andrews, James Donald, Daniel Massey, Michael Horden, Gabriella Licudi, Lotte Tarp, Frank Finlay, Warren Mitchell, Mark Burns, Rachel Kempson, Edward Fox, Michael Goodliffe, Peter Gilmore, Basil Dignam, Freda Jackson, Nicky Henson, Julian Holloway.

Nominated for Hollywood Golden Globe as Best Comedy of the Year.

1967 *I'll Never Forget What's'isname.* Production Company: Scimitar Films. Distributor: Universal. Producer and Director: Michael Winner. Script: Peter Draper. Music: Francis Lai. Photography: Otto Heller. Editor: Bernard Gribble. Leading Players: Oliver Reed, Orson Welles, Carol White, Harry Andrews, Michael Horden, Wendy Craig, Marianne Faithfull, Frank Finlay, Mark Burns, Ann Lynn, Mark Eden, Edward Fox, Norman Rodway, Stuart Cooper, Lyn Ashley, Bessie Love.

1968 *Hannibal Brooks.* Production Company: Scimitar Films. Distributor: United Artists. Producer and Director: Michael Winner. Original story: Michael Winner and Tom Wright. Screenplay: Dick Clement and Ian La Frenais. Music: Francis Lai. Photography: Robert Paynter. Editor: Peter Austen Hunt. Leading Players: Oliver Reed, Michael J. Pollard, John Alderton, Wolfgang Preiss, Helmut Lohner, Karin Baal, Jurgen Draeger.

1969 *The Games.* Production Company and Distributor: Twentieth Century-Fox. A Michael Winner–Lester Linsk Production. Producer: Lester Linsk. Director: Michael Winner. Script: Erich Segal from the book by Hugh Atkinson. Music: Francis Lai. Photography: Robert Paynter. Editors: Bernard Gribble and Arnold Crust. Leading Players: Ryan O'Neal, Michael Crawford, Stanley Baker, Charles Aznavour, Jeremy Kemp, Elaine Taylor, Athol Compton, Fritz Wepper, Leigh Taylor-Young, Sam Elliott, Rafer Johnson, Mona Washbourne, Stephanie Beacham, Kent Smith.

1970 *Lawman*. Production Company: Scimitar Films. Distributor: United Artists. Producer and Director: Michael Winner. Script: Gerald Wilson. Music: Jerry Fielding. Photography: Robert Paynter. Supervising Editor: Freddie Wilson. Editor: Arnold Crust. Leading Players: Burt Lancaster, Robert Ryan, Lee J. Cobb, Robert Duvall, J. D. Cannon, Sheree North, Richard Jordan, John Beck, Ralph Waite, William Watson, John McGiver, Joseph Wiseman, Robert Emhardt, Albert Salmi, Walter Brooke, John Hillerman, Lou Frizell, Charles Tyner, Richard Bull.

1971 *The Nightcomers*. Great Britain. Production Company: Scimitar Films. Distributor: Avco Embassy. Executive Producers: Elliott Kastner, Jay Kanter, Alan Ladd. Producer and Director: Michael Winner. Script: Michael Hastings. Based on characters from *The Turn of the Screw* by Henry James. Music: Jerry Fielding, Photography: Robert Paynter. Supervising Editor: Freddie Wilson. Editor: Arnold Crust. Leading Players: Marlon Brando, Stephanie Beacham, Thora Hird, Christopher Ellis, Verna Harvey, Anna Palk, Harry Andrews.
    Invited entry at Venice Film Festival. Invited entry at San Francisco Film Festival.

1971 *Chato's Land*. (USA) Production Company: Scimitar Films. Distributor: United Artists. Producer and Director: Michael Winner. Script: Gerald Wilson. Music: Jerry Fielding. Photography: Robert Paynter. Supervising Editor: Freddie Wilson. Editor: Arnold Crust. Leading Players: Charles Bronson, Jack Palance, Richard Basehart, James Whitmore, Ralph Waite, Richard Jordan, Victor French, William Watson, Roddy McMillan, Paul Young, Sonia Rangan, Lee Patterson, Simon Oakland, Raul Castro, Verna Harvey.

1972 *The Mechanic*. Production Company: Chartoff-Winkler. Distributor: United Artists. Producers: Robert Chartoff and Irwin Winkler. Director: Michael Winner. Script: Lewis John Carlino. Music: Jerry Fielding. Photography: Richard Kline. European Photography: Robert Paynter. Supervising Editor: Freddie Wilson. Editor: Arnold Crust. Leading Players: Charles Bronson, Keenan

Wynn, Jan-Michael Vincent, Jill Ireland, Linda Ridgeway, Lindsay Crosby, Frank De Kova.

1972 *Scorpio*. Production Company: Scimitar Films. Distributor: United Artists. Producer: Walter Mirisch. Director: Michael Winner. Script: David W. Rintels and Gerald Wilson. Original Story: David W. Rintels. Music: Jerry Fielding. Photography: Robert Paynter. Editor: Arnold Crust. Leading Players: Burt Lancaster, Alain Delon, Paul Scofield, Gayle Hunnicutt, John Colicos, J. D. Cannon, William Smithers, Schmuel Rudensky, Joanne Linville, James Sikking, Mel Stewart, Robert Emhardt, Frederick Jaeger, George Mikell, Jack Colvin, Vladek Sheybal, Sandor Eles, Douglas Lambert.

1973 *The Stone Killer*. Production Company: Interproduction Film Service. A Dino de Laurentiis presentation. Distributor: Columbia. Producer and Director: Michael Winner. Script: Gerald Wilson from the book *A Complete State of Death* by John Gardner. Music: Roy Budd. Photography: Richard Moore. New York Photography: Richard Kline. Editor: Arnold Crust. Leading Players: Charles Bronson, Martin Balsam, Stuart Margolin, David Sheiner, Norman Fell, Ralph Waite, Eddie Firestone, Walter Burke, Jack Colvin, David Moody, Charles Tyner, Paul Koslo, John Ritter, Byron Morrow, Frank Campanella, Alfred Ryder, Lisabeth Hush, Frenchia Guizon, Robert Emhardt, Richard Armbruster, Kelly Miles, Morgan Farley.

1974 *Death Wish*. Production Company: Dino de Laurentiis Corporation. Distributor: Paramount. Co-Producer and Director: Michael Winner. Script: Wendell Mayes from the book *Death Wish* by Brian Garfield. Music: Herbie Hancock. Photography: Arthur Ornitz. Hawaii and Arizona Photography: Richard Kline. Executive Editor: Bernard Gribble. Editor: Arnold Crust. Leading Players: Charles Bronson, Vincent Gardenia, Hope Lange, Steven Keats, Stuart Margolin, William Redfield, Kathleen Tolan, Jack Wallace, Stephen Elliott, Ed Grover, Helen Martin, Olympia Dukakis, Jeff Goldblum.

1975 *Won Ton Ton the Dog Who Saved Hollywood*. Production Company/Distributor: Paramount Pictures. Producers: David V. Picker, Michael Winner, Arnold Schulman. Director: Michael Winner. Script: Arnold Schulman and Cy Howard. Music: Neal Hefti. Photography: Richard Kline. Executive Editor: Bernard Gribble. Editor: Arnold Crust. Leading Players: Bruce Dern, Madeline Kahn, Phil Silvers, Art Carney, Victor Mature, Virginia Mayo, Henny Youngman, Shecky Greene, Dennis Morgan, Rory Calhoun, Henry Wilcoxon, Ricardo Montalban, Jackie Coogan, Aldo Ray, Ethel Merman, Yvonne De Carlo, Joan Blondell, Andy Devine, Broderick Crawford, Richard Arlen, Jack La Rue, Dorothy Lamour, Nancy Walker, Gloria De Haven, Louis Nye, Johnny Weissmuller, Stepin Fetchit, Rudy Vallee, George Jessel, Rhonda Fleming, Ann Miller, Dean Stockwell, Dick Haymes, Tab Hunter, Robert Alda, Ron Leibman, Fritz Feld, Janet Blair, Dennis Day, The Ritz Brothers, Jack Carter, Barbara Nicholls, Fernando Lamas, Zsa Zsa Gabor, Cyd Charisse, Huntz Hall, Edgar Bergen, Peter Lawford, Guy Madison, Alice Fay, Milton Berle, John Carradine, Walter Pidgeon, Teri Garr, William Demarest.

1976 *The Sentinel*. Production Company/Distributor: Universal Pictures. Producers: Michael Winner, Jeffrey Konvitz. Director: Michael Winner. Screenplay: Michael Winner, Jeffrey Konvitz from the book by Jeffrey Konvitz. Photography: Dick Kratina. Music: Gil Melée. Executive Editor: Bernard Gribble. Editor: Arnold Crust. Leading Players: Chris Sarandon, Cristina Raines, Martin Balsam, John Carradine, Jose Ferrer, Ava Gardner, Arthur Kennedy, Burgess Meredith, Sylvia Miles, Deborah Raffin, Eli Wallach, Christopher Walken, Beverly D'Angelo, Tom Berenger, Jerry Orbach.

1977 *The Big Sleep*. Production Company: Winkast. Distributor: ITC. Producers: Elliott Kastner, Michael Winner. Director: Michael Winner. Script: Michael Winner from the book by Raymond Chandler. Music: Jerry Fielding. Photography: Robert Paynter. Editor: Arnold Crust. Leading Players: Robert Mitchum, Sarah Miles, Richard Boone, Candy Clark, Joan Collins, Edward Fox, John Mills, James Stewart, Oliver Reed, Richard Todd, James Donald, Harry Andrews, Diana Quick, Colin Blakely.

1978 *Firepower*. Production Company: Michael Winner Ltd. Distributor: ITC. Producer-Director: Michael Winner. Script: Gerald Wilson. Story: Michael Winner, Bill Kirby. Music: Gato Barbieri. Photography: Robert Paynter. Editor: Arnold Crust. Leading Players: Sophia Loren, James Coburn, O. J. Simpson, Anthony Franciosa, Eli Wallach, George Grizzard, Victor Mature, Vincent Gardenia.

1981 *Death Wish Two*. Production Company: Cannon. Distributor: Filmways/Columbia. Producers: Menahem Golan, Yoram Globus. Director: Michael Winner. Script: David Englebach. Music: Jimmy Page. Photography: Richard Kline. Editor: Arnold Crust. Leading Players: Charles Bronson, Jill Ireland, Vincent Gardenia, J. D. Cannon, Anthony Franciosa, Laurence Fishburne.

1982 *The Wicked Lady*. Production Company: Cannon. Distributor: MGM/UA/Columbia. Producers: Menahem Golan, Yoram Globus. Director: Michael Winner. Script: Leslie Arliss, Michael Winner. From the book by Magdalen King-Hall. Music: Tony Banks. Photography: Jack Cardiff. Editor: Arnold Crust. Leading Players: Faye Dunaway, Alan Bates, John Gielgud, Denholm Elliott, Prunella Scales, Glynis Barber, Oliver Tobias.

1983 *Scream for Help*. Production Company: Lorimar. Producer-Director: Michael Winner. Executive Producer: Irwin Yablans. Script: Tom Holland. Music: John Paul Jones. Photography: Robert Paynter, Dick Kratina. Editor: Arnold Crust. Leading Players: Rachael Kelly, Marie Masters, David Brooks, Rocco Sisto, Lolita Lorre, Sandra Clark, Corey Parker.

1985 *Death Wish Three*. Production/Distribution: Cannon. Producers: Menahem Golan and Yoram Globus. Director and Co-Producer: Michael Winner. Script: Don Jakoby. Music: Jimmy Page. Photography: John Stanier. Editor: Arnold Crust. Leading Players: Charles Bronson, Martin Balsam, Ed Lauter, Deborah Raffin, Alex Winter.

1987 *Appointment with Death*. Production/Distribution: Cannon. Executive Producers: Menahem Golan, Yoram Globus. Producer-Director: Michael Winner. Screenplay: Anthony Shaffer, Peter Buckman and Michael Winner. Based on the book by Agatha Christie. Music: Pino Donaggio. Photography: David Gurfinkel. Editor: Arnold Crust. Leading Players: Peter Ustinov, Lauren Bacall, Carrie Fisher, John Gielgud, Piper Laurie, Hayley Mills, Jenny Seagrove, David Soul.

1988 *A Chorus of Disapproval*. An Elliott Kastner/Andre Blay Presentation. Producer-Director: Michael Winner. Screenplay: Alan Ayckbourn and Michael Winner. From the play by Alan Ayckbourn. Music: John Du Prez. Photography: Alan Jones. Editor: Arnold Crust. Leading Players: Anthony Hopkins, Jeremy Irons, Prunella Scales, Jenny Seagrove, Richard Briers, Patsy Kensit, Alexandra Pigg, Lionel Jeffries, Sylvia Syms, Barbara Ferris, Gareth Hunt.
    Winner of Grand Jury Prize at Cologne Film Festival.

1989 *Bullseye!* Production: 21st Century. Producer-Director: Michael Winner. Executive Producer: Menahem Golan. Screenplay: Leslie Bricusse, Laurence Marks and Maurice Gran, Michael Winner and Nick Mead. Music: John Du Prez. Photography: Alan Jones. Editor: Arnold Crust. Leading Players: Michael Caine, Roger Moore, Sally Kirkland. Guest appearances by John Cleese, Patsy Kensit, Jenny Seagrove.

1992–93 *Dirty Weekend*. Production: Scimitar Films. Distributor: UIP. Producers: Michael Winner and Robert Earl. Director: Michael Winner. Screenplay: Michael Winner and Helen Zahavi from the book by Helen Zahavi. Music: David Fanshawe. Photography: Alan Jones. Editor: Arnold Crust. Leading Players: Lia Williams, Rufus Sewell, David McCallum, Sylvia Syms, Ian Richardson.

1997–98 *Parting Shots*. Production: Scimitar Films. Distributor: UIP. Producer-Director: Michael Winner. Screenplay: Michael Winner and Nick Mead from a story by Michael Winner. Music: Les Reed. Main themes by Chris Rea. Photography: Ousama Rawi.

Editor: Arnold Crust. Leading Players: Chris Rea, Felicity Kendal, Bob Hoskins, Ben Kingsley, Joanna Lumley, Oliver Reed, Diana Rigg, John Cleese.

As actor/performer/personality
For The Greater Good (BBC Television) – Sir Randolph Spence. Director Danny Boyle.
Decadence – club member. Director Steven Berkoff.
Radio: panellist on *Any Questions* for six years.
TV series: *Michael Winner's True Crimes* (LWT) – presenter.
TV shows include: *Kenny Everett, Reeves and Mortimer, Celebrity Sleepover, Mrs Merton, Question Time, Shooting Stars, This Is Dom Joly, Banzai, This Is Your Life, God Almighty, Night of 1000 Stars, Diners, Meet Ricky Gervais, Gayle's World, Noel's House Party, Room 101, Have I Got News For You.*

Index